D1090573

The American CITIZENS HANDBOOK

REVISED EDITION
Edited by JOY ELMER MORGAN
WITH 200 ILLUSTRATIONS

National Council for the Social Studies
A Department of the National Education Association
1201 Sixteenth Street, N. W., Washington, D.C. 20036

First Edition, 1941
Second Edition, 1941
Third Edition, 1946
Fourth Edition, 1951
Fifth Edition, 1960
Sixth Edition, 1968

Library of Congress Catalog Card Number 68-56052

Foreword

THE *American Citizens Handbook* was compiled by Joy Elmer Morgan, Editor of the *Journal* of the National Education Association from 1920 thru 1954 who then became president of Senior Citizens of America. The *Handbook* was first published in 1941 in connection with the observance of National Citizenship Day which comes on September 17 of each year.

Believing the *Handbook* to be a useful reference in introducing citizens to the ideals that have inspired the goals and continued development of a democracy of liberty, equal opportunity, and personal growth, Dr. Morgan generously offered it to the National Council for the Social Studies and contributed his services in preparing this edition. It was felt that a reference work containing basic documents upon which our culture is built, along with samples of literature and interpretations of these documents and the values underlying them, would be useful in helping individuals evaluate and refine their own understanding of citizenship and its responsibilities. The *Handbook* is inspirational and informative, whereas other publications of the National Council deal with the professional or academic aspects of social studies instruction.

However, one of the most important, if not *the* most important purpose for teaching the social studies is citizenship education. Man is both an emotional and intellectual being. To slight either aspect or to fail to develop a functional relationship between the two is to be ineffective or even harmful in developing responsible citizenship. Man *does* make commitments and social studies instruction has often been shown to be less than adequate in developing responsible citizenship.

In a diverse society such as we have in the United States, it may be expected that no one will agree with every item in the *Handbook*. Indeed, sound citizenship is developed by confrontations with conflicting interpretations of the basic values underlying our system. It is hoped that out of exposure to varying interpretations will come a synthesis leading to a richer, fuller, more productive citizen.—LESLIE A. WOOD, *Publications Committee*, National Council for the Social Studies.

Life is no brief candle to me. It is a sort of splendid torch which I have got hold of for the moment, and I want to make it burn as brightly as possible before handing it on to future generations—GEORGE BERNARD SHAW.

This Book Belongs to You

To be a good friend, brother, sister, father, mother;
To be a dependable, faithful, and skilled worker in home, school, field, factory, or office;
To be an intelligent, honest, useful, and loyal citizen, with faith in God and love of fellowman;
To recognize the brotherhood of man and to live by the Golden Rule—

These are the aspirations that have brought happiness and achievement to the America we all love. These are the aspirations that must help us find our way to new glory and grace in the midst of worldwide change. A great civilization must have its roots in the soil of the past and its branches reaching to the stars of the future. Otherwise it lacks the experience and motive necessary for noble achievement in the present. Has the nation lost its way? Let it return again to the faith of its youth. This faith is found at its best in the lives and writings of great leaders who have quickened and purified the national spirit.

This book belongs to you as an American citizen. In it you will find the ideals that have inspired generations of the best men and women to work out on this continent a democracy of liberty, equal opportunity, and personal growth. Read this book carefully; study the documents on which your rights as a citizen are based; memorize its songs and poetry; enjoy the inspiring statements which have given purpose, hope, and courage to millions of Americans.—JOY ELMER MORGAN.

A Word About the Sixth Edition

BEGINNING with this SIXTH edition *The American Citizens Handbook* is published by the National Council for the Social Studies, a Department of the National Education Association. It continues under the editorship of Joy Elmer Morgan in cooperation with the Publications Committee of the Council, consisting of Dr. Ruth Ellsworth, Wayne State University, *Chairman;* Dr. Leslie A. Wood, Indiana University; and Dr. Jack Allen, George Peabody College for Teachers. Mrs. Willadene Price of the Council's staff assisted in the production and editing. There has been a substantial revision and reorganization of the text in this edition, and much new material and many new illustrations have been added. The following is a partial list of new selections:

"Our Schools Have Kept Us Free" by Henry Steele Commager
"Goals for Americans" by The President's Commission on National Goals
"Characteristics of the Good Democratic Citizen" by National Council for the Social Studies
Speeches by such notables as President John F. Kennedy, President Franklin D. Roosevelt and Dr. Martin Luther King, Jr.
Latest additions to the Hall of Fame and United Nations
Latest information under Roll Call of the States
"The Children's Charter" by the White House Conference.

The American Citizens Handbook is designed for citizens of every age and in every walk of life. The volume should be in every home library and on the desk of every teacher and statesman. For years it has been a standard work in public libraries thruout the world. It was originally prepared for presentation to young citizens as they reach voting age and is often used in that way by service clubs interested in promoting good citizenship and preserving our American Heritage.—MERRILL F. HARTSHORN, *Executive Secretary,* National Council for the Social Studies.

Contents

Illustrations

PART I

Your Citizenship in the Making

YOU, AT THIS MOMENT *have the honor to belong to a generation whose lips are touched by fire . . . The human race now passes thru one of its great crises. New ideas, new issues—a new call for men to carry on the work of righteousness, of charity, of courage, of patience, and of loyalty—all these things have come and are daily coming to you.*

When you are old . . . however memory brings back this moment to your minds, let it be able to say to you: That was a great moment. It was the beginning of a new era . . . This world in its crisis called for volunteers, for men of faith in life, of patience in service, of charity, and of insight. I responded to the call however I could. I volunteered to give myself to my master—the cause of humane and brave living. I studied, I loved, I labored, unsparingly and hopefully, to be worthy of my generation.

—JOSIAH ROYCE.

THE UNITED STATES CAPITOL *shown on the following page is situated on the brow of a hill overlooking the city. The National Art Gallery, the Museum of Natural History, and the Museum of History and Technology may be seen to the right of the Mall. Facing the Capitol at the far end of the Mall are the Washington Monument and the Lincoln Memorial on an east-west axis.*

Photograph, Architect's Office, Capitol

Your Citizenship in the Making

JOY ELMER MORGAN

Editor, Journal of the National Education Association, 1920–1954; founder of Future Teachers of America; founder and president of Senior Citizens of America and editor of its magazine SENIOR CITIZEN, *1954—*

IT IS a high privilege to be a citizen of the United States. There are those in less fortunate circumstances who would gladly give all they possess for the mere chance to come here to live. Although serious problems have to be solved, ours is known as a land of opportunity, equality, democracy and progress. The development of our uniquely American civilization is due to at least four factors: adequate natural resources; the variety of ethnic groups in our population; a common system of purpose and ideals inculcated into the lives of all the people by a system of free public schools; and a high level of technical skill based upon a high level of general education. It is for each of us as individual citizens to do his part to preserve and enrich our inheritance. By becoming active and responsible citizens we can help to build a future worthy of the pioneer men and women who made possible the opportunities we now enjoy.

Our National Heritage

There is first the country itself. What a rich and beautiful continent we are privileged to inhabit! As one rides its farflung railroads or motors over its thousands of miles of paved highways, or follows its streams, or penetrates its forests, or takes the airplane and skimming thru the sky looks down upon the panorama beneath, it is an inspiring picture of a mighty God-given gift; truly "America the Beautiful" as described in Katharine Lee Bates' inspiring poem:

O beautiful for spacious skies,
For amber waves of grain,
For purple mountain majesties
Above the fruited plain!
America! America!
God shed His grace on thee
And crown thy good with brotherhood
From sea to shining sea!

We have not always been appreciative of this gift. We have been wasteful of our forests and minerals, careless of our water power, ruthless in the wastage of our soil. We have come now to the day of reckoning when by flood, dust storm, air and water pollution we are forced to face our national destiny and our relation as a people to the soil from which we draw our life. But with all the wastage, with all the lack of planning and of vision, we still have the greatest heritage of natural resources and climate to be found upon the face of the earth.

Our Heritage of Leadership

There is too the mighty heritage that has come to us in the memory of great deeds performed by the pioneer men and women who have established this nation in so brief a span of years. Some of their names are recorded in the account of the Hall of Fame in this book. Every American should be encouraged to read biography because it gives examples of the nobility to which mankind can aspire. It lifts one above the petty and trivial to go again with George Washington, with Benjamin Franklin and Thomas Jefferson, with Horace Mann or with Abraham Lincoln, thru the struggles that have created our national being, that have given us our freedom, and that have kept us going forward in continual efforts to improve our democracy. Every American is entitled to know these creators and guardians of our liberty, and we may be sure that a knowledge of their great deeds as well as their human frailties will reinforce and inspire our own purposes. We have attached great importance in this country to literacy, to the ability to read and write. We have not attached enough importance to reading itself as a lifelong enterprise in the life of the citizen. The mere fact of being able to read does not of itself guarantee intelligent citizenship. There must be wisdom in the choice of reading. Formal schooling is too short, even if pursued thruout the college years, to enable any citizen to read all the things which he should know about the founding and growth of our Republic.

Charters of American Liberty

Beyond the heritage which is found in the lives of the men and women who have made America, *stands the Republic itself,* one of the greatest examples of constitutional government among free men. The full text of our American Constitution is given in this book. Every American should know its content. It is the greatest single document in the entire struggle of mankind for orderly self-government. We need not review here the story of the Constitution. You are familiar with the history of the colonies and their difficulties, with the Declaration of

Independence, with the Revolutionary War, and the difficult years under the Articles of Confederation. You are familiar with the struggles of the Constitutional Convention itself. You know the patience and nobility of Washington as he presided over the convention; the difficulty of reaching agreement; the willingness of the men who took part to subordinate personal and sectional interests to the general good; and the narrow margin by which the Constitution was adopted and put into force when it was submitted to the states.

Religious Ideals the Foundation

It is difficult to read this history without seeing in it the hand of a Providence, for the struggle which was then taking place in America was a chapter in the continuous human struggle upward, a struggle against despotism, against the destructive forces often found within man himself. The birth of our democracy is partially the result of the teachings of religious leaders going back hundreds of years. Democracy can find its fullest expression in the roots of religion, which has ever emphasized the Fatherhood of God and the Brotherhood of Man. For democracy to reach its highest fruition, our society must include that larger liberty and justice preached so eloquently by the Hebrew Prophets and by Jesus.

No one would contend that the Constitution is a perfect document. The very men who framed it were conscious of its shortcomings. And the fact of the Civil War proves that it could not meet all the needs of the young republic—a war to test, in the words of Lincoln, whether any nation conceived in liberty and dedicated to the proposition that all men are created equal can long endure. We have our difficulties in these days also in agreeing among ourselves as to what we want the Constitution to be and how we want it to be interpreted or administered. But these are small matters as compared with the great fact of the Constitution itself standing between us and chaos, between us and a return to the brutalities and confusion of earlier centuries.

Education, the Safeguard of Democracy

We must also include in our great American heritage, along with the land itself, the memory of noble men and women, and our system of free government, *the common school*—which is yours to cherish, to improve, and to use as the instrument of your intelligence. The importance of education in a democracy is eloquently stated elsewhere in this book by Horace Mann, who because of his courageous, dynamic and eloquent leadership of the nineteenth century educational revival, is known as the *father of our free public schools.*

We have in our schools millions of young people—a population many times as large as the total population of the colonies when the Declaration of Independence was signed. But we have come to see that education of adults is no less important than the education of children. We already have the beginnings of a nationwide system of tax-supported free public education of adults. It is essential that adult education grow to a point where in every school building in the land there will be classes and discussion groups of people in the community dealing with the important issues of their lives. Events in our country and in the world are occurring so rapidly that new problems of life and government arise overnight and if people are to meet them with full intelligence, they must continue their study and education thruout the years.

The End of an Epoch

We live in one of the greatest transition ages of all history. We think of the dawn of history, the breaking up of the Roman Empire, and the reorganization of the world's life which followed the discovery of America as marking great turning points in man's existence. But the change that is taking place in human life today is even greater than the change which took place in the Middle Ages or during the fall of the Roman Empire; it can be compared only with the dawn of history itself. The world is entering upon a new epoch, mankind has reached a point where it can, if it will, move forward into a new period of light, selfgovernment, and justice.

The big event of our age is not the atom bomb, or World War II, or the United Nations, or any of the things that have been featured in press and radio. It is something that lies deeper than all these— a new kind of growth that is taking place in the minds and hearts of men. It is working its way among the billions of inhabitants of this earth with a power that no man can estimate. It dwarfs all the statesmen that ever lived. The seed for this new growth was sown back in the centuries by great teachers who saw with prophetic clarity that men could not advance by magnifying their antipathies, but that by exalting their common brotherhood they could enjoy the earth and the fulness thereof. They knew as all intelligent men must know that love is more powerful than hate, and that intelligence is stronger than force in the life of humanity.

Never during the long slow struggle of man against

the forces around him and within himself has he risen to greater heights than now. Never has man recognized the need to be more willing to sacrifice and fight when the odds were strong against him, more willing to live and die for the larger good. Never has the mind of man been broader in its reach and grasp. Never has he been more inventive, ingenious, and resourceful. Never before have the sympathies of man been so greatly challenged to reach out to so many of his fellow creatures. Never before has the spirit of man been called upon to rise above all the creeds and conflicts of religion and race to a feeling of universal brotherhood for his fellowmen everywhere.

How to Build Influence

Our task as citizens seeking to shape the larger affairs of humanity is to make our influence felt as widely as possible. We cannot expect to agree upon all our problems. In the end we shall have to adjust our differences in the spirit of goodwill and subordinate our lesser interests to the general welfare. The important thing is for you as a citizen to look at our problems with an open mind in a spirit of fairness, willing and eager to listen to all sides, the slave of no man and no party, determined to find the truth, to serve the people as a whole, and to accept and follow the sovereignty of your own mind.

There are too many people in our country today who get their political information and attitudes from one newspaper or from one source on radio or TV, who consult their prejudices rather than their intelligence. Under such conditions political discussion degenerates to the level of propaganda; every statesman is dragged down and lied about; facts are obscured; special privilege gets possession of the powerful agencies for the distribution of public information; and the Ship of State is torn and threatened by conflicting gales of uninformed public prejudice. It is not easy to know the truth and there is always the possibility that the citizen will make mistakes in his judgment, but he can at least make sure that he is honest and sincere in his attempt to get at the truth and to serve not any selfish interest but the people as a whole. That is the principle upon which democratic government was founded. It is the only principle upon which it can survive and adapt itself to the new and difficult conditions of our time.

The Citizen's Responsibility

What of the citizen's obligation to cherish and improve the great inheritance of democracy and selfgovernment? Think for a moment of what it means to be endowed with the highest gift the community can bestow—that of having a part in the government of humanity. For untold centuries men have fought and labored thru long and tortuous years that the rights which we enjoy might be ours, and under our system we intrust this precious heritage in the hands of the people themselves. We say to every young man and young woman who reaches voting age:

> You have become a sovereign citizen. You are the source of the authority of our government. You have upon your shoulders the preservation of this great boon of freedom and opportunity for which others have paid so dearly. If you do not appreciate the importance of this sovereign privilege, if you do not exercise it and

exercise it wisely, it will be lost and the age-long cycle of confusion and suffering will be once more ahead.

Your Many-Sided Life

There is always the danger that we shall think of our citizenship too narrowly, that we shall fail to realize its relationship to our lives as a whole. When we think of citizenship, we are likely to think of voting, of helping to choose good candidates, of serving in public office, on a jury, perhaps of being drafted into the armed services. *These are specific tasks that cannot be neglected if the individual is to count himself as a good citizen.* But back of these duties stands life itself, the art of living so that life shall be good and worthy of the human race.

You cannot separate your citizenship and the exercise of your civic duties from the rest of your life. Your aspirations, interests, ideals, tastes, and habits influence the performance of your civic duties. If your life is noble and rich, your citizenship will express that nobility. If you are a good mother or a good father, you are more likely to be a good voter. The purpose you have as a father or as a mother will carry over and influence your decisions at the ballot box. If you are a good workman with joy and a sense of perfection in your daily task, you will make a better member of a jury, because thru your labor you will have penetrated the common heart of humanity. If in your relations with your family and your neighbors, you have a spirit of goodwill and mutual helpfulness, that spirit will be your contribution toward a wholesome state of the common mind. If you are dishonest in your thinking and indifferent to the wellbeing of others, these qualities will degrade the public life.

The world today needs you at your best with such qualities as these:

A determination to earn your own way in the world by useful service.

A personal interest in human welfare that seizes every opportunity to help others improve their lives.

A deep concern for good government combined with sustained study and action.

Begin Your Citizenship in the Home

The foundations of your whole life—physical, emotional, and mental—are usually laid in the home. The well-ordered home based on love, mutual helpfulness, and intelligent cooperation is the highest achievement of mankind. It is the cradle of civilization. By living and working together in the home we acquire the virtues, habits, and skills needed for the highest success in life. By doing your part in the tasks about the home; by helping to keep it clean, orderly, and beautiful; by seeking to make it a peaceful, friendly, and happy place; you learn to think, to plan, and to work with others in ways that will help you to perform well your part in school and community. Exalt, enrich, and beautify your home. It is the foundation of your life and happiness; it can be the first school of citizenship and democracy.

Improve Your Community Citizenship

Make a list of things which you can and will do to contribute most to the welfare and happiness of all in the community, including such items as:

[1] Keeping the premises about your home clean, orderly, and beautiful.

[2] Obeying traffic rules and showing courtesy as motorist or pedestrian.

[3] Taking an active interest in government and public affairs.

[4] Taking part in religious, civic, and cultural activities.

[5] Maintaining a friendly and cooperative attitude toward members of all racial, ethnic and religious groups.

[6] Helping to free the community from influences that weaken and degrade the lives of the people.

[7] Voting when you are of proper age and encouraging others to vote for officers who will honestly and efficiently serve the interests of all the people.

Your Political Citizenship

Your citizenship in the political community is made effective thru voting, public sentiment, legislation, and public administration. The two points which are most weakened thru neglect are the government of the locality and the primary election. If people do not take an interest in and learn to control and to manage honestly and efficiently local political affairs, which are nearest them, they will not know how to manage well the larger affairs of state and nation. Political bosses often gain control for their own selfish interests by concentrating on the primary, where a few votes often control the result. Attend first therefore to local government and the primary election. Gather facts about local government; encourage public discussion.

The Government of Industry

In the days when each man owned his farm or shop, people did not need to give much thought to the government of industry. They thought only of political government. With the coming of large corporations, people came to see that their lives, liberties, and happiness were involved in the industrial community as much and sometimes more than in the political community. In what ways may you have a part in the government of industry? First, thru your political citizenship you can give attention to the charters which create the corporations and the laws and commissions which regulate them. Second, thru organization as a worker you can encourage justice and fair play. Third, as a consumer, you can patronize only industries which abide by the letter and spirit of the principle of fair play. If they violate this principle, you can join others in the consumers cooperative movement.

There Is Power in the People

Dictators have discovered the physical force of great masses of people. Democracies must discover and release the intellectual and moral force that resides in the people—in their energy, in their aspirations, in their purposes, in their experience, in their love of neighbors and dear ones. Jesus built a religion out of the wisdom of plain people. He turned their homely experience into devotion, faith, hope, and good works. The founders of America instituted our Republic on the conviction that people could rule themselves better than kings could rule for them. Horace Mann laid the foundations of the world's noblest school system in the ambition of the common people to improve themselves. Release the power that is in the people and out of a great people will come an abundance of great and inspired leaders. May you as a sovereign citizen, carrying upon your shoulders the responsibility for selfgovernment, ever be watchful of your priceless and hard-won heritage. May you build into your life the best that mankind has thought or dreamed thruout the ages, knowing full well that if your life is right, your citizenship will be worthy. May you ever realize that all human institutions, including government, must be born anew in the hearts and minds of each generation. May we all accept our trusteeship for government of the people, by the people, for the people; matching every right with a corresponding duty.

The United Nations

The coming of United Nations and the urgent necessity that it evolve into a more comprehensive form of world government places upon citizens of the United States an increased obligation to make the most of their citizenship which now widens into active world citizenship. No nation can teach more than it is; and what we make of ourselves and our country will determine what we can do for a greater world order. The world is being drawn closer and closer together by modern communication and transportation. Nationalities with different ideals, religions, customs, and languages see more of each other. Trade interests cross and often conflict. Dictator countries threaten the peace of neighbors. These wider interests must in some way be brought under law and order. Their nature must be better understood. Public sentiment must be created on behalf of the ideal of fair play. Ideals of mutual respect and helpfulness must be developed. World machinery must be perfected to deal with world issues. This will require creative thinking and courageous action. Considering what we now have to work with, the problems presented are at least as great as those associated with the preparation and adoption of the Constitution of the United States.

Your Challenge

As you read this book, ask yourself what you as a citizen can do to pass on the torch of democracy and to make the nation better and stronger. Determine to do your part to keep democracy true to the ideals of its founders. Ask yourself again and again thru the years: "What kind of a country and what kind of world do I really want? What kind of a life for myself and my loved ones?" Ask yourself what you can do to achieve the following personal goals:

[1] To keep fit physically, mentally, and ethically thru a careful routine of living.

[2] To exalt the family and the community of neighbors as the foundation of civilized culture.

[3] To give attention to civic duty with a determination to maintain our democratic personal rights, political liberties, and representative institutions.

[4] To take the long look even beyond our generation and to sow the seeds of a better day.

[5] To find my part and to do it patiently, consistently, and well; one day at a time; without thought of reward; losing myself in the common good.

[6] To hold fast to the ideals of the Golden Rule and the brotherhood of man.

[7] To help perfect a world order enabling all people everywhere to enjoy what they cherish for themselves.

Democratic government can rise no higher than the intelligence, purpose, and conscience of the individual citizen.

Characteristics of the Good Democratic Citizen

In the winter of 1949-50, the Armed Forces Information and Education Division, Department of Defense, asked the executive secretary of the National Council for the Social Studies for a description of the good democratic citizen. The executive secretary immediately organized a working committee on citizenship. The committee wrote to leading authorities in the field of civic education requesting a list of characteristics essential to effective democratic citizenship. The committee also compiled a list and eventually the two lists were combined in a questionnaire, which was mailed to more than 300 leaders in practically every field of American life. The response was amazing, and the agreement on essentials gratifying. The following report, which was made on February 6, 1950, represents, therefore, the consensus of a considerable number of Americans.

THE GOOD CITIZEN

[1] Believes in equality of opportunity for all people:

[a] treats all men with respect, regardless of their station in life,

[b] rejects distinctions based on race, creed, or class,

[c] exerts his influence to secure equal opportunity for all, in accordance with ability,

[d] upholds the principle that all men are equal before the law and entitled to the equal protection of the law,

[e] believes that the right to vote should not be denied on the basis of race, sex, creed, or economic status.

[2] Values, respects, and defends basic human rights and privileges guaranteed by the US Constitution:

[a] knows the provisions of the Bill of Rights,

[b] upholds freedom of speech for ideas he doesn't like,

[c] goes beyond legal requirements by observing the spirit of the Bill of Rights in situations not covered by law.

[3] Respects and upholds the law and its agencies:

[a] upholds the idea of government by law,

[b] insists upon equality before the law and equal protection of the law for all,

[c] insists upon the use of due process in all legal action,

[d] obeys the law, condemns lawbreaking, and supports officials in their work of law enforcement,

[e] willingly performs jury service, regarding it as one of his contributions toward law enforcement,

[f] respects and supports officers who enforce the law, but does not permit his zeal for law enforcement to encourage officials to infringe upon guaranteed civil rights,

[g] understands what perjury means and testifies honestly.

[4] Understands and accepts the following democratic principles as guides in evaluating his own behavior and the policies and practices of other persons and groups, and judges his own behavior and the behavior of others by them:

[a] that each individual possesses dignity and worth as a person and is entitled to consideration as a person,

[b] that governments exist by the consent of the governed,

[c] that each citizen has certain civil rights guaranteed by the Constitution,

[d] that government is by law, not by men,

[e] that in a large nation with diverse social and economic groups compromise is frequently necessary,

[f] that since the people are intelligent enough to govern themselves, they do not need protection by censorship—hence free speech, a free press, and academic freedom are necessary.

[5] Understands that, in the long run, people will govern themselves better than any selfappointed group would govern them:

[a] rejects all group claims to special privilege based on birth, wealth, place of origin, or place of residence,

[b] consults the advice of experts within their field of competence by considering their recommendations within a framework of total needs,

[c] expands his range of interests to gain some basic knowledge in many fields where his vote may help make a decision,

[d] favors better and more education as a means for improving the quality of government,

[e] realizes that democracy is, and has been, challenged by ideologies which reject its principles and base the claim of a small group to hold all power on the assumption that the people are unable to govern themselves.

[6] Puts the general welfare above his own whenever a choice between them is necessary:

[a] avoids the abuse of public benefits (e.g., the misuse of unemployment compensation by a process of malingering),

[b] devotes time to community organizations and services without pay,

[c] has enough insight to realize that in the general welfare may be his own long-term welfare.

[7] Feels that he has inherited an unfinished experiment in selfgovernment which it is his duty and privilege to carry on:

[a] realizes the dangers to democracy from internal pressures arising from bigotry and prejudice,

[b] realizes that methods for meeting current economic problems such as labor-management relations and boom-depression cycles can be improved,

[c] denies to any group the right to use illegal or extra-legal methods of installing or enforcing its program,

[d] recognizes the dangers to democracy of a totalitarian philosophy based on fascism, communism, or excessive nationalism,

[e] is critically aware of differences between democratic ideals and accomplishments, but works to improve accomplishment and refuses to become cynical about the differences; recognizes that one function of idealism is to achieve a better reality.

[8] Exercises his right to vote:

[a] rejects emotional appeals when such appeals have little relation to the issues discussed,

[b] realizes that in a community where voters are apathetic a minority may hold the power to govern,

[c] will find out how, when, where to register in order to vote,

[d] votes habitually in primaries, recognizing the importance of the primary in selecting candidates,

[e] avoids narrow advantages based on parochialism and provincialism in consideration of candidates and issues,

[f] studies the main issue in each bond issue, referendum on public questions and other issues to be decided by the electorate at the polls.

[9] Accepts civic responsibilities and discharges them to the best of his ability:

[a] regards a public office as a public trust,

[b] gives the holding of public office a high priority among the obligations he owes to society,

[c] refuses to act arbitrarily or approve of arbitrary official action even when his own party or faction stands to gain from it,

[d] recognizes his obligation to render military service or other appropriate service in time of war.

[10] Knows technics of social action (e.g., how to win support for desirable legislation) and can cooperate with others in achieving such action:

[a] relies upon persuasion within a framework of fair play for gaining adherents to his cause,

[b] avoids exaggerated claims for his program which may encourage a reaction when the promised benefits fail to appear,

[c] does not allow his enthusiasm for the success of his project to lead him to accept compromises which are prejudicial to the general welfare,

[d] accepts the necessity for honest compromise as a part of the democratic process,

[e] realizes that the best opportunity for a single individual to influence public decision is thru cooperation,

[f] participates in organizational activity at the neighborhood level and knows how to relate this activity to larger social units,

[g] attends meetings, uses forums, letters to the papers, and petitions to contribute to plans and programs that lead to public action.

[b] recognizes achievements made by international organizations in the interest of peace, order, and human welfare,

[c] has enough perspective to see in events in other countries threats to peace and freedom in his own,

[d] studies proposals for preventing future wars and avoids feelings of unjustified optimism or irrational despondency,

[e] is willing to consider modifying national policies, when democratic values are not at stake, in the interest of international peace,

[f] looks with favor upon effective international controls over special phases of technology to prevent war or limit its destructiveness,

[g] does not allow his love for peace, or his dread of war, to lead him to abandon democratic values or submit to unilateral pressure from an aggressor,

[h] appreciates the role of the armed services (under civilian control) of his country and supports measures to keep them as strong and effective as necessary.

[20] Is deeply aware of the interdependence of people and realizes that a good life can be attained only by the organized cooperation of millions of people all over the world:

[a] supports the maximum use of scientific research for improving human living and human relations,

[b] supports all measures for better and more accurate communication among classes and nations,

[c] understands the organization and functions of the United Nations and its specialized agencies.

[21] Understands cultures and ways of life other than his own:

[a] recognizes that other cultures have made contributions to our own,

[b] realizes that attempts to impose our way of life on others may bring resentment,

[c] conducts himself as a worthy representative of his country in his personal and public relations with people he meets at home and abroad.

[22] Cultivates qualities of character and personality that have a high value in his culture:

[a] is honest in his relationships with others,

[b] plays fair, follows the rules of the game, asks for no personal advantage, and refuses to cheat,

[c] cultivates physical and moral courage,

[d] is loyal to his ideals,

[e] is courteous and considerate of the rights and feelings of others,

[f] is industrious in his work and respects the time of others,

[g] protects his health and safety and is concerned for the health and safety of others.

[23] Is a responsible family member and assumes his full responsibilities for maintaining the civic standards of his neighborhood and community:

[a] does his part to make his family a competent social and economic unit,

[b] maintains family property, works out plans and acts with his family to build neighborhood attitudes of friendliness and cooperation,

[c] takes a deep interest in questions of general concern to the neighborhood,

[d] has the courage to report any unlawful activity in his neighborhood and insist on police and court action for its removal.

[24] Recognizes taxes as payment for community services and pays them promptly:

[a] reviews the services provided by the community and evaluates them against his tax bill,

[b] in considering all proposals for spending public money, considers ability to pay, public needs, and other relevant factors before voting,

[c] opposes proposals for lower taxes if they mean inadequate community services.

Franklin's Plan of Selfimprovement

Arranged by
JOY ELMER MORGAN
from Franklin's Autobiography

IT WAS about this time I conceived the bold and arduous project of arriving at moral perfection. I wished to live without committing any fault at any time; I would conquer all that either natural inclination, custom, or company might lead me into. As I knew, or thought I knew, what was right and wrong, I did not see why I might not always do the one and avoid the other. But I soon found I had undertaken a task of more difficulty than I had imagined. While my care was employed in guarding against one fault, I was often surprised by another; habit took the advantage of inattention; inclination was sometimes too strong for reason. I concluded, at length, that the mere speculative conviction that it was our interest to be completely virtuous was not sufficient to prevent our slipping; and that the contrary habits must be broken, and good ones established, before we can have any dependence on a steady, uniform rectitude of conduct. For this purpose I contrived the following method.

In the various enumerations of the moral virtues I found that different writers included more or fewer ideas under the same name. Temperance, for example,

Architect's Office, Capitol

BENJAMIN FRANKLIN

This symbolic Portrait of Franklin depicts History. It was painted by Constantino Brumidi and is part of a mural on the ceiling of the President's Room, Senate wing, Capitol.

was by some confined to eating and drinking, while by others it was extended to mean the moderating of every other pleasure, appetite, inclination, or passion, bodily or mental. I proposed to myself, for the sake of clearness, to use rather more names, with fewer ideas annexed to each, than a few names with more ideas; and I included under thirteen names all that at that time occurred to me as necessary or desirable, and annexed to each a short precept.

The Virtues and Their Precepts

[1] *Temperance.* Eat not to dullness; drink not to elevation.

[2] *Silence.* Speak not but what may benefit others or yourself.

[3] *Order.* Let all your things have their places; each activity its time.

[4] *Resolution.* Resolve to perform what you ought. Perform what you resolve.

[5] *Frugality.* Make no expense but to do good to others or yourself.

[6] *Industry.* Lose no time; be always employed in something useful.

[7] *Sincerity.* Think and speak justly.

[8] *Justice.* Wrong none by doing injuries, or omitting benefits that are your duty.

[9] *Moderation.* Avoid extremes.

[10] *Cleanliness.* Tolerate no uncleanliness in body, clothes, or habitation.

[11] *Tranquility.* Be not disturbed at trifles, or at unavoidable accidents.

[12] *Chastity.* Clean thoughts and wholesome activities lead to clean living.

[13] *Humility.* Imitate Jesus and Socrates.

One Virtue at a Time

My intention being to acquire the habitude of all these virtues, I judged it would be well not to distract my attention by attempting the whole at once, but to fix it on one of them at a time; and, when I should be master of that, then to proceed to another, and so on, till I should have gone thru the thirteen; and as the previous acquisition of some might facilitate the acquisition of certain others, I arranged them with that view, as they stand above. *Temperance* first, as it tends to procure that coolness and clearness of head, which is so necessary where constant vigilance was to be kept up, and guard maintained against the unremitting attraction of ancient habits, and the force of perpetual temptations. This being acquired and established, *Silence* would be more easy. This and the next, *Order,* I expected would allow me more time for attending to my project and my studies. *Resolution,* once become habitual, would keep me firm in my endeavors; *Frugality* and *Industry* freeing me from my remaining debt, and producing affluence and independence, would make more easy the practice of *Sincerity* and *Justice,* etc. Conceiving that daily examination would be necessary, I contrived the following method for conducting that examination.

I made a little book, in which I allotted a page for each of the virtues. I ruled each page with red ink, so as to have seven columns, one for each day of the week. I crossed these columns with thirteen red lines, one for each of the virtues, on which line, and in its proper column I marked by a black spot every fault I found upon examination to have been committed respecting that virtue upon that day.

Form of the Record Pages

TEMPERANCE

Eat not to dullness
Drink not to elevation

	S	M	T	W	T	F	S
Temperance							
Silence							
Order							
Resolution							
Frugality							
Industry							
Sincerity							
Justice							
Moderation							
Cleanliness							
Tranquility							
Chastity							
Humility							

One Week to Each Virtue

I determined to give a week's strict attention to each of the virtues successively. Thus, in the first week, my great guard was to avoid even the least offense against *Temper-*

ance, leaving the other virtues to their ordinary chance, only marking every evening the faults of the day. Thus, if in the first week I could keep my first line, marked *Temperance,* clear of spots, I supposed the habit of that virtue so much strengthened, and its opposite weakened, that I might venture extending my attention to include the next, *Silence,* and for the following week keep both lines clear of spots. Proceeding thus to the last, I could go thru a course complete in thirteen weeks, and four courses in a year; till in the end, by a number of courses, I should be happy in viewing a clean book, after a thirteen weeks' daily examination.

The Wisdom of the Ages

Thus my little book had for its motto these lines from Addison's Cato:

"Here will I hold. If there's a power above us [and that there is, all nature cries aloud thru her works], He must delight in virtue; and that which He delights in must be happy."

And conceiving God to be the fountain of wisdom, I thought it right and necessary to solicit His assistance in obtaining it; to this end I formed the following little prayer, which was prefixed to my tables of examination, for daily use:

"O powerful Goodness! bountiful Father! merciful Guide! Increase in me that wisdom which discovers my truest interest. Strengthen my resolutions to perform what that wisdom dictates. Accept my kind offices to Thy other children as the only return in my power for Thy continual favors to me."

The Daily Program

The precept of Order requiring that *every part of my business should have its allotted time,* one page in my little book contained the following scheme of employment for the twenty-four hours of the day.

MORNING *Question. What good shall I do this day?*	5 6 7	Rise, wash, and address powerful Goodness! Contrive day's business and take the resolution of the day; prosecute the present study, and breakfast.
FORENOON	8-11	Work.
NOON	12 1	Read, look over my accounts, and dine.
AFTERNOON	2-5	Work.
EVENING *Question. What good have I done today?*	6 7 8 9	Put things in their places. Supper. Music or diversion, or conversation. Examination of the day.
NIGHT	10-4	Sleep.

The Art of Virtue

It will be remarked that, tho my scheme was not wholly without religion, there was in it no mark of any of the distinguishing tenets of any particular sect. I had purposely avoided them; for, being fully persuaded of the utility and excellency of my method, and that it might be serviceable to people in all religions, and intend-

Library of Congress Collections

"FRANKLIN, THE PRINTER"

Benjamin Franklin, one of the most interesting men of history, was born in Boston, January 17, 1706. At 8 years of age he was sent to school; at 10 taken out to assist his father; at 12 apprenticed in his brother's printing office. At 17 he ran away to Philadelphia. At 23 he became a publisher and at 26 began "Poor Richard's Almanac." That was in 1732, the year George Washington was born. Always a student and inventor, Franklin studied languages and experimented with electricity. He became postmaster first of Philadelphia and in 1753 of the Colonies. He was much in London as agent for the Colonies. He began his famous Autobiography in 1771. He greatly aided the Revolution and helped negotiate the treaty in which it ended. He was a most influential member of the Constitutional Convention. He died April 17, 1790. The picture above is from a mural of Franklin's life by Charles E. Mills in the Franklin Union, Boston.

ing some time or other to publish it, I would not have anything in it that should prejudice anyone, of any sect, against it. I purposed writing a little comment on each virtue, in which I would have shown the advantages of possessing it, and the mischiefs attending its opposite vice; and I should have called my book *The Art of Virtue,* because it would have shown the means and manner of obtaining virtue, which would have distinguished it from the mere exhortation to be good, that does not instruct and indicate the means, but is like the apostle's man of verbal charity, who only without showing to the naked and hungry how or where they might get clothes or victuals exhorted them to be fed and clothed. [*James 2: 15, 16.*]

In this piece it was my design to explain and enforce this doctrine, that vicious actions are not hurtful because they are forbidden, but forbidden because they are hurtful, the nature of man alone considered; that it was, therefore, everyone's interest to be virtuous who wished to be happy in this world; and I should, from this circumstance, have endeavored to convince young persons that no qualities were so likely to make a poor man's fortune as those of probity and integrity.

Humility Added to My List

My list of virtues contained at first but twelve; but a Quaker friend having kindly informed me that I was generally thought proud; that my pride showed itself frequently in conversation; that I was not content with being in the right when discussing any point, but was overbearing, and rather insolent, of which he convinced me by mentioning several instances; I determined to cure myself, if I could, of this vice or folly, and added *Humility* to my list, giving an extensive meaning to the word. I cannot boast of much success in acquiring the *reality* of this virtue, but I had a good deal with regard to the *appearance* of it. I made it a rule to forbear all direct contradiction to the sentiments of others, and all positive assertion of my own. I even forbid myself the use of every word or expression in the language that imported a fixed opinion, such as certainly, undoubtedly, and I adopted, instead of them, *I conceive, I apprehend,* or *I imagine* a thing to be so or so; or it *so appears to me at present.* When another asserted something that I thought an error, I denied myself the pleasure of contradicting him abruptly; and in answering I began by observing that in certain cases his opinion would be right, but in the present case there *appeared* to me some difference. I soon found the advantage of this change in my manner; the conversations I engaged in went on more pleasantly. The way in which I proposed my opinions procured them a readier reception and less contradiction; I had less mortification when found to be in the wrong, and I more easily prevailed with others to give up their mistakes and join with me when I happened to be in the right.

That man is great, and he alone,
Who serves a greatness not his own,
  For neither praise nor pelf:
Content to know and be unknown:
  Whole in himself.

—From *A Great Man* by Owen Meredith, Pseudonym of Edward Robert Bulwer-Lytton, first Earl of Lytton, born November 8, 1831; died November 24, 1891

The Greatest Club in the World

Consider also the Junto, *in Philadelphia, a club organized by Benjamin Franklin in 1727. It had only twelve members, and, of course, every club cannot have a Franklin for its head, but we may count the American Philosophical Society, The Franklin Institute, the University of Pennsylvania, the first American public library, and the first Philadelphia mutual fire insurance company as off-shoots of the talks at this club.—From* Frontiers of American Culture *by James Truslow Adams. Charles Scribner's Sons, 1944. Pages 157-58. [The text as here given is taken from "The Works of Benjamin Franklin" by Jared Sparks, published by Benjamin Franklin Stevens. London 1882. Volume 2: Pages 9-12.]*

THE CLUB called *The Junto* which Benjamin Franklin organized in 1727 is important for practical suggestions which would be immensely useful today to any group which wished to follow them for the mutual improvement of its own members. Franklin sought to make sure of two things. First, that the members were mutually agreeable and that they had some contribution to make to the personal growth of each other. Then, that they had a program of questions dealing with concrete everyday things. It was required that any person to be qualified as a member stand up, lay his hand upon his breast, and be asked these questions:

[1] Have you any particular disrespect to any present members? *Answer*. I have not.

[2] Do you sincerely declare, that you love mankind in general, of what profession or religion soever? *A*. I do.

[3] Do you think any person ought to be harmed in his body, name, or goods, for mere speculative opinions, or his external way of worship? *Answer.* No.

[4] Do you love truth for truth's sake, and will you endeavor impartially to find and receive it yourself, and communicate it to others? *Answer.* Yes.

Then in 1728 a list of rules was drawn up which each member was asked to read on the morning before the meeting in order that he might consider what he had to offer the Junto touching any one of them. Rules:

[1] Have you met with anything in the author you last read, remarkable, or suitable to be communicated to the Junto? particularly in history, morality, poetry, physic, travels, mechanic arts, or other parts of knowledge.

[2] What new story have you lately heard agreeable for telling in conversation?

[3] Hath any citizen in your knowledge failed in his business lately, and what have you heard of the cause?

[4] Have you lately heard of any citizen's thriving well, and by what means?

[5] Have you lately heard how any present rich man, here or elsewhere, got his estate?

[6] Do you know of a fellow citizen, who has lately done a worthy action, deserving praise and imitation; or who has lately committed an error, proper for us to be warned against and avoid?

[7] What unhappy effects of intemperance have you lately observed or heard; of imprudence, of passion, or of any other vice or folly?

[8] What happy effects of temperance, of prudence, of moderation, or of any other virtue?

[9] Have you or any of your acquaintance been lately sick or wounded? If so, what remedies were used, and what were their effects?

[10] Whom do you know that are shortly going journeys, if one should have occasion to send by them?

[11] Do you think of any thing at present, in which the Junto may be serviceable to *mankind*, to their country, to their friends, or to themselves?

[12] Hath any deserving stranger arrived in town since last meeting, that you have heard of? And what have you heard or observed of his character or merits? And whether, think you, it lies in the power of the Junto to oblige him, or encourage him as he deserves?

[13] Do you know of any deserving young beginner lately set up, whom it lies in the power of the Junto any way to encourage?

[14] Have you lately observed any defect in the laws of your *country*, of which it would be proper to move the legislature for an amendment? Or do you know of any beneficial law that is wanting?

[15] Have you lately observed any encroachment on the just liberties of the people?

[16] Hath any body attacked your reputation lately? And what can the Junto do towards securing it?

[17] Is there any man whose friendship you want, and which the Junto, or any of them, can procure for you?

[18] Have you lately heard any member's character attacked, and have you defended it?

[19] Hath any man injured you, from whom it is in the power of the Junto to procure redress?

[20] In what manner can the Junto, or any of them, assist you in any of your honorable designs?

[21] Have you any weighty affair on hand, in which you think the advice of the Junto may be of service?

[22] What benefits have you lately received from any man not present?

[23] Is there any difficulty in matters of opinion, of justice, and injustice, which you would gladly have discussed at this time?

[24] Do you see any thing amiss in the present customs or proceedings of the Junto, which might be amended?

WISDOM FROM FRANKLIN'S ALMANACS

[Hanging near the fireplace in the Colonial home, the almanac was a guide to the seasons—a record of sun, moon, and tides. It contained other useful information and took the place of today's calendar, newspaper, magazine, and radio. Family data written on the margins of its pages made it a sort of family history. Franklin, seeing the need for wiser living, had the idea of using this means to emphasize fundamental ideals and virtues. He began in 1732 to publish his almanac, pretending it was written by Richard Saunders. After 25 years, he gathered the proverbial sentences that had been scattered thru "Poor Richard's Almanac" into a connected discourse, which was prefixed to the edition of 1757.]

He that would please all, and himself, too, takes more in hand than he is like to do.

He that lieth down with dogs, shall rise up with fleas.

Distrust and caution are the parents of security.

Better slip with foot than tongue.

Without justice courage is weak.

Would you live with ease, do what you ought, and not what you please.

Take this remark from Richard, the poor and lame, What e'er's begun in anger, ends in shame.

No man was ever glorious, who was not laborious.

All things are easy to industry. All things difficult to sloth.

Would you persuade, speak of interest, not reason.

Teach your child to hold his tongue, he'll learn fast enough to speak.

A Message to Garcia

ELBERT HUBBARD

It was in a casual conversation between Elbert Hubbard and his son when the latter suggested that Rowan, the man who carried the message to Garcia, was the real hero of the Cuban war. The boy's father, after a hard day of prodding indifferent employes, needed only this remark to inspire him to write in one hour the article which he said, in 1913, attained "a larger circulation than any other literary venture during the lifetime of the author." After its publication without a heading in the Philistine *in 1899 orders came in for a dozen, a hundred, and finally, for 100,000 reprints of the article. A visiting Russian prince distributed it to every railroad employe in his country. Eventually it was translated into every written language. Thus, "thru a series of lucky accidents"* A Message to Garcia *traveled around the world.*

IN ALL this Cuban business there is one man who stands out on the horizon of my memory like Mars at perihelion.

When war broke out between Spain and the United States, it was very necessary to communicate quickly with the leader of the Insurgents. Garcia was somewhere in the mountain fastnesses of Cuba—no one knew where. No mail or telegraph message could reach him. The President must secure his cooperation, and quickly.

What to do!

Someone said to the President, "There is a fellow by the name of Rowan will find Garcia for you, if anybody can."

Rowan was sent for and given a letter to be delivered to Garcia. How the "fellow by the name of Rowan" took the letter, sealed it up in an oilskin pouch, strapped it over his heart, in four days landed by night off the coast of Cuba from an open boat, disappeared into the jungle, and in three weeks came out on the other side of the Island, having traversed a hostile country on foot, and delivered his letter to Garcia—are things I have no special desire now to tell in detail. The point that I wish to make is this: McKinley gave Rowan a letter to be delivered to Garcia; Rowan took the letter and did not ask, "Where is he at?"

By the Eternal! there is a man whose form should be cast in deathless bronze and the statue placed in every college of the land. It is not book-learning young men need, nor instruction about this and that, but a stiffening of the vertebrae which will cause them to be loyal to a trust, to act promptly, concentrate their energies: Do the thing—"Carry a message to Garcia."

General Garcia is dead now, but there are other Garcias. No man who has endeavored to carry out an enterprise where many hands are needed, but has been well-nigh appalled at times by the imbecility of the average man—the inability or unwillingness to concentrate on a thing and do it.

Slipshod assistance, foolish inattention, dowdy indifference, and halfhearted work seem the rule; and no man succeeds, unless by hook or crook or threat he forces or bribes other men to assist him; or mayhap, God in His goodness performs a miracle, and sends him an Angel of Light for an assistant.

You, reader, put this matter to a test: You are sitting

now in your office—six clerks are within call. Summon any one and make this request: "Please look in the encyclopedia and make a brief memorandum for me concerning the life of Correggio."

Will the clerk quietly say, "Yes, sir," and go do the task?

On your life he will not. He will look at you out of a fishy eye and ask one or more of the following questions:

Who was he?

Which encyclopedia?

Where is the encyclopedia?

Was I hired for that?

Don't you mean Bismarck?

What's the matter with Charlie doing it? Is he dead?

Is there any hurry?

Sha'n't I bring you the book and let you look it up yourself?

What do you want to know for?

And I will lay you ten to one that after you have answered the questions, and explained how to find the information, and why you want it, the clerk will go off and get one of the other clerks to help him try to find Garcia—and then come back and tell you there is no such man. Of course I may lose my bet, but according to the Law of Average I will not.

Now, if you are wise, you will not bother to explain to your "assistant" that Correggio is indexed under the C's, not in the K's, but you will smile very sweetly and say, "Never mind," and go look it up yourself. And this incapacity for independent action, this moral stupidity, this infirmity of the will, this unwillingness to cheerfully catch hold and lift—these are the things that put pure

Socialism so far into the future. If men will not act for themselves, what will they do when the benefit of their effort is for all?

A first mate with knotted club seems necessary; and the dread of getting "the bounce" Saturday night holds many a worker to his place. Advertise for a stenographer, and nine out of ten who apply can neither spell nor punctuate—and do not think it necessary to.

Can such a one write a letter to Garcia?

"You see that bookkeeper," said the foreman to me in a large factory.

"Yes; what about him?"

"Well, he's a fine accountant, but if I'd send him up to town on an errand, he might accomplish the errand all right, and on the other hand, might stop at four saloons on the way, and when he got to Main Street would forget what he had been sent for."

Can such a man be entrusted to carry a message to Garcia?

We have recently been hearing much maudlin sympathy expressed for the "down-trodden denizens of the sweatshop" and the "homeless wanderer searching for honest employment," and with it all often go many hard words for the men in power.

Nothing is said about the employer who grows old before his time in a vain attempt to get frowsy ne'er-do-wells to do intelligent work; and his long, patient striving after "help" that does nothing but loaf when his back is turned. In every store and factory there is a constant weeding out process going on. The employer is constantly sending away "help" that have shown their incapacity to further the interests of the business, and others are being taken on. No matter how good times are, this sorting continues: Only, if times are hard and work is scarce, the sorting is done finer—but out and forever out the incompetent and unworthy go. It is the survival of the fittest. Selfinterest prompts every employer to keep the best—those who can carry a message to Garcia.

I know one man of really brilliant parts who has not the ability to manage a business of his own, and yet who is absolutely worthless to anyone else, because he carries with him constantly the insane suspicion that his employer is oppressing, or intending to oppress, him. He cannot give orders, and he will not receive them. Should a message be given him to take to Garcia, his answer would probably be, "Take it yourself!"

Tonight this man walks the streets looking for work, the wind whistling thru his threadbare coat. No one who knows him dare employ him, for he is a regular firebrand of discontent. He is impervious to reason, and the only thing that can impress him is the toe of a thick-soled number nine boot.

Of course, I know that one so morally deformed is no less to be pitied than a physical cripple; but in our pitying let us drop a tear, too, for the men who are striving to carry on a great enterprise, whose working hours are not limited by the whistle, and whose hair is fast turning white thru the struggle to hold in line dowdy indifference, slipshod imbecility, and the heartless ingratitude which, but for their enterprise, would be both hungry and homeless.

Have I put the matter too strongly? Possibly I have; but when all the world has gone a-slumming I wish to speak a word of sympathy for the man who succeeds—

the man who, against great odds, has directed the efforts of others, and having succeeded, finds there's nothing in it: Nothing but bare board and clothes. I have carried a dinner-pail and worked for day's wages, and I have also been an employer of labor, and I know there is something to be said on both sides. There is no excellence, *per se*, in poverty, rags are no recommendation; and all employers are not rapacious and high-handed, any more than all poor men are virtuous. My heart goes out to the man who does his work when the "boss" is away, as well as when he is at home. And the man who, when given a letter for Garcia, quietly takes the missive, without asking any idiotic questions, and with no lurking intention of chucking it into the nearest sewer, or of doing aught else but deliver it, never gets "laid off," nor has to go on a strike for higher wages. Civilization is one long, anxious search for just such individuals. Anything such a man asks shall be granted. He is wanted in every city, town, and village —in every office, shop, store, and factory. The world cries out for such; he is needed and needed badly—the man who can "Carry a Message to Garcia."—*This article has been reprinted with the generous permission of Elbert Hubbard II.*

The greatest discovery of my generation is that human beings can alter their lives by altering their attitudes of mind.—William James.

Citizenship in an Age of Change

From Promising Practices in Civic Education *published by the National Council for the Social Studies in 1967.*

IN ONE sense, desirable citizenship traits in a democratic society remain the same today, in the midst of rapid cultural change, as they were hundreds of years ago. Effective participation by the individual in public affairs continues to require the same four essentials: knowledge, thought, commitment, and action. In application, however, each generation redefines good citizenship to fit the demands of its times. Effective participation in American society during the remaining decades of the 20th century clearly calls for many different traits and competencies than were appropriate in 16th-century England or colonial America. . . .

The most important factor contributing to the evolution of the meaning of good citizenship in the United States has been the nation's expanding concept of democracy, from colonial times and the Jeffersonian and Jacksonian eras through the civil rights movement of the 1960's. This concept of democracy embraces the right of the individual to his own unique combination of traits and interests and the right and responsibility of citizens to participate fully in public affairs. It is a concept of human worth that has been alternately advanced and jeopardized by the accelerated tempo of change in the 20th century.

Many changes in 20th century life have resulted from scientific and technological developments. One profile of the scope and speed of change can be found in March's *Thesaurus,* which lists and defines 1,800 words and phrases that came into use during this century. Under the letter "A," for example, the entries include A-bomb, accelerator, aircraft, allergy, amino acids, anti-acids, anti-freeze, antihistamine, and automation.

Other yardsticks can be used to measure the pace of contemporary change. Today's large industries—automobiles, aviation, radio, television, computers, plastics, and dozens more—did not exist 65 years ago. At least half of today's occupations have come into existence within the past 40 years.

As other technological advances have done in the past, development of atomic energy and automation of industrial processes will inevitably bring unemployment and empty leisure to some categories of workers while it stimulates the aspirations and creativity of others. Another inevitable byproduct of technological transformations, population mobility, is already a prominent feature of American life.

Gradually, society adapts to reconcile the social structure to the technological innovation, but in today's world, this adaptation also entails centralization of power and leadership, particularly in creating new roles for government. In response to the problems that arise as the small town gives way to megalopolis, the Federal government established the Department of Housing and Urban Development. As automation spreads, the Federal and state governments have instituted retraining projects. Because the inadequacies of one area are often carried to another by mobile pupils and teachers, complicating the problems of teaching and learning, the Federal government has extended more programs of financial assistance to schools. The program of the Great Society is largely an effort to deal with the dislocations and inequities resulting from technological change. In responding to problems arising from technology, however, government draws attention to another concern: Can centralization of power and leadership be reconciled with autonomy for the individual?

Equally important questions are raised by the influence of technological change on international relations. Some nations, thrust into pivotal positions in the balance of power between East and West, pursue intense nationalism and divisive internal struggle while proliferation of nuclear weapons continues. Technology has transformed some agricultural economies within a single generation, while in others, the problems of famine, disease, and poverty are not likely to be solved within the foreseeable future. Underlying these concerns are the Cold War, Vietnam, and the ever-present hazard of nuclear warfare.

The Nation in 1965

The year 1965 was one of dramatic advances. An astronaut walked in space, as his earthbound colleagues pushed ahead with plans for a rendezvous of four astronauts travelling at 17,000 miles per hour. Man's arrival on the moon was scheduled to occur in less than five years. The economy surged, as employment reached an all-time high. The automobile industry set another record; color television gained widespread use; and stock market averages reached a new peak. Continuing efforts to bring civil

National Aeronautics and Space Administration

AN ASTRONAUT FLOATING IN SPACE

Astronaut Edward H. White II is shown performing his spectacular space feat during the third orbit of the Gemini-Titan 4 flight. White floats into space, secured to the spacecraft by a 25-foot umbilical line and a 23-foot tether line, both wrapped together with gold tape to form one cord. White became the first American astronaut to egress his spacecraft while in orbit. He remained outside the spacecraft for 21 minutes. He wears a specially designed space suit for his extravehicular activities and holds a selfmanuevering unit which he used to move about in the weightless environment. He wears an emergency oxygen supply chest pack. White and the GT-4 command pilot, Astronaut James A. McDivitt, performed other scientific and engineering experiments before completing their 62-revolutions mission and returning safely to earth.

equality for Negroes took a step forward with the Civil Rights Act of 1965. Congress passed legislation on voting rights, poverty, medicare, and education.

The year 1965 was also one of trouble. Violence erupted in Selma, Montgomery, and Watts. In other parts of the world—Laos, the Dominican Republic, the Congo, and on the India-Pakistan border—brutal fighting occurred. The war in Vietnam escalated to a full-scale military involvement, with no end in sight. While the national economy boomed, with a gross national product of more than $650 billion, 35 million Americans continued to live in poverty. While the ecumenical movement in religion made gains, the idea that God is "dead" provided a popular source of controversy. In almost every city in the nation, urban planners faced increasingly complex problems in meeting man's spiritual and practical needs. Throughout the world, the population explosion and depletion of natural resources caused increased concern. . . .

Redefining Civic Education For Today's World

The problems confronting citizens today give urgency to the search for effective civic education. Our responses to the challenges are shaped by the nature of our democratic society. Unlike a closed society, in which an officially authorized ideology can be imposed on the young without deviation, our democratic society relies on continual reexamination of beliefs, so that outworn convictions may be discarded without sacrifice of the essentials of our democratic heritage. Thomas Jefferson said it well:

I am not an advocate for frequent changes in laws and constitutions. But laws and institutions must go hand in hand with progress of the human mind as that becomes more developed, more enlightened, as new discoveries are made, new truths discovered, and manners of opinions change with the change of circumstances. Institutions must advance also to keep pace with the times. We might as well require a man to wear, still, the coat which fitted him when a boy, as civilized society to remain ever under the regimen of their barbarous ancestors.

Also unlike a closed society, in which citizens have well defined roles, our democratic society encourages individuality and diversity. In a nation as diverse as ours, it is neither desirable nor realistic to insist on a single definition of good citizenship and a single set of traits and competencies for all to share in full measure. Can we say, for example, that the foreign affairs expert is a poor citizen if he fails to take an interest in each local election? Can an active, sensitive citizen be condemned because he resists knowledge of economics, art, or science?

The open-ended responsibility democracy places on its citizens makes it difficult to define civic education in precise terms. Citizenship in our society does not depend on the individual's acceptance of an externally imposed role; instead it depends on his participation in the processes of society. Civic education in a democratic society does not require fixed adherence to a static ideology; instead, it calls for flexible responses to changing conditions. . . .

Aspirations for Citizenship

The 11 goals . . . [below] collectively represent aspirations for citizenship in our society; individually they may be found in good citizens in varying measures and with differing emphases. The school can serve its role in civic education, however, by exposing students to the full spectrum of goals for citizenship and trusting that these students will, as citizens, incorporate some—if not all—into their own lives. . . .

[1] *Knowledge and skills to assist in solving the problems of our times.*

[2] *Awareness of the effects of science on civilization and its use to improve the quality of life.*

[3] *Readiness for effective economic life.*

[4] *Ability to make value judgments for effective life in a changing world.*

[5] *Recognition that we live in an open-ended world which requires receptivity to new facts, new ideas, and new ways of life.*

[6] *Participation in the process of decision-making through expression of views to representatives, experts, and specialists.*

[7] *Belief in both liberty for the individual and equality for all, as guaranteed by the Constitution of the United States.*

[8] *Pride in the achievements of the United States, appreciation of the contributions of other peoples, and support for international peace and cooperation.*

[9] *Use of the creative arts to sensitize oneself to universal human experience and to the uniqueness of the individual.*

[10] *Compassion and sensitivity for the needs, feelings, and aspirations of other human beings.*

[11] *Development of democratic principles and application to daily life.*

HEADQUARTERS OF THE NATIONAL EDUCATION ASSOCIATION IN WASHINGTON, D.C.

The National Education Association of the United States is an outgrowth of the National Teachers Association which was organized August 26, 1857, at Philadelphia. The purpose of the NEA, as stated in its Charter, is "to elevate the character and advance the interests of the profession of teaching and to promote the cause of education in the United States."

Our Schools Have Kept Us Free

This eloquent statement by Henry Steele Commager, professor of history at Columbia University, New York, N.Y. appeared as an editorial in LIFE Magazine for October 16, 1950, a special issue devoted to education. It is reprinted here by courteous permission.

NO OTHER people ever demanded so much of education as have the American. None other was ever served so well by its schools and educators.

From the beginning education has had very special, and very heavy tasks to perform. Democracy could not work without an enlightened electorate. The various states and regions could not achieve unity without a sentiment of nationalism. The nation could not absorb tens of millions of immigrants from all parts of the globe without rapid and effective Americanization. Economic and social distinctions and privileges, severe enough to corrode democracy itself, had to be fought. To our schools went the momentous responsibility of inspiring a people to pledge and hold allegiance to these historic principles of democracy, nationalism, Americanism and egalitarianism.

Because we are a "new" nation we sometimes forget how very old are some of our institutions and practices. The U.S.—today the oldest democracy in the world and the oldest republic—also has the oldest public school system in the world. The famous Ould Deluder Satan law of 1647 which set up a system of community-supported schools in Massachusetts Bay Colony was, in its day, something new under the sun. "As a fact," wrote Horace Mann, himself one of its later products, "it had no precedent in world history, and as a theory it could have been refuted and silenced by a . . . formidable array of argument and experience. . . ." What compels our interest, however, is not only the daring of that law but the accuracy with which it reflected our national character and foreshadowed our history.

How did it happen that this little frontier colony of some 15 or 20,000 souls, clinging precariously to the wilderness shelf, should within a few years have established a Latin School, Harvard College and a system of public education? Why this instant and persistent concern for education—so great that education became the American religion? For it is in education that we have put our faith; it is our schools and colleges that are the peculiar objects of public largess and private benefaction. Even in architecture we have proclaimed our devotion, building schools like cathedrals.

None of this reflects any peculiar respect for learning or for scholarship. There has never been much of that, and there is probably less of it today than at any previous time in our history. Only in the U.S. could the term "brain trust" be one of opprobrium; only here is the college professor a stereotype of absent-mindedness and general woolliness.

Yet the paradox in all this is more apparent than real. It is not because education advances scholarship that it has been so prized in America—but rather because it promised to bring to real life the American dream of the good society. So declared the great Northwest Ordinance of 1787: "Religion, morality, and knowledge, being necessary to good government and the happiness of mankind, schools and the means of education shall forever be encouraged." And the generation that fought the Revolution had energy enough left to create a dozen new colleges, establish state universities and provide for common schools by munificent land grants. Even the Encyclopaedia Britannica could observe sourly of this generation that "notwithstanding their addiction to those occupations of which lucre is the sole object, Americans were duly attentive to cultivate the field of learning, and they have ever since their first foundation been particularly careful to provide for the education of the rising progeny." And, in our generation today, when the critical pedant of the Old World disparages American academic traditions, we are prone—and with much reason—to answer tartly: it has never been the Americans who succumbed to the evil and meretricious appeals of Fascism, Nazism or Communism.

Let us look at the specific tasks which our triumphant faith in education imposed on our schools. *The first and greatest task* was to provide an enlightened citizenry in order that selfgovernment might work. Though the earliest settlers in New England used the word democracy only as a rebuke, they had in fact embarked upon an experiment in democracy. With independence the problem of selfgovernment became urgent. It is important to remember that selfgovernment had not been tried before on such a scale. The founding fathers confidently believed they had found the key. "To be longlived," as Benjamin Rush observed, "republics must invest in education." It is their first and last line of defense.

Has our investment succeeded? None can doubt that it has. Americans have, in short, made democracy work. They established a nation, held it together, and expanded the original 13 to 48 states—while steadily pursuing the grand objectives of the framers of the Constitution: their "more perfect union" *did* establish justice and domestic tranquillity, and secure the blessings of liberty. Thru all their history, they elected some mediocre presidents but never a wicked or a dangerous one; they never yielded to a military dictator; they avoided revolutions; they settled all problems by compromise except the greatest one, slavery, and perhaps that could not be settled by compromise; they revealed in every crisis an ability to select able leaders. Only a people taught selfgovernment could record these achievements.

The second great task imposed upon education and on the schools—the creation of national unity—was equally difficult. In 1789 no one took for granted the blessing of the "more perfect union"—for what, after all, was the basis for an American nation? Its geographical basis was so large as to defeat itself, for how hold together an area of continental dimensions thinly inhabited by some four million people? The historical basis was almost non-existent: differences that separated South Carolinians from Connecticut Yankees seemed to be greater than the bonds that united them.

Yet, we created unity out of diversity, nationalism out of particularism. Powerful material forces—the westward movement, canals and railroads, a liberal land policy—sped this achievement. But just as important were intellectual and emotional factors—what Lincoln called those "mystic chords of memory, stretching from every battlefield and patriot grave to every living heart and hearthstone." These were the contribution of poets and novelists, editors and naturalists, historians and jurists, orators and painters—and the medium thru which they worked was the school. Thru the whole 19th Century, novelists like Cooper and Simms and Hawthorne, poets like Bryant and Longfellow and Whittier, painters like Trumbull and Stuart and Peale, historians like Jared Sparks and George Bancroft, schoolmen like Noah Webster with his Spellers and the McGuffeys with their Readers—all these and scores of others created and popularized that common group of heroes and villains, that common store of poems and stories, of images and values of which national spirit is born. These men gave to Americans, old and new alike, a people's common language with which to voice a people's common heritage:

> **God sifted a whole nation that He might send choice grain over into this wilderness; As for me, give me liberty or give me death; If they mean to have a war, let it begin here; One if by land, and two if by sea; These are the times that try men's souls; I only regret that I have but one life to lose for my country; I have just begun to fight; Millions for defence, but not one cent for tribute; Don't give up the ship; We have met the enemy and they are ours; Liberty and union, now and forever, one and inseparable; I propose to fight it out on this line if it takes all summer; Damn the torpedoes; Government of the people, by the people, for the people; With malice toward none, with charity for all.**

And then there were the songs and the pictures, too.

In school and lyceum, children came to learn and remember at least snatches of the "Concord Hymn" or "Old Ironsides" or the "Midnight Ride of Paul Revere." From famed paintings they learned to recognize Wolfe dying on the Plains of Abraham, Penn making a treaty with the Indians, Washington crossing the Delaware, Boone pushing his way thru the Cumberland Gap. Thru its young eyes the young people came to see itself as one nation. Thus was born the feeling of national unity.

The third task imposed on education, and particularly on the public schools, was that which we call Americanization. Each decade after 1840 saw from two to eight million immigrants pour into America. No other people had ever absorbed such large or varied racial stocks so rapidly. In this, America could proclaim both its pride and its welcome in the inscription chiseled in the base of the Statue of Liberty:

> Give me your tired, your poor,
> Your huddled masses yearning to breathe free,
> The wretched refuse of your teeming shore.
> Send these, the homeless, tempest-tost to me;
> I lift my lamp beside the golden door.

How, after all, were these millions of newcomers to be "Americans"—in language, in ways of life and thought, in citizenship? The nation's first and main answer was the public school. Most of the new millions, eager though they were to be Americanized, were too old for school, but their children went to the public schools, adapting themselves with children's speed to American ways, and taking home with them the idiom, the habits, the very thoughts and standards they picked up in the schoolroom and on the playground. Mary Antin tells us, in her moving *Promised Land*, what school meant to the new masses: "Education was free. . . . It was the one thing that [my father] was able to promise us when he sent for us; surer, safer than bread or shelter. On our second day I was thrilled with the realization of what this freedom of education meant. A little girl from across the alley came and offered to conduct us to school. My father was out, but we five between us had a few words of English by this time. We knew the word school. We understood. This child who had never seen us until yesterday, who could not pronounce our names, who was not much better dressed than we, was able to offer us the freedom of the schools of Boston! No application made, no questions asked, no examinations, rulings, exclusions; no machinations, no fees. The doors stood open for every one of us."

That magic open door imposed upon American schools such a responsibility as the schools of no other country have ever had to meet. Doubtless the necessity of teaching immigrant children even the most elementary subjects slowed up the processes of formal education in many schools. Yet those schools have done the astounding job asked of them: they have literally made millions of Americans.

There is a fourth and final service the schools have rendered the cause of American democracy. This most heterogeneous of modern societies—profoundly varied in racial background, religious faith, social and economic interest—has ever seemed the most easy prey to forces of riotous privilege and ruinous division. These forces have not prevailed; they have been routed, above all, in the schoolrooms and on the playgrounds of America. In the classroom, the nation's children have lived and learned equality—all subject to the same educational processes and the same disciplines. On the playground and the athletic field, the same code has ruled—with the reward of honor and applause heartfully given to achievements to which all could aspire equally. The roster of "foreign" names on our highschool and college football teams has seemed worth a feeble joke to many an unwitty radio comedian. Who can seriously doubt that the cause of democracy is served when it is a Murphy, a Schwartz, a Groglio or a Levitsky that the cheering stands applaud?

If, thru the 19th and well into the 20th Century, American schools performed such magnificent service, the question remains: do they still serve the nation well? And is education still the American religion?

The evidence is conflicting. Americans in many ways still confess their faith in education, still impose upon it tasks performed elsewhere by home, church or industry. More young people are going to college and university today than went to highschool only 30 years ago. Public appropriations have mounted to $5 billion * annually. While the federal government has accepted a larger share of responsibility for education than ever before, private philanthropy continues unabated and we still build colleges with the fervor that other ages gave only to their cathedrals.

Yet there is other evidence of a more sobering nature. The *proportion* of our national income devoted to education has declined in the last decades, and $5 billion * for public education compares rather poorly with the $8 billion * spent on liquor or the $19 billion * on automobiles

* Figures are for expenditures in 1950.

each year. Most schoolteachers are underpaid, many buildings are antiquated, most colleges and universities are in desperate financial plight. And—even graver than the material picture—the decade that has witnessed the greatest rush to American universities has also witnessed savage attacks upon their intellectual integrity and independence.

The American mind today seems deeply worried about its school system as it never has been before. In the vast literature on education there is more discontent than complacency, more blame than praise. There is an uneasy feeling that the schools have somehow failed to do their job.

Yet no one seems very positive as to what the job of the schools is today. It is oddly ironic—to say the kindest—to hear people who rear their children on comics complain that the schools fail to instil a love of literature. It is shocking—to say the truth—to hear the very people who support teachers' oaths and textbook censorship contend that the schools are failing to encourage greater intellectual independence.

We need to get our standards straight and clear. Many of the old purposes and criteria have disappeared, and the people have not defined new ones to take their place. The 19th Century school, for example, had an enormous job in "Americanization"—but it was a clearly defined job, universally willed by the people. Today's school faces a nice problem in deciding whether its education should reinforce nationalism—or inspire internationalism.

Two developments have further blurred the picture inherited from the 19th Century. First: schools no longer have anything like the monopoly in education they then exercised. Today they share responsibility with the movies, the radio and television and, to a far larger extent than before, with the newspaper and the magazine: for millions of Americans *Life* and the *Reader's Digest* have supplanted the McGuffey Readers. Second: with the phenomenal growth of higher education, the new demands of industry and the professions, the government and the military, the function of elementary and secondary education has become more narrowly educational than ever before. In a day of specialization schools are called on more and more to prepare not so much for life, citizenship or democracy as for particular tasks and competences.

This means that we have placed our schools in a crossfire of conflicting demands. While we still want them to perform broad social functions, we impose upon them narrower educational functions. The old expectation persists that schools be training grounds for democracy and nationalism. The new demands are implacable—that schools not only prepare young people for college but somehow manage to teach domestic economy, driving, machine shop, current events, world history and typewriting at the same time.

There is a further difficulty—the one that most of us are reluctant to recognize. Schools reflect the society they serve. Many of the failures we ascribe to contemporary education are in fact failures of our society as a whole. A society that is indifferent to its own heritage cannot expect schools to make good the indifference. A society that slurs over fundamental principles and takes refuge in the superficial and the ephemeral cannot demand that its schools instruct in abiding moral values. A society proudly preoccupied with its own material accomplishments and wellbeing cannot fairly expect its schools to teach that the snug warmth of security is less meaningful than the bracing venture of freedom. In all this, to reform our schools is first to reform ourselves.

For a century and a half American schools have served and strengthened the commonwealth. They provided a citizenry as enlightened as any on earth. They justified and vindicated democracy's promise. If society clearly defines the new duties it wishes our schools to fulfill and if it steadfastly supports them not only with money but also with faith, they will surely justify that faith in the future as they have in the past.

THE FREEMAN SCHOOL

The Freeman School of School District 21, Gage County, Nebraska was used continuously from the Spring of 1872 until June, 1967. The old school is now owned by the Homestead Historical Association pending possible Congressional action to make it a part of nearby Homestead National Monument.

National Park Service

The Objectives of Civic Responsibility

These Objectives were formulated by the Educational Policies Commission, appointed by the National Education Association and the American Association of School Administrators. The Objectives appeared in the report of the Commission, The Purposes of Education in American Democracy, *published in 1938.*

Social Justice. The educated citizen is sensitive to the disparities of human circumstance.

Social Activity. The educated citizen acts to correct unsatisfactory conditions.

Social Understanding. The educated citizen seeks to understand social structures and social processes.

Critical Judgment. The educated citizen has defenses against propaganda.

Tolerance. The educated citizen respects honest differences of opinion.

Conservation. The educated citizen has a regard for the nation's resources.

Social Applications of Science. The educated citizen measures scientific advance by its contribution to the general welfare.

World Citizenship. The educated citizen is a cooperating member of the world community.

Law Observance. The educated citizen respects the law.

Economic Literacy. The educated citizen is economically literate.

Political Citizenship. The educated citizen accepts his civic duties.

Devotion to Democracy. The educated citizen acts upon an unswerving loyalty to democratic ideals.

PART II

The Hall of Fame

THE HALL OF FAME *belongs to every American. It is a unique way of identifying and recognizing greatness. The memory of the lives and achievements of noble men and women is our most precious possession. Because of it we can all hold our heads higher, walk straighter and cherish nobler aspirations for the future.*

The Hall of Fame is held in trust by New York University and the method of nominating and choosing candidates assures as representative a judgment as it is possible to obtain. Candidates are nominated and voted upon every five years. They must have been dead for at least 25 years which gives time for perspective. Not more than seven can be added at any election and usually the number is less than that.

Thus thru the years the Hall of Fame grows in significance. Amid all the distractions of a busy and changing world, it helps us to keep fresh in our minds the key figures in our national growth and development. A handbook entitled The Hall of Fame for Great Americans *tells the story of its establishment and operation, lists the names of the electors and the names of persons voted upon at each election since the beginning in 1900. Portraits and sketches covering the 93 persons so honored are included. Copies of* The Handbook *may be purchased from The Hall of Fame for Great Americans, Executive Offices, 1009 Fifth Avenue, New York City, New York 10028.*

SECTOR OF THE COLONNADE, HALL OF FAME

The above photo shows a sector of the Colonnade of the Hall of Fame on the campus of New York University. At present the Hall of Fame colonnade contains approximately 100 niches for busts, of which 93 have been filled. Beneath each bronze bust is a quotation on a bronze plaque recessed in the wall. Many of these quotations are given with the brief biographies on the following pages.

Americans Honored In The Hall of Fame

AUTHORS

EDUCATORS

THEOLOGIANS

HUMANITARIANS, SOCIAL AND ECONOMIC REFORMERS

SCIENTISTS

ENGINEERS, ARCHITECTS

PHYSICIANS, SURGEONS

INVENTORS

MISSIONARIES, EXPLORERS

MILITARY

LAWYERS, JUDGES

STATESMEN

BUSINESS MEN, PHILANTHROPISTS

ARTISTS, MUSICIANS, ACTORS

Story of the Hall of Fame

The Hall of Fame For Great Americans, on the campus of New York University on University Heights, overlooking the palisades and the Hudson and Harlem River Valleys, was originated by Dr. Henry M. MacCracken, one of the former Chancellors of New York University, and was made possible by the generosity of Mrs. Finley J. Shepard Helen Gould. It is one of the last examples of the architecture of Stanford White of McKim, Mead and White.

The open air colonnade, ten feet, three inches wide and 630 feet long, and the massive substructure which constitute the Hall of Fame and Museum of the Hall of Fame, form an important and distinctive feature of the western group of New York University buildings, making that group, the dominating feature of which is the Gould Memorial Library, one of surpassing architectural beauty. To this commanding site, certain parts of the work of the undergraduate colleges were moved in 1894 from their old location at Washington Square. The Hall of Fame, however, was not officially dedicated until May 30, 1901.

While the University holds the title to the Hall of Fame, it regards itself as a trustee under sacred obligations to administer the gift in such a manner as to conserve the patriotic and educational aims of the donor. The gift was to the American people, and the University in administering it keeps constantly in mind the fact that the Hall of Fame is a national, and not a local, institution.

Early in 1900, the public was invited to submit nominations for the Hall of Fame, and provisions were made to inscribe the names of 50 that year, provided that number should be chosen.

By May 1, 1900, more than 1000 nominations had been placed before the Senate of New York University by the public. The Senate, having secured the cooperation of approximately 100 wellknown persons thruout the country as electors, submitted to them the 100 names which had received the largest public support, adding to these, 100 selected by the Senate, and inviting the electors to suggest other candidates. This resulted in the submisson of 234 names on the final list of nominations, and of these 29 received a majority of the votes and were elected.

In 1905 eight names were added; in 1910, ten; in 1915, nine; in 1920, seven; in 1925, two; in 1930, four; in 1935, three; in 1940, one; in 1945, four; in 1950, six; in 1955, three; in 1960, three; and in 1965, four, thus making the total number elected to date 93.

Under the original Constitution governing the Hall of Fame, no foreign-born citizen was eligible for election. The Senate of the University soon saw the injustice of this distinction and in 1904 it was decided to establish a Hall of Fame for foreign-born Americans. In 1914 this was abandoned, and the Constitution changed striking out every discrimination between native citizens and Americans of foreign birth.

Also, in 1914, the University set apart a site in the Colonnade for a Hall of Fame for Women, but in 1922, after seven names had been chosen, all discrimination as to sex in future elections was abolished and in the same year it was decided to classify the names of the women with those of the men.

In 1922, the margin of time after death at which a person becomes eligible for consideration was extended from ten to twenty five years.

In connection with the Hall of Fame it is planned, as funds may be provided, to establish a Museum of letters, books, portraits and other important mementoes of the Americans whose names have been placed in the Colonnade.—From *Handbook of the Hall of Fame*, New York University, University Heights, New York City. October 1956.

COLONNADE OF THE HALL OF FAME

The Hall of Fame

AUTHORS

GEORGE BANCROFT 1800-1891

Bust by Rudulph Evans

George Bancroft, historian, was born in Worcester, Mass., October 3, 1800. He was Secretary of the Navy under Polk. He was Minister to Great Britain and Germany. "*History interposes with evidence that tyranny and wrong lead inevitably to decay; that freedom and right, however hard may be the struggle, always prove resistless.*"

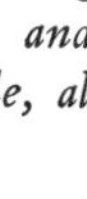

WILLIAM CULLEN BRYANT 1794-1878

Bust by Herbert Adams

William Cullen Bryant, poet and editor, was born at Cunningham, Mass., November 3, 1794. He was editor of the New York Evening Post. His poems include "Thanatopsis." "*So live that when thy summons comes . . . thou go not like the quarry slave at night scourged to his dungeon, but, sustained and soothed by an unfaltering trust, approach thy grave like one who wraps the drapery of his couch about him and lies down to pleasant dreams.*"

SAMUEL LANGHORNE CLEMENS 1835-1910

Bust by Albert Humphreys

Samuel Langhorne Clemens ["Mark Twain"] was born at Florida, Mo., November 30, 1835. He served as a pilot on the Mississippi, was a reporter and editor, and traveled extensively. He was one of the first seven members of the American Academy of Arts and Letters. His better known works are "Tom Sawyer," "Innocents Abroad," "Huckleberry Finn," and "Joan of Arc." "*Loyalty to petrified opinion never yet broke a chain or freed a human soul.*"

JAMES FENIMORE COOPER 1789-1851

Bust by Victor Salvatore

James Fenimore Cooper, writer of romance, was born at Burlington, N. J., September 15, 1789. He shipped on a merchantman and later won a commission as midshipman in the navy. His "Leather-stocking Tales" immortalized the American Indian and his sea stories revolutionized the literature of the sea. *"I now feel mortified and grieved when I meet with an American gentleman who professes anything but liberal opinions as respects the rights of his fellow-creatures."*

RALPH WALDO EMERSON 1803-1882

Bust by Daniel Chester French

Ralph Waldo Emerson, poet and essayist, was born in Boston, May 25, 1803. Among his chief books are "Representative Men," "English Traits," and "Conduct of Life." Because of the wisdom and philosophy of his essays, poems, and addresses he was known as "the Sage of Concord." *"The day is always his who works in it with serenity and great aims. The unstable estimates of men crowd to him whose mind is filled with the truth as the heaped waves of the Atlantic follow the moon."*

NATHANIEL HAWTHORNE 1804-1864

Bust by Daniel Chester French

Nathaniel Hawthorne, writer of romance, was born in Salem, Mass., July 4, 1804. He showed indomitable energy for writing, altho he failed to receive encouragement until 1831. The first series of his "Twice-Told Tales" appeared in 1837. "The Scarlet Letter" and "The House of Seven Gables" attained immediate success. Later he was United States Consul at Liverpool, England. *"Living in solitude till the fullness of time, I still kept the dew of my youth and the freshness of my heart."*

OLIVER WENDELL HOLMES 1809-1894
Bust by Edmond T. Quinn

Oliver Wendell Holmes was born in Cambridge, Mass., August 29, 1809. He was a doctor; his works on medicine are still regarded as authoritative. His poem "Old Ironsides" brought him national fame. He is the author of "The Autocrat of the Breakfast Table" and of three novels. His "Chambered Nautilus," "The Last Leaf," "The Iron Gate," and one or two hymns gave him high rank as poet-philosopher. *"Build thee more stately mansions, O my soul, as the swift seasons roll!"*

WASHINGTON IRVING 1783-1859
Bust by Edward McCartan

Washington Irving, historian and essayist, was born in New York City, April 3, 1783. His works include "The History of New York by Diedrich Knickerbocker," "The Sketch Book," "The Life of Washington," "The Life of Columbus," and "The Alhambra." He was appointed minister to Spain in 1842. *"The intercourse between the author and his fellowmen is ever new, active, and immediate. Well may the world cherish his renown. It has been purchased by the diligent dispensation of pleasure."*

SIDNEY LANIER 1842-1881
Bust by Hans Schuler

Sidney Lanier was born in 1842. He is perhaps best known for his poetry altho he was an enthusiastic musician as well. When he was 17 he graduated from Oglethorpe College in Georgia. From 1879 until his death he was a lecturer in English Literature at Johns Hopkins University. His works include: *Science of English Verse, The Boy's King Arthur, The Song of the Chattahoochee. "Weakness, in freedom, grows stronger than strength with a chain."*

HENRY WADSWORTH LONGFELLOW 1807-1882
Bust by Rudulph Evans

Henry Wadsworth Longfellow, poet, was born in Portland, Me., February 27, 1807. He was a professor at Bowdoin and professor of modern languages and literature at Harvard. He translated Dante into English verse. Much of his poetry, which has wide popularity, has been translated into foreign languages. *"The heights by great men reached and kept were not attained by sudden flight, but they, while their companions slept, were toiling upward in the night."*

JAMES RUSSELL LOWELL 1819-1891
Bust by Allan Clark

James Russell Lowell, poet and critic, was born at Cambridge, Mass., February 22, 1819. He was editor of the Atlantic Monthly and of the North American Review; published many poems and essays; was a professor at Harvard; was United States Minister to Spain and England. He was chosen Lord Rector of Saint Andrews in 1883. *"No power can die that ever wrought for truth; thereby a law of nature it became and lives unwithered in its blithesome youth when he who calls it forth is but a name."*

JOHN LOTHROP MOTLEY 1814-1877
Bust by Frederick MacMonnies

John Lothrop Motley, historian, was born at Dorchester, Mass., April 15, 1814. He was U. S. Minister to Austria and Great Britain. He was eminent as a historian of Holland, his best-known works being "The Rise of the Dutch Republic," "History of the United Netherlands," and "The Life and Death of John of Barneveld." *"I venture to hope that the lovers of human progress and the admirers of disinterested virtue may find encouragement in the deep-taled history of an heroic people in its most eventful period."*

THOMAS PAINE 1737-1809

Bust by Malvina Hoffman

Thomas Paine was born in Thetford, England, January 29, 1737, and died in New York City, June 8, 1809. His only formal education was obtained at grammar school, which he had to leave when he was thirteen, owing to the poverty of his family. His interest in science probably led to his contact with Franklin in 1774, who gave him letters of introduction to bring to America, where he became editor of the *Pennsylvania* Gazette. He wrote the famous pamphlet *Common Sense* which had a profound influence in crystallizing sentiment for the Revolution. *"Those who expect to reap the blessings of freedom, must, like men, undergo the fatigues of supporting it. . . ."*

FRANCIS PARKMAN 1823-1893

Bust by Hermon A. MacNeil

Francis Parkman, historian, was born in Boston, September 16, 1823. He dedicated his life to the writing of American history. He was professor of horticulture at Harvard. He wrote "The Oregon Trail," "The Conspiracy of Pontiac," "France and England in the New World," "Montcalm and Wolfe," and "A Half Century of Conflict." *"The narrator must seek to imbue himself with the life and spirit of the time. He must himself be, as it were, a sharer or a spectator of the action he describes."*

EDGAR ALLAN POE 1809-1849

Bust by Daniel Chester French

Edgar Allan Poe, poet and writer of short stories, was born in Boston, January 19, 1809. He was editor of many papers and magazines. His romantic poetry and prose are among the classics of American literature and he ranks with Hawthorne as an imaginative genius. His better known works are "The Raven," "Tales of the Arabesque and Grotesque," and "The Murders in the Rue Morgue." *"A poem deserves its title only inasmuch as it excites by elevating the soul."*

HARRIET BEECHER STOWE 1811-1896
Bust by Brenda Putnam

Harriet Beecher Stowe was born at Litchfield, Conn., June 14, 1811. When her "Uncle Tom's Cabin," first published as a serial, was issued in book form, more than half a million copies were sold within five years. It became a powerful factor in the anti-slavery agitation. Other stories by her were "The Minister's Wooing," and "Agnes of Sorrento." *"I would write something that would make this whole nation feel what a cursed thing slavery is."*

HENRY DAVID THOREAU 1817-1862
Bust by Malvina Hoffman

Henry David Thoreau, essayist and naturalist, was born in Concord, Mass., July 12, 1817. He graduated from Harvard in 1837 and joined his brother in conducting a private school in Concord until 1841 when he went to live at Emerson's home. He built a cabin on Emerson's land at Walden Pond in 1845 and lived the simple life there for 26 months. In 1853 he filled his journals with antislavery denunciations, later incorporated into *Walden,* his most famous work, published August 9, 1854.

WALT WHITMAN 1819-1892
Bust by Chester Beach

Walt Whitman was born at West Hills, L. I., May 31, 1819. His first literary work was in journalism. His first volume of poems, "Leaves of Grass," made a sensation in England and America for its freedom of method and expression. He is one of the most eloquent American poets. *"In this broad earth of ours, amid the measureless grossness and the slag, enclosed and safe within its central heart, nestles the seed Perfection."*

JOHN GREENLEAF WHITTIER 1807-1892
Bust by Rudulph Evans

John Greenleaf Whittier, poet, was born at Haverhill, Mass., December 17, 1807. He was the editor of several newspapers and magazines, a member of the Massachusetts legislature. He preserved in narrative and ballad poems many American legends and traditions; he wrote many anti-slavery poems. He is called "The Quaker Poet." "*Making his rustic reed of song a weapon in the war with wrong, yoking his fancy to the breaking plough that beam-deep turned the soil for truth to spring and grow.*"

EDUCATORS

MARK HOPKINS 1802-1887
Bust by Hans Hoerbst

Mark Hopkins was born at Stockbridge, Mass., February 4, 1802. He practised medicine, but gave it up to become a professor at Williams College; he was president at Williams for 36 years. He was a lecturer and author. "*What higher conception of virtue can we have than that at every point of a man's life his conscience should demand and he should render that love which is the fulfilling of the law.*"

MARY LYON 1797-1849
Bust by Laura Gardin Fraser

Mary Lyon was born at Buckland, Mass., February 28, 1797. She began teaching when 18 years old and devoted her life to founding Mt. Holyoke Female Seminary—now Mt. Holyoke College—a place where girls could obtain an education at a low price. She was president of the Seminary for twelve years. She wrote many books on educational teaching and methods. "*There is nothing in the universe that I fear but that I shall not know all my duty or fail to do it.*"

HORACE MANN 1796-1859
Bust by Adolph A. Wienman

Horace Mann was born at Franklin, Mass., May 4, 1796. He served in the Massachusetts legislature and in Congress. In 1837 he became secretary of the Massachusetts State Board of Education, the first in America. His work here earned for him the title of "Father of the Public Schools." He aided in founding the first normal school in America. He later became president of Antioch College. *"The common school is the greatest discovery ever made by man."*

ALICE FREEMAN PALMER 1855-1902
Bust by Evelyn Longman

Alice Freeman Palmer was born at Colesville, N. Y., February 21, 1855. She was president of Wellesley College; nonresident dean of the Woman's Department of the University of Chicago; and member of the Massachusetts State Board of Education. She lectured on educational and municipal topics. *"The smallest village, the plainest home, give ample space for the resources of the college-trained woman."*

SYLVANUS THAYER 1785-1872
Bust by Joseph Kiselewski

Sylvanus Thayer, military engineer and educator, was born at Braintree, Mass., June 9, 1875. Graduated at Dartmouth, he entered the U. S. Military Academy at West Point in 1807 and in 1808 was graduated and commissioned second lieutenant in the Corps of Engineers. In 1817 he was made head of West Point and during 16 years until July 1, 1833 built so brilliantly that he became known as the "Father of the Military Academy." From 1833 until his retirement as a colonel in 1863, Thayer was engineer in charge of Boston Harbor fortifications. He is buried at West Point.

BOOKER T. WASHINGTON 1858-1915
Bust by Richmond Barthé

Booker T. Washington, American Negro educator, was born near Hale's Ford, Franklin County, Va., about 1858. He acquired an education, in spite of many difficulties. Tuskegee Institute, established to give Negroes education and industrial training, was founded by him. His books include: *Up from Slavery* and *Tuskegee and Its People*. *"The highest test of the civilization of a race is its willingness to extend a helping hand to the less fortunate."*

EMMA WILLARD 1787-1870
Bust by Frances Grimes

Emma Willard, a pioneer in the education of girls, was born at Berlin, Conn., February 23, 1787. She was principal of two girls' academies and helped found girls' seminaries in Waterford, N. Y., and at Athens, Greece. She was the author of schoolbooks which have been translated into many languages. *"Reason and religion teach us that we too are primary existences, that it is for us to move in the orbit of our duty around the holy center of perfection, the companions not the satellites of men."*

PREACHERS, THEOLOGIANS

HENRY WARD BEECHER 1813-1887
Bust by Massey Rhind

Henry Ward Beecher was born at Litchfield, Conn., June 24, 1813. After serving as pastor of two western churches, he became pastor of the Plymouth Congregational Church in Brooklyn, where his rare eloquence drew large audiences. He spoke for freedom, temperance, civic honesty, and the Union. *"It matters little to me what school of theology rises or falls, so only that Christ may rise in all his father's glory, full-orbed upon the darkness of this world."*

PHILLIPS BROOKS 1835-1893
Bust by Daniel Chester French

Phillips Brooks was born in Boston, December 13, 1835. He was rector of two churches in Philadelphia before becoming rector of Trinity Church in Boston where he served until he became Bishop of Massachusetts. As a pulpit orator he was almost unrivaled. He was the author of many books. *"If you limit the search for truth and forbid men anywhere, in any way, to seek knowledge, you paralyze the vital force of truth itself."*

WILLIAM ELLERY CHANNING 1780-1842
Bust by Herbert Adams

William Ellery Channing was born in Newport, R. I., April 7, 1780. He became the leader of the movement in the Congregational Church in New England known as Unitarianism. He was an ardent abolitionist and championed temperance and education. His writings have been translated into many languages. *"I think of God as the Father and Inspirer of the Soul—of Christ as its Redeemer and model; of Christianity as given to enlighten, perfect, and glorify it."*

JONATHAN EDWARDS 1703-1758
Bust by Charles Grafly

Jonathan Edwards was born at East Windsor, Conn., October 5, 1703. He served for twenty-three years as Presbyterian minister at Northampton, Massachusetts. His sermon, "God Glorified Man's Dependence," started a religious revival in the colonies and Great Britain. His most famous work is the "Essay on the Freedom of the Will." *"God is the head of a universal system of existence, from whom all is perfectly derived and on whom all is most absolutely dependent."*

ROGER WILLIAMS 1603-1684
Bust by Hermon A. MacNeil

Roger Williams was born in Wales, probably in 1603. He came to this country in 1631 after trouble with the ecclesiastical and civil authorities in England. He founded Rhode Island, opening the colony to anyone seeking religious freedom. *"To proclaim a true and absolute soul freedom to all the people of the land impartially so that no person be forced to pray, nor pray otherwise than as his soul believeth and consenteth."*

HUMANITARIANS, SOCIAL AND ECONOMIC REFORMERS

JANE ADDAMS 1860-1935
Bust by Granville W. Carter

Jane Addams, social reformer, was born Sept. 6, 1860 at Cedarville, Ill. After graduation from Rockford College, where she was active in the incipient feminist movement, she entered medical college, but failing health sent her on a two year pilgrimage to Europe. On her second trip abroad, a visit to an adult education center in London's shabby Whitechapel district led to her work with the poor in the development of world-famous Hull House in Chicago.

SUSAN BROWNELL ANTHONY 1820-1906
Bust by Brenda Putnam

Susan Brownell Anthony, crusader for women's rights, was born at Adams, Mass., Feb. 15, 1820; died at Rochester, N. Y., March 13, 1906. As president of the National Woman Suffrage Association she led the fight for the right of women to vote. *"The day will come when man will recognize woman as his peer, not only at the fireside but in the councils of the nation. Then . . . will there be the perfect comradeship . . . between the sexes that shall result in the highest development of the race. . . ."*

FRANCES ELIZABETH WILLARD 1839-1898
Bust by Lorado Taft

Frances Elizabeth Willard was born at Churchville, N. Y., September 28, 1839. She was professor of esthetics in Northwestern University and dean of the women's college there. She was secretary and later president of the Woman's Christian Temperance Union and was a strong supporter of equal suffrage. *"Were I asked to define in a sentence the thought and purpose of the Woman's Christian Temperance Union, I should reply it is to make the whole world homelike."*

SCIENTISTS

LOUIS AGASSIZ 1807-1873
Bust by Anna Hyatt Huntington

Louis Agassiz, zoologist, was born at Motier, Switzerland, May 28, 1807. He was professor of zoology at Harvard. He founded a summer school for the study of zoology. He ranks as the most influential of American naturalists, and is regarded as a great teacher and inspirer of scientists. *"Scientific investigations should be inspired by a purpose as animating to the general sympathy as was the religious zeal which built the Cathedral of Cologne and the Basilica of St. Peter."*

JOHN JAMES AUDUBON 1785-1851
Bust by A. Stirling Calder

John James Audubon, naturalist, was born at Aux Cayes, Haiti, April 26, 1785. Altho nominally engaged in commercial ventures, his time was spent in ornithological investigation. He published "Birds of America" and "Ornithological Biographies." Many European art and science societies made him an honorary member or foreign associate. *"The productions of nature soon became my playmates. I felt that an intimacy with them not consisting of friendship, merely, but bordering on phrenzy, must accompany my steps thru life."*

JOSIAH WILLARD GIBBS 1839-1903

Bust by Stanley Martineau

Josiah Willard Gibbs, discoverer and interpreter of the laws of chemical equilibrium, was born February 11, 1839 at New Haven, Conn. He is regarded as one of the greatest scientific geniuses of his century. Although his work was that of a mathematician dealing with the problems of physics and chemistry, his investigations have profoundly affected the science of mineralogy, and have had an influence on such matters as the constitution of Portland cement. He served as professor of mathematics at Yale University from 1871 until his death.

ASA GRAY 1810-1888

Bust by Chester Beach

Asa Gray, botanist, was born at Paris, N. Y., November 18, 1810. He was curator of the New York Lyceum of Natural History, was professor of natural history at Harvard, received academic honors from Edinburgh, Cambridge, and Oxford, and was president of the American Academy of Arts and Sciences. "*I confidently expect that in the future even more than in the past, faith in an order, which is the basis of science, will not be dissevered from faith in an Ordainer, the basis of religion.*"

JOSEPH HENRY 1797-1878

Bust by John Flanagan

Joseph Henry was born in Albany, N. Y., December 17, 1797. He perfected the magnetic telegraph. He was secretary of the Smithsonian Institution, an authority on acoustics, and president of the National Academy of Sciences and the Philosophical Society of Washington. "*I may say I was the first to bring the electro magnet into the condition necessary to its use in telegraphy and also to point out its application to the telegraph.*"

MATTHEW FONTAINE MAURY 1806-1873
Bust by F. William Sievers

Matthew Fontaine Maury was born in Spotsylvania County, Va., January 24, 1806. He was an important scientist in the fields of hydrography, meteorology, and oceanography. The fundamental principles which Maury enunciated are the groundwork upon which hydrographic activities are carried on to this day. The security of vessels at sea is still enhanced by aid of the investigations made by him. He was largely responsible for the establishment of the U. S. Naval Academy and of the Weather Bureau. *"Pathfinder of the Seas."*

MARIA MITCHELL 1818-1889
Bust by Emma F. Brigham

Maria Mitchell was born at Nantucket, Mass., August 1, 1818. She was librarian of the Nantucket Athenæum and professor of astronomy at Vassar. She discovered a comet in 1847. She was an honorary member of the American Academy of Arts and Sciences, president of the American Association for the Advancement of Women. *"Every formula which expresses a law of nature is a hymn of praise to God."*

SIMON NEWCOMB 1835-1909
Bust by Frederick MacMonnies

Simon Newcomb was born at Wallace, Nova Scotia, March 12, 1835. He became professor of mathematics and astronomy at Johns Hopkins University in 1884; in 1895 he was elected one of eight foreign associates of the Paris Academy of Science; Franklin and Agassiz being the other Americans so honored. *"The world owes two debts to the science of astronomy: One for its practical uses, and the other for the ideas it has afforded us of the immensity of creation."*

ENGINEERS, ARCHITECTS

JAMES BUCHANAN EADS 1820-1887
Bust by Charles Grafly

James Buchanan Eads, engineer, was born at Lawrenceburg, Ind., May 23, 1820. He early designed useful boats for raising sunken steamers, and during the Civil War built ironclads for the Union forces. He built an arched bridge over the Mississippi River at St. Louis, improved the delta of the South Pass of the Mississippi, and planned the deepening of that river. "*I cannot die; I have not finished my work.*"

PHYSICIANS, SURGEONS

WILLIAM CRAWFORD GORGAS 1854-1920
Bust by Bryant Baker

William Crawford Gorgas, American Army Surgeon, was born at Toulminville, near Mobile, Alabama, October 3, 1854, and died in London, England, July 4, 1920. He is buried in Arlington National Cemetery. He was appointed surgeon general of the Army in 1880. He translated the discoveries of Dr. Walter Reed concerning yellow fever and Malaria into practical accomplishment, practically rid the Canal zone of yellow fever and made possible the construction of the Canal. "*. . . If there were no way to control yellow fever and malaria, the hot countries would be left to the inertia of the ages. . . .*"

WILLIAM T. G. MORTON 1819-1868
Bust by Helen Farnsworth Mears

William Thomas Green Morton was born at Charlton, Mass., August 19, 1819. He was the first to give to the world a demonstration of the use of sulphuric ether as a practical surgical anesthetic, in a major operation performed in the Massachusetts General Hospital, in 1846. "*I leave it to surgeons and physicians to speak the praises of ether in the various operations in which it is now universally used whenever the relief of pain is an object of importance.*"

WALTER REED 1851-1902

Bust by Cecil Howard

Walter Reed, American military surgeon and bacteriologist, entered the Army Medical Corps in 1874 and later was made professor of bacteriology in the Army Medical School. He is perhaps best known for his work as chairman of the committee which proved that yellow fever is carried by certain mosquitoes. In 1893 Reed began his work as curator of the Army Medical Museum in Wash., D. C.

INVENTORS

ALEXANDER GRAHAM BELL 1847-1922

Bust by Stanley Martineau

Alexander Graham Bell, inventor of the telephone and outstanding leader in the education of the deaf, was born in Edinburgh, Scotland, March 3, 1847 and died near Baddeck, Nova Scotia, August 2, 1922. His father, Alexander Melville Bell, was the inventor of Visible Speech, a system of symbols that showed the vocal organs. Bell secured a copy of Helmholtz's *The Sensations of Tone* which aided him in establishing his theory of sound. In 1871 Bell went to Boston to teach visible speech. On March 10, 1876 Bell spoke the first words over his instrument for which the patent had been issued on March 7.

THOMAS ALVA EDISON 1847-1931

Bust by Bryant Baker

Thomas Alva Edison was born in Milan, Ohio, February 11, 1847. His interest in science began with a chemical laboratory in his cellar at age 11. Starting as a telegrapher in the Midwest he became interested in inventions and went to Boston in 1868. Later he built laboratories at Menlo Park and West Orange, New Jersey. He invented the phonograph in 1877 and the motion-picture camera in 1891. On October 21, 1879, he perfected the first feasible incandescent electric lamp.

ROBERT FULTON 1765-1815
Bust by Jean-Antoine Houdon

Robert Fulton, inventor of the steamboat, was born in Lancaster County, Pa., November 14, 1765. His first steamboat was launched on the River Seine, but was unsuccessful. In 1807 he launched the "Clermont" on the Hudson River. The first steam-propelled warship was built from his plans. *"To direct the genius and resources of our country to useful improvements, to the sciences, the arts, education, the amendment of the public mind and morals, in such pursuits lie . . . the nation's glory."*

ELIAS HOWE 1819-1867
Bust by Charles Keck

Elias Howe, inventor of the sewing machine, was born at Spencer, Mass., July 9, 1819. He began life as a machinist. He secured his first patent in 1846 but it was not until fourteen years later that he reaped any benefit from his invention. *"Be it known that I have invented a new and useful machine for sewing seams in cloth and other articles requiring to be sewed, and I do hereby declare a full and exact description thereof."*

SAMUEL F. B. MORSE 1791-1872
Bust by Chester Beach

Samuel F. B. Morse was born at Charlestown, Mass., April 27, 1791. He was the inventor of the recording electric telegraph, which was exhibited in 1837, and the originator of submarine telegraphy. He was the first president of the National Academy of Design. He was a professor in New York University. *"I am persuaded that whatever facilitates intercourse between the different portions of the human family will have the effect . . . to promote the best interests of man."*

GEORGE WESTINGHOUSE 1846-1914
Bust by Edmondo Quattrocchi

George Westinghouse, inventor, engineer, and manufacturer was born October 6, 1846, at Central Bridge, New York and died March 12, 1914 in New York City. His father, once a Vermont farmer, later became an inventor and manufacturer of farm machinery. It was in his father's shop that George acquired his interest in mechanics. His name is usually associated with the Westinghouse Air Brake which transformed the operation of railroads. Among other inventions credited to him are a shock absorbing system to minimize damage in railroad cars; a motor for trolley cars; an electric brake for subway trains; and apparatus to perfect electrification of the locomotive.

ELI WHITNEY 1765-1825
Bust by Chester Beach

Eli Whitney was born at Westborough, Mass., December 8, 1765. In 1792 he invented the cotton gin, which revolutionized the cotton industry. He failed to enjoy the fruits of his invention because of a robbery. He later manufactured firearms. *"The machine, it is true, operates in the first instance, on mere physical elements, to produce an accumulation and distribution of property. But do not all the arts of civilization follow in its train?"*

ORVILLE WRIGHT 1871-1948
Bust by Paul Fjelde

Orville Wright was born August 19, 1871 in Dayton, Ohio. He was elected to the Hall of Fame in 1965—ten years after his brother and coworker Wilbur was accorded that honor. Experiments with gliders at Kitty Hawk, N. C., and wind tunnel studies led to their first plane, powered by a four-cylinder motor. On Dec. 17, 1903 Orville made history's first successful flight at Kitty Hawk, N. C.—a 12-second hop that ended 120 feet from the takeoff point. The same day, Wilbur, on the fourth flight travelled 852 feet.

WILBUR WRIGHT 1867-1912
Bust by Vincent Glinsky

Wilbur Wright was born April 16, 1867, at Millville near New Castle, Indiana, and died in Dayton, Ohio, May 30, 1912. Early in life, Wilbur and Orville started a printing business and later organized the Wright Cycle Company. In 1896 they became interested in Aeronautics and at Kitty Hawk, North Carolina, on December 17, 1903, made the first successful flight in a heavier-than-air mechanically propelled airplane.

MISSIONARIES, EXPLORERS

DANIEL BOONE 1734-1820
Bust by Albin Polasek

Daniel Boone, explorer, was born in Berks County, Pa., February 11, 1734. He explored the headwaters of the Tennessee and Kentucky River valleys and made it possible for pioneers to settle the land by his work among the Indians. He fought in the Revolution with the rank of Colonel. In his later years he explored what is now the state of Missouri.

THE MILITARY

DAVID GLASGOW FARRAGUT 1801-1870
Bust by Charles Grafly

David Glasgow Farragut was born near Knoxville, Tenn., July 5, 1801. He served in the War of 1812, and in the Civil War commanded the fleets that forced the surrender of New Orleans and defeated the Confederate forces in Mobile Bay. He received the rank of Admiral in 1866. "*As to being prepared for defeat, I certainly am not. Any man who is prepared for defeat would be half defeated before he commenced.*"

ULYSSES SIMPSON GRANT 1822-1885

Bust by James Earle Fraser

Ulysses Simpson Grant was born at Point Pleasant, Ohio, April 27, 1822. He was lieutenant-general of the Union forces which defeated Lee. He served two terms as President of the U. S. His "Memoirs" are a valuable historic record. During his last illness he was made General of the Army. *"I determined, first, to use the greatest number of troops practicable; second, to hammer continuously against the enemy until by mere attrition, if in no other way, there should be nothing left to him but submission."*

"STONEWALL" JACKSON 1824-1863

Bust by Bryant Baker

Thomas Jonathan "Stonewall" Jackson was born in Clarksburg, Virginia, now West Virginia, January 21, 1824 and died May 10, 1863. Jackson's parents died during his early childhood and his education was acquired in a small country school and in West Point. He served in the Mexican War and in 1852 resigned from the Army to teach at the Virginia Military Institute at Lexington. When Virginia seceded in April 1861, the Lexington Cadets were ordered to Richmond with Jackson in command. His rise to fame as one of Robert E. Lee's ablest officers was rapid. *"You may be whatever you resolve to be. . . . Never take counsel of your fears."*

JOHN PAUL JONES 1747-1792

Bust by Charles Grafly

John Paul Jones was born in Kirkcudbrightshire, Scotland, July 6, 1747. During the Revolutionary War he had a romantic and brilliant career of distinguished service. In 1778 with the "Ranger" he captured the "Drake," a British sloop of war. September 23, 1779, as Commodore, in the "Bonhomme Richard," he captured the "Serapis" in one of the greatest naval engagements in history. *"He hath made the flag of America respected among the flags of other nations."*

ROBERT EDWARD LEE 1807-1870
Bust by George T. Brewster

Robert Edward Lee was born at Stratford, Va., January 19, 1807. He won a colonelcy in the Mexican War, was superintendent of the West Point Military Academy, guarded the Texas frontier, and captured John Brown. He resigned his commission to take command of the Virginia forces when that state seceded, and later became commander-in-chief of the Confederate Army. After the Civil War he became president of Washington College. *"Duty then is the sublimest word in our language."*

WILLIAM TECUMSEH SHERMAN 1820-1891
Bust by Augustus Saint-Gaudens

William Tecumseh Sherman was born at Lancaster, Ohio, February 8, 1820. He fought at Shiloh and Vicksburg and Chattanooga, invaded Georgia and led the march from Atlanta to the sea. He was made lieutenant-general and later general. *"War is cruelty and you cannot refine it. I want peace and believe it can only be reached thru union and war, and I will ever conduct war with a view to perfect and early success."*

LAWYERS, JUDGES

RUFUS CHOATE 1799-1859
Bust by Hermon A. MacNeil

Rufus Choate was born at Ipswich, Mass., October 1, 1799. A distinguished orator, he served in the House of Representatives and the Senate. *"The profession of the Bar has seemed to possess a twofold nature. It has resisted despotism and yet taught obedience. It has recognized the rights of man, and yet has reckoned it always among the most sacred of those rights to be shielded and led by the divine nature and immortal reason of law."*

OLIVER WENDELL HOLMES, JR. 1841-1935
Bust not yet unveiled

Oliver Wendell Homes, Jr., was born March 8, 1841 in Boston and died March 6, 1935 in Washington, D. C. He left Harvard in 1861 to volunteer for the Civil War. He was wounded three times and rose to the rank of brevet lieutenant colonel. He was graduated from the Harvard Law School in 1866 and established himself as a lawyer and writer. On Dec. 5, 1882, after a year as Weld Professor at Harvard Law School he was appointed to the Massachusetts Supreme Court where he served until in 1902 he was appointed by President Theodore Roosevelt to the U. S. Supreme Court which he served with distinction until 1932. He is buried in Arlington National Cemetery.

JAMES KENT 1763-1847
Bust by Edmond T. Quinn

James Kent was born in Putnam County, N. Y., July 31, 1763. He lectured on law at Columbia College, was chief justice of the New York supreme court, was chancellor of the state of New York, and the author of "Commentaries on American Law." "*We ought not to separate the science of public law from that of ethics. States or bodies politic are to be considered as moral persons having a public will capable and free to do right and wrong.*"

JOHN MARSHALL 1755-1835
Bust by Herbert Adams

John Marshall was born in Fauquier Co., Va., September 24, 1755. He served as an officer in the Revolution, was U. S. envoy to France, a member of Congress, and Secretary of State. He was a Judge of the Supreme Court for thirty-four years. "*The Constitution and the laws made in pursuance thereof are supreme; they control the constitution and laws of the respective states and cannot be controlled by them.*"

JOSEPH STORY 1779-1845

Bust by Herbert Adams

Joseph Story was born at Marblehead, Mass., September 18, 1779. He served in the Massachusetts Legislature and in the House of Representatives and he was associate justice of the United States Supreme Court. He was a prolific writer of works that rank with the highest authorities on law. "*The founders of the Constitution, with profound wisdom, laid the cornerstone of our national republic in the permanent independence of the judicial establishment.*"

STATESMEN

JOHN ADAMS 1735-1826

Bust by John Francis Paramino

John Adams was born at Braintree, Mass., October 30, 1735. He was a member of the First and Second Continental Congresses, signed the Declaration of Independence, was the first American minister to Great Britain, the first Vicepresident and the second President of the U. S. "*As a government so popular can be supported only by universal knowledge and virtue, it is the duty of all ranks to promote the means of education as well as true religion, purity of manners, and integrity of life.*"

JOHN QUINCY ADAMS 1767-1848

Bust by Edmond T. Quinn

John Quincy Adams was born at Braintree, Mass., July 11, 1767. He was educated at Harvard and abroad. He served in the Massachusetts Senate and in the U. S. Senate, was successively Minister to The Hague, to Prussia, to Russia, and to England, was Secretary of State under Monroe, and sixth President of the United States. "*I live in the faith and hope of the progressive advancement of Christian liberty and expect to abide by the same in death.*"

HENRY CLAY 1777-1852
Bust by Robert Aitken

Henry Clay, Representative, Senator, and Cabinet member, was born in Hanover County, Va., April 12, 1777. He was noted for his efforts to settle the slavery question thru compromise measures. He was three times defeated for the presidency. *"That patriotism which, catching its inspiration from the immortal God, animates and prompts to deeds of self-sacrifice, of valor, of devotion, and of death itself—that is public virtue."*

GROVER CLEVELAND 1837-1908
Bust by Rudulph Evans

Grover Cleveland was born at Caldwell, N. J., March 18, 1837. He became a lawyer and was elected mayor of Buffalo in 1881. Two years later he became governor of New York. At the age of 48, in 1885 he became President of the United States, and served a second term in 1892. He promoted reforms in the civil service and the tariff system. *"Let us look for guidance to the principles of true Democracy, which are enduring because they are right, and invincible because they are just."*

BENJAMIN FRANKLIN 1706-1790
Bust by Robert Aitken

Benjamin Franklin, editor, author, diplomat, scientist, public teacher, and philosopher, was born in Boston, January 17, 1706. He made important discoveries in electricity. He helped draw up the Declaration of Independence and the Constitution and helped negotiate the treaty recognizing the independence of the United States. *"This Constitution can end in despotism, as other forms have done before it, only when the people shall become so corrupted as to need despotic government."*

ALEXANDER HAMILTON 1757-1804

Bust by Giuseppe Ceracchi

Alexander Hamilton was born in the West Indies, January 11, 1757. He originated the national system of taxation, served in the Continental Congress, the Constitutional Convention, and the New York legislature. He was the first Secretary of the Treasury, and chief author of "The Federalist." "*The establishment of a constitution in time of profound peace by the voluntary consent of a whole people is a prodigy to the completion of which I look forward with trembling anxiety.*"

PATRICK HENRY 1736-1799

Bust by Charles Keck

Patrick Henry was born in Hanover Co., Va., May 29, 1736. In the Virginia House of Burgesses he made notable speeches. He represented Virginia in the first Continental Congress and commanded the Virginia troops in 1775-76. He served four terms as Governor of Virginia. He offered a series of resolutions declaring the Stamp Act unconstitutional and was an eloquent supporter of the Revolution. "*Give me liberty or give me death.*"

ANDREW JACKSON 1767-1845

Bust by Belle Kinney

Andrew Jackson was born in Waxhaw settlement, S. C., March 15, 1767. He served in the House of Representatives and the U. S. Senate, and was a supreme court judge in Tennessee. He commanded the U. S. forces at the Battle of New Orleans. He subjugated Florida and became its military governor. He served two terms as President of the United States. He was the successful opponent of nullification. "*Our federal union! It must and shall be preserved.*"

THOMAS JEFFERSON 1743-1826
Bust by Robert Aitken

Thomas Jefferson was born at Shadwell, Va., April 13, 1743. He drafted the Declaration of Independence, was Vicepresident and third President of the United States. During his administration, the Louisiana Purchase was made. "*We hold these truths to be selfevident: that all men are created equal; that they are endowed by their Creator with certain inalienable rights; that among these are life, liberty, and the pursuit of happiness.*"

ABRAHAM LINCOLN 1809-1865
Bust by Augustus Saint-Gaudens

Abraham Lincoln was born in Hardin Co., Ky., February 12, 1809. He served in the Illinois legislature and in the House of Representatives. As President of the United States during the Civil War, he issued the Emancipation Proclamation. "*With malice towards none, with charity for all, with firmness in the right as God gives us to see the right, let us strive on to finish the work we are in.*"

JAMES MADISON 1751-1836
Bust by Charles Keck

James Madison was born at Port Conway, Va., March 16, 1751. He was a member of the Constitutional Convention and one of the chief framers of the Constitution, a member of the Continental Congress, Secretary of State under Jefferson, and twice President of the United States. He was the author of "Virginia Resolutions." "*Governments do better without kings and nobles than with them; religion flourishes in greater purity without than with the aid of government.*"

JAMES MONROE 1758-1831
Bust by Hermon A. MacNeil

James Monroe was born in Westmoreland County, Va., April 28, 1758. He fought in the Revolutionary War, served in Congress, was Minister to France, Governor of Virginia, and served two terms as President of the U. S. He was the author of the Monroe Doctrine. *"The cause of liberty . . . animated my youthful days; it has engaged the zealous attention of my maturer years; it will command my best efforts in its support so long as I shall be permitted to live."*

WILLIAM PENN 1644-1718
Bust by A. Stirling Calder

William Penn was born in London, England, October 24, 1644. He was chief author of the Concessions and Agreements of 1676 and 1677, setting forth the right of petition, trial by jury, and other ideas which were followed in the provinces founded and developed under his influence: Pennsylvania, New Jersey, and Delaware. *"Governments rather depend upon men, than men upon governments . . . if men be bad, let the government be never so good, they will endeavor to warp and spoil it to their turn."*

THEODORE ROOSEVELT 1858-1919
Bust by Georg Lober

Theodore Roosevelt was born in New York City, October 27, 1858. He served in the state legislature and was elected governor in 1898. During the Spanish-American War he was leader of the "Rough Riders." Under President McKinley he served as Assistant Secretary of the Navy, then as Vicepresident. When President McKinley was assassinated in 1901, he became President of the United States and in 1904 was elected to the office. *"I wish to preach not the doctrine of ignoble ease, but the doctrine of the strenuous life."*

GEORGE WASHINGTON 1732-1799
Bust by Jean-Antoine Houdon

George Washington, "The Father of his Country," was born in Westmoreland County, Va., February 22, 1732. He was a colonel in the French and Indian War, a member of the First and Second Continental Congresses, Commander-in-Chief of the Army of the Revolution, presiding officer of the first Constitutional Convention, and first President of the United States. "*Promote, then, as an object of primary importance, institutions for the general diffusion of knowledge.*"

DANIEL WEBSTER 1782-1852
Bust by Robert Aitken

Daniel Webster was born at Salisbury, N. H., January 18, 1782. He practiced law in New Hampshire and Massachusetts, served in the House of Representatives and the Senate, and was Secretary of State during three administrations. Considered the greatest political orator of his time, he was an exponent and defender of the Constitution. "*I profess, in my career hitherto, to have kept steadily in view the prosperity and honor of the whole country and the preservation of our federal union.*"

WOODROW WILSON 1856-1924
Bust by Walker K. Hancock

Woodrow Wilson was born in Staunton, Va., Dec. 28, 1856. He served as president of Princeton University, Governor of New Jersey, and as 28th President of the United States. He inspired the League of Nations, a heroic attempt to organize the nations of the world for international justice and cooperation. "*A general association of nations must be formed under specific covenants for the purpose of affording mutual guaranties of political independence and territorial integrity to great and small states alike.*"

BUSINESS MEN, PHILANTHROPISTS

PETER COOPER 1791-1883
Bust by Chester Beach

Peter Cooper was born in New York City, February 12, 1791. He founded the Canton Iron Works, where the first locomotive engine in America was built. He was president of the first Atlantic Cable Company. He founded Cooper Union in New York City. He ran for the presidency of the United States in 1876. "*The great object I desire to accomplish is to open the avenue of scientific knowledge to youth, so that the young may see the beauties of creation, enjoy its blessings, and learn to love the Author.*"

GEORGE PEABODY 1795-1869
Bust by Hans Schuler

George Peabody was born at Danvers [now Peabody], Mass., February 18, 1795. He established the banking house of George Peabody in London, founded the Peabody Institute and Library of Baltimore, and financed scientific expeditions. His greatest gift was the "Peabody Fund" for education. "*Looking forward beyond my stay on earth I see our country becoming richer and more powerful. But to make her prosperity more than superficial, her moral and intellectual development should keep pace with her material growth.*"

ARTISTS

EDWIN BOOTH 1833-1893
Bust by Edmond T. Quinn

Edwin Booth, actor, was born at Belair, Md., November 13, 1833. As Hamlet, Richard III, Iago, Shylock, and Cardinal Richelieu he made memorable success. He is usually considered the foremost American tragedian. In voice, carriage, and dramatic resource he was notable. "*Hamlet was the epitome of mankind, not an individual, a sort of magic mirror in which all men and women see the reflex of themselves.*"

CHARLOTTE SAUNDERS CUSHMAN 1816-1876

Bust by Frances Grimes

Charlotte Saunders Cushman was born in Boston, July 23, 1816. She made her first appearance in opera in 1834 and appeared as Lady Macbeth in 1835. She toured the United States playing Shakespearean roles. She is in the front rank of American tragedienness. "*To be thoroly in earnest, intensely in earnest in all my thoughts and in all my actions, whether in my profession or out of it, became my one single idea.*"

STEPHEN COLLINS FOSTER 1826-1864

Bust by Walker Hancock

Stephen Collins Foster was born July 4, 1826, in Pittsburgh, Pa., where most of his best music was written. He entered Jefferson College in 1841, but his love for music impelled him to leave after a week's trial and his formal education was continued with tutors. His earliest composition, "The Tioga Waltz" for flutes, was written in 1840 when he was 14 years old. Among his best known compositions [more than 200 in number] depicting American home life, life on the Ohio and Mississippi Rivers, slavery, plantation life, and political scenes, are: "Old Folks at Home," and "My Old Kentucky Home."

EDWARD ALEXANDER MacDOWELL 1861-1908

Bust by C. Paul Jennewein

Edward Alexander MacDowell, composer, was born in New York City December 18, 1861 and died there January 23, 1908. The product of a home rich in culture and affection, he studied the piano while attending public school. In 1876 his mother took him to Paris to continue his musical education at the Conservatoire. Later, he studied in Germany. At the age of 20 he was nominated by Carl Heymann, the brilliant pianist, to succeed him on the Frankfort Conservatory faculty. He produced orchestral and piano compositions and songs. In 1888 he returned to Boston to devote himself to teaching, composing, and giving recitals.

AUGUSTUS SAINT-GAUDENS 1848-1907
Bust by James Earle Fraser

Augustus Saint-Gaudens was born at Dublin, Ireland, March 1, 1848. In 1871 he produced his first figure, called "Hiawatha." Among his better known works are the President Lincoln statue in Chicago; the Shaw monument in Boston; the Adams figure in Rock Creek Cemetery, Washington; and the Sherman and Farragut statues in New York City. He was one of the first seven members of the American Academy. *"Too much time cannot be spent in a task that is to endure for centuries."*

GILBERT CHARLES STUART 1755-1828
Bust by Laura Gardin Fraser

Gilbert Charles Stuart was born at Narragansett, R. I., December 3, 1755. He began the painting of portraits before he was fifteen years old, but it was not until 1788 that he received recognition. Among his subjects, besides George Washington, were Thomas Jefferson, James Madison, and John Quincy Adams. His portraits are notably faithful. *"The portrait of George Washington was undertaken by me. It has been indeed the object of the most valuable years of my life to obtain the portrait."*

JAMES ABBOTT McNEILL WHISTLER 1834-1903
Bust by Frederick MacMonnies

James Abbott McNeill Whistler was born at Lowell, Mass., July 10, 1834. He is best known by his portraits and etchings of Venetian scenes, and his nocturnes. His portrait of his mother is one of his finest works. *"Nature contains the elements in color and form, of all pictures, as the keyboard contains the notes of all music. But the artist is born to pick and choose and group with science, these elements, that the result may be beautiful."*

Chronological List of Notables

The 93 Americans honored in the Hall of Fame arranged according to the year of their election are given below.

1900

John Adams
John James Audubon
Henry Ward Beecher
William Ellery Channing
Henry Clay
Peter Cooper
Jonathan Edwards
Ralph Waldo Emerson
David Glasgow Farragut
Benjamin Franklin
Robert Fulton
Ulysses Simpson Grant
Asa Gray
Nathaniel Hawthorne
Washington Irving
Thomas Jefferson
James Kent
Robert Edward Lee
Abraham Lincoln
Henry Wadsworth Longfellow
Horace Mann
John Marshall
Samuel Finley Breese Morse
George Peabody
Joseph Story
Gilbert Charles Stuart
George Washington
Daniel Webster
Eli Whitney

1905

John Quincy Adams
James Russell Lowell
Mary Lyon
James Madison
Maria Mitchell
William Tecumseh Sherman
John Greenleaf Whittier
Emma Willard

1910

George Bancroft
Phillips Brooks
William Cullen Bryant
James Fenimore Cooper
Oliver Wendell Holmes
Andrew Jackson
John Lothrop Motley
Edgar Allan Poe
Harriet Beecher Stowe
Frances Elizabeth Willard

1915

Louis Agassiz
Daniel Boone
Rufus Choate
Charlotte Saunders Cushman
Alexander Hamilton
Joseph Henry
Mark Hopkins
Elias Howe
Francis Parkman

1920

Samuel Langhorne Clemens (Mark Twain)
James Buchanan Eads
Patrick Henry
William Thomas Green Morton
Alice Freeman Palmer
Augustus Saint-Gaudens
Roger Williams

1925

Edwin Booth
John Paul Jones

1930

Matthew Fontaine Maury
James Monroe
James Abbott McNeill Whistler
Walt Whitman

1935

Grover Cleveland
Simon Newcomb
William Penn

1940

Stephen Collins Foster

1945

Sidney Lanier
Thomas Paine
Walter Reed
Booker T. Washington

1950

Susan B. Anthony
Alexander Graham Bell
Josiah Willard Gibbs
William Crawford Gorgas
Theodore Roosevelt
Woodrow Wilson

1955

Thomas Jonathan "Stonewall" Jackson
George Westinghouse
Wilbur Wright

1960

Thomas Alva Edison
Edward Alexander MacDowell
Henry David Thoreau

1965

Jane Addams
Oliver Wendell Holmes, Jr.
Sylvanus Thayer
Orville Wright

PART III

The Statue of Liberty

THE STATUE OF LIBERTY, *featured on the following page, is the most famous example of colossal art in the world. It is located on Liberty Island in New York City Harbor and is one of the first sights the newcomer glimpses from shipboard. The sculptor, Frederic Auguste Bartholdi, spent 20 years creating the monument, which as a gift from the French nation to the United States was to commemorate the centennial of American Independence, and perpetuate the friendship which began between the two nations when Lafayette and other Frenchmen cast their lot with the new-world colonies in the cause of freedom.*

To the left of the entrance to the statue is a bronze tablet inscribed with a poem, "The New Colossus," by Emma Lazarus.

Not like the brazen giant of Greek fame,
With conquering limbs astride from land to land
Here at our sea-washed sunset gates shall stand
A mighty woman with a torch, whose flame
Is the imprisoned lightning, and her name
Mother of Exiles. From her beacon-hand
Glows world-wide welcome; her mild eyes command
The air-bridged harbour that twin cities frame.
"Keep, ancient lands, your storied pomp!"
cries she
With silent lips. "Give me your tired, your poor,
Your huddled masses yearning to breathe free,
The wretched refuse of your teeming shore.
Send these, the homeless, the tempest-tost to me,
I lift my lamp beside the golden door!"

Photograph, Jack Boucher, National Park Service

JULY
IV
MDCCLXXVI

Liberty Enlightening the World

WILLADENE PRICE

Adapted from Boys' Life, published by permission of the Boy Scouts of America.

ON A grey October day in 1886, a million Americans, including the President of the United States, braved a cold rain to attend the dedication of the Statue of Liberty in New York. Of those who looked upward at her serene face there were few who realized what hardships she had survived in the 20 years it had taken her to reach her pedestal.

It was in the summer of 1865 that a group of Frenchmen met to discuss how France might take part in the anniversary celebration of American independence. One of the guests was Auguste Bartholdi, a young sculptor from Alsace. Bartholdi wrote down much of what was said that day. Looking over his notes later, he read, "*If a monument should rise in the United States as a memorial to their independence, I should think it only natural if it were built by united effort—a common work of both our nations,*" and he began to dream. But it was years before he saw his dream come true.

However, while busy making a name for himself as an artist in Paris, Bartholdi was ever aware of his dream of a monument for America. He even became friendly with a little group of Americans who lived in France so that he might learn more about the United States.

Then suddenly France was at war with Prussia. Bartholdi's native province, Alsace, was put under German rule. More than ever, America became for him a haven of peace and hope.

After the French defeat America had supplied food for a hungry France, and now a grateful Bartholdi spoke out for a French gift to the coming celebration of the signing of the Declaration of Independence, which was to be held in Philadelphia. He proposed a statue of liberty so large that it could "be seen from the shores of America to the coast of France." Backed by the enthusiasm of other Frenchmen, Bartholdi set off for America to talk about his plans.

As he approached the shores of the United States, he was so stirred by feelings of peace and security that for the first time he was able to put on paper his idea for a statue. It took him but a few moments to complete his design and he promptly named the tall, proud lady in his drawing "Liberty Enlightening the World."

Bartholdi toured the United States for five months and interested President Grant, the poet Henry Wadsworth Longfellow, and many others in his project. He returned to a France that was still recovering from war wounds so it took some time to start a campaign to collect funds to build the statue. Meanwhile the people of America were to supply the pedestal for the statue.

Bartholdi put 20 men to work ten hours a day on his colossal Liberty. It was no longer just a work of art; it became an engineering feat. A nine-foot plaster model of the statue was first reproduced four times its original height. Then section by section the 36-foot model was enlarged to its existing scale. Copper sheets of about the

Album des Travaux de Construction de la Statue Colossale de la Liberte, Paris, 1883

BARTHOLDI AT WORK ON MISS LIBERTY'S LEFT HAND

thickness of a silver dollar were pressed into wooden patterns and hammered into shape by hand. Liberty's copper body took shape over a steel and iron skeleton designed by Gustave Eiffel, who later built the famous Eiffel Tower. By 1876 only the right arm holding the torch was ready for the Centennial celebration in Philadelphia.

The money to pay for Miss Liberty trickled in from the French people, and she grew slowly in the yard of a gigantic workshop in Paris.

By Christmas of 1882 Miss Liberty began towering over the French housetops. Cranes lifted the magnificent head, which had been on display at an exposition in Paris, and it was riveted into place.

The left arm, which clutched a giant law book inscribed July IV MDCCLXXVI, and the right arm, which had been shipped back from America, were also put into place. On July 4, 1884, the completed Miss Liberty was formally presented to the American ambassador in Paris.

But people in the United States seemed to be in no hurry to arrange her homecoming. A group of Americans who lived in Paris were so embarrassed by this indifference to the statue that they decided to express appreciation to France with a gift of a small Statue of Liberty, and they secured from Bartholdi the 35-foot original plaster working model. The presentation of the model was made the day before the original statue finally set sail for America. Later a bronze model of the miniature was completed, and it now stands at the end of a little island in the River Seine, in the heart of Paris.

When Miss Liberty arrived on Bedloe's Island—now called Liberty Island—her pedestal was still not ready. The 214 crates in which she was packed had to be stored in a warehouse. A Pedestal Fund Committee, organized long before the arrival of the statue, was still $100,000 short of enough money to complete the pedestal.

It was a newspaper man who finally came to the rescue of Miss Liberty. He was Joseph Pulitzer, owner of the New York *World*. "*The World*," said Mr. Pulitzer, "is the people's paper, and it now appeals to the people to come forward and raise this money."

The money came in—five cents, fifty cents, dollars and more dollars. Much of it came from school children. In a few months *The World* had collected $102,006.39.

When the 225-ton Goddess of Liberty had finally risen to her majestic height of 300 feet from pedestal to torch, President Grover Cleveland officially welcomed her with the promise that "We will not forget that Liberty has here made her home." This was on October 27, 1886.

PART IV

Documents of Freedom

THIS SECTION *is an attempt to bring together certain writings that belong to mankind the world over. These writings express the aspirations, ideals, purposes, and spirit of our people so clearly that they should become the property of every American Youth and form the basis for cooperation and understanding with other peoples.*

The form of government and rights which we sometimes take for granted have been inherited thru the labor of our ancestors and the benevolence of our Creator. We have also inherited the responsibility of continuing to refine these values so that they are increasingly effective and universal. In this sense Civilization must be born anew with each generation. The entire population requires not only knowledge but purpose, spirit and aspiration.

As Mrs. Eleanor Roosevelt points out in The Moral Basis of Democracy: "*The principle of the responsibility of the individual for the well being of his neighbors which is akin to: 'Love thy neighbor as thyself,' in the Bible, seems always to have been a part of the democratic ideal which has differentiated it from all other forms of government." The growth of the idea of brotherhood gave us the concept of democracy in government. It emphasized the sacredness of the human personality and gave rise to the idea of personal rights which all mankind should respect. It leads to the doctrine of equality of opportunity.*

Magna Charta, Charter of Liberties

THE United States is a democracy, a country in which the people or their representatives make their own laws and choose their leaders. Many of these American liberties had their beginnings in England with the signing of Magna Charta, one of the first great milestones of political freedom. This document, granted June 15, 1215, by King John to the barons, fixed in writing a recognition of the rights of the people so that kings could no longer override them at will. In the original Latin the charter contains about 3500 words and over 5000 when translated into English. Historians and scholars have divided it into 63 "chapters" or articles, many of which were temporary in influence. The nine points on which the English judicial system is based were summarized by William Penn in 1687:

[1] No man shall be taken or imprisoned
[2] No man shall be disseised [dispossessed of land]
[3] No man shall be outlawed [from the privileges of the law]
[4] No man shall be banished
[5] No man shall in any sort be destroyed
[6] No man shall be condemned but by the judgment of his peers [trial by jury]
[7] We shall SELL to no man justice or right
[8] We shall DENY to no man justice or right.
[9] We shall DEFER to no man justice or right.

Other important articles limited the king in taxation: "No scutage or aid shall be imposed in our kingdom unless by the general council of our kingdom."

The Mayflower Compact

AS THE spirit of liberty grew stronger in England—religious oppression making it keener—little bands began to brave uncharted seas to new America where they would have freedom of thought and action. They brought with them such ideals as those stated in the Magna Charta. In Cape Cod Bay [now Provincetown] on board the *Mayflower*, was signed on November 11, 1620, a compact in which the Pilgrim Fathers voluntarily agreed on self-government. Governor Bradford thus describes the event: "This day before we came to harbor, observing some now well affected to unity and concord, but gave some appearance of faction, it was thought that there should be an association and agreement, that we should combine together in one body, and to submit to such government and governors as we should by common consent agree to make and choose, and set our hands to this that follows:

"In the name of God, Amen. We, whose names are underwritten, the loyal subjects of our dread sovereign Lord, King James, by the grace of God of Great Britain, France, & Ireland King, defender of the faith, etc., having undertaken for the glory of God and advancement of the Christian faith, and the honor of our King and country, a voyage to plant the first colony in the northern parts of Virginia, do by these presents, solemnly and mutually in the presence of God and one another, covenant and combine ourselves together into a civil body politic for our better ordering and preservation and furtherance of the ends aforesaid; and by virtue hereof do enact, constitute, and frame such just and equal laws, ordinances, acts, constitutions, and offices, from time to time, as shall be thought most meet and convenient for the general good of the colony; unto which we promise all due submission and obedience."

National Archives Collections

DOCUMENTS OF AMERICAN LIBERTY

A family group examining the original handwritten copies of the Declaration of Independence, the Constitution of the United States, and the Bill of Rights in Exhibition Hall, National Archives Building, Washington, D. C. The documents are so arranged that when not on exhibition they can be lowered into a fireproof, bombproof vault designed to be safe against all contingencies. Such are the precautions taken to guard these precious charters of liberty, the heritage and pride of the American people.

The Story of the Declaration of Independence

EACH year thousands of visitors to the nation's capital look with reverent interest upon the precious documents of American liberty as they are preserved in the shrine in Exhibition Hall in the Archives Building. We do well to read again and again these two great documents, and thus to renew our faith in democracy and our devotion to the American way of life.

The two documents should always be considered together, for as John Quincy Adams said a hundred years ago, the Constitution is the complement of the earlier Declaration, founded upon the same principles, but providing the means by which they could be carried out. The citizen should also remember the background of history which shaped these two documents: the growing difficulties between the American colonies and Great Britain during the third quarter of the 18th century; the gradual spread of the idea of complete separation from the mother country; the Declaration of Independence in 1776; the long hard years of the Revolutionary War; the anxious days during which the Constitution was drafted and finally adopted by the Constitutional Convention in 1787.

Coloring these events are the leaders who helped shape the thought of the people: Thomas Paine, Patrick Henry, Samuel Adams, Thomas Jefferson, George Washington, Franklin, Madison, Hamilton, and others.

Keep in mind that at the first Continental Congress, held in 1774, separation from the mother country was not yet considered. The colonial representatives used their right of petition to state their grievances to England.

In January 1776 Tom Paine's pamphlet, *Common Sense,* was published. Thomas Jefferson called this pamphlet "one of the most powerful and influential pamphlets ever published in the English language." Paine wrote, in popular form, the practical ideas of representative government which could be established upon this continent. His pamphlet stirred thousands of colonists to demand freedom from Britain. In May, Virginia set up an independent state, adopted a bill of rights, and put the power of government in the hands of the people.

On July 4, the Second Continental Congress voted to adopt the Declaration of Independence which had been drawn up by Thomas Jefferson with the suggestions of a committee including Benjamin Franklin, John Adams, Robert R. Livingston, and Roger Sherman. This Declaration stated that "all men are created equal" and that they have certain "unalienable rights" including the right to "life, liberty, and the pursuit of happiness." The Declaration was signed in the State House at Philadelphia which thereafter was known as Independence Hall [pictured on page 124], and here on July 8 the Liberty Bell proclaimed the adoption of the Declaration to all the people. The Bell, now on view in the Hall, bears the following inscription: *Proclaim Liberty throughout all the land unto all the inhabitants thereof.*—LEV. XXV, 10.

THE DECLARATION OF INDEPENDENCE

A Declaration by the Representatives of the United States of America, in Congress Assembled, July 4, 1776

WHEN in the course of human events, it becomes necessary for one people to dissolve the political bands which have connected them with another, and to assume, among the powers of the earth, the separate and equal station to which the laws of nature and of nature's God entitle them, a decent respect to the opinions of mankind requires that they should declare the causes which impel them to the separation.

We hold these truths to be self-evident: That all men are created equal; that they are endowed by their Creator with certain unalienable rights; that among these are life, liberty, and the pursuit of happiness. That to secure these rights, governments are instituted among men, deriving their just powers from the consent of the governed; that, whenever any form of government becomes destructive of these ends, it is the right of the people to alter or to abolish it, and to institute new government, laying its foundation on such principles, and organizing its powers in such form, as to them shall seem most likely to effect their safety and happiness. Prudence, indeed, will dictate that governments long established should not be changed for light and transient causes; and accordingly all experience has shown that mankind are more disposed to suffer, while evils are sufferable, than to right themselves by abolishing the forms to which they are accustomed. But when a long train of abuses and usurpations, pursuing invariably the same object, evinces a design to reduce them under absolute despotism, it is their right, it is their duty, to throw off such government, and to provide new guards for their future security. Such has been the patient sufferance of these colonies; and such is now the necessity which constrains them to alter their former systems of government. The history of the present King of Great Britain is a history of repeated injuries and usurpations, all having in direct object the establishment of an absolute tyranny over these states. To prove this, let facts be submitted to a candid world.

He has refused his assent to laws, the most wholesome and necessary for the public good.

He has forbidden his governors to pass laws of immediate and pressing importance, unless suspended in their operation till his assent should be obtained; and when so suspended, he has utterly neglected to attend to them.

He has refused to pass other laws for the accommodation of large districts of people, unless those people would relinquish the right of representation in the legislature, a right inestimable to them and formidable to tyrants only.

He has called together legislative bodies at places unusual, uncomfortable, and distant from the depository of their public records, for the sole purpose of fatiguing them into compliance with his measures.

He has dissolved Representative Houses repeatedly, for opposing with manly firmness his invasions on the rights of the people.

He has refused for a long time after such dissolutions, to cause others to be elected; whereby the legislative powers, incapable of annihilation, have returned to the people at large for their exercise; the state remaining in the meantime, exposed to all the dangers of invasions from without, and convulsions within.

He has endeavored to prevent the population of these states; for that purpose obstructing the laws for the naturalization of foreigners; refusing to pass others to encourage their migration hither, and raising the conditions of new appropriations of lands.

He has obstructed the administration of justice, by refusing his assent to laws for establishing judiciary powers.

He has made judges dependent on his will alone, for the tenure of their offices, and the amount and payment of their salaries.

He has erected a multitude of new offices, and sent hither swarms of officers to harass our people and eat out their substance.

He has kept among us in times of peace, standing armies without the consent of our legislatures.

He has affected to render the military independent of and superior to the civil power.

He has combined with others to subject us to a jurisdiction foreign to our constitution, and unacknowledged by our laws; giving his assent to their acts of pretended legislation:

For quartering large bodies of armed troops among us;

For protecting them, by a mock trial, from punishment for any murders which they should commit on the inhabitants of these states;

For cutting off our trade with all parts of the world;

For imposing taxes on us without our consent;

For depriving us, in many cases, of the benefits of trial by jury;

For transporting us beyond seas to be tried for pretended offences;

For abolishing the free system of English laws in a neighboring province, establishing therein an arbitrary government, and enlarging its boundaries so as to render it at once an example and fit instrument for introducing the same absolute rule into these colonies;

For taking away our charters, abolishing our most valuable laws, and altering fundamentally the forms of our governments;

For suspending our own legislatures, and declaring themselves invested with power to legislate for us in all cases whatsoever.

He has abdicated government here, by declaring us out of his protection and waging war against us.

He has plundered our seas, ravaged our coasts, burned our towns, and destroyed the lives of our people.

He is at this time transporting large armies of foreign mercenaries to complete the works of death, desolation, and tyranny, already begun with circumstances of cruelty and perfidy scarcely paralleled in the most barbarous ages, and totally unworthy the head of a civilized nation.

He has constrained our fellow-citizens, taken captive on the high seas, to bear arms against their country, to become the executioners of their friends and brethren, or to fall themselves by their hands.

He has excited domestic insurrections among us, and has endeavored to bring on the inhabitants of our frontiers, the merciless Indian savages, whose known rule of warfare is an undistinguished destruction of all ages, sexes, and conditions.

Painting by Charles Willson Peale, 1791,
Independence National Historical Park collections

THOMAS JEFFERSON, 1743-1826

Thomas Jefferson, third President of the United States, was born at Shadwell, Virginia, April 13, 1743. Educated at William and Mary College, he was admitted to the bar in 1767. In 1779 he succeeded Patrick Henry as governor of Virginia. Until 1789 he was in France, as Franklin's successor as minister. Under President Washington he became Secretary of State and was elected to the Presidency in 1801 and again in 1804. The Louisiana Purchase was made during his administration. He died July 4, 1826, the fiftieth anniversary of the signing of the Declaration of Independence, and on the same day as Second President John Adams. Jefferson had written his own epitaph: "Here was buried Thomas Jefferson, author of the Declaration of Independence, of the Statute of Virginia for Religious Freedom, and Father of the University of Virginia."

In every stage of these oppressions we have petitioned for redress in the most humble terms; our repeated petitions have been answered only by repeated injury. A prince, whose character is thus marked by every act which may define a tyrant, is unfit to be the ruler of a free people.

Nor have we been wanting in attentions to our British brethren. We have warned them, from time to time, of attempts by their legislature to extend an unwarrantable jurisdiction over us. We have reminded them of the circumstances of our emigration and settlement here. We have appealed to their native justice and magnanimity; and we have conjured them, by the ties of our common kindred, to disavow these usurpations, which would inevitably interrupt our connections and correspondence. They, too, have been deaf to the voice of justice and consanguinity. We must, therefore, acquiesce in the necessity which denounces our separation, and hold them, as we hold the rest of mankind, enemies in war, in peace friends.

We, therefore, the representatives of the United States of America, in General Congress assembled, appealing to the Supreme Judge of the world for the rectitude of our intentions, do, in the name and by authority of the good people of these colonies, solemnly publish and declare, That these United Colonies are, and of right ought to be, free and independent states; that they are absolved from all allegiance to the British crown, and that all political connection between them and the state of Great Britain is, and ought to be, totally dissolved; and that, as free and independent states, they have full power to levy war, conclude peace, contract alliances, establish commerce, and do all other acts and things which independent states may of right do. And for the support of this Declaration, with a firm reliance on the protection of Divine Providence, we mutually pledge to each other our lives, our fortunes, and our sacred honor.

Signed by Order and in Behalf of the Congress,
John Hancock, *President.*

Attest. Charles Thomson, *Secretary.*

NEW HAMPSHIRE

Josiah Bartlett
William Whipple
Matthew Thornton

MASSACHUSETTS BAY

Samuel Adams
John Adams
Robert Treat Paine
Elbridge Gerry

RHODE ISLAND

Stephen Hopkins
William Ellery

CONNECTICUT

Roger Sherman
Samuel Huntington
William Williams
Oliver Wolcott

NEW YORK

William Floyd
Philip Livingston
Francis Lewis
Lewis Morris

NEW JERSEY

Richard Stockton
John Witherspoon
Francis Hopkinson
John Hart
Abraham Clark

PENNSYLVANIA

Robert Morris
Benjamin Rush
Benjamin Franklin
John Morton
George Clymer
James Smith
George Taylor
James Wilson
George Ross

DELAWARE

Caesar Rodney
George Read
Thomas McKean

MARYLAND

Samuel Chase
William Paca
Thomas Stone
Charles Carroll

VIRGINIA

George Wythe
Richard Henry Lee
Thomas Jefferson
Benjamin Harrison
Thomas Nelson, Jr.
Francis Lightfoot Lee
Carter Braxton

NORTH CAROLINA

William Hooper
Joseph Hewes
John Penn

SOUTH CAROLINA

Edward Rutledge
Thomas Heyward, Jr.
Thomas Lynch, Jr.
Arthur Middleton

GEORGIA

Button Gwinnett
Lyman Hall
George Walton

INDEPENDENCE HALL

Independence Hall in Philadelphia where the Declaration of Independence was signed and where the Constitutional Convention met in 1787.

The Story of the Constitution

THE Revolutionary War which followed the Declaration of Independence dragged along thru weary years of uncertainty and suffering to be finally terminated by the surrender of Yorktown on October 19, 1781, and the Treaty of Peace signed in 1783. The new nation drew up the Articles of Confederation, which were "destitute of even a shadow of a constitutional power to enforce the execution of its own laws" and were therefore too weak to govern adequately the newly created states. But the Articles did serve as a transition government to tide the new nation along until the Constitution could be put into force.

The framers of the Constitution met in May 1787 at Independence Hall [pictured on the preceding page]. They encountered problems of the most complicated nature. The world was not accustomed to democracy. The selfgovernment of nations seemed to be a mere dream. Yet in 87 working days, the delegates by September 17, 1787, had completed the framework of a system that was "new in human experience, well-suited to the American situation, equitable as between states, and so wisely conceived that it has survived over 150 years, during which all important nations of the world have revised their forms of government." Small wonder that the English statesman, Gladstone, declared that "the American Constitution is, so far as I can see, the most wonderful work ever struck off at a given time by the brain and purpose of man."

George Washington, hero of the Revolutionary War, who had presided with wisdom and patience over the meetings of the delegates, was directed to send the new Constitution to the Congress of the Confederation. The fight for adoption was long and bitter. From the many pamphlets that were prepared for and against adoption came a series of articles known as *The Federalist*, a classic that has come down to us as a monumental work on the nature of our government.

The first state to ratify the Constitution was Delaware on December 7, 1787. Pennsylvania approved it on December 12; next New Jersey, then Georgia, Connecticut, Massachusetts, Maryland, and South Carolina. With ratification by the ninth state, New Hampshire, the Constitution became effective in the nine states which had approved it. Virginia was the tenth state to accept it, and New York the eleventh. North Carolina and Rhode Island refused to act. It was not until after the new government was organized and Washington was President that these two states came into the Union.

The struggle to adopt the Constitution may well be regarded as one of the major political conflicts in the history of our country. The debates and discussions on the new government constituted our first great school of democracy.

The Constitution is written so that everyone can understand its meaning. It can be read in 15 minutes. It should be, as William Hickey called it, "the fireside companion of the American citizen." For the convenience of the reader, headings have been added in the following version, and spelling and capitalization have been changed to conform to modern usage.

THE CONSTITUTION OF THE UNITED STATES

Preamble

WE THE PEOPLE of the United States, in order to form a more perfect union, establish justice, insure domestic tranquillity, provide for the common defense, promote the general welfare, and secure the blessings of liberty to ourselves and our posterity, do ordain and establish this Constitution for the United States of America.

ARTICLE I

Legislative Department

SECTION 1. *Congress*

All legislative powers herein granted shall be vested in a Congress of the United States, which shall consist of a Senate and House of Representatives.

SECTION 2. *House of Representatives*

[1] *Election and term of members.* The House of Representatives shall be composed of members chosen every second year by the people of the several states, and the electors in each state shall have the qualifications requisite for electors of the most numerous branch of the state legislature.

[2] *Qualifications of members.* No person shall be a Representative who shall not have attained to the age of twenty-five years, and been seven years a citizen of the United States, and who shall not, when elected, be an inhabitant of that state in which he shall be chosen.

[3] *Apportionment of representatives and of direct*

taxes. [Representatives and direct taxes shall be apportioned among the several states which may be included within this Union, according to their respective numbers, which shall be determined by adding to the whole number of free persons, including those bound to service for a term of years, and excluding Indians not taxed, three-fifths of all other persons][1] The actual enumeration shall be made within three years after the first meeting of the Congress of the United States, and within every subsequent term of ten years, in such manner as they shall by law direct. The number of Representatives shall not exceed one for every thirty thousand, but each state shall have at least one representative; [and until such enumeration shall be made, the State of New Hampshire shall be entitled to choose three, Massachusetts eight, Rhode Island and Providence Plantations one, Connecticut five, New York six, New Jersey four, Pennsylvania eight, Delaware one, Maryland six, Virginia ten, North Carolina five, South Carolina five, and Georgia three.][2]

[4] *Filling vacancies.* When vacancies happen in the representation from any state, the Executive authority thereof shall issue writs of election to fill such vacancies.

[5] *Officers; power of impeachment.* The House of Representatives shall choose their Speaker and other officers; and shall have the sole power of impeachment.

SECTION 3. *Senate*

[1] *Number and election of members.* The Senate of the United States shall be composed of two Senators from

[1] The final word "persons" refers to slaves. This sentence has been modified by the Fourteenth Amendment.

[2] Obsolete since 1793.

each state, chosen [by the legislature thereof],[3] for six years; and each Senator shall have one vote.

[2] *Classification.* Immediately after they shall be assembled in consequence of the first election, they shall be divided as equally as may be into three classes. The seats of the Senators of the first class shall be vacated at the expiration of the second year, of the second class at the expiration of the fourth year, and of the third class at the expiration of the sixth year, so that one-third may be chosen every second year; [and if vacancies happen by resignation, or otherwise, during the recess of the legislature of any state, the Executive thereof may make temporary appointments until the next meeting of the legislature, which shall then fill such vacancies.][4]

[3] *Qualifications of members.* No person shall be a Senator who shall not have attained to the age of thirty years, and been nine years a citizen of the United States, and who shall not, when elected, be an inhabitant of that state for which he shall be chosen.

[4] *President of the Senate.* The Vice-President of the United States shall be President of the Senate, but shall have no vote, unless they be equally divided.

[5] *Other officers.* The Senate shall choose their other officers, and also a President *pro tempore,* in the absence of the Vice-President, or when he shall exercise the office of President of the United States.

[6] *Trials of impeachment.* The Senate shall have the sole power to try all impeachments. When sitting for

---

[3] The method of electing Senators was changed by the Seventeenth Amendment.

[4] The method of filling Senatorial vacancies was modified by the Seventeenth Amendment.

that purpose, they shall be on oath or affirmation. When the President of the United States is tried, the Chief Justice shall preside; and no person shall be convicted without the concurrence of two-thirds of the members present.

[7] *Judgment of convicted official.* Judgment in cases of impeachment shall not extend further than to removal from office, and disqualification to hold and enjoy any office of honor, trust or profit under the United States; but the party convicted shall nevertheless be liable and subject to indictment, trial, judgment and punishment, according to law.

SECTION 4. *Both Houses*

[1] *Method of holding elections.* The times, places and manner of holding elections for Senators and Representatives shall be prescribed in each state by the legislature thereof; but the Congress may at any time by law make or alter such regulations, [except as to the places of choosing Senators.] [5]

[2] *Meetings of Congress.* [The Congress shall assemble at least once in every year, and such meeting shall be on the first Monday in December, unless they shall by law appoint a different day.] [6]

---

[5] This was to prevent Congress from fixing the meeting places of state legislatures. The Seventeenth Amendment changed the condition.

[6] Changed by the Twentieth Amendment. The December session was done away with, and Congress now meets on January 3.

SECTION 5. *The Houses Separately*

[1] *Organization.* Each House shall be the judge of the elections, returns and qualifications of its own members, and a majority of each shall constitute a quorum to do business; but a smaller number may adjourn from day to day, and may be authorized to compel the attendance of absent members, in such manner, and under such penalties, as each House may provide.

[2] *Rules of procedure.* Each House may determine the rules of its proceedings, punish its members for disorderly behavior, and with the concurrence of two-thirds, expel a member.

[3] *Journal of proceedings.* Each House shall keep a journal of its proceedings, and from time to time publish the same, excepting such parts as may in their judgment require secrecy; and the yeas and nays of the members of either House on any question shall, at the desire of one-fifth of those present, be entered on the journal.

[4] *Adjournment.* Neither House, during the session of Congress, shall, without the consent of the other, adjourn for more than three days, nor to any other place than that in which the two Houses shall be sitting.

SECTION 6. *Privileges and Disabilities of Members*

[1] *Compensation and privileges.* The Senators and Representatives shall receive a compensation for their services, to be ascertained by law and paid out of the treasury of the United States. They shall in all cases except treason, felony and breach of the peace, be privileged from arrest during their attendance at the session of their respective Houses, and in going to and returning

from the same; and for any speech or debate in either House, they shall not be questioned in any other place.

[2] *Holding other public office forbidden.* No Senator or Representative shall, during the time for which he was elected, be appointed to any civil office under the authority of the United States, which shall have been created, or the emoluments whereof shall have been increased, during such time; and no person holding any office under the United States shall be a member of either House during his continuance in office.

SECTION 7. *Manner of Making Laws*

[1] *Revenue bills.* All bills for raising revenue shall originate in the House of Representatives; but the Senate may propose or concur with amendments as on other bills.

[2] *How bills become laws.* Every bill which shall have passed the House of Representatives and the Senate, shall, before it become a law, be presented to the President of the United States; if he approve he shall sign it, but if not he shall return it with his objections to that House in which it shall have originated, who shall enter the objections at large on their journal, and proceed to reconsider it. If after such reconsideration two-thirds of that House shall agree to pass the bill, it shall be sent, together with the objections, to the other House, by which it shall likewise be reconsidered, and, if approved by two-thirds of that House, it shall become a law. But in all such cases the votes of both Houses shall be determined by yeas and nays, and the names of the persons voting for and against the bill shall be entered on the journal of each House respectively. If any bill shall not be returned by the Presi-

dent within ten days (Sundays excepted) after it shall have been presented to him, the same shall be a law, in like manner as if he had signed it, unless the Congress by their adjournment prevent its return, in which case it shall not be a law.

[3] *Approval by the President.* Every order, resolution, or vote to which the concurrence of the Senate and House of Representatives may be necessary (except on a question of adjournment) shall be presented to the President of the United States; and before the same shall take effect, shall be approved by him, or being disapproved by him, shall be repassed by two-thirds of the Senate and House of Representatives, according to the rules and limitations prescribed in the case of a bill.

SECTION 8. *Powers Granted to Congress*

1-17. The Congress shall have power:

[1] To lay and collect taxes, duties, imposts and excises, to pay the debts and provide for the common defense and general welfare of the United States; but all duties, imposts and excises shall be uniform thruout the United States;

[2] To borrow money on the credit of the United States;

[3] To regulate commerce with foreign nations, and among the several states, and with the Indian tribes;

[4] To establish an uniform rule of naturalization, and uniform laws on the subject of bankruptcies thruout the United States;

[5] To coin money, regulate the value thereof, and of foreign coin, and fix the standard of weights and measures;

[6] To provide for the punishment of counterfeiting the securities and current coin of the United States;

[7] To establish post offices and post roads;

[8] To promote the progress of science and useful arts by securing for limited times to authors and inventors the exclusive right to their respective writings and discoveries;

[9] To constitute tribunals inferior to the Supreme Court;

[10] To define and punish piracies and felonies committed on the high seas and offenses against the law of nations;

[11] To declare war, grant letters of marque and reprisal, and make rules concerning captures on land and water;

[12] To raise and support armies, but no appropriation of money to that use shall be for a longer term than two years;

[13] To provide and maintain a navy;

[14] To make rules for the government and regulation of the land and naval forces;

[15] To provide for calling forth the militia to execute the laws of the Union, suppress insurrections, and repel invasions;

[16] To provide for organizing, arming, and disciplining the militia, and for governing such part of them as may be employed in the service of the United States, reserving to the states respectively the appointment of the officers, and the authority of training the militia according to the discipline prescribed by Congress;

[17] To exercise exclusive legislation in all cases whatsoever, over such district (not exceeding ten miles square)

as may, by cession of particular states, and the acceptance of Congress, become the seat of the government of the United States,[7] and to exercise like authority over all places purchased by the consent of the legislature of the state in which the same shall be, for the erection of forts, magazines, arsenals, dock-yards, and other needful buildings; and

[18] *Implied powers.* To make all laws which shall be necessary and proper for carrying into execution the foregoing powers, and all other powers vested by this Constitution in the government of the United States, or in any department or office thereof.[8]

SECTION 9. *Powers Forbidden to the United States*[9]

[1] The migration or importation of such persons as any of the states now existing shall think proper to admit shall not be prohibited by the Congress prior to the year one thousand eight hundred and eight; but a tax or duty may be imposed on such importation, not exceeding ten dollars for each person.[10]

[2] The privilege of the writ of *habeas corpus* shall not be suspended, unless when in cases of rebellion or invasion the public safety may require it.

[3] No bill of attainder or *ex post facto* law shall be passed.

---

[7] Gives the federal government its authority over the District of Columbia.

[8] This is the famous so-called "elastic clause" of the Constitution.

[9] Other powers forbidden to the United States are found in Amendments One to Ten.

[10] This paragraph refers to the slave trade, which was prohibited by Congress after 1808. The only force of the clause at present is to authorize a tax on immigrants.

[4] [No capitation, or other direct tax shall be laid, unless in proportion to the census or enumeration herein-before directed to be taken.][11]

[5] No tax or duty shall be laid on articles exported from any state.

[6] No preference shall be given by any regulation of commerce or revenue to the ports of one state over those of another; nor shall vessels bound to, or from, one state, be obliged to enter, clear, or pay duties in another.

[7] No money shall be drawn from the treasury, but in consequence of appropriations made by law; and a regular statement and account of the receipts and expenditures of all public money shall be published from time to time.

[8] No title of nobility shall be granted by the United States; and no person holding any office of profit or trust under them, shall, without the consent of the Congress, accept of any present, emolument, office, or title, of any kind whatever, from any king, prince, or foreign state.

SECTION 10. *Various Powers Denied the States*

[1] No state shall enter into any treaty, alliance, or confederation; grant letters of marque and reprisal; coin money; emit bills of credit; making anything but gold and silver coin a tender in payment of debts; pass any bill of attainder, *ex post facto* law, or law impairing the obligation of contracts, or grant any title of nobility.

[2] No state shall, without the consent of the Con-

[11] Modified by the Sixteenth Amendment establishing a Federal Income Tax.

gress, lay any imposts or duties on imports or exports, except what may be absolutely necessary for executing its inspection laws; and the net produce of all duties and imposts, laid by any state on imports or exports, shall be for the use of the treasury of the United States; and all such laws shall be subject to the revision and control of the Congress.

[3] No state shall, without the consent of Congress, lay any duty of tonnage, keep troops, or ships of war in time of peace, enter into any agreement or compact with another state, or with a foreign power, or engage in war, unless actually invaded, or in such imminent danger as will not admit of delay.

ARTICLE II

Executive Department

SECTION 1. *President and Vice-President*

[1] *Term of office.* The executive power shall be vested in a President of the United States of America. He shall hold his office during the term of four years, and together with the Vice-President, chosen for the same term, be elected as follows:

[2] *Electors.* Each state shall appoint, in such manner as the legislature thereof may direct, a number of electors, equal to the whole number of Senators and Representatives to which the state may be entitled in the Congress; but no Senator or Representative, or person holding an office of trust or profit under the United States, shall be appointed an elector.

Original method of electing President and Vice-Presi-

dent. [The electors shall meet in their respective states, and vote by ballot for two persons, of whom one at least shall not be an inhabitant of the same state with themselves. And they shall make a list of all the persons voted for, and of the number of votes for each; which list they shall sign and certify, and transmit sealed to the seat of the government of the United States, directed to the President of the Senate. The President of the Senate shall, in the presence of the Senate and House of Representatives, open all the certificates, and the votes shall then be counted. The person having the greatest number of votes shall be the President, if such number be a majority of the whole number of electors appointed; and if there be more than one who have such majority, and have an equal number of votes, then the House of Representatives shall immediately choose by ballot one of them for President; and if no person have a majority, then from the five highest on the list the said House shall in like manner choose the President. But in choosing the President the votes shall be taken by states, the representation from each state having one vote; a quorum for this purpose shall consist of a member or members from two-thirds of the states, and a majority of all the states shall be necessary to a choice. In every case, after the choice of the President, the person having the greatest number of votes of the electors shall be the Vice-President. But if there should remain two or more who have equal votes, the Senate shall choose from them by ballot the Vice-President.] [12]

[3] *Time of choosing electors.* The Congress may determine the time of choosing the electors, and the day on

---

[12] This paragraph has been superseded by the Twelfth Amendment.

which they shall give their votes; which day shall be the same thruout the United States.[13]

[4] *Qualifications of the President.* No person except a natural born citizen, [or a citizen of the United States, at the time of the adoption of this Constitution,][14] shall be eligible to the office of President; neither shall any person be eligible to that office who shall not have attained to the age of thirty-five years, and been fourteen years a resident within the United States.

[5] *Vacancy.* In case of the removal of the President from office, or of his death, resignation, or inability to discharge the powers and duties of the said office, the same shall devolve on the Vice-President, and the Congress may by law provide for the case of removal, death, resignation, or inability, both of the President and Vice-President, declaring what officer shall then act as President, and such officer shall act accordingly, until the disability be removed, or a President shall be elected.[15]

[6] *The President's salary.* The President shall, at stated times, receive for his services, a compensation, which shall neither be increased nor diminished during the period for which he shall have been elected, and he

---

[13] Since the passage of the Twentieth Amendment, the electors vote, by Act of Congress, on the first Monday after the second Wednesday in December. Ballots are sent to the President of the Senate before the fourth Wednesday in December. Congress counts the votes on January 6, following.

[14] Obsolete.

[15] In 1886 Congress passed the Presidential Succession Act establishing the order of succession by Cabinet officers in case of the death or disability of both President and Vice-President. This paragraph is further supplemented by Sections 3 and 4 of Amendment XX and by Amendment XXV.

shall not receive within that period any other emolument from the United States, or any of them.

[7] *The Presidential oath of office.* Before he enter on the execution of his office, he shall take the following oath or affirmation: "I do solemnly swear (or affirm) that I will faithfully execute the office of President of the United States, and will to the best of my ability, preserve, protect and defend the Constitution of the United States."

SECTION 2. *Powers of the President*

[1] *Military powers; reprieves and pardons.* The President shall be commander-in-chief of the Army and Navy of the United States, and of the militia of the several states, when called into the actual service of the United States; he may require the opinion, in writing, of the principal officer in each of the executive departments, upon any subject relating to the duties of their respective offices, and he shall have power to grant reprieves and pardons for offences against the United States, except in cases of impeachment.

[2] *Treaties; appointments.* He shall have power, by and with the advice and consent of the Senate, to make treaties, provided two-thirds of the Senators present concur; and he shall nominate, and by and with the advice and consent of the Senate, shall appoint ambassadors, other public ministers and consuls, judges of the Supreme Court, and all other officers of the United States, whose appointments are not herein otherwise provided for, and which shall be established by law; but the Congress may by law vest the appointment of such inferior officers, as they think proper, in the President alone, in the courts of law, or in the heads of departments.

[3] *Filling of vacancies.* The President shall have power to fill up all vacancies that may happen during the recess of the Senate, by granting commissions which shall expire at the end of their next session.

SECTION 3. *Duties of the President*

He shall from time to time give to the Congress information of the state of the Union, and recommend to their consideration such measures as he shall judge necessary and expedient; he may, on extraordinary occasions, convene both Houses, or either of them, and in case of disagreement between them, with respect to the time of adjournment, he may adjourn them to such time as he shall think proper; he shall receive ambassadors and other public ministers; he shall take care that the laws be faithfully executed, and shall commission all the officers of the United States.

SECTION 4. *Impeachment*

The President, Vice-President, and all civil officers of the United States, shall be removed from office on impeachment for, and on conviction of, treason, bribery, or other high crimes and misdemeanors.

ARTICLE III

Judicial Department

SECTION 1. *United States Courts*

The judicial power of the United States shall be vested in one Supreme Court, and in such inferior courts as

Congress may from time to time ordain and establish. The judges, both of the supreme and inferior courts, shall hold their offices during good behavior, and shall, at stated times, receive for their services, a compensation, which shall not be diminished during their continuance in office.

SECTION 2. *Jurisdiction of United States Courts*

[1] *Federal courts in general.* The judicial power shall extend to all cases, in law and equity, arising under this Constitution, the laws of the United States, and treaties made or which shall be made, under their authority;—to all cases affecting ambassadors, other public ministers and consuls;—to all cases of admiralty and maritime jurisdiction;—to controversies to which the United States shall be a party;—to controversies between two or more states;—between a state and citizens of another state;[16]—between citizens of different states;—between citizens of the same state claiming lands under grants of different states, and between a state, or the citizens thereof, and foreign states, citizens or subjects.

[2] *The Supreme Court.* In all cases affecting ambassadors, other public ministers and consuls, and those in which a state shall be party, the Supreme Court shall have original jurisdiction. In all the other cases before mentioned, the Supreme Court shall have appellate jurisdiction, both as to law and fact, with such exceptions, and under such regulations as the Congress shall make.

[3] *Rules respecting trials.* The trial of all crimes,

[16] The Eleventh Amendment restricts this clause to suits by a state against citizens of another state.

except in cases of impeachment, shall be by jury; and such trial shall be held in the state where the said crimes shall have been committed; but when not committed within any state, the trial shall be at such place or places as the Congress may by law have directed.

SECTION 3. *Treason*

[1] *Definition of treason.* Treason against the United States shall consist only in levying war against them, or in adhering to their enemies, giving them aid and comfort. No person shall be convicted of treason unless on the testimony of two witnesses to the same overt act, or on confession in open court.

[2] *Punishment of treason.* The Congress shall have power to declare the punishment of treason, but no attainder of treason shall work corruption of blood, or forfeiture except during the life of the person attainted.

ARTICLE IV

Relations of the States

SECTION 1. *Full Credit to Official Acts*

Full faith and credit shall be given in each state to the public acts, records, and judicial proceedings of every other state. And the Congress may by general laws prescribe the manner in which such acts, records, and proceedings shall be proved, and the effect thereof.

SECTION 2. *Privileges of Citizens*

[1] *In general.* The citizens of each state shall be en-

titled to all privileges and immunities of citizens in the several states.

[2] *Return of fugitives from justice.* A person charged in any state with treason, felony, or other crime, who shall flee from justice, and be found in another state, shall on demand of the executive authority of the state from which he fled, be delivered up, to be removed to the state having jurisdiction of the crime.

[3] *Fugitive slaves.* [No person held to service or labor in one state, under the laws thereof, escaping into another, shall, in consequence of any law or regulation therein, be discharged from such service or labor, but shall be delivered up on claim of the party to whom such service or labor may be due.][17]

SECTION 3. *New States and Territories*

[1] *Admission of new states.* New states may be admitted by the Congress into this Union; but no new state shall be formed or erected within the jurisdiction of any other state; nor any state be formed by the junction of two or more states, or parts of states, without the consent of the legislatures of the states concerned as well as of the Congress.

[2] *Power of Congress over territory and property of the United States.* The Congress shall have power to dispose of and make all needful rules and regulations respecting the territory or other property belonging to the

[17] This paragraph was the basis of the Fugitive Slave Laws. It was practically superseded by the Thirteenth Amendment which prohibits slavery.

United States; and nothing in this Constitution shall be so construed as to prejudice any claims of the United States, or of any particular state.

SECTION 4. *Protection to the States*

The United States shall guarantee to every state in this Union a republican form of government, and shall protect each of them against invasion; and on application of the legislature, or of the executive (when the legislature cannot be convened) against domestic violence.

ARTICLE V

Amendments to the Constitution

The Congress, whenever two-thirds of both Houses shall deem it necessary, shall propose amendments to this Constitution, or, on the application of the legislatures of two-thirds of the several states, shall call a convention for proposing amendments, which, in either case shall be valid to all intents and purposes, as part of this Constitution, when ratified by the legislatures of three-fourths of the several states, or by conventions in three-fourths thereof, as the one or the other mode of ratification may be proposed by the Congress; provided [that no amendments which may be made prior to the year one thousand eight hundred and eight shall in any manner affect the first and fourth clauses in the ninth section of the first article; and][18] that no state, without its consent, shall be deprived of its equal suffrage in the Senate.

[18] Obsolete since 1808.

ARTICLE VI

General Provisions

[1] *Public debts valid.* All debts contracted and engagements entered into, before the adoption of this Constitution, shall be as valid against the United States under this Constitution, as under the Confederation.

[2] *The Constitution supreme.* This Constitution, and the laws of the United States which shall be made in pursuance thereof; and all treaties made, or which shall be made, under the authority of the United States, shall be the supreme law of the land; and the judges in every state shall be bound thereby, anything in the Constitution or laws of any state to the contrary notwithstanding.

[3] *Official oath; no religious test.* The Senators and Representatives before mentioned, and the members of the several state legislatures, and all executive and judicial officers, both of the United States and of the several states, shall be bound by oath or affirmation, to support this Constitution; but no religious test shall ever be required as a qualification to any office or public trust under the United States.

ARTICLE VII

Ratification

The ratification of the conventions of nine states, shall be sufficient for the establishment of this Constitution between the states so ratifying the same.

Done in Convention by the unanimous consent of the states present, the seventeenth day of September in the year of our Lord one thousand seven hundred and eighty-seven and of the Independence of the United States of America the twelfth. In witness whereof we have hereunto subscribed our names.

George Washington, President, and Deputy from Virginia.
Attested, William Jackson, *Secretary*

NEW HAMPSHIRE
John Langdon
Nicholas Gilman

MASSACHUSETTS
Nathaniel Gorham
Rufus King

CONNECTICUT
William Samuel Johnson
Roger Sherman

NEW YORK
Alexander Hamilton

NEW JERSEY
William Livingston
David Brearley
William Paterson
Jonathan Dayton

PENNSYLVANIA
Benjamin Franklin
Thomas Mifflin
Robert Morris
George Clymer
Thomas FitzSimons
Jared Ingersoll
James Wilson
Gouverneur Morris

DELAWARE
George Read
Gunning Bedford, Jr.
John Dickinson
Richard Bassett
Jacob Broom

MARYLAND
James McHenry
Daniel of St. Thomas Jenifer
Daniel Carroll

VIRGINIA
John Blair
James Madison, Jr.

NORTH CAROLINA
William Blount
Richard Dobbs Spaight
Hugh Williamson

SOUTH CAROLINA
John Rutledge
Charles Cotesworth Pinckney
Charles Pinckney
Pierce Butler

GEORGIA
William Few
Abraham Baldwin

AMENDMENTS TO THE CONSTITUTION

The Bill of Rights—Amendments I-X[20]

Adopted 1791

AMENDMENT I

Freedom of Religion, Speech, Press, Assembly, and Petition

Congress shall make no law respecting an establishment of religion, or prohibiting the free exercise thereof; or abridging the freedom of speech, or of the press; or the right of the people peaceably to assemble, and to petition the government for a redress of grievances.

AMENDMENT II

Right To Bear Arms

A well-regulated militia, being necessary to the security of a free state, the right of the people to keep and bear arms, shall not be infringed.

AMENDMENT III

Quartering of Soldiers

No soldier shall, in time of peace be quartered in any house, without the consent of the owner, nor in time of war, but in a manner to be prescribed by law.

---

[20] The first ten amendments were adopted at one time within three years after the Constitution was ratified. They are often called the American Bill of Rights because their purpose is to safeguard more fully the rights of the people and of the states.

AMENDMENT IV

Protection Against Search and Seizure

The right of the people to be secure in their persons, houses, papers, and effects, against unreasonable searches and seizures, shall not be violated, and no warrants shall issue but upon probable cause, supported by oath or affirmation, and particularly describing the place to be searched, and the persons or things to be seized.

AMENDMENT V

Right to Due Process of Law

No person shall be held to answer for a capital, or otherwise infamous crime, unless on a presentment or indictment of a grand jury, except in cases arising in the land or naval forces, or in the militia, when in actual service in time of war or public danger; nor shall any person be subject for the same offense to be twice put in jeopardy of life or limb; nor shall be compelled in any criminal case to be a witness against himself, nor be deprived of life, liberty, or property, without due process of law; nor shall private property be taken for public use without just compensation.

AMENDMENT VI

Rights of Trial by Jury, Counsel

In all criminal prosecutions the accused shall enjoy the right to a speedy and public trial, by an impartial jury of the state and district wherein the crime shall have been committed, which district shall have been previously ascertained by law, and to be informed of the nature and cause of the accusation; to be confronted with the witnesses against him; to have compulsory process for obtaining witnesses in his favor, and to have the assistance of counsel for his defense.

AMENDMENT VII

Suits at Common Law

In suits at common law, where the value in controversy shall exceed twenty dollars, the right of trial by jury shall be preserved, and no fact tried by a jury shall be otherwise reexamined in any court of the United States, than according to the rules of the common law.

AMENDMENT VIII

Bail, Fines, and Punishments

Excessive bail shall not be required, nor excessive fines imposed, nor cruel and unusual punishments inflicted.

AMENDMENT IX

Rights Retained by the People

The enumeration in the Constitution, of certain rights, shall not be construed to deny or disparage others retained by the people.

AMENDMENT X

Powers Reserved to the States or the People

The powers not delegated to the United States by the Constitution, nor prohibited by it to the States, are reserved to the States respectively, or to the people.

[End of Bill of Rights]

AMENDMENT XI

[*Adopted 1798*]

Limiting Federal Judicial Powers Against States

The judicial power of the United States shall not be construed to extend to any suit in law or equity, commenced or prosecuted against one of the United States by citizens of another state, or by citizens or subjects of any foreign state.[21]

AMENDMENT XII

[*Adopted 1804*]

Election of President and Vice-President

The electors shall meet in their respective states, and vote by ballot for President and Vice-President, one of whom, at least, shall not be an inhabitant of the same state with themselves; they shall name in their ballots the person voted for as President, and in distinct ballots the person voted for as Vice-President, and they shall make distinct lists of all persons voted for as President, and of all persons voted for as Vice-President, and of the number of votes for each, which lists they shall sign and certify, and transmit sealed to the seat of government of the United States, directed to the President of the Senate;—the President of the Senate shall, in the presence of the Senate and House of Representatives, open all the certificates and the votes shall then be counted; the person having the greatest number of votes for President shall be the President, if such number be a majority of the whole number of electors appointed; and if no person have such majority, then from the persons having the

[21] This amendment modifies Paragraph 1, Section 2, Article III, of the original Constitution.

highest numbers not exceeding three on the list of those voted for as President, the House of Representatives shall choose immediately, by ballot, the President. But in choosing the President, the votes shall be taken by states, the representation from each state having one vote; a quorum for this purpose shall consist of a member or members from two-thirds of the states, and a majority of all the states shall be necessary to a choice. And if the House of Representatives shall not choose a President whenever the right of choice shall devolve upon them, before the fourth day of March next following, then the Vice-President shall act as President, as in the case of the death or other constitutional disability of the President. —The person having the greatest number of votes as Vice-President, shall be the Vice-President, if such number be a majority of the whole number of electors appointed, and if no person have a majority, then from the two highest numbers on the list, the Senate shall choose the Vice-President; a quorum for the purpose shall consist of two-thirds of the whole number of Senators, and a majority of the whole number shall be necessary to a choice. But no person constitutionally ineligible to the office of President shall be eligible to that of Vice-President of the United States.[22]

AMENDMENT XIII
[*Adopted 1865*]

Abolition of Slavery

SECTION 1. *Slavery abolished.* Neither slavery nor involuntary servitude, except as a punishment for crime

[22] This amendment replaces the major portion of Paragraph 2, Section 1, Article II, of the original Constitution.

whereof the party shall have been duly convicted, shall exist within the United States, or any place subject to their jurisdiction.

SECTION 2. *Enforcement.* Congress shall have power to enforce this article by appropriate legislation.

AMENDMENT XIV

[*Adopted 1868*]

Citizenship, Representation, and the Public Debt

SECTION 1. *National and state citizenship.* All persons born or naturalized in the United States, and subject to the jurisdiction thereof, are citizens of the United States and of the state wherein they reside. No state shall make or enforce any law which shall abridge the privileges or immunities of citizens of the United States; nor shall any state deprive any person of life, liberty, or property, without due process of law; nor deny to any person within its jurisdiction the equal protection of the laws.

SECTION 2. *Apportionment of Representatives.* Representatives shall be apportioned among the several states according to their respective numbers, counting the whole number of persons in each state, excluding Indians not taxed. But when the right to vote at any election for the choice of electors for President and Vice-President of the United States, Representatives in Congress, the executive and judicial officers of a state, or the members of the legislature thereof, is denied to any of the male inhabitants of such state, being twenty-one years of age and citizens of the United States, or in any way abridged, except for participation in rebellion, or other crime, the basis of representation therein shall be reduced in the proportion which the number of such male citizens shall bear to the whole number of male citizens twenty-one years of age in such state.[23]

SECTION 3. *Loss of political privilege.* No person shall be a Senator or Representative in Congress, or elector of President and Vice-President, or hold any office, civil or military, under the United States, or under any state, who, having previously taken an oath, as a member of Congress, or as an officer of the United States, or as a member of any state legislature, or as an executive or judicial officer of any state, to support the Constitution of the United States, shall have engaged in insurrection or rebellion against the same, or given aid or comfort to the enemies thereof. But Congress may by vote of two-thirds of each House, remove such disability.[24]

SECTION 4. *Validity of public debts.* The validity of the public debt of the United States, authorized by law, including debts incurred for payment of pensions and bounties for services in suppressing insurrection or rebellion, shall not be questioned. But neither the United States nor any state shall assume or pay any debt or obligation incurred in aid of insurrection or rebellion against the United States, or any claim for the loss or emancipation of any slave; but all such debts, obligations, and claims shall be held illegal and void.

SECTION 5. *Enforcement.* The Congress shall have power to enforce by appropriate legislation the provisions of this article.

---

[23] Sections 1 and 2 of this amendment modify Paragraph 3, Section 2, Article I, of the original Constitution.

[24] Section 3 of this amendment supplements Paragraph 2, Section 2, Article I; Paragraph 3, Section 3, Article I; and Paragraph 2, Section 1, Article II, of the original Constitution.

AMENDMENT XV
[*Adopted 1870*]

Negro Suffrage

SECTION 1. *Right to vote affirmed.* The right of citizens of the United States to vote shall not be denied or abridged by the United States or by any state on account of race, color, or previous condition of servitude.

SECTION 2. *Enforcement.* The Congress shall have power to enforce this article by appropriate legislation.

AMENDMENT XVI
[*Adopted 1913*]

Income Tax

The Congress shall have power to lay and collect taxes on incomes, from whatever source derived, without apportionment among the several states, and without regard to any census or enumeration.[25]

AMENDMENT XVII
[*Adopted 1913*]

Direct Election of Senators

[1] *Election by the people.* The Senate of the United States shall be composed of two Senators from each state, elected by the people thereof, for six years; and each Senator shall have one vote. The electors in each state shall have the qualifications requisite for electors of the most numerous branch of the state legislatures.

[2] *Vacancies.* When vacancies happen in the representation of any state in the Senate, the executive au-

[25] This amendment modifies Paragraph 4, Section 9, Article I, of the original Constitution.

thority of such state shall issue writs of election to fill such vacancies: Provided that the legislature of any state may empower the executive thereof to make temporary appointments until the people fill the vacancies by election as the legislature may direct.

[3] *Not retroactive.* This amendment shall not be so construed as to affect the election or term of any Senator chosen before it becomes valid as part of the Constitution.[26]

AMENDMENT XVIII
[*Adopted 1919*]

National Prohibition

SECTION 1. *Intoxicating liquors prohibited.* After one year from the ratification of this article the manufacture, sale, or transportation of intoxicating liquors within, the importation thereof into, or the exportation thereof from, the United States and all territory subject to the jurisdiction thereof for beverage purposes is hereby prohibited.

SECTION 2. *Enforcement.* The Congress and the several states shall have concurrent power to enforce this article by appropriate legislation.

SECTION 3. *Limited time for ratification.* This article shall be inoperative unless it shall have been ratified as an amendment to the Constitution by the legislatures of the several states, as provided in the Constitution, within seven years from the date of the submission hereof to the states by the Congress.[27]

---

[26] This amendment modifies Paragraphs 1 and 2, Section 3, Article I, and Paragraph 1, Section 4, Article I, of the original Constitution.

[27] This amendment was repealed by the Twenty-first Amendment.

AMENDMENT XIX
[*Adopted 1920*]

Woman Suffrage

SECTION 1. *Right to vote affirmed.* The right of citizens of the United States to vote shall not be denied or abridged by the United States or by any state on account of sex.

SECTION 2. *Enforcement.* The Congress shall have power to enforce this article by appropriate legislation.

AMENDMENT XX
[*Adopted 1933*]

Abolishing the "Lame-duck" Session of Congress

SECTION 1. *Terms of President, Vice-President, and members of Congress.* The terms of the President and Vice-President shall end at noon on the 20th day of January, and the terms of Senators and Representatives at noon on the 3rd day of January, of the years in which such terms would have ended if this article had not been ratified; and the terms of their successors shall then begin.[28]

SECTION 2. *Meetings of Congress.* The Congress shall assemble at least once in every year, and such meeting shall begin at noon on the 3d day of January, unless they shall by law appoint a different day.[29]

---

[28] Thus defeated Congressmen do not hold over to attend a "lame-duck" session.

[29] This section modifies Paragraph 2, Section 4, Article I, of the original Constitution.

SECTION 3. *Succession to the Presidency.* If, at the time fixed for the beginning of the term of the President, the President elect shall have died, the Vice-President elect shall become President. If a President shall not have been chosen before the time fixed for the beginning of his term, or if the President elect shall have failed to qualify, then the Vice-President elect shall act as President until a President shall have qualified; and the Congress may by law provide for the case wherein neither a President elect nor a Vice-President elect shall have qualified, declaring who shall then act as President, or the manner in which one who is to act shall be selected, and such person shall act accordingly until a President or Vice-President shall have qualified.

SECTION 4. The Congress may by law provide for the case of the death of any of the persons from whom the House of Representatives may choose a President whenever the right of choice shall have devolved upon them, and for the case of the death of any of the persons from whom the Senate may choose a Vice-President whenever the right of choice shall have devolved upon them.[30]

SECTION 5. *When effective. Sections* 1 and 2 shall take effect on the 15th day of October following the ratification of this article.

SECTION 6. *Limited time for ratification.* This article shall be inoperative unless it shall have been ratified as an amendment to the Constitution by the legislatures of three-fourths of the several states within seven years from the date of its submission.

---

[30] Sections 3 and 4 supplement Paragraph 5, Section 1, Article II, of the original Constitution, and Amendment XII.

AMENDMENT XXI

[*Adopted 1933*]

Repeal of National Prohibition

SECTION 1. *Repealing the Eighteenth Amendment.* The Eighteenth article of amendment to the Constitution of the United States is hereby repealed.

SECTION 2. *Protection of states.* The transportation or importation into any state, territory, or possession of the United States for delivery or use therein of intoxicating liquors in violation of the laws thereof is hereby prohibited.

SECTION 3. *Ratification by state conventions within limited time.* This article shall be inoperative unless it shall have been ratified as an amendment to the Constitution by convention in the several states, as provided in the Constitution, within seven years from the date of the submission hereof to the states by the Congress.

AMENDMENT XXII

[*Adopted 1951*]

Limiting the Term of the President

SECTION 1. No person shall be elected to the office of the President more than twice, and no person who has held the office of President, or acted as President, for more than two years of a term to which some other person was elected President shall be elected to the office of the President more than once. But this Article shall not apply to any person holding the office of President when this Article was proposed by the Congress, and shall not prevent any person who may be holding the office of

President, or acting as President during the term within which this Article becomes operative, from holding the office of President or acting as President during the remainder of such term.

SECTION 2. This article shall be inoperative unless it shall have been ratified as an amendment to the Constitution by the legislatures of three-fourths of the several States within seven years from the date of its submission to the States by the Congress.

AMENDMENT XXIII
[*Adopted 1961*]

Presidential Electors for the District of Columbia

SECTION 1. The District constituting the seat of Government of the United States shall appoint in such manner as the Congress may direct:

A number of electors of President and Vice President equal to the whole number of Senators and Representatives in Congress to which the District would be entitled if it were a State, but in no event more than the least populous State; they shall be in addition to those appointed by the States, but they shall be considered, for the purposes of the election of President and Vice President, to be electors appointed by a State; and they shall meet in the District and perform such duties as provided by the twelfth article of amendment.

SECTION 2. The Congress shall have power to enforce this article by appropriate legislation.

AMENDMENT XXIV
[*Adopted 1964*]

Voter Qualifications in Federal Elections

SECTION 1. The right of citizens of the United States to vote in any primary or other election for President or Vice President, for elections for President or Vice President, or for Senator or Representative in Congress, shall not be denied or abridged by the United States or any State by reason of failure to pay any poll tax or other tax.

SECTION 2. The Congress shall have power to enforce this article by appropriate legislation.

AMENDMENT XXV
[*Adopted 1967*]

Presidential Disability and Succession

SECTION 1. In case of the removal of the President from office or his death or resignation , the Vice President shall become President.

SECTION 2. Whenever there is a vacancy in the office of the Vice President, the President shall nominate a Vice President who shall take the office upon confirmation by a majority vote of both houses of Congress.

SECTION 3. Whenever the President transmits to the President pro tempore of the Senate and the Speaker of the House of Representatives his written declaration that he is unable to discharge the powers and duties of his office, and until he transmits to them a written declaration to the contrary, such powers and duties shall be discharged by the Vice President as Acting President.

SECTION 4. Whenever the Vice President and a majority of either the principal officers of the executive departments or of such other body as Congress may by law provide, transmit to the President pro tempore of the Senate and the Speaker of the House of Representatives their written declaration that the President is unable to discharge the powers and duties of his office, the Vice President shall immediately assume the powers and duties of the office as Acting President.

Thereafter, when the President transmits to the President pro tempore of the Senate and the Speaker of the House of Representatives his written declaration that no inability exists, he shall resume the powers and duties of his office unless the Vice President and a majority of either the principal officers of the executive department or of such other body as Congress may by law provide, transmit within four days to the President pro tempore of the Senate and the Speaker of the House of Representatives their written declaration that the President is unable to discharge the powers and duties of his office. Thereupon Congress shall decide the issue, assembling within 48 hours for that purpose if not in session. If the Congress, within 21 days after receipt of the latter written declaration, or, if Congress is not in session, within 21 days after Congress is required to assemble, determines by two-thirds vote of both houses that the President is unable to discharge the powers and duties of his office, the Vice President shall continue to discharge the same as Acting President; otherwise, the President shall resume the powers and duties of his office.[31]

---

[31] This Amendment supplements Paragraph 5, Section 1, Article II, of the original Constitution.

The Children's Charter

Introductory—In the face of danger or disaster on a sinking ship we would strike down anyone who attempted to save himself at the expense of a child. Children come first not only on sinking ships but in our hearts, our homes, our schools, and our churches. They ARE first. The race can save itself—can lift itself higher—only as children are lifted up. It was in this spirit that the 1930 White House Conference on Child Health and Protection, meeting in the midst of the severest depression in American history, drew up The Children's Charter *which was widely published thruout the country in newspapers and magazines. It appears in* The Journal of the National Education Association *for April 1931. Like our* Declaration of Independence, The Children's Charter *stands as a challenge to Americans and to people thruout the world to make civilization worthy of the promise of childhood.*

PRESIDENT Hoover's White House Conference on Child Health and Protection recognizing the rights of the child as the first rights of citizenship pledges itself to these aims for the children of America:

[1] For every child spiritual and moral training to help him to stand firm under the pressure of life.

[2] For every child understanding and the guarding of his personality as his most precious right.

[3] For every child a home and that love and security which a home provides; and for that child who must receive foster care, the nearest substitute for his own home.

[4] For every child full preparation for his birth, his

mother receiving prenatal, natal, and postnatal care; and the establishment of such protective measures as will make childbearing safer.

[5] For every child health protection from birth thru adolescence including: periodical health examinations and, where needed, care of specialists and hospital treatment; regular dental examinations and care of the teeth; protective and preventive measures against communicable diseases; the insuring of pure food, pure milk, and pure water.

[6] For every child from birth thru adolescence, promotion of health, including health instruction and a health program, wholesome physical and mental recreation, with teachers and leaders adequately trained.

[7] For every child a dwelling place safe, sanitary, and wholesome, with reasonable provisions for privacy, free from conditions which tend to thwart his development; and a home environment harmonious and enriching.

[8] For every child a school which is safe from hazards, sanitary, properly equipped, lighted, and ventilated. For younger children nursery schools and kindergartens to supplement home care.

[9] For every child a community which recognizes and plans for his needs, protects him against physical dangers, moral hazards, and disease; provides him with safe and wholesome places for play and recreation; and makes provision for his cultural and social needs.

[10] For every child an education which, thru the discovery and development of his individual abilities, prepares him for life; and thru training and vocational guidance prepares him for a living which will yield him the maximum of satisfaction.

[11] For every child such teaching and training as will prepare him for successful parenthood, homemaking, and the rights of citizenship; and, for parents, supplementary training to fit them to deal wisely with the problems of parenthood.

[12] For every child education for safety and protection against accidents to which modern conditions subject him—those to which he is directly exposed and those which, thru loss or maiming of his parents, affect him indirectly.

[13] For every child who is blind, deaf, crippled, or otherwise physically handicapped, and for the child who is mentally handicapped, such measures as will early discover and diagnose his handicap, provide care and treatment, and so train him that he may become an asset to society rather than a liability. Expenses of these services should be borne publicly where they cannot be privately met.

[14] For every child who is in conflict with society the right to be dealt with intelligently as society's charge, not society's outcast; with the home, the school, the church, the court and institutions when needed, shaped to return him whenever possible to the normal stream of life.

[15] For every child the right to grow up in a family with an adequate standard of living and the security of a stable income as the surest safeguard against social handicaps.

[16] For every child protection against labor that stunts growth, either physical or mental, that limits education, that deprives children of their right of comradeship, of play, and of joy.

[17] For every rural child as satisfactory schooling and health services as for the city child, and an extension to rural families of social, recreational, and cultural facilities.

[18] To supplement the home and the school in the training of youth, and to return to them those interests of which modern life tends to cheat children, every stimulation and encouragement should be given to the extension and development of the voluntary youth organizations.

[19] To make everywhere available these minimum protections of the health and welfare of children, there should be a district, county, or community organization for health, education, and welfare, with fulltime officials, coordinating with a statewide program which will be responsive to a nationwide program of general information, statistics, and scientific research. This should include:

[a] Trained, fulltime public health officials, with public health nurses, sanitary inspection, and laboratory workers.

[b] Available hospital beds.

[c] Fulltime public welfare service for the relief, aid, and guidance of children in special need due to poverty, misfortune, or behavior difficulties, and for the protection of children from abuse, neglect, exploitation, or moral hazard.

For EVERY child these rights, regardless of race, or color, or situation, wherever he may live.

Farewell Address to the People of the United States

GEORGE WASHINGTON

Introductory—This address was written by President Washington primarily to eliminate himself as a candidate for a third term. It was never read by the President in public, but was printed in Claypoole's *American Daily Advertiser*, Philadelphia, September 19, 1796. The address is in two parts: In the first, Washington definitely declines a third term, gives reasons, and acknowledges a debt of gratitude for the honors conferred upon him and for the confident support of the people. In the second more important part, he presents, as a result of his experience and as a last legacy of advice, thoughts upon the government.—From *The Story of the Constitution* published by the United States Constitution Sesquicentennial Commission, 1937.

FAREWELL ADDRESS TO THE PEOPLE OF THE UNITED STATES, SEPTEMBER 17, 1796

FRIENDS *and Fellow Citizens:* The Period for a new election of a citizen, to administer the executive government of the United States, being not far distant, and the time actually arrived, when your thoughts must be employed in designating the person, who is to be clothed with that important trust, it appears to me proper, especially as it may conduce to a more distinct expression

Portrait by Gilbert Stuart

GEORGE WASHINGTON, 1732-1799

Born on a plantation in the English colony of Virginia, February 22, 1732, George Washington came into a world of pioneer cavaliers, living on the land, united by the many arms of Chesapeake Bay. There was hard work and little schooling except as children were sent to England. Washington grew into a strong young man, learning to live, work, hunt, and fight in the wilderness. When revolt against England came in 1776, he was placed at the head of the army and brought the almost hopeless cause to victory. In 1787 he presided over the Constitutional Convention; then was elected and reelected President of the new Republic, serving from 1789 to 1797. He died December 14, 1799.

of the public voice, that I should now apprise you of the resolution I have formed, to decline being considered among the number of those, out of whom a choice is to be made.

I beg you, at the same time, to do me the justice to be assured, that this resolution has not been taken without a strict regard to all the considerations appertaining to the relation, which binds a dutiful citizen to his country —and that, in withdrawing the tender of service which silence in my situation might imply, I am influenced by no diminution of zeal for your future interest, no deficiency of grateful respect for your past kindness; but am supported by a full conviction that the step is compatible with both.

The acceptance of, and continuance hitherto in, the office to which your suffrages have twice called me, have been a uniform sacrifice of inclination to the opinion of duty, and to a deference for what appeared to be your desire. I constantly hoped, that it would have been much earlier in my power, consistently with motives, which I was not at liberty to disregard, to return to that retirement, from which I had been reluctantly drawn. The strength of my inclination to do this, previous to the last election, had even led to the preparation of an address to declare it to you; but mature reflection on the then perplexed and critical posture of our affairs with foreign nations, and the unanimous advice of persons entitled to my confidence, impelled me to abandon the idea.

I rejoice that the state of your concerns, external as well as internal, no longer renders the pursuit of inclination incompatible with the sentiment of duty, or propriety; and am persuaded whatever partiality may be retained for my services, that in the present circumstances of our country, you will not disapprove my determination to retire.

The impressions, with which I first undertook the arduous trust, were explained on the proper occasion. In the discharge of this trust, I will only say, that I have, with good intentions, contributed towards the organization and administration of the government, the best exertions of which a very fallible judgment was capable. Not unconscious, in the outset, of the inferiority of my qualifications, experience in my own eyes, perhaps still more in the eyes of others, has strengthened the motives to diffidence of myself; and every day the increasing weight of years admonishes me more and more that the shade of retirement is as necessary to me as it will be welcome. Satisfied that if any circumstances have given peculiar value to my services, they were temporary, I have the consolation to believe, that while choice and prudence invite me to quit the political scene, patriotism does not forbid it.

In looking forward to the moment, which is intended to terminate the career of my public life, my feelings do not permit me to suspend the deep acknowledgment of that debt of gratitude which I owe to my beloved country for the many honors it has conferred upon me; still more for the steadfast confidence with which it has supported me; and for the opportunities I have thence enjoyed of manifesting my inviolable attachment, by services faithful and persevering, tho in usefulness unequal to my zeal. If benefits have resulted to our country from these services, let it always be remembered to your praise, and as an instructive example in our annals, that under circumstances in which the passions agitated in every direction were liable to mislead, amidst appearances sometimes dubious, vicissitudes of fortune often discouraging, in situations in which not unfrequently want of success has countenanced the spirit of criticism, the constancy of your support was the essential prop of the efforts, and a guarantee of the plans by which they were effected. Profoundly penetrated with this idea, I shall carry it with me to my grave, as a strong incitement to unceasing vows that Heaven may continue to you the choicest tokens of its beneficence; that your union and brotherly affection may be perpetual; that the free Constitution, which is the work of your hands, may be sacredly maintained; that its administration in every department may be stamped with wisdom and virtue; that, in fine, the happiness of the people of these states, under the auspices of liberty, may be made complete, by so careful a preservation and so prudent a use of this blessing, as will acquire to them the glory of recommending it to the applause, the affection, and adoption of every nation, which is yet a stranger to it.

Here, perhaps, I ought to stop. But a solicitude for your welfare, which cannot end but with my life, and the apprehension of danger, natural to that solicitude, urge me on an occasion like the present, to offer to your solemn contemplation, and to recommend to your frequent review, some sentiments, which are the result of much reflection, of no inconsiderable observation, and which appear to me all-important to the permanency of your felicity as a people. These will be offered to you with the more freedom, as you can only see in them the disinterested warnings of a parting friend, who can possibly have no personal motive to bias his counsel. Nor can I forget, as an encouragement to it, your indulgent reception of my sentiments on a former and not dissimilar occasion.

Interwoven as is the love of liberty with every ligament of your hearts, no recommendation of mine is necessary to fortify or confirm the attachment.

The unity of government, which constitutes you one people, is also now dear to you. It is justly so: for it is a main pillar in the edifice of your real independence, the support of your tranquillity at home, your peace abroad; of your safety; of your prosperity; of that very liberty, which you so highly prize. But as it is easy to foresee, that from different causes and from different quarters, much pains will be taken, many artifices employed, to weaken in your minds the conviction of this truth; as this is the point in your political fortress against which the batteries of internal and external enemies will be most constantly and actively (tho often covertly and insidiously) directed, it is of infinite moment, that you should properly estimate the immense value of your national union to your collective and individual happiness; that you should cherish a cordial, habitual, and immovable attachment to it; accustoming yourselves to think and speak of it as of the Palladium of your political safety and prosperity; watching for its preservation with jealous anxiety; discountenancing whatever may suggest even a suspicion that it can in any event be abandoned; and indignantly frowning upon the first dawning of every attempt to alienate any portion of our country from the rest, or to enfeeble the sacred ties which now link together the various parts.

For this you have every inducement of sympathy and interest. Citizens by birth or choice, of a common country, that country has a right to concentrate your affections. The name of *American*, which belongs to you, in your national capacity, must always exalt the just pride of patriotism, more than any appellation derived from local discriminations. With slight shades of difference, you have the same religion, manners, habits, and political principles. You have in a common cause fought and triumphed together; the independence and liberty you possess are the work of joint councils, and joint efforts, of common dangers, sufferings, and successes.

But these considerations, however powerfully they address themselves to your sensibility, are greatly outweighed by those which apply more immediately to your interest. Here every portion of our country finds the most commanding motives for carefully guarding and preserving the union of the whole.

The *North*, in an unrestrained intercourse with the *South*, protected by the equal laws of a common government, finds in the productions of the latter, great additional resources of maritime and commercial enterprise and precious materials of manufacturing industry. The *South*, in the same intercourse, benefiting by the agency of the *North*, sees its agriculture grow and its commerce expand. Turning partly into its own channels the seamen of the *North*, it finds its particular navigation invigorated; and while it contributes, in different ways, to nourish and increase the general mass of the national navigation, it looks forward to the protection of a maritime strength, to which itself is unequally adapted. The *East*, in a like intercourse with the *West*, already finds, and in the progressive improvement of interior communications by land and water, will more and more find a valuable vent for the commodities which it brings from abroad, or manufactures at home. The *West* derives from the *East* supplies requisite to its growth and comfort, and what is perhaps of still greater consequence, it must of necessity owe the *secure* enjoyment of indispensable *outlets* for its own productions to the weight, influence, and the future maritime strength of the Atlantic side of the Union, directed by an indissoluble community of interest as *one nation*. Any other tenure by which the *West* can hold this essential advantage, whether derived from its own separate strength, or from an apostate and unnatural connection with any foreign power, must be intrinsically precarious.

While, then, every part of our country thus feels an immediate and particular interest in union, all the parts combined cannot fail to find in the united mass of means and efforts greater strength, greater resource, proportionably greater security from external danger, a less frequent interruption of their peace by foreign nations; and, what is of inestimable value, they must derive from union an exemption from those broils and wars between themselves, which so frequently afflict neighboring countries not tied together by the same governments, which their own rivalships alone would be sufficient to produce but which opposite foreign alliances, attachments, and intrigues would stimulate and embitter. Hence, likewise, they will avoid the necessity of those overgrown military establishments, which under any form of government, are inauspicious to liberty, and which are to be regarded as particularly hostile to republican liberty. In this sense it is, that your union ought to be considered as a main prop of your liberty, and that the love of the one ought to endear to you the preservation of the other.

These considerations speak a persuasive language to every reflecting and virtuous mind, and exhibit the continuance of the union as a primary object of patriotic desire. Is there a doubt whether a common government can embrace so large a sphere? Let experience solve it. To listen to mere speculation in such a case were criminal. We are authorized to hope that a proper organization of the whole, with the auxiliary agency of governments for the respective subdivisions, will afford a happy issue to the experiment. It is well worth a fair and full experiment. With such powerful and obvious motives to union, affecting all parts of our country, while experience shall not have demonstrated its impracticability, there will always be reason to distrust the patriotism of those, who in any quarter may endeavour to weaken its bands.

In contemplating the causes which may disturb our Union, it occurs as matter of serious concern, that any ground should have been furnished for characterizing parties by *geographical* discriminations—*Northern* and *Southern, Atlantic* and *Western;* whence designing man may endeavour to excite a belief that there is a real difference of local interests and views. One of the expedients of party to acquire influence, within particular districts, is to misrepresent the opinions and aims of other districts. You cannot shield yourselves too much against the jealousies and heart-burnings, which spring from these misrepresentations. They tend to render alien to each other, those who ought to be bound together by fraternal affection. The inhabitants of our western country have lately had a useful lesson on this head. They have seen, in the negotiation by the Executive, and in the unanimous ratification by the Senate, of the treaty with Spain, and in the universal satisfaction at that event, thruout the United States, a decisive proof how unfounded were the suspicions propagated among them of a policy in the General Government and in the Atlantic States unfriendly to their interests in regard to the Mississippi. They have been witnesses to the formation of two treaties, that with Great Britain, and that with Spain, which secure to them everything they could desire, in respect to our foreign relations, towards confirming their prosperity. Will it not be their wisdom to rely for the preservation of these advantages on the *Union* by which they were procured? Will they not henceforth be deaf to those advisers, if such they are, who would sever them from their brethren, and connect them with aliens?

To the efficacy and permanency of your Union, a government for the whole is indispensable. No alliances, however strict, between the parts can be an adequate substitute. They must inevitably experience the infractions and interruptions, which all alliances in all times have experienced. Sensible of this momentous truth, you have improved upon your first essay, by the adoption of a Constitution of government better calculated than your former for an intimate union, and for the efficacious management of your common concerns. This government, the offspring of our own choice, uninfluenced and unawed, adopted upon full investigation and mature deliberation, completely free in its principles, in the distribution of its powers, uniting security with energy, and containing within itself a provision for its own amendment, has a just claim to your confidence and your support. Respect for its authority, compliance with its laws, acquiescence in its measures, are duties enjoined by the fundamental maxims of true liberty. The basis of our political systems is the right of the people to make and to alter their constitutions of government. But the constitution which at any time exists, till changed by an explicit and authentic act of the whole people, is sacredly obligatory upon all. The very idea of the power and the right of the people to establish government presupposes the duty of every individual to obey the established government.

All obstructions to the execution of the laws, all combinations and associations, under whatever plausible character, with the real design to direct, control, counteract, or awe the regular deliberation and action of the constituted authorities, are destructive of this fundamental principle and of fatal tendency. They serve to organize faction, to give it an artificial and extraordinary force; to put, in the place of the delegated will of the nation, the will of a party, often a small but artful and enterprising minority of the community; and, according to the alternate triumphs of different parties, to make the public administration the mirror of the ill-concerted and incongruous projects of faction, rather than the organ of consistent and wholesome plans digested by common counsels, and modified by mutual interests.

However combinations or associations of the above descriptions may now and then answer popular ends, they are likely, in the course of time and things, to become potent engines, by which cunning, ambitious, and unprincipled men will be enabled to subvert the power of the people, and to usurp for themselves the reins of government; destroying afterwards the very engines which have lifted them to unjust dominion.

Towards the preservation of your government, and the permanency of your present happy state, it is requisite, not only that you steadily discountenance irregular oppositions to its acknowledged authority, but also that you resist with care the spirit of innovation upon its principles, however specious the pretexts. One method of assault may be to effect, in the forms of the Constitution, alterations which will impair the energy of the system, and thus to undermine what cannot be directly overthrown. In all the changes to which you may be invited, remember that time and habit are at least as necessary to fix the true character of governments, as of other human institutions; that experience is the surest standard, by which to test the real tendency of the existing constitution of a country; that facility in changes, upon the credit of mere hypotheses and opinion, exposes to perpetual change, from the endless variety of hypotheses and opinion; and remember, especially, that for the efficient management of your common interests, in a country so extensive as ours, a government of as much vigor as is consistent with the perfect security of liberty is indispensable. Liberty itself will find in such a government, with powers properly distributed and adjusted, its surest guardian. It is indeed, little else than a name, where the government is too feeble to withstand the enterprises of faction, to confine each member of the society within the limits prescribed by the laws, and to maintain all in the secure and tranquil enjoyment of the rights of person and property.

I have already intimated to you the danger of parties in the state, with particular reference to the founding of them on geographical discriminations. Let me now take a more comprehensive view, and warn you in the most solemn manner against the baneful effects of the spirit of party, generally.

The spirit, unfortunately, is inseparable from our nature, having its root in the strongest passions of the human mind. It exists under different shapes in all governments, more or less stifled, controlled, or repressed; but, in those of the popular form, it is seen in its greatest rankness, and is truly their worst enemy.

The alternate domination of one faction over another, sharpened by the spirit of revenge natural to party dissension, which in different ages and countries has perpetrated the most horrid enormities, is itself a frightful despotism. But this leads at length to a more formal and permanent despotism. The disorders and miseries, which result, gradually incline the minds of men to seek security and repose in the absolute power of an individual; and sooner or later the chief of some prevailing faction, more able or more fortunate than his competitors, turns this disposition to the purposes of his own elevation, on the ruins of public liberty.

Without looking forward to an extremity of this kind (which nevertheless ought not to be entirely out of sight), the common and continual mischiefs of the spirit of party are sufficient to make it the interest and the duty of a wise people to discourage and restrain it.

It serves always to distract the public councils and enfeeble the public administration. It agitates the community with ill-founded jealousies and false alarms, kindles the animosity of one part against another, foments occasionally riot and insurrection. It opens the door to foreign influence and corruption, which find a facilitated access to the government itself thru the channels of party passions. Thus the policy and the will of one country are subjected to the policy and will of another.

There is an opinion, that parties in free countries are useful checks upon the administration of the government and serve to keep alive the spirit of liberty. This within certain limits is probably true; and in governments of a monarchial cast, patriotism may look with indulgence, if not with favor, upon the spirit of party. But in those of the popular character, in governments purely elective, it is a spirit not to be encouraged. From their natural tendency, it is certain there will always be enough of that spirit for every salutary purpose. And, there being constant danger of excess, the effort ought to be, by force of public opinion, to mitigate and assuage it. A fire not to be quenched, it demands a uniform vigilance to prevent its bursting into a flame, lest instead of warming, it should consume.

It is important, likewise, that the habits of thinking in a free country should inspire caution in those intrusted with its administration, to confine themselves within their respective constitutional spheres, avoiding in the exercise of the powers of one department to encroach upon another. The spirit of encroachment tends to consolidate the powers of all the departments in one, and thus to create, whatever the form of government, a real despotism. A just estimate of that love of power, and proneness to abuse it, which predominates in the human heart, is sufficient to satisfy us of the truth of this position. The necessity of reciprocal checks in the exercise of political power, by dividing and distributing it into different depositories, and constituting each the guardian of the public weal against invasions by the others, has been evinced by experiments ancient and modern; some of them in our country and under our own eyes. To preserve them must be as necessary as to institute them. If, in the opinion of the people, the distribution or modification of the Constitutional powers be in any particular wrong, let it be corrected by an amendment in the way which the Constitution designates. But let there be no change by usurpation, for, tho this, in one instance, may be the instrument of good, it is the customary weapon by which free governments are destroyed. The precedent must always greatly overbalance in permanent evil any partial or transient benefit which the use can at any time yield.

Of all the dispositions and habits which lead to political prosperity, religion and morality are indispensable supports. In vain would that man claim the tribute of patriotism, who should labor to subvert these great pillars of human happiness, these firmest props of the duties of men and citizens. The mere politician, equally with the pious man, ought to respect and to cherish them. A volume could not trace all their connections with private and public felicity. Let it simply be asked, Where is the security for property, for reputation, for life, if the sense of religious obligation *desert* the oaths, which are the instruments of investigation in courts of justice? And let us with caution indulge the supposition that morality can be maintained without religion. Whatever may be conceded to the influence of refined education on minds of peculiar structure—reason and experience both forbid us to expect that national morality can prevail in exclusion of religious principle.

It is substantially true, that virtue or morality is a necessary spring of popular government. The rule, indeed, extends with more or less force to every species of free government. Who that is a sincere friend to it, can look with indifference upon attempts to shake the foundation of the fabric?

Promote, then, as an object of primary importance, institutions for the general diffusion of knowledge. In proportion as the structure of a government gives force to public opinion, it is essential that public opinion should be enlightened.

As a very important source of strength and security, cherish public credit. One method of preserving it is to use it as sparingly as possible; avoiding occasions of expense by cultivating peace, but remembering also that timely disbursements to prepare for danger frequently prevent much greater disbursements to repel it; avoiding likewise the accumulation of debt, not only by shunning occasions of expense, but by vigorous exertions in time of peace to discharge the debts which unavoidable wars may have occasioned, not ungenerously throwing upon posterity the burden which we ourselves ought to bear. The execution of these maxims belongs to your Representatives, but it is necessary that public opinion should cooperate. To facilitate to them the performance of their duty, it is essential that you should practically bear in mind, that towards the payment of debts there must be revenue; that to have revenue there must be taxes; that no taxes can be devised which are not more or less inconvenient and unpleasant; that the intrinsic embarrassment, inseparable from the selection of the proper objects (which is always a choice of difficulties), ought to be a decisive motive for a candid construction of the conduct of the government in making it, and for a spirit of acquiescence in the measures for obtaining revenue, which the public exigencies may at any time dictate.

Observe good faith and justice towards all nations. Cultivate peace and harmony with all. Religion and morality enjoin this conduct; and can it be that good policy does not equally enjoin it? It will be worthy of a free, enlightened, and, at no distant period, a great nation, to give to mankind the magnanimous and too novel example of a people always guided by an exalted justice and benevolence. Who can doubt that in the course of time and things, the fruits of such a plan would richly repay any temporary advantages which might be lost by a steady adherence to it? Can it be that Providence has not connected the permanent felicity of a nation with its virtue? The experiment, at least, is recommended by every sentiment which ennobles human nature. Alas! is it rendered impossible by its vices?

In the execution of such a plan, nothing is more essential than that permanent, inveterate antipathies against particular nations and passionate attachments for others should be excluded; and that, in place of them, just and amicable feelings towards all should be cultivated. The nation which indulges towards another an habitual hatred, or an habitual fondness, is in some degree a slave. It is a slave to its animosity or to its affection, either of which is sufficient to lead it astray from its duty and its interest. Antipathy in one nation against another disposes each more readily to offer insult and injury, to lay hold of slight causes of umbrage, and to be haughty and intractable, when accidental or trifling occasions of dispute occur. Hence frequent collisions, obstinate, envenomed, and bloody contests. The nation, prompted by ill-will and resentment, sometimes impels to war the government, contrary to the best calculations of policy. The government sometimes participates in the national propensity, and adopts thru passion what reason would reject; at other times, it makes the animosity of the nation subservient to projects of hostility instigated by pride, ambition, and other sinister and pernicious motives. The peace often, sometimes perhaps the liberty, of nations has been the victim.

So likewise, a passionate attachment of one nation for another produces a variety of evils. Sympathy for the favorite nation, facilitating the illusion of an imaginary common interest, in cases where no real common interest exists, and infusing into one the enmities of the other, betrays the former into a participation in the quarrels and wars of the latter, without adequate inducement or justification. It leads also to concessions to the favorite nation of privileges denied to others, which is apt doubly to injure the nation making the concessions, by unnecessarily parting with what ought to have been retained; and by exciting jealousy, ill-will, and a disposition to retaliate, in the parties from whom equal privileges are withheld. And it gives to ambitious, corrupted, or deluded citizens (who devote themselves to the favorite nation) facility to betray or sacrifice the interests of their own country, without odium, sometimes even with popularity; gliding, with the appearances of a virtuous sense of obligation, a commendable deference for public opinion, or a laudable zeal for public good, the base of foolish compliances of ambition, corruption, or infatuation.

As avenues to foreign influence in innumerable ways, such attachments are particularly alarming to the truly enlightened and independent patriot. How many opportunities do they afford to tamper with domestic factions, to practice the arts of seduction, to mislead public opinion, to influence or awe the public councils! Such an attachment of a small or weak, towards a great and powerful nation, dooms the former to be the satellite of the latter.

Against the insidious wiles of foreign influence (I conjure you to believe me, fellow-citizens) the jealousy of a free people ought to be *constantly* awake; since history and experience prove that foreign influence is one of the most baneful foes of republican government. But that jealousy, to be useful, must be impartial; else it becomes the instrument of the very influence to be avoided, instead of a defense against it. Excessive partiality for one foreign nation and excessive dislike of another, cause those whom they actuate to see danger only on one side, and serve to veil and even second the arts of influence on the other. Real patriots, who may resist the intrigues of the favorite, are liable to become suspected and odious; while its tools and dupes usurp the applause and confidence of the people, to surrender their interests.

The great rule of conduct for us, in regard to foreign nations, is, in extending our commercial relations, to have with them as little *political* connection as possible. So far as we have already formed engagements, let them be fulfilled with perfect good faith. Here let us stop.

Europe has a set of primary interests, which to us have none, or a very remote relation. Hence she must be engaged in frequent controversies, the causes of which are essentially foreign to our concerns. Hence, therefore, it must be unwise in us to implicate ourselves, by artificial ties, in the ordinary vicissitudes of her politics, or the ordinary combinations and collisions of her friendships or enmities.

Our detached and distant situation invites and enables us to pursue a different course. If we remain one people, under an efficient government, the period is not far off, when we may defy material injury from external annoyance; when we may take such an attitude as will cause the neutrality we may at any time resolve upon to be scrupulously respected; when belligerent nations, under the impossibility of making acquisitions upon us, will not lightly hazard the giving us provocation; when we may choose peace or war, as our interest, guided by justice, shall counsel.

Why forego the advantages of so peculiar a situation? Why quit our own to stand upon foreign ground? Why, by interweaving our destiny with that of any part of Europe, entangle our peace and prosperity in the toils of European ambition, rivalship, interest, humor, or caprice?

It is our true policy to steer clear of permanent alliances with any portion of the foreign world; so far, I mean, as we are now at liberty to do it; for let me not be understood as capable of patronizing infidelity to existing engagements. (I hold the maxim no less applicable to public than to private affairs, that honesty is always the best policy.) I repeat it, therefore, let those engagements be observed in their genuine sense. But in my opinion, it is unnecessary and would be unwise to extend them.

Taking care always to keep ourselves, by suitable establishments, on a respectably defensive posture, we may safely trust to temporary alliances for extraordinary emergencies.

Harmony, liberal intercourse with all nations, are recommended by policy, humanity, and interest. But even our commercial policy should hold an equal and impartial hand; neither seeking nor granting exclusive favors or preferences; consulting the natural course of things; diffusing and diversifying by gentle means the streams of commerce, but forcing nothing; establishing, with powers so disposed, in order to give trade a stable course, to define the rights of our merchants, and to enable the government to support them, conventional rules of intercourse, the best that present circumstances and mutual opinion will admit, but temporary, and liable to be from time to time abandoned or varied, as experience and circumstances shall dictate; constantly keeping in view, that it is folly in one nation to look for disinterested favors from another; that it must pay with a portion of its independence for whatever it may accept under that character; that, by such acceptance, it may place itself in the condition of having given equivalents for nominal favors, and yet of being reproached with ingratitude for not giving more. There can be no greater error than to expect or calculate upon real favors from nation to nation. It is an illusion, which experience must cure, which a just pride ought to discard.

In offering to you, my countrymen, these counsels of

an old and affectionate friend, I dare not hope they will make the strong and lasting impression I could wish; that they will control the usual current of the passions, or prevent our nation from running the course which has hitherto marked the destiny of nations. But if I may even flatter myself that they may be productive of some partial benefit, some occasional good; that they may now and then recur to moderate the fury of party spirit, to warn against the mischiefs of foreign intrigue, to guard against the impostures of pretended patriotism—this hope will be a full recompense for the solicitude for your welfare, by which they have been dictated.

How far in the discharge of my official duties I have been guided by the principles which have been delineated, the public records and other evidences of my conduct must witness to you and to the world. To myself, the assurance of my own conscience is, that I have at least believed myself to be guided by them.

In relation to the still subsisting war in Europe, my Proclamation of the 22d of April 1793 is the index to my plan. Sanctioned by your approving voice, and by that of your Representatives in both Houses of Congress, the spirit of that measure has continually governed me, uninfluenced by any attempts to deter or divert me from it.

After deliberate examination with the aid of the best lights I could obtain, I was well satisfied that our country, under all the circumstances of the case, had a right to take, and was bound in duty and interest, to take a neutral position. Having taken it, I determined, as far as should depend upon me, to maintain it, with moderation, perseverance, and firmness.

The considerations, which respect the right to hold this

conduct, it is not necessary on this occasion to detail. I will only observe, that according to my understanding of the matter, that right, so far from being denied by any of the belligerent powers, has been virtually admitted by all.

The duty of holding a neutral conduct may be inferred, without any thing more, from the obligation which justice and humanity impose on every nation, in cases in which it is free to act, to maintain inviolate the relations of peace and amity towards other nations.

The inducements of interest for observing that conduct will best be referred to your own reflections and experience. With me, a predominant motive has been to endeavor to gain time to our country to settle and mature its yet recent institutions, and to progress without interruption to that degree of strength and consistency, which is necessary to give it, humanly speaking, a command of its own fortunes.

Tho in reviewing the incidents of my administration, I am unconscious of international error, I am nevertheless too sensible of my defects not to think it probable that I may have committed many errors. Whatever they may be, I fervently beseech the Almighty to avert or mitigate the evils to which they may tend. I shall also carry with me the hope that my country will never cease to view them with indulgence; and that after forty-five years of my life dedicated to its service with an upright zeal, the faults of incompetent abilities will be consigned to oblivion, as myself must soon be to the mansions of rest.

Relying on its kindness in this as in other things, and actuated by that fervent love towards it, which is so natural to a man, who views in it the native soil of himself and his progenitors for several generations; I anticipate with pleasing expectation that retreat, in which I promise myself to realize, without alloy, the sweet enjoyment of partaking, in the midst of my fellow-citizens, the benign influence of good laws under a free government—the ever favorite object of my heart, and the happy reward, as I trust, of our mutual cares, labors, and dangers.

MOUNT VERNON, HOME OF GEORGE WASHINGTON

Mount Vernon, home of George Washington on the Potomac River, 15 miles from Washington, has universal appeal as an American shrine. Restored by the Mount Vernon Ladies' Association, it recaptures the leisurely charm and stately decorum of the eighteenth-century estate of the great patriot-farmer.

Abbie Rowe, National Park Service

Go Forth and Teach

HORACE MANN

Introductory—It is an incalculable loss to America that the national birthday—the Fourth of July—falls at a season when the schools are not generally in session. The force of the occasion is thus largely lost, for most communities pass it lightly by or give it over to commercialized mirth and noisemaking. The best celebrations are thoughtful occasions such as were held in Boston during the years following the Revolution when the young Republic was seeking to establish itself. In those days no higher tribute could be made to an orator than to be selected to deliver the Fourth of July Oration to the citizens of Boston, the nation's leading city. In 1842 that honor came to Horace Mann and he made the most of it in an address which ranks as the greatest of our Independence Day orations—an address that looks far into the future. It is in such pieces as this that youthful aspirations are aroused and directed.

GO FORTH AND TEACH

From Horace Mann's Fourth of July Oration, Boston, July 4, 1842

ON ONE of those oft-recurring days, when the fate of the state or the Union is to be decided at the polls; when, over all the land, the votes are falling thick as hail, and we seem to hear them rattle like the clangor of arms

HORACE MANN, 1796-1859

Horace Mann, father of the American system of free public education, was born at Franklin, Massachusetts, on May 4, 1796. During his young manhood he was surrounded by the patriotic fervor associated with the veterans of the Revolution and the War of 1812. Amid great difficulties he secured his education, graduating from Brown University in 1819 and later from the famous law school at Litchfield, Connecticut. As a lawyer of unusual integrity he rose rapidly in influence, advanced to the legislature, and became president of the Massachusetts Senate. It was then that the opportunity came to become the first secretary of the Massachusetts Board of Education where he gave twelve years of such inspired leadership as to turn the tide markedly in the direction of free public education in keeping with the democratic purpose of the new Republic.

—is it not enough to make the lover of his country turn pale to reflect upon the motives under which they may be given and the consequences to which they may lead? By the votes of a few wicked men, or even of one wicked man, honorable men may be hurled from office and miscreants elevated to their places; useful offices abolished and sinecures created; the public wealth, which had supported industry, squandered upon mercenaries; enterprise crippled, and thus capital which had been honestly and laboriously accumulated, turned into dross; in fine, the whole policy of the government may be reversed and the social condition of millions changed to gratify one man's grudge, or prejudice, or revenge. In a word, if the votes, which fall so copiously into the ballot-box on our days of election, emanate from wise counsels and a loyalty to truth, they will descend, like benedictions from heaven, to bless the land and fill it with song and gladness, but if, on the other hand, these votes come from ignorance and crime, the fire and brimstone that were rained on Sodom and Gomorrah would be more tolerable.

So if, at the time when that almost anarchical state of things which immediately followed the Revolutionary War, subsided and took shape and character in the republican form of our national and state constitutions—if, at that time, there was a large class of men more wealthy and better educated than the mass, that class of men had one of the most solemn duties to perform ever imposed upon human beings. If they had a superior knowledge of the past and a greater stake in the future, it was alike their duty and their interest to stifle all considerations of person and caste, to reconcile themselves to their new condition, and to concentrate all their energies in providing some refuge from impending evils. With our change from a monarchical to a popular government, from a government where all rule descended from "our Lord the King," to one where all rule ascended from "our Lords the People," the whole condition and relations of men were changed. It was like a change in the order of nature. Before this epoch, the few, by force of rank, wealth, dress, equipage, accomplishments, governed the many; after it, the many were to govern the few. Before this, birth and family were words of potent signification; but the revolution worked the most thorough attainder of all such blood. Before this, the deference paid to the opinions of different men, varied in the ratio of thousands to one; but after this, the vote of the veriest ignoramus or scoundrel would balance that of Franklin or Washington.

About the expediency, and especially about the *extent* of that change, a wide difference of opinion prevailed. But the change being made, was it not the duty of its opponents to yield to the inevitable course of events and to prepare for coming exigencies? And could not every really noble soul find an ample compensation for the loss of personal influence or family distinction in the greater dignity and elevation of his fellow beings? From whom should instruction come, if not from the most educated? Where should generosity towards the poor begin, if not with those whom Providence had blessed with abundance? Whence should magnanimity proceed, if not from minds expanded by culture? If there were an order of men who lost something of patrician rank by this political change, instead of holding themselves aloof from the people, they should have walked among them as Plato and Socrates did among their contemporaries, and expounded to them the nature and the vastness of the work they had undertaken to do—nay, if need were, they should have drained the poisoned bowl to sanctify the truths which they taught. For want of that interest and sympathy in the condition of the poor and the ignorant which the new circumstances required, they and their descendants have been and will be compelled to drink potions more bitter than hemlock as their daily beverage. . . .

With the change in the organic structure of our government, there should have been corresponding changes in all public measures and institutions. For every dollar given by the wealthy, or by the state, to colleges to cultivate the higher branches of knowledge, a hundred should have been given to primary education. For every acre of land bestowed upon an academy, a province should have been granted to common schools. Select schools for select children should have been discarded, and universal education joined hands with universal suffrage. Instead of the old order of nobility, with its baubles and puerilities, a new order should have been created—an order of *teachers,* wise, benevolent, filled with Christian enthusiasm, and rewarded and honored by all—an order looking *forwards* to a noble line of benefactors which they might help to rear, rather than *backwards* to ancestors from whom they had basely degenerated. In these schools, the first great principle of a republican government, that of native, inborn equality, should have been practically inculcated by their being open to all, good enough for all, and attended by all. Here, too, the second great principle of a republican government should have been taught, that all men, 'tho natively equal, become inherently unequal the moment that one grows wiser or better than his fellow. The doctrine of "higher" and "lower" classes in society should have been retained, but with a change in application. Those who had done the most good to mankind should have been honored as the "highest"; while those who had done no good to the race, either by the labors of the hand or by the labors of the mind, who had lived without requital upon the earnings of others, and left the world no better or made it worse, than they found it, should have been thrust down in the scale of social consideration to "low" and "lower," thru all the degrees of comparison. Whatever of leisure or of knowledge was possessed by the more wealthy or educated should have been freely expended to enlighten the laboring classes. Lectures, libraries, lyceums, mechanics' institutes, should everywhere have been fostered; scientific tracts gratuitously distributed; and a drowning child should not have been snatched from a watery grave with more promptness and alacrity than an ignorant or an abandoned one should have been sought out and brought under elevating and reforming influences. The noblest public edifices, the most splendid galleries of art, theatres, gardens, monuments, should all have been deemed a reproach to any people, while there was a child amongst them without ample and improved means of education. The nature and functions of our government, the laws of political economy, the *duties* as well as the *rights* of citizens, should have been made familiar as household words. The right to vote should have been held up as the most sacred of human rights, as involving all civil and religious rights, and therefore to be *constrained* by all civil and religious obligations. The great truth should everywhere have been inculcated, by example as well as by precept, that for the dependent to vote from malice, or envy, or wantonness, involves substantially the moral guilt of treason; and for the superior to compel the dependent, thru fear or bribery, to vote against his judgment, involves the baseness as well as the guilt of subornation of treason. Had this been done, our days of election would never have been, as they now so often are, days of turbulence and bacchanalian riot, of insulting triumph or revengeful defeat; but they would have been days of thoughtfulness and of solemnity, such as befit a day whose setting sun will witness the ruin or the rescue of so much of human welfare. . . .

And until all this work of improvement is done, until this indifference of the wealthy and the educated towards the masses shall cease, and legislative bounty shall atone for past penuriousness, there can be no security for any class or description of men, nor for any interest, human or divine. With additional thousands of voters every year crossing the line of manhood to decree the destiny of the nation, without additional knowledge and morality, things must accelerate from worse to worse. Amid increasing darkness and degeneracy, every man's rights may be invaded thru legislation—thru the annulment of charters or the abrogation of remedies—and thru the corruption of jurors, or even of one juror on the panel of twelve, every man's right of redress may be denied for the grossest aggressions. . . .

I have said that schools should have been established for the education of the whole people. These schools should have been of a more perfect character than any which have ever yet existed. In them the principles of morality should have been copiously intermingled with the principles of science. Cases of conscience should have alternated with lessons in the rudiments. The multiplication table should not have been more familiar, nor more frequently applied, than the rule to do to others as we would that they should do unto us. The lives of great and good men should have been held up for admiration and example; and especially the life and character of Jesus Christ, as the sublimest pattern of benevolence, of purity, of selfsacrifice, ever exhibited to mortals. In every course of studies, all the practical and preceptive parts of the Gospel should have been sacredly included; and all dogmatical theology and sectarianism sacredly excluded. In no school should the Bible have been opened to reveal the sword of the polemic, but to unloose the dove of peace.

I have thus endeavored to show that with universal suffrage there must be universal elevation of character, intellectual and moral, or there will be universal mismanagement and calamity. . . .

No, Fellow-Citizens, we have not for years past, and we shall not have, at least for many years to come, an election of a President, or a Congress, or a governor of a state, chosen under written constitutions and to legislate and act under written constitutions, whose choice will not be dependent upon, and determinable by, *legal* voters unable to read and write—voters who do not know and cannot know whether they vote for King Log or King Stork. The illustrious and noble band who framed the Constitution of the Union—Washington, Adams, Franklin, Jefferson, Madison—who adjusted all the principles which it contains by the line and the plummet, and weighed the words which describe them in scales so nice as to tremble beneath the dust of the balance—expended the energies of their mighty minds to perfect an instrument which, before half a century should pass away, was doomed to be administered, controled, expounded, by men unable to read and write. The power of Congress over all the great social and economical interests of this vast country; the orbits in which the states are to move around the central body in the system; the functions of the Executive who holds in his hands the Army and the Navy, manages all diplomatic relations with foreign powers, and can involve the country at any time in the horrors of war; and that grand poising power, the Supreme Judiciary, appointed to be the presiding intelligence over the system, to harmonize its motions and to hold its attracting and divergent tendencies in equilibrium—all this splendid structure, the vastest and the nicest ever devised by mortals, is under the control of men who are incapable of reading one word of the language which describes its framework and defines its objects and its guards, unable to read one word of contemporaneous exposition, of antecedent history, or of subsequent developments, and therefore ready to make it include anything, or exclude anything, as their blind passions may dictate.

I have spoken of those only who might as well have lived before Cadmus invented letters, as in the middle of this nineteenth century. But it is to be remembered there is no unoccupied space, no broad line of demarcation between the totally ignorant and the competently learned.

If the seven hundred thousand who, in one particular, surpass the most learned of ancient or modern times because to them all written languages are alike—if these are the most numerous class—probably the next most numerous consists of those who know next to nothing—and in reaching the summit of the highest intelligence, we should ascend by very easy gradations. Very many people learn to write their name for business purposes, whose attainments at the point become stationary; and it is one thing to be just able to read a verse in the Bible, and quite another to understand the forty thousand words in common use among intelligent men. Nay, if a few of the words, used by an intelligent man, are lost to the hearer, thru his ignorance of their meaning, the whole drift and object of the speaking or writing are lost. The custom so prevalent at the West and South, of *stump-speaking* had its origin in the voters' incapacity to read. How otherwise can a candidate for office communicate with ignorant voters? Should he publish his views and send them abroad, he must send an interpreter with them; but at a *barbecue*—amid the sympathy of numbers, the excitement of visible objects, the feast, the flow, the roar—the most abstruse points of the Constitution, the profoundest questions of national policy can all be expounded, and men and measures decided upon, to universal satisfaction!

A clear corollary is deducible from this demonstration. If the majority of a selfgoverning people are sober-minded, enlightened, studious of right, capable of comparing and balancing opposite interpretations of a fundamental law, or opposite views of a particular system of policy; then all appeals addressed to them in messages, speeches, pamphlets, and from the thousand-tongued newspaper press, will be calm, dispassionate, adapted at once to elucidate the subject under consideration and to instruct and elevate the mind of the arbiters. But, on the other hand, if the people are ignorant, fickle, averse to, or incapable of, patient inquiry, prone to hasty decisions from plausible appearances, or reckless from prejudice or passion, then the demagogues who address, will adapt themselves to the dupes who hear, just as certainly as the hunter adapts his lure to the animal he would ensnare; and flattery, imposture, falsehood, the vindication and eulogy of fellow-partisans however wicked, and the defamation of opponents however virtuous, will be the instruments by which a warfare, destructive in the end alike to victors and vanquished, will be waged. Let the spirit and tone of our congressional and legislative speechmakers, and the language of the political press throughout the country, decide the question, which of the above described classes they consider themselves as addressing. . . .

Let those, then, whose wealth is lost or jeoparded by fraud or misgovernment; let those who quake with apprehension for the fate of all they hold dear; let those who behold and lament the desecration of all that is holy; let rulers whose counsels are perplexed, whose plans are baffled, whose laws defied or evaded, let them all know that whatever ills they feel or fear, are but the just retributions of a righteous heaven for neglected childhood.

Remember, then, the child whose voice first lisps, today, before that voice shall whisper sedition in secret or thunder treason at the head of an armed band. Remember the child whose hand, today, first lifts its tiny bauble, before that hand shall scatter firebrands, arrows, and death. Remember those sportive groups of youth in whose halcyon bosoms there sleeps an ocean, as yet scarcely ruffled by the passions which soon shall heave it as with the tempest's strength. Remember that whatever station in life you may fill, these mortals—these immortals—are your care. Devote, expend, consecrate yourselves to the holy work of their improvement. Pour out light and truth, as God pours sunshine and rain. No longer seek knowledge as the luxury of a few, but dispense it amongst all as the bread of life. Learn only how the ignorant may learn; how the innocent may be preserved; the vicious reclaimed. Call down the astronomer from the skies; call up the geologist from his subterranean explorations; summon, if need be, the mightiest intellects from the council chamber of the nation; enter cloistered halls where the scholiast muses over superfluous annotations; dissolve conclave and synod where subtle polemics are vainly discussing their barren dogmas; collect whatever of talent, or erudition, or eloquence, or authority, the broad land can supply, *and go forth,* AND TEACH THIS PEOPLE. For, in the name of the living God, it must be proclaimed that licentiousness shall be the liberty; and violence and chicanery shall be the law; and superstition and craft shall be the religion; and the selfdestructive indulgence of all sensual and unhallowed passions shall be the only happiness of that people who neglect the education of their children.

Gettysburg and Second Inaugural Addresses

ABRAHAM LINCOLN

Introductory—Because of the peculiar circumstances of his life, character, and achievement, Lincoln more than any other American has become the hero of the poor and lowly thruout the world who aspire to better things. His utterances have a noble simplicity and sincerity that suggest the style of the Old Testament of which Lincoln was an earnest student. The two addresses which follow reveal Lincoln at his best. In form and thought they deserve a place with the great utterances of all time. Both are on the walls of the Lincoln Memorial in the nation's capitol.

THE GETTYSBURG ADDRESS

Delivered at the Dedication of the National Cemetery at Gettysburg, Pennsylvania, November 19, 1863

FOURSCORE and seven years ago our fathers brought forth on this continent a new nation, conceived in liberty, and dedicated to the proposition that all men are created equal.

Now we are engaged in a great civil war, testing whether that nation, or any nation so conceived and so dedicated, can long endure. We are met on a great battlefield of that war. We have come to dedicate a portion of that field as a final resting-place for those who here gave

Abbie Rowe, National Park Service

THE LINCOLN MEMORIAL STATUE
DANIEL CHESTER FRENCH, SCULPTOR

their lives that that nation might live. It is altogether fitting and proper that we should do this.

But, in a larger sense we cannot dedicate—we cannot consecrate—we cannot hallow—this ground. The brave men, living and dead, who struggled here, have consecrated it far above our poor power to add or detract. The world will little note nor long remember what we say here, but it can never forget what they did here. It is for us, the living, rather, to be dedicated here to the unfinished work which they who fought here have thus far so nobly advanced. It is rather for us to be here dedicated to the great task remaining before us—that from these honored dead we take increased devotion to that cause for which they gave the last full measure of devotion; that we here highly resolve that these dead shall not have died in vain; that this nation, under God, shall have a new birth of freedom; and that government of the people, by the people, for the people, shall not perish from the earth.

SECOND INAUGURAL ADDRESS

Washington, D. C., March 4, 1865

FELLOW-COUNTRYMEN: At this second appearing to take the oath of the presidential office, there is less occasion for an extended address than there was at the first. Then a statement, somewhat in detail, of a course to be pursued, seemed fitting and proper. Now, at the expiration of four years, during which public declarations have been constantly called forth on every point and phase of the great contest which still absorbs the attention and engrosses the energies of the nation, little that

America's Independent Electric Light and Power Companies

LINCOLN SITTING ON A PARK BENCH

The above statue by Gutzon Borglum is on the Court House steps in Newark, New Jersey. When Theodore Roosevelt saw the statue at the unveiling on Decoration Day, 1911, he exclaimed, "This doesn't look like a monument at all. It looks real!" Today, almost any time of day, a child or an adult may be seen admiring Lincoln or sitting beside him on the park bench.

is new could be presented. The progress of our arms, upon which all else chiefly depends, is as well-known to the public as to myself; and it is, I trust, reasonably satisfactory and encouraging to all. With high hope for the future, no prediction in regard to it is ventured.

On the occasion corresponding to this four years ago, all thoughts were anxiously directed to an impending civil war. All dreaded it—all sought to avert it. While the inaugural address was being delivered from this place, devoted altogether to saving the Union without war, insurgent agents were in the city seeking to destroy it without war—seeking to dissolve the Union, and divide effects, by negotiation. Both parties deprecated war; but one of them would make war rather than let the nation survive; and the other would accept war rather than let it perish. And the war came.

One-eighth of the whole population were colored slaves, not distributed generally over the Union, but localized in the southern part of it. These slaves constituted a peculiar and powerful interest. All knew that this interest was, somehow, the cause of the war. To strengthen, perpetuate, and extend this interest was the object for which the insurgents would rend the Union even by war; while the Government claimed no right to do more than to restrict the territorial enlargement of it.

Neither party expected for the war the magnitude or the duration which it has already attained. Neither anticipated that the cause of the conflict might cease with, or even before, the conflict itself should cease. Each looked for an easier triumph, and a result less fundamental and astounding. Both read the same Bible, and pray to the same God; and each invokes His aid against the other. It may seem strange that any men should dare to ask a just God's assistance in wringing their bread from the sweat of other men's faces; but let us judge not, that we be not judged. The prayers of both could not be answered—that of neither has been answered fully.

The Almighty has His own purpose. "Woe unto the world because of offenses! for it must needs be that offenses come; but woe to that man by whom the offense cometh." If we shall suppose that American slavery is one of those offenses which, in the providence of God, must needs come, but which, having continued thru His appointed time, He now wills to remove, and that He gives to both North and South this terrible war, as the woe to those by whom the offense came, shall we discern therein any departure from those divine attributes which the believers in a living God always ascribe to Him? Fondly do we hope—fervently do we pray—that this mighty scourge of war may speedily pass away. Yet, if God will that it continue until all the wealth piled by the bondman's two hundred and fifty years of unrequited toil shall be sunk, and until every drop of blood drawn with the lash shall be paid by another drawn with the sword, as was said three thousand years ago, so still it must be said, "The judgments of the Lord are true and righteous altogether."

With malice toward none; with charity for all; with firmness in the right, as God gives us to see the right, let us strive on to finish the work we are in; to bind up the nation's wounds; to care for him who shall have borne the battle, and for his widow, and his orphan—to do all which may achieve and cherish a just and a lasting peace among ourselves, and with all nations.

The Road Away From Revolution

BY WOODROW WILSON

When Daniel L. Marsh, then President of Boston University, brought together in 1939 in *The American Canon* the seven great documents which he considered the finest expression of the American spirit, he included this essay by Woodrow Wilson along with the Declaration of Independence and Lincoln's Second Inaugural Address. Says Dr. Marsh: "With the possible exception of Thomas Jefferson, Woodrow Wilson was the keenest analytical mind that has ever occupied the White House. With the possible exceptions of George Washington and Abraham Lincoln, he stands without a peer as a patriot among all our Presidents. He was reviled and persecuted, vilified and lied about, but no more than were Washington and Lincoln in their days. For excellence of literary style, incisiveness of thought, and clarity of expression he stands unsurpassed.

"Following his break in health and his retirement from the White House, Wilson was not able to carry on his more vigorous activities. Nevertheless, he kept mentally alert to what was happening. Mrs. Wilson tells us that in the spring of 1923 Woodrow Wilson began to display a sense of anxiety over the turn of affairs in the nation. He seemed to have a premonition of the troubles that finally did come in 1929 and following. He expressed a wish to write an article, but he had the use of only his right hand, and the return of neuritis in that hand made it practically impossible for him to hold a pen. He then turned to his typewriter again, but since he could pick out the letters with only one hand, he found that labor a burden. So he began to dictate to Mrs. Wilson what he wanted to say. Slowly, sometimes giving a single sentence in the middle of night, sometimes stopping in the midst of recreation and dictating another sentence, he finally had a short article written that he called *The Road Away From Revolution*. He polished the article again and again, smoothing up its diction, sharpening its style, making sure it said what he wanted it to say, and then he sent it to *The Atlantic Monthly*, in which it was published."
This article written a few months before Wilson died on February 3,

1924, was published in "Atlantic Monthly" August, 1923. It is used here thru the courteous permission of Edith Bolling Wilson.

In these doubtful and anxious days, when all the world is at unrest and, look which way you will, the road ahead seems darkened by shadows which portend dangers of many kinds, it is only common prudence that we should look about us and attempt to assess the causes of distress and the most likely means of removing them.

There must be some real ground for the universal unrest and perturbation. It is not to be found in superficial politics or in mere economic blunders. It probably lies deep at the sources of the spiritual life of our time. It leads to revolution; and perhaps if we take the case of the Russian Revolution, the outstanding event of its kind in our age, we may find a good deal of instruction for our judgment of present critical situations and circumstances.

What gave rise to the Russian Revolution? The answer can only be that it was the product of a whole social system. It was not in fact a sudden thing. It had been gathering head for several generations. It was due to the systematic denial to the great body of Russians of the rights and privileges which all normal men desire and must have if they are to be contented and within reach of happiness. The lives of the great mass of the Russian people contained no opportunities, but were hemmed in by barriers against which they were constantly flinging their spirits, only to fall back bruised and dispirited. Only the powerful were suffered to secure their rights or even to gain access to the means of material success.

It is to be noted as a leading fact of our time that it was against "capitalism" that the Russian leaders directed their attack. It was capitalism that made them see red;

Library of Congress Collections

WOODROW WILSON

WOODROW WILSON *was born in Staunton, Virginia, on December 28, 1856. After outstanding service as president of Princeton University he became Governor of New Jersey. In 1912 he was elected 28th President of the United States. His program of domestic reform—crowned by such victories as creation of the Federal Reserve System and the Federal Trade Commission—was interrupted by World War I.*

Wilson's prayer thruout the war was "that if this contest has no other result, it will at least have the result of creating an international tribunal and producing some sort of joint guarantee of peace on the part of the great nations of the world." Father and advocate of the League of Nations, he warned his countrymen in 1919, with a foresight vindicated by the events of two decades later: "I can predict with absolute certainty that within another generation there will be another World War if the nations of the world do not concert the method by which to prevent it."

Woodrow Wilson died on February 3, 1924, but his dream lives on in the United Nations.

and it is against capitalism under one name or another that the discontented classes everywhere draw their indictment.

There are thoughtful and well-informed men all over the world who believe, with much apparently sound reason, that the abstract thing, the system, which we call capitalism, is indispensable to the industrial support and development of modern civilization. And yet everyone who has an intelligent knowledge of social forces must know that great and widespread reactions like that which is now unquestionably manifesting itself against capitalism do not occur without cause or provocation; and before we commit ourselves irreconcilably to an attitude of hostility to this movement of the time, we ought frankly to put to ourselves the question, Is the capitalistic system unimpeachable? which is another way of asking, Have capitalists generally used their power for the benefit of the countries in which their capital is employed and for the benefit of their fellowmen?

Is it not, on the contrary, too true that capitalists have often seemed to regard the men whom they used as mere instruments of profit, whose physical and mental powers it was legitimate to exploit with as slight cost to themselves as possible, either of money or of sympathy? Have not many fine men who were actuated by the highest principles in every other relationship of life seemed to hold that generosity and humane feeling were not among the imperative mandates of conscience in the conduct of a banking business, or in the development of an industrial or commercial enterprise?

And if these offenses against high morality and true citizenship have been frequently observable, are we to say that the blame for the present discontent and turbulence is wholly on the side of those who are in revolt against them?

Ought we not, rather, to seek a way to remove such offenses and make life itself clean for those who will share honorably and cleanly in it?

The world has been made safe for democracy. There need now be no fear that any such mad design as that entertained by the insolent and ignorant Hohenzollerns and their counselors may prevail against it. But democracy has not yet made the world safe against irrational revolution. That supreme task, which is nothing less than the salvation of civilization, now faces democracy, insistent, imperative. There is no escaping it, unless everything we have built up is presently to fall in ruin about us; and the United States, as the greatest of democracies, must undertake it.

The road that leads away from revolution is clearly marked, for it is defined by the nature of man and of organized society. It therefore behooves us to study very carefully and very candidly the exact nature of the task and the means of its successful accomplishment.

The nature of men and of organized society dictates the maintenance, in every field of action, of the highest and purest standards of justice and of right dealing; and it is essential to efficacious thinking in this critical matter that we should not entertain a narrow or technical conception of justice. By justice the lawyer generally means the prompt, fair, and open application of impartial rules; but we call ours a Christian civilization, and a Christian conception of justice must be much higher. It must include sympathy and helpfulness and a willingness to forgo selfinterest in order to promote the welfare, happiness, and contentment of others and of the community as a whole. This is what our age is blindly feeling after in its reaction against what it deems the too great selfishness of the capitalistic system.

The sum of the whole matter is this, that our civilization cannot survive materially unless it be redeemed spiritually. It can be saved only by becoming permeated with the spirit of Christ and being made free and happy by the practices which spring out of that spirit. Only thus can discontent be driven out and all the shadows lifted from the road ahead.

Here is the final challenge to our churches, to our political organizations, and to our capitalists—to everyone who fears God or loves his country. Shall we not all earnestly cooperate to bring in the new day?

We in this country, in this generation, are—by destiny rather than choice—the watchmen on the walls of world freedom. We ask, therefore, that we may be worthy of our power and responsibility—that we may exercise our strength with wisdom and restraint—and that we may achieve in our time and for all time the ancient vision of peace on earth, good will toward men. That must always be our goal—and the righteousness of our cause must always underlie our strength. For as was written long ago: "Except the Lord keep the city, the watchman waketh but in vain."

John Fitzgerald Kennedy
The Undelivered Speech
November, 1963

PART V

The United Nations

THE UNITED NATIONS *is another step toward the realization of the age-old faith that men can govern themselves in love, peace, and mutual helpfulness. It is the immediate successor of The League of Nations which was established after World War I, and in which the United States refused to participate. The UN Charter was drafted at a conference of nations which opened in San Francisco on April 25, 1945. The Charter was unanimously approved by vote of the delegates on June, 25, 1945 and the next day members of the delegations signed the official documents. The charter came into effect October 24, 1945, having been ratified by the five permanent members of the Security Council, and a majority of the other signatories.*

It was ratified by the United States Senate on July 28, 1945 by a vote of 89 to 2 and is now a part of the basic law governing every American citizen.

During the few brief years of its existence the United Nations and its related organizations have performed many international services of the greatest importance and on one occasion after another have taken the lead in helping to preserve the peace of the world. It is only thru long and patient effort that such an organization can be brought to its full strength and usefulness. The only other alternative in our modern technological world is chaos or reversion to primitive ways of life, following near destruction of the human race by modern weapons of warfare.

STRUCTURE OF THE UNITED NATIONS

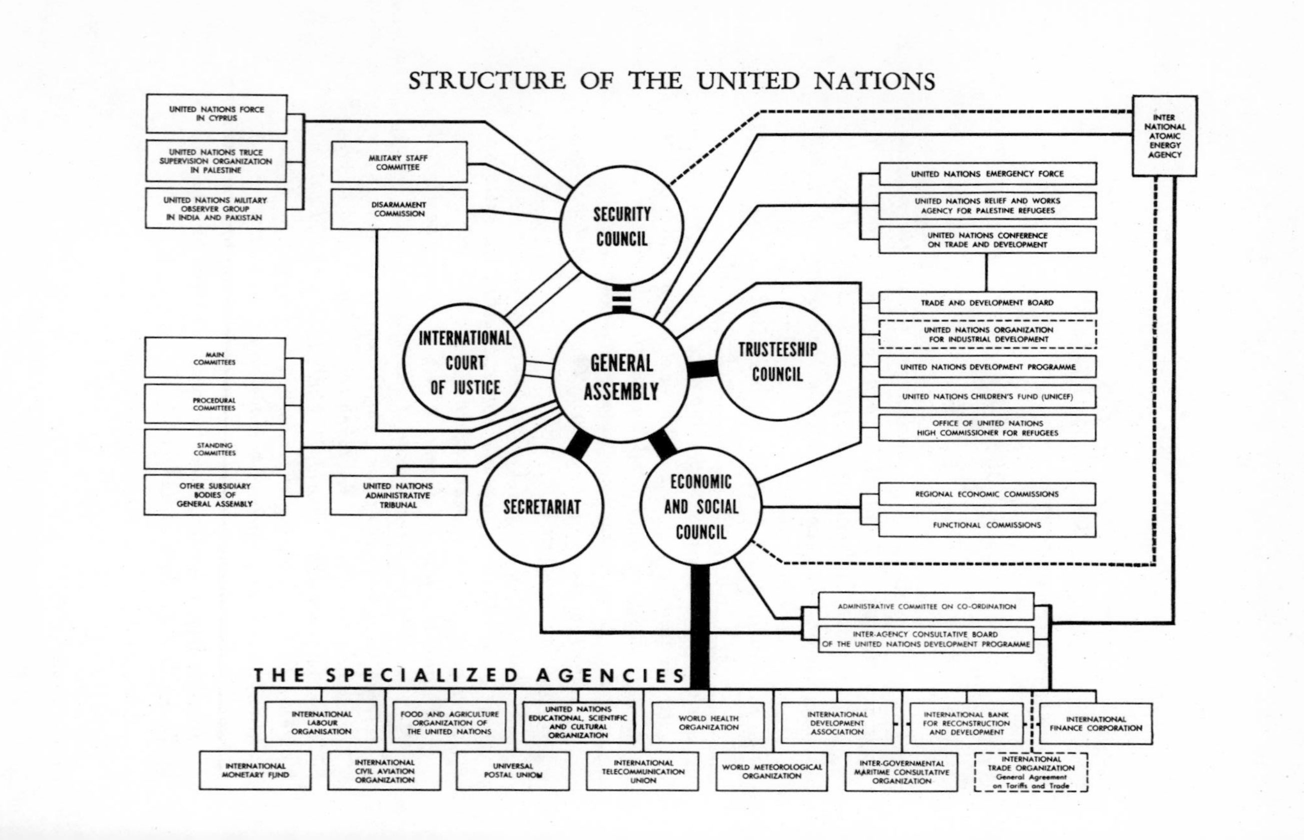

Membership of the United Nations

The 124 members of the United Nations, as of 1 September 1968, and the date of their admission, are:

Afghanistan	19 Nov. 1946
Albania	14 Dec. 1955
Algeria	8 Oct. 1962
*Argentina	24 Oct. 1945
*Australia	1 Nov. 1945
Austria	14 Dec. 1955
Barbados	9 Dec. 1966
*Belgium	27 Dec. 1945
*Bolivia	14 Nov. 1945
Botswana	17 Oct. 1966
*Brazil	24 Oct. 1945
Bulgaria	14 Dec. 1955
Burma	19 Apr. 1948
Burundi	18 Sept. 1962
*Byelorussian SSR	24 Oct. 1945
Cambodia	14 Dec. 1955
Cameroon	20 Sept. 1960
*Canada	9 Nov. 1945
Central African Republic	20 Sept. 1960
Ceylon	14 Dec. 1955
Chad	20 Sept. 1960
*Chile	24 Oct. 1945
*China	24 Oct. 1945
*Colombia	5 Nov. 1945
Congo (Brazzaville)	20 Sept. 1960
Congo (Democratic Republic of)	20 Sept. 1960
*Costa Rica	2 Nov. 1945
*Cuba	24 Oct. 1945
Cyprus	20 Sept. 1960
*Czechoslovakia	24 Oct. 1945
Dahomey	20 Sept. 1960
*Demark	24 Oct. 1945
*Dominican Republic	24 Oct. 1945
*Ecuador	21 Dec. 1945
*El Salvador	24 Oct. 1945
*Ethiopia	13 Nov. 1945
Finland	14 Dec. 1955
*France	24 Oct. 1945
Gabon	20 Sept. 1960
Gambia	21 Sept. 1965
Ghana	8 Mar. 1957
*Greece	25 Oct. 1945
*Guatemala	21 Nov. 1945
Guinea	12 Dec. 1958
Guyana	20 Sept. 1966
*Haiti	24 Oct. 1945
*Honduras	17 Dec. 1945
Hungary	14 Dec. 1955
Iceland	19 Nov. 1946
*India	30 Oct. 1945
Indonesia	28 Sept. 1950
*Iran	24 Oct. 1945
*Iraq	21 Dec. 1945
Ireland	14 Dec. 1955
Israel	11 May 1949

**Original member.*

Italy	14 Dec. 1955	*Poland	24 Oct. 1945
Ivory Coast	20 Sept. 1960	Portugal	14 Dec. 1955
Jamaica	18 Sept. 1962	Romania	14 Dec. 1955
Japan	18 Dec. 1956	Rwanda	18 Sept. 1962
Jordan	14 Dec. 1955	*Saudia Arabia	24 Oct. 1945
Kenya	16 Dec. 1963	Senegal	28 Sept. 1960
Kuwait	14 May 1963	Sierra Leone	27 Sept. 1961
Laos	14 Dec. 1955	Singapore	21 Sept. 1965
*Lebanon	24 Oct. 1945	Somalia	20 Sept. 1960
Lesotho	17 Oct. 1966	*South Africa	7 Nov. 1945
*Liberia	2 Nov. 1945	Southern Yemen	14 Dec. 1967
Libya	14 Dec. 1955	Spain	14 Dec. 1955
*Luxembourg	24 Oct. 1945	Sudan	12 Nov. 1956
Madagascar	20 Sept. 1960	Sweden	19 Nov. 1946
Malawi	1 Dec. 1964	*Syria	24 Oct. 1945
Malaysia	17 Sept. 1957	Thailand	16 Dec. 1946
Maldive Islands	21 Sept. 1965	Togo	20 Sept. 1960
Mali	28 Sept. 1960	Trinidad and	
Malta	1 Dec. 1964	Tobago	18 Sept. 1962
Mauritania	27 Oct. 1961	Tunisia	12 Nov. 1956
Mauritius	24 Apr. 1968	*Turkey	24 Oct. 1945
*Mexico	7 Nov. 1945	Uganda	25 Oct. 1962
Mongolia	27 Oct. 1961	*Ukrainian SSR	24 Oct. 1945
Morocco	12 Nov. 1956	*USSR	24 Oct. 1945
Nepal	14 Dec. 1955	*United Arab	
*Netherlands	10 Dec. 1945	Republic	24 Oct. 1945
*New Zealand	24 Oct. 1945	*United Kingdom	24 Oct. 1945
*Nicaragua	24 Oct. 1945	United Republic	
Niger	20 Sept. 1960	of Tanzania	14 Dec. 1961
Nigeria	7 Oct. 1960	*United States	24 Oct. 1945
*Norway	27 Nov. 1945	Upper Volta	20 Sept. 1960
Pakistan	30 Sept. 1947	*Uruguay	18 Dec. 1945
*Panama	13 Nov. 1945	*Venezuela	15 Nov. 1945
*Paraguay	24 Oct. 1945	Yemen	30 Sept. 1947
*Peru	31 Oct. 1945	*Yugoslavia	24 Oct. 1945
*Philippines	24 Oct. 1945	Zambia	1 Dec. 1964

**Original member.*

Charter of the United Nations

WE *the peoples of the United Nations determined*

to save succeeding generations from the scourge of war, which twice in our lifetime has brought untold sorrow to mankind, and

to reaffirm faith in fundamental human rights, in the dignity and worth of the human person, in the equal rights of men and women and of nations large and small, and

to establish conditions under which justice and respect for the obligations arising from treaties and other sources of international law can be maintained, and

to promote social progress and better standards of life in larger freedom,

and for these ends

to practice tolerance and live together in peace with one another as good neighbors, and

to unite our strength to maintain international peace and security, and

to ensure, by the acceptance of principles and the institution of methods, that armed force shall not be used, save in the common interest, and

to employ international machinery for the promotion of the economic and social advancement of all peoples,

have resolved to combine our efforts to accomplish these aims.

Accordingly, our respective Governments, thru representatives assembled in the city of San Francisco, who have exhibited their full powers found to be in good and due form, have agreed to the present Charter of the United Nations and do hereby establish an international organization to be known as the United Nations.

CHAPTER I

Purposes and Principles

Article 1—The Purposes of the United Nations are:

1. To maintain international peace and security, and to that end: to take effective collective measures for the prevention and removal of threats to the peace, and for the suppression of acts of aggression or other breaches of the peace, and to bring about by peaceful means, and in conformity with the principles of justice and international law, adjustment or settlement of international disputes or situations which might lead to a breach of the peace;

2. To develop friendly relations among nations based on respect for the principle of equal rights and self-determination of peoples, and to take other appropriate measures to strengthen universal peace;

3. To achieve international cooperation in solving international problems of an economic, social, cultural, or humanitarian character, and in promoting and encouraging respect for human rights and for fundamental freedoms for all without distinction as to race, sex, language, or religion; and

4. To be a center for harmonizing the actions of nations in the attainment of these common ends.

Article 2—The Organization and its Members, in pursuit of the Purposes stated in Article 1, shall act in accordance with the following Principles.

1. The Organization is based on the principle of the sovereign equality of all its Members.

2. All Members, in order to ensure to all of them the rights and benefits resulting from membership, shall fulfil in good faith the obligations assumed by them in accordance with the present Charter.

3. All Members shall settle their international disputes by peaceful means in such a manner that international peace and security, and justice, are not endangered.

4. All Members shall refrain in their international relations from the threat or use of force against the territorial integrity or political independence of any state, or any other manner inconsistent with the Purposes of the United Nations.

5. All Members shall give the United Nations every assistance in any action it takes in accordance with the present Charter, and shall refrain from giving assistance to any state against which the United Nations is taking preventive or enforcement action.

6. The Organization shall ensure that states which are not Members of the United Nations act in accordance with these Principles so far as may be necessary for the maintenance of international peace and security.

7. Nothing contained in the present Charter shall authorize the United Nations to intervene in matters which are essentially within the domestic jurisdiction of any state or shall require the Members to submit such matters to settlement under the present Charter; but this principle shall not prejudice the application of enforcement measures under Chapter VII.

CHAPTER II

Membership

Article 3—The original Members of the United Nations shall be the states which, having participated in the United Nations Conference on International Organization at San Francisco, or having previously signed the Declaration by United Nations of January 1, 1942, sign the present Charter and ratify it in accordance with Article 110.

Article 4—1. Membership in the United Nations is open to all other peace-loving states which accept the obligations contained in the present Charter and, in the judgment of the Organization, are able and willing to carry out these obligations.

2. The admission of any such state to membership in the United Nations will be effected by a decision of the General Assembly upon the recommendation of the Security Council.

Article 5—A Member of the United Nations against which preventive or enforcement action has been taken by the Security Council may be suspended from the exercise of the rights and privileges of membership by the General Assembly upon the recommendation of the Security Council. The exercise of these rights and privileges may be restored by the Security Council.

Article 6—A Member of the United Nations which has persistently violated the Principles contained in the present Charter may be expelled from the Organization by the General Assembly upon the recommendation of the Security Council.

CHAPTER III

Organs

Article 7—1. There are established as the principal organs of the United Nations: a General Assembly, a Security Council, an Economic and Social Council, a Trusteeship Council, an International Court of Justice, and a Secretariat.

2. Such subsidiary organs as may be found necessary may be established in accordance with the present Charter.

Article 8—The United Nations shall place no restrictions on the eligibility of men and women to participate in any capacity and under conditions of equality in its principal and subsidiary organs.

CHAPTER IV

The General Assembly

COMPOSITION

Article 9—1. The General Assembly shall consist of all the Members of the United Nations.

2. Each Member shall have not more than five representatives in the General Assembly.

FUNCTIONS AND POWERS

Article 10—The General Assembly may discuss any questions or any matters within the scope of the present Charter or relating to the powers and functions of any organs provided for in the present Charter, and, except as provided in Article 12, may make recommendations to the Members of the United Nations or to the Security Council or to both on any such questions or matters.

Article 11—1. The General Assembly may consider the general principles of cooperation in the maintenance of international peace and security, including the principles governing disarmament and the regulation of armaments, and may make recommendations with regard to such principles to the Members or to the Security Council or to both.

2. The General Assembly may discuss any questions relating to the maintenance of international peace and security brought before it by any Member of the United Nations, or by the Security Council, or by a state which is not a Member of the United Nations in accordance with Article 35, paragraph 2, and, except as provided in Article 12, may make recommendations with regard to any such questions to the state or states concerned or to the Security Council or to both. Any such questions on which action is necessary shall be referred to the Security Council by the General Assembly either before or after discussion.

3. The General Assembly may call the attention of the Security Council to situations which are likely to endanger international peace and security.

4. The powers of the General Assembly set forth in this Article shall not limit the general scope of Article 10.

Article 12—1. While the Security Council is exercising in respect of any dispute or situation the functions assigned to it in the present Charter, the General Assembly shall not make any recommendation with regard to that dispute or situation unless the Security Council so requests.

2. The Secretary-General, with the consent of the Security Council, shall notify the General Assembly at each session of any matters relative to the maintenance of international peace and security which are being dealt with by the Security Council and shall similarly notify the General Assembly, or the Members of the United Nations if the General Assembly is not in session, immediately the Security Council ceases to deal with such matters.

Article 13—1. The General Assembly shall initiate studies and make recommendations for the purpose of:

a. promoting international cooperation in the political field and encouraging the progressive development of international law and its codification;

b. promoting international cooperation in the economic, social, cultural, educational, and health fields, and assisting in the realization of human rights and fundamental freedoms for all without distinction as to race, sex, language, or religion.

2. The further responsibilities, functions, and powers of the General Assembly with respect to matters mentioned in paragraph 1 (b) above are set forth in Chapters IX and X.

Article 14—Subject to the provisions of Article 12, the General Assembly may recommend measures for the peaceful adjustment of any situation, regardless of origin, which it deems likely to impair the general welfare or friendly relations among nations, including situations resulting from a violation of the provisions of the present Charter setting forth the Purposes and Principles of the United Nations.

Article 15—1. The General Assembly shall receive and consider annual and special reports from the Security Council; these reports shall include an account of the measures that the Security Council has decided upon or taken to maintain international peace and security.

2. The General Assembly shall receive and consider reports from the other organs of the United Nations.

Article 16—The General Assembly shall perform such functions with respect to the international trusteeship system as are assigned to it under Chapters XII and XIII, including the approval of the trusteeship agreements for areas not designated as strategic.

Article 17—1. The General Assembly shall consider and approve the budget of the Organization.

2. The expenses of the Organization shall be borne by the Members as apportioned by the General Assembly.

3. The General Assembly shall consider and approve any financial and budgetary arrangements with specialized agencies referred to in Article 57 and shall examine the administrative budgets of such specialized agencies with a view to making recommendations to the agencies concerned.

VOTING

Article 18—1. Each member of the General Assembly shall have one vote.

2. Decisions of the General Assembly on important questions shall be made by a two-thirds majority of the members present and voting. These questions shall include: recommendations with respect to the maintenance of international peace and security, the election of the non-permanent members of the Security Council, the election of the members of the Economic and Social Council, the election of

members of the Trusteeship Council in accordance with paragraph 1 (c) of Article 86, the admission of new Members to the United Nations, the suspension of the rights and privileges of membership, the expulsion of Members, questions relating to the operation of the trusteeship system, and budgetary questions.

3. Decisions on other questions, including the determination of additional categories of questions to be decided by a two-thirds majority, shall be made by a majority of the members present and voting.

Article 19—A Member of the United Nations which is in arrears in the payment of its financial contributions to the Organization shall have no vote in the General Assembly if the amount of its arrears equals or exceeds the amount of the contributions due from it for the preceding two full years. The General Assembly may, nevertheless, permit such a Member to vote if it is satisfied that the failure to pay is due to conditions beyond the control of the Member.

PROCEDURE

Article 20—The General Assembly shall meet in regular annual sessions and in such special sessions as occasion may require. Special sessions shall be convoked by the Secretary-General at the request of the Security Council or of a majority of the Members of the United Nations.

Article 21—The General Assembly shall adopt its own rules of procedure. It shall elect its President for each session.

Article 22—The General Assembly may establish such subsidiary organs as it deems necessary for the performance of its functions.

CHAPTER V

The Security Council

COMPOSITION

Article 23—1. The Security Council shall consist of eleven* Members of the United Nations. The Republic of China, France, the Union of Soviet Socialist Republics, the United Kingdom of Great Britain and Northern Ireland, and the United States of America

* Amendment adopted December 17, 1963, increased Security Council to fifteen members.

shall be permanent members of the Security Council. The General Assembly shall elect six other Members of the United Nations to be non-permanent members of the Security Council, due regard being specially paid, in the first instance to the contribution of Members of the United Nations to the maintenance of international peace and security and to the other purposes of the Organization, and also to equitable geographical distribution.

2. The non-permanent members of the Security Council shall be elected for a term of two years. In the first election of the non-permanent members, however, three shall be chosen for a term of one year. A retiring member shall not be eligible for immediate re-election.

3. Each member of the Security Council shall have one representative.

FUNCTIONS AND POWERS

Article 24—1. In order to ensure prompt and effective action by the United Nations, its Members confer on the Security Council primary responsibility for the maintenance of international peace and security, and agree that in carrying out its duties under this responsibility the Security Council acts on their behalf.

2. In discharging these duties the Security Council shall act in accordance with the Purposes and Principles of the United Nations. The specific powers granted to the Security Council for the discharge of these duties are laid down in Chapters VI, VII, VIII, and XII.

3. The Security Council shall submit annual and, when necessary, special reports to the General Assembly for its consideration.

Article 25—The Members of the United Nations agree to accept and carry out the decisions of the Security Council in accordance with the present Charter.

Article 26—In order to promote the establishment and maintenance of international peace and security with the least diversion for armaments of the world's human and economic resources, the Security Council shall be responsible for formulating, with the assistance of the Military Staff Committee referred to in Article 47, plans to be submitted to the Members of the United Nations for the establishment of a system for the regulation of armaments.

VOTING

Article 27—1. Each member of the Security Council shall have one vote.

2. Decisions of the Security Council on procedural matters shall be made by an affirmative vote of seven* members.

3. Decisions of the Security Council on all other matters shall be made by an affirmative vote of seven* members including the concurring votes of the permanent members; provided that, in decisions under Chapter VI, and under paragraph 3 of Article 52, a party to a dispute shall abstain from voting.

PROCEDURE

Article 28—1. The Security Council shall be so organized as to be able to function continuously. Each member of the Security Council shall for this purpose be represented at all times at the seat of the Organization.

2. The Security Council shall hold periodic meetings at which each of its members may, if it so desires, be represented by a member of the government or by some other specially designated representative.

3. The Security Council may hold meetings at such places other than the seat of the Organization as in its judgment will best facilitate its work.

Article 29—The Security Council may establish such subsidiary organs as it deems necessary for the performance of its functions.

Article 30—The Security Council shall adopt its own rules of procedure, including the method of selecting its President.

Article 31—Any Member of the United Nations which is not a member of the Security Council may participate, without vote, in the discussion of any question brought before the Security Council whenever the latter considers that the interests of that Member are specially affected.

Article 32—Any Member of the United Nations which is not a member of the Security Council or any state which is not a Member of the United Nations, if it is a party to a dispute under consideration by the Security Council, shall be invited to participate,

---

* Amendment adopted December 17, 1963, increased this to nine members.

without vote, in the discussion relating to the dispute. The Security Council shall lay down such conditions as it deems just for the participation of a state which is not a Member of the United Nations.

CHAPTER VI

Pacific Settlement of Disputes

Article 33—1. The parties to any dispute, the continuance of which is likely to endanger the maintenance of international peace and security, shall, first of all, seek a solution by negotiation, enquiry, mediation, conciliation, arbitration, judicial settlement, resort to regional agencies or arrangements, or other peaceful means of their own choice.

2. The Security Council shall, when it deems necessary, call upon the parties to settle their dispute by such means.

Article 34—The Security Council may investigate any dispute, or any situation which might lead to international friction or give rise to a dispute, in order to determine whether the continuance of the dispute or situation is likely to endanger the maintenance of international peace and security.

Article 35—1. Any Member of the United Nations may bring any dispute, or any situation of the nature referred to in Article 34, to the attention of the Security Council or of the General Assembly.

2. A state which is not a Member of the United Nations may bring to the attention of the Security Council or of the General Assembly any dispute to which it is a party if it accepts in advance, for the purposes of the dispute, the obligations of pacific settlement provided in the present Charter.

3. The proceedings of the General Assembly in respect of matters brought to its attention under this Article will be subject to the provisions of Articles 11 and 12.

Article 36—1. The Security Council may, at any stage of a dispute of the nature referred to in Article 33 or of a situation of like nature, recommend appropriate procedures or methods of adjustment.

2. The Security Council should take into consideration any procedures for the settlement of the dispute which have already been adopted by the parties.

3. In making recommendations under this Article the Security Council should also take into consideration that legal disputes should as a general rule be referred by the parties to the International Court of Justice in accordance with the provisions of the Statute of the Court.

Article 37—1. Should the parties to a dispute of the nature referred to in Article 33 fail to settle it by the means indicated in that Article, they shall refer it to the Security Council.

2. If the Security Council deems that the continuance of the dispute is in fact likely to endanger the maintenance of international peace and security, it shall decide whether to take action under Article 36 or to recommend such terms of settlement as it may consider appropriate.

Article 38—Without prejudice to the provisions of Articles 33 to 37, the Security Council may, if all the parties to any dispute so request, make recommendations to the parties with a view to a pacific settlement of the dispute.

CHAPTER VII

Action with Respect to Threats to the Peace, Breaches of the Peace, and Acts of Aggression

Article 39—The Security Council shall determine the existence of any threat to the peace, breach of the peace, or act of aggression and shall make recommendations, or decide what measures shall be taken in accordance with Articles 41 and 42, to maintain or restore international peace and security.

Article 40—In order to prevent an aggravation of the situation, the Security Council may, before making the recommendations or deciding upon the measures provided for in Article 39, call upon the parties concerned to comply with such provisional measures as it deems necessary or desirable. Such provisional measures shall be without prejudice to the rights, claims, or position of the parties concerned. The Security Council shall duly take account of failure to comply with such provisional measures.

Article 41—The Security Council may decide what measures not involving the use of armed force are to be employed to give effect to its decisions, and it may call upon the Members of the United Nations to apply such measures. These may include complete or partial interruption of economic relations and of rail, sea, air, postal, telegraphic, radio, and other means of communication, and the severance of diplomatic relations.

Article 42—Should the Security Council consider that measures provided for in Article 41 would be inadequate or have proved to be inadequate, it may take such action by air, sea, or land forces as may be necessary to maintain or restore international peace and security. Such action may include demonstrations, blockade, and other operations by air, sea, or land forces of Members of the United Nations.

Article 43—1. All Members of the United Nations, in order to contribute to the maintenance of international peace and security, undertake to make available to the Security Council on its call and in accordance with a special agreement or agreements, armed forces, assistance, and facilities, including rights of passage, necessary for the purpose of maintaining international peace and security.

2. Such agreement or agreements shall govern the numbers and types of forces, their degree of readiness and general location, and the nature of the facilities and assistance to be provided.

3. The agreement or agreements shall be negotiated as soon as possible on the initiative of the Security Council. They shall be concluded between the Security Council and Members or between the Security Council and groups of Members and shall be subject to ratification by the signatory states in accordance with their respective constitutional processes.

Article 44—When the Security Council has decided to use force it shall, before calling upon a Member not represented on it to provide armed forces in fulfillment of the obligations assumed under Article 43, invite that Member, if the Member so desires, to participate in the decisions of the Security Council concerning the employment of contingents of that Member's armed forces.

Article 45—In order to enable the United Nations to take urgent military measures, Members shall hold immediately available national air-force contingents for combined international enforcement action. The strength and degree of readiness of these contingents and plans for their combined action shall be determined, within the limits laid down in the special agreement or agreements referred to in

Article 43, by the Security Council with the assistance of the Military Staff Committee.

Article 46—Plans for the application of armed force shall be made by the Security Council with the assistance of the Military Staff Committee.

Article 47—1. There shall be established a Military Staff Committee to advise and assist the Security Council on all questions relating to the Security Council's military requirements for the maintenance of international peace and security, the employment and command of forces placed at its disposal, the regulation of armaments, and possible disarmament.

2. The Military Staff Committee shall consist of the Chiefs of Staff of the permanent members of the Security Council or their representatives. Any Member of the United Nations not permanently represented on the Committee shall be invited by the Committee to be associated with it when the efficient discharge of the Committee's responsibilities requires the participation of that Member in its work.

3. The Military Staff Committee shall be responsible under the Security Council for the strategic direction of any armed forces placed at the disposal of the Security Council. Questions relating to the command of such forces shall be worked out subsequently.

4. The Military Staff Committee, with the authorization of the Security Council and after consultation with appropriate regional agencies, may establish regional subcommittees.

Article 48—1. The action required to carry out the decisions of the Security Council for the maintenance of international peace and security shall be taken by all the Members of the United Nations or by some of them, as the Security Council may determine.

2. Such decisions shall be carried out by the Members of the United Nations directly and through their action in the appropriate international agencies of which they are members.

Article 49—The Members of the United Nations shall join in affording mutual assistance in carrying out the measures decided upon by the Security Council.

Article 50—If preventative or enforcement measures against any state are taken by the Security Council, any other state, whether a Member of the United Nations or not, which finds itself confronted with special economic problems arising from the carrying out of those measures shall have the right to consult the Security Council with regard to a solution of those problems.

Article 51—Nothing in the present Charter shall impair the inherent right of individual or collective self-defense if an armed attack occurs against a Member of the United Nations, until the Security Council has taken the measures necessary to maintain international peace and security. Measures taken by Members in the exercise of this right of self-defense shall be immediately reported to the Security Council and shall not in any way affect the authority and responsibility of the Security Council under the present Charter to take at any time such action as it deems necessary in order to maintain or restore international peace and security.

CHAPTER VIII

Regional Arrangements

Article 52—1. Nothing in the present Charter precludes the existence of regional arrangements or agencies for dealing with such matters relating to the maintenance of international peace and security as are appropriate for regional action, provided that such arrangements or agencies and their activities are consistent with the Purposes and Principles of the United Nations.

2. The Members of the United Nations entering into such arrangements or constituting such agencies shall make every effort to achieve pacific settlement of local disputes thru such regional arrangements or by such regional agencies before referring them to the Security Council.

3. The Security Council shall encourage the development of pacific settlement of local disputes thru such regional arrangements or by such regional agencies either on the initiative of the states concerned or by reference from the Security Council.

4. This Article in no way impairs the application of Articles 34 and 35.

Article 53—1. The Security Council shall, where appropriate, utilize such regional arrangements or agencies for enforcement action under its authority. But no enforcement action shall be taken under regional arrangements or by regional agencies without the authorization of the Security Council, with the exception of measures against any enemy state, as defined in paragraph 2 of this Article, provided for pursuant to Article 107 or in regional arrangements directed against renewal of aggressive policy on the part of any such state, until such time as the Organization may, on request of the Governments concerned, be charged with the responsibility for preventing further aggression by such a state.

2. The term enemy state as used in paragraph 1 of this Article applies to any state which during the Second World War has been an enemy of any signatory of the present Charter.

Article 54—The Security Council shall at all times be kept fully informed of activities undertaken or in contemplation under regional arrangements or by regional agencies for the maintenance of international peace and security.

CHAPTER IX

International Economic and Social Cooperation

Article 55—With a view to the creation of conditions of stability and well-being which are necessary for peaceful and friendly relations among nations based on respect for the principle of equal rights and self-determination of peoples, the United Nations shall promote:

a. higher standards of living, full employment, and conditions of economic and social progress and development;

b. solutions of international economic, social, health, and related problems; and international cultural and educational co-operation; and

c. universal respect for, and observance of, human rights and fundamental freedoms for all without distinction as to race, sex, language, or religion.

Article 56—All Members pledge themselves to take joint and separate action in cooperation with the Organization for the achievement of the purposes set forth in Article 55.

Article 57—1. The various specialized agencies, established by intergovernmental agreement and having wide international responsibilities, as defined in their basic instruments, in economic, social, cultural, educational, health, and related fields, shall be brought into relationship with the United Nations in accordance with the provisions of Article 63.

2. Such agencies thus brought into relationship with the United Nations are hereinafter referred to as specialized agencies.

Article 58—The Organization shall make recommendations for the coordination of the policies and activities of the specialized agencies.

Article 59—The Organization shall, where appropriate, initiate negotiations among the states concerned for the creation of any new specialized agencies required for the accomplishment of the purposes set forth in Article 55.

Article 60—Responsibility for the discharge of the functions of the Organization set forth in this Chapter shall be vested in the General Assembly and, under the authority of the General Assembly, in the Economic and Social Council, which shall have for this purpose the powers set forth in Chapter X.

CHAPTER X

The Economic and Social Council

COMPOSITION

Article 61—1. The Economic and Social Council shall consist of eighteen* Members of the United Nations elected by the General Assembly.

2. Subject to the provisions of paragraph 3, six members of the Economic and Social Council shall be elected each year for a term of three years. A retiring member shall be eligible for immediate re-election.

3. At the first election, eighteen members of the Economic and Social Council shall be chosen. The term of office of six members so chosen shall expire at the end of one year, and of six other members at the end of two years, in accordance with arrangements made by the General Assembly.

4. Each member of the Economic and Social Council shall have one representative.

FUNCTIONS AND POWERS

Article 62—1. The Economic and Social Council may make or initiate studies and reports with respect to international economic,

* Enlarged to twenty-seven by amendment adopted December 17, 1963.

social, cultural, educational, health, and related matters and may make recommendations with respect to any such matters to the General Assembly, to the Members of the United Nations, and to the specialized agencies concerned.

2. It may make recommendations for the purpose of promoting respect for, and observance of human rights and fundamental freedoms for all.

3. It may prepare draft conventions for submission to the General Assembly, with respect to matters falling within its competence.

4. It may call, in accordance with the rules prescribed by the United Nations, international conferences on matters falling within its competence.

Article 63—1. The Economic and Social Council may enter into agreements with any of the agencies referred to in Article 57, defining the terms on which the agency concerned shall be brought into relationship with the United Nations. Such agreements shall be subject to approval by the General Assembly.

2. It may coordinate the activities of the specialized agencies thru consultation with and recommendations to such agencies and thru recommendations to the General Assembly and to the Members of the United Nations.

Article 64—1. The Economic and Social Council may take appropriate steps to obtain regular reports from the specialized agencies. It may make arrangements with the Members of the United Nations and with the specialized agencies to obtain reports on the steps taken to give effect to its own recommendations and to recommendations on matters falling within its competence made by the General Assembly.

2. It may communicate its observations on these reports to the General Assembly.

Article 65—The Economic and Social Council may furnish information to the Security Council and shall assist the Security Council upon its request.

Article 66—1. The Economic and Social Council shall perform such functions as fall within its competence in connection with the carrying out of the recommendations of the General Assembly.

2. It may, with the approval of the General Assembly, perform services at the request of Members of the United Nations and at the request of specialized agencies.

3. It shall perform such other functions as are specified elsewhere in the present Charter or as may be assigned to it by the General Assembly.

VOTING

Article 67—1. Each member of the Economic and Social Council shall have one vote.

2. Decisions of the Economic and Social Council shall be made by a majority of the members present and voting.

PROCEDURE

Article 68—The Economic and Social Council shall set up commissions in economic and social fields and for the promotion of human rights, and such other commissions as may be required for the performance of its functions.

Article 69—The Economic and Social Council shall invite any Member of the United Nations to participate, without vote, in its deliberations on any matter of particular concern to that Member.

Article 70—The Economic and Social Council may make arrangements for representatives of the specialized agencies to participate, without vote, in its deliberations and in those of the commissions established by it, and for its representatives to participate in the deliberations of the specialized agencies.

Article 71—The Economic and Social Council may make suitable arrangements for consultation with non-governmental organizations which are concerned with matters within its competence. Such arrangements may be made with international organizations and, where appropriate, with national organizations after consultation with the Member of the United Nations concerned.

Article 72—1. The Economic and Social Council shall adopt its own rules of procedure, including the method of selecting its President.

2. The Economic and Social Council shall meet as required in accordance with its rules which shall include provision for the convening of meetings on the request of a majority of its members.

CHAPTER XI

Declaration Regarding Non-Self-Governing Territories

Article 73—Members of the United Nations which have or assume responsibilities for the administration of territories whose peoples have not yet attained a full measure of self-government recognize the principle that the interests of the inhabitants of these territories are paramount, and accept as a sacred trust the obligation to promote to the utmost, within the system of international peace and security established by the present Charter, the well-being of the inhabitants of these territories, and, to this end:

a. to ensure, with due respect for the culture of the peoples concerned, their political, economic, social, and educational advancement, their just treatment, and their protection against abuses;

b. to develop self-government, to take due account of the political aspirations of the peoples, and to assist them in the progressive development of their free political institutions, according to the particular circumstances of each territory and its peoples and their varying stages of advancement;

c. to further international peace and security;

d. to promote constructive measures of development, to encourage research, and to cooperate with one another and, when and where appropriate, with specialized international bodies with a view to the practical achievement of the social, economic, and scientific purposes set forth in this Article; and

e. to transmit regularly to the Secretary-General for information purposes, subject to such limitation as security and constitutional considerations may require, statistical and other information of a technical nature relating to economic, social, and educational conditions in the territories for which they are respectively responsible other than those territories to which Chapters XII and XIII apply.

Article 74—Members of the United Nations also agree that their policy in respect of the territories to which this Chapter applies, no less than in respect of their metropolitan areas, must be based on the general principle of good-neighborliness, due account being taken of the interests and well-being of the rest of the world, in social, economic, and commercial matters.

United Nations

UNITED NATIONS, NEW YORK

The Headquarters of the United Nations and New York's mid-Manhattan skyline, as seen from the southern tip of Welfare Island, in the middle of the East River. The 39-story skyscraper houses the Secretariat's offices; council chambers and conference rooms are located in the low building at the river's edge, and the General Assembly in the domed building at right.

CHAPTER XII

International Trusteeship System

Article 75—The United Nations shall establish under its authority an international trusteeship system for the administration and supervision of such territories as may be placed thereunder by subsequent individual agreements. These territories are hereinafter referred to as trust territories.

Article 76—The basic objectives of the trusteeship system, in accordance with the Purposes of the United Nations laid down in Article 1 of the present Charter, shall be:

a. to further international peace and security;

b. to promote the political, economic, social, and educational advancement of the inhabitants of the trust territories, and their progressive development towards self-government or independence as may be appropriate to the particular circumstances of each territory and its peoples and the freely expressed wishes of the peoples concerned, and as may be provided by the terms of each trusteeship agreement;

c. to encourage respect for human rights and for fundamental freedoms for all without distinction as to race, sex, language, or religion, and to encourage recognition of the interdependence of the peoples of the world; and

d. to ensure equal treatment in social, economic, and commercial matters for all Members of the United Nations and their nationals, and also equal treatment for the latter in the administration of justice, without prejudice to the attainment of the foregoing objectives and subject to the provisions of Article 80.

Article 77—1. The trusteeship system shall apply to such territories in the following categories as may be placed thereunder by means of trusteeship agreements:

a. territories now held under mandate;

b. territories which may be detached from enemy states as a result of the Second World War; and

c. territories voluntarily placed under the system by states responsible for their administration.

2. It will be a matter for subsequent agreement as to which territories in the foregoing categories will be brought under the trusteeship system and upon what terms.

Article 78—The trusteeship system shall not apply to territories which have become Members of the United Nations, relationship among which shall be based on respect for the principle of sovereign equality.

Article 79—The terms of trusteeship for each territory to be placed under the trusteeship system, including any alteration or amendment, shall be agreed upon by the states directly concerned, including the mandatory power in the case of territories held under mandate by a Member of the United Nations, and shall be approved as provided for in Articles 83 and 85.

Article 80—1. Except as may be agreed upon in individual trusteeship agreements, made under Articles 77, 79, and 81, placing each territory under the trusteeship system, and until such agreements have been concluded, nothing in this Chapter shall be construed in or of itself to alter in any manner the rights whatsoever of any states or any peoples or the terms of existing international instruments to which Members of the United Nations may respectively be parties.

2. Paragraph 1 of this Article shall not be interpreted as giving grounds for delay or postponement of the negotiation and conclusion of agreements for placing mandated and other territories under the trusteeship system as provided for in Article 77.

Article 81—The trusteeship agreement shall in each case include the terms under which the trust territory will be administered and designate the authority which will exercise the administration of the trust territory. Such authority, hereinafter called the administering authority, may be one or more states or the Organization itself.

Article 82—There may be designated, in any trusteeship agreement, a strategic area or areas which may include part or all of the trust territory to which the agreement applies, without prejudice to any special agreement or agreements made under Article 43.

Article 83—1. All functions of the United Nations relating to strategic areas, including the approval of the terms of the trusteeship agreements and of their alteration or amendment, shall be exercised by the Security Council.

2. The basic objectives set forth in Article 76 shall be applicable to the people of each strategic area.

3. The Security Council shall, subject to the provisions of the trusteeship agreements and without prejudice to security considerations, avail itself of the assistance of the Trusteeship Council to perform those functions of the United Nations under the trusteeship system relating to political, economic, social, and educational matters in the strategic areas.

Article 84—It shall be the duty of the administering authority to ensure that the trust territory shall play its part in the maintenance of international peace and security. To this end the administering authority may make use of volunteer forces, facilities, and assistance from the trust territory in carrying out the obligations towards the Security Council undertaken in this regard by the administering authority, as well as for local defense and the maintenance of law and order within the trust territory.

Article 85—1. The functions of the United Nations with regard to trusteeship agreements for all areas not designated as strategic, including the approval of the terms of the trusteeship agreements and of their alteration or amendment, shall be exercised by the General Assembly.

2. The Trusteeship Council, operating under the authority of the General Assembly, shall assist the General Assembly in carrying out these functions.

CHAPTER XIII

The Trusteeship Council

COMPOSITION

Article 86—1. The Trusteeship Council shall consist of the following Members of the United Nations:

a. those Members administering trust territories;

b. such of those Members mentioned by name in Article 23 as are not administering trust territories; and

The Dumbarton Oaks Collection

THE MAIN HOUSE, DUMBARTON OAKS

In 1944 in this fine old Georgian estate in Georgetown were held the conversations between representatives of the United States, Great Britain, Russia and China that resulted in the first draft of the United Nations charter. Once the home of John C. Calhoun, this estate was presented by its last owners, Mr. and Mrs. Robert Woods Bliss, along with their research library and famous collection of pre-Columbian, Byzantine and early Christian art to Harvard University, which maintains it as a center for study.

c. as many other Members elected for three-year terms by the General Assembly as may be necessary to ensure that the total number of members of the Trusteeship Council is equally divided between those Members of the United Nations which administer trust territories and those which do not.

2. Each member of the Trusteeship Council shall designate one specially qualified person to represent it therein.

FUNCTIONS AND POWERS

Article 87—The General Assembly and, under its authority, the Trusteeship Council, in carrying out their functions, may:

a. consider reports submitted by the administering authority;

b. accept petitions and examine them in consultation with the administering authority;

c. provide for periodic visits to the respective trust territories at times agreed upon with the administering authority; and

d. take these and other actions in conformity with the terms of the trusteeship agreements.

Article 88—The Trusteeship Council shall formulate a questionnaire on the political, economic, social, and educational advancement of the inhabitants of each trust territory, and the administering authority for each trust territory within the competence of the General Assembly shall make an annual report to the General Assembly upon the basis of such questionnaire.

VOTING

Article 89—1. Each member of the Trusteeship Council shall have one vote.

2. Decisions of the Trusteeship Council shall be made by a majority of the members present and voting.

PROCEDURE

Article 90—1. The Trusteeship Council shall adopt its own rules of procedure, including the method of selecting its President.

2. The Trusteeship Council shall meet as required in accordance with its rules, which shall include provision for the convening of meetings on the request of a majority of its members.

Article 91—The Trusteeship Council shall, when appropriate, avail itself of the assistance of the Economic and Social Council and of the specialized agencies in regard to matters with which they are respectively concerned.

CHAPTER XIV

The International Court of Justice

Article 92—The International Court of Justice shall be the principal judicial organ of the United Nations. It shall function in accordance with the annexed Statute, which is based upon the Statute of the Permanent Court of International Justice and forms an integral part of the present Charter.

Article 93—1. All Members of the United Nations are *ipso facto* parties to the Statute of the International Court of Justice.

2. A state which is not a Member of the United Nations may become a party to the Statute of the International Court of Justice on conditions to be determined in each case by the General Assembly upon the recommendation of the Security Council.

Article 94—1. Each Member of the United Nations undertakes to comply with the decision of the International Court of Justice in any case to which it is a party.

2. If any party to a case fails to perform the obligations incumbent upon it under a judgment rendered by the Court, the other party may have recourse to the Security Council, which may, if it deems necessary, make recommendations or decide upon measures to be taken to give effect to the judgment.

Article 95—Nothing in the present Charter shall prevent Members of the United Nations from entrusting the solution of their differences to other tribunals by virtue of agreements already in existence or which may be concluded in the future.

Article 96—1. The General Assembly or the Security Council may request the International Court of Justice to give an advisory opinion on any legal question.

2. Other organs of the United Nations and specialized agencies, which may at any time be so authorized by the General Assembly, may also request advisory opinions of the Court on legal questions arising within the scope of their activities.

CHAPTER XV

The Secretariat

Article 97—The Secretariat shall comprise a Secretary-General and such staff as the Organization may require. The Secretary-General shall be appointed by the General Assembly upon the recommendation of the Security Council. He shall be the chief administrative officer of the Organization.

Article 98—The Secretary-General shall act in that capacity in all meetings of the General Assembly, of the Security Council, of the Economic and Social Council, and of the Trusteeship Council, and shall perform such other functions as are entrusted to him by these organs. The Secretary-General shall make an annual report to the General Assembly on the work of the Organization.

Article 99—The Secretary-General may bring to the attention of the Security Council any matter which in his opinion may threaten the maintenance of international peace and security.

Article 100—1. In the performance of their duties the Secretary-General and the staff shall not seek or receive instructions from any government or from any other authority external to the Organization. They shall refrain from any action which might reflect on their position as international officials responsible only to the Organization.

2. Each Member of the United Nations undertakes to respect the exclusively international character of the responsibilities of the Secretary-General and the staff and not to seek to influence them in the discharge of their responsibilities.

Article 101—1. The staff shall be appointed by the Secretary-General under regulations established by the General Assembly.

2. Appropriate staffs shall be permanently assigned to the Economic and Social Council, the Trusteeship Council, and, as required, to other organs of the United Nations. These staffs shall form a part of the Secretariat.

3. The paramount consideration in the employment of the staff and in the determination of the conditions of service shall be the necessity of securing the highest standards of efficiency, competence, and integrity. Due regard shall be paid to the importance of recruiting the staff on as wide a geographical basis as possible.

CHAPTER XVI

Miscellaneous Provisions

Article 102—1. Every treaty and every international agreement entered into by any Member of the United Nations after the present Charter comes into force shall as soon as possible be registered with the Secretariat and published by it.

2. No party to any such treaty or international agreement which has not been registered in accordance with the provisions of paragraph 1 of this Article may invoke that treaty or agreement before any organ of the United Nations.

Article 103—In the event of a conflict between the obligations of the Members of the United Nations under the present Charter and their obligations under any other international agreement, their obligations under the present Charter shall prevail.

Article 104—The Organization shall enjoy in the territory of each of its Members such legal capacity as may be necessary for the exercise of its functions and the fulfillment of its purposes.

Article 105—1. The Organization shall enjoy in the territory of each of its Members such privileges and immunities as are necessary for the fulfillment of its purposes.

2. Representatives of the Members of the United Nations and officials of the Organization shall similarly enjoy such privileges and immunities as are necessary for the independent exercise of their functions in connection with the Organization.

3. The General Assembly may make recommendations with a view to determining the details of the application of paragraphs 1 and 2 of this Article or may propose conventions to the Members of the United Nations for this purpose.

CHAPTER XVII

Transitional Security Arrangements

Article 106—Pending the coming into force of such special agreements referred to in Article 43 as in the opinion of the Security Council enable it to begin the exercise of its responsibilities under Article 42, the parties to the Four-Nation Declaration, signed at Moscow,

October 30, 1943, and France, shall, in accordance with the provisions of paragraph 5 of that Declaration, consult with one another and as occasion requires with other Members of the United Nations with a view to such joint action on behalf of the Organization as may be necessary for the purpose of maintaining international peace and security.

Article 107—Nothing in the present Charter shall invalidate or preclude action, in relation to any state which during the Second World War has been an enemy of any signatory to the present Charter, taken or authorized as a result of that war by the Governments having responsibility for such action.

CHAPTER XVIII
Amendments

Article 108—Amendments to the present Charter shall come into force for all Members of the United Nations when they have been adopted by a vote of two thirds of the members of the General Assembly and ratified in accordance with their respective constitutional processes by two thirds of the Members of the United Nations, including all the permanent members of the Security Council.

Article 109—1. A General Conference of the Members of the United Nations for the purpose of reviewing the present Charter may be held at a date and place to be fixed by a two-thirds vote of the members of the General Assembly and by a vote of any seven* members of the Security Council. Each Member of the United Nations shall have one vote in the conference.

2. Any alteration of the present Charter recommended by a two-thirds vote of the conference shall take effect when ratified in accordance with their respective constitutional processes by two thirds of the Members of the United Nations including all the permanent members of the Security Council.

3. If such a conference has not been held before the tenth annual session of the General Assembly following the coming into force of the present Charter, the proposal to call such a conference shall be placed on the agenda of that session of the General Assembly, and the conference shall be held if so decided by a majority vote of the members of the General Assembly and by a vote of any seven members of the Security Council.

---

* Increased to nine members by amendment adopted December 20, 1965.

CHAPTER XIX

Ratification and Signature

Article 110—1. The present Charter shall be ratified by the signatory states in accordance with their respective constitutional processes.

2. The ratifications shall be deposited with the Government of the United States of America, which shall notify all the signatory states of each deposit as well as the Secretary-General of the Organization when he has been appointed.

3. The present Charter shall come into force upon the deposit of ratifications by the Republic of China, France, the Union of Soviet Socialist Republics, the United Kingdom of Great Britain and Northern Ireland, and the United States of America, and by a majority of the other signatory states. A protocol of the ratifications deposited shall thereupon be drawn up by the Government of the United States of America which shall communicate copies thereof to all the signatory states.

4. The states signatory to the present Charter which ratify it after it has come into force will become original Members of the United Nations on the date of the deposit of their respective ratifications.

Article 111—The present Charter, of which the Chinese, French, Russian, English, and Spanish texts are equally authentic, shall remain deposited in the archives of the Government of the United States of America. Duly certified copies thereof shall be transmitted by that Government to the Governments of the other signatory states.

For Further Information

Information on the United Nations and its related agencies may be obtained by directing inquiries to: Public Inquiries Unit, United Nations, New York. Information concerning the availability of United Nations publications may be obtained from: Sales Section, United Nations, New York.

Constitution of the United Nations Educational, Scientific and Cultural Organization

[*Adopted in London on November 16, 1945 and amended at later Conferences. The text used here is from the* UNESCO Manual of the General Conference, *1967 edition.*]

The Governments of the States Parties to This Constitution, on Behalf of Their Peoples, Declare

that since wars begin in the minds of men, it is in the minds of men that the defenses of peace must be constructed;
that ignorance of each other's ways and lives has been a common cause, thruout the history of mankind, of that suspicion and mistrust between the peoples of the world thru which their differences have all too often broken into war;
that the great and terrible war which has now ended was a war made possible by the denial of the democratic principles of the dignity, equality and mutual respect of men, and by the propagation, in their place, thru ignorance and prejudice, of the doctrine of the inequality of men and races;
that the wide diffusion of culture, and the education of humanity for justice and liberty and peace are indispensable to the dignity of man and constitute a sacred duty which all the nations must fulfil in a spirit of mutual assistance and concern;
that a peace based exclusively upon the political and economic arrangements of governments would not be a peace which could secure the unanimous, lasting and sincere support of the peoples of the world, and that the peace must therefore be founded, if it is not to fail, upon the intellectual and moral solidarity of mankind.

For These Reasons,

the States Parties to this Constitution, believing in full and equal opportunities for education for all, in the unrestricted pursuit of objective truth, and in the free exchange of ideas and knowledge are agreed and determined to develop and to increase the means of communication between their peoples and to employ these means for the purposes of mutual understanding and a truer and more perfect knowledge of each other's lives;

In Consequence Whereof

they do hereby create the United Nations Educational, Scientific and Cultural Organization for the purpose of advancing, thru the educational and scientific and cultural relations of the peoples of the world, the objectives of international peace and of the common welfare of mankind for which the United Nations Organization was established and which its Charter proclaims.

ARTICLE I—PURPOSES AND FUNCTIONS

1. The purpose of the Organization is to contribute to peace and security by promoting collaboration among the nations thru education, science and culture in order to further universal respect for justice, for the rule of law and for the human rights and fundamental freedoms which are affirmed for the peoples of the world, without distinction of race, sex, language or religion, by the Charter of the United Nations.

2. To realize this purpose the Organization will:

[*a*] collaborate in the work of advancing the mutual knowledge and understanding of peoples, thru all means of mass communication and to that end recommend such international agreements as may be necessary to promote the free flow of ideas by word and image;

[*b*] give fresh impulse to popular education and to the spread of culture;

by collaborating with Members, at their request, in the development of educational activities;

by instituting collaboration among the nations to advance the ideal of equality of educational opportunity without regard to race, sex or any distinctions, economic or social;

by suggesting educational methods best suited to prepare the children of the world for the responsibilities of freedom;

[*c*] maintain, increase and diffuse knowledge;

by assuring the conservation and protection of the world's inheritance of books, works of art and monuments of history and science, and recommending to the nations concerned the necessary international conventions;

by encouraging cooperation among the nations in all branches of intellectual activity, including the international exchange of persons active in the fields of education, science and culture and the exchange of publications, objects of artistic and scientific interest and other materials of information;

by initiating methods of international cooperation calculated to give the people of all countries access to the printed and published materials produced by any of them.

3. With a view to preserving the independence, integrity and fruitful diversity of the cultures and educational systems of the States Members of this Organization, the Organization is prohibited from intervening in matters which are essentially within their domestic jurisdiction.

ARTICLE II—MEMBERSHIP

1. Membership of the United Nations Organization shall carry with it the right to membership of the United Nations Educational, Scientific and Cultural Organization.

2. Subject to the conditions of the agreement between this Organization and the United Nations Organization, approved pursuant to Article X of this Constitution, States not members of the United Nations Organization may be admitted to membership of the Organization, upon recommendation of the Executive Board, by a two-thirds majority vote of the General Conference.

3. Territories or groups of territories which are not responsible for the conduct of their international relations may be admitted as Associate Members by the General Conference by a two-thirds majority of Members present and voting, upon application made on behalf of such territory or group of territories by the Member or other authority having responsibility for their international relations. The nature and extent of the rights and obligations of Associate Members shall be determined by the General Conference.

4. Members of the Organization which are suspended from the exercise of the rights and privileges of membership of the United

Nations Organization shall, upon the request of the latter, be suspended from the rights and privileges of this Organization.

5. Members of the Organization which are expelled from the United Nations Organization shall automatically cease to be members of this Organization.

6. Any Member State or Associate Member of the Organization may withdraw from the Organization by notice addressed to the Director-General. Such notice shall take effect on 31 December of the year following that during which the notice was given. No such withdrawal shall affect the financial obligations owed to the Organization on the date the withdrawal takes effect. Notice of withdrawal by an Associate Member shall be given on its behalf by the Member State or other authority having responsibility for its international relations.

ARTICLE III—ORGANS

The Organization shall include a General Conference, an Executive Board and a Secretariat.

ARTICLE IV—THE GENERAL CONFERENCE

A. Composition 1. The General Conference shall consist of the representatives of the States Members of the Organization. The Government of each Member State shall appoint not more than five delegates, who shall be selected after consultation with the National Commission, if established, or with educational, scientific and cultural bodies.

B. Functions 2. The General Conference shall determine the policies and the main lines of work of the Organization. It shall take decisions on programs submitted to it by the Executive Board.

3. The General Conference shall, when it deems desirable and in accordance with the regulations to be made by it, summon international conferences of States on education, the sciences and humanities or the dissemination of knowledge; nongovernmental conferences on the same subjects may be summoned by the General Conference or by the Executive Board in accordance with such regulations.

4. The General Conference shall, in adopting proposals for submission to the Member States, distinguish between recommendations and international conventions submitted for their approval. In the former case a majority vote shall suffice; in the latter case a two-thirds majority shall be required. Each of the Member States shall

submit recommendations or conventions to its competent authorities within a period of one year from the close of the session of the General Conference at which they were adopted.

5. Subject to the provisions of Article V, paragraph 5(c), the General Conference shall advise the United Nations Organization on the educational, scientific and cultural aspects of matters of concern to the latter, in accordance with the terms and procedure agreed upon between the appropriate authorities of the two Organizations.

6. The General Conference shall receive and consider the reports submitted periodically by Member States as provided by Article VIII.

7. The General Conference shall elect the members of the Executive Board and, on the recommendation of the Board, shall appoint the Director-General.

C. Voting 8. [a] Each Member State shall have one vote in the General Conference. Decisions shall be made by a simple majority except in cases in which a two-thirds majority is required by the provisions of this Constitution. A majority shall be a majority of the Members present and voting.

[b] A Member State shall have no vote in the General Conference if the total amount of contributions due from it exceeds the total amount of contributions payable by it for the current year and the immediately preceding calendar year.

[c] The General Conference may nevertheless permit such a Member State to vote, if it is satisfied that the failure to pay is due to conditions beyond the control of the Member Nation.

D. Procedure 9. [a] The General Conference shall meet in ordinary session every two years. It may meet in extraordinary session if it decides to do so itself or if summoned by the Executive Board, or on the demand of at least one-third of the Member States.

[b] At each session the location of its next ordinary session shall be designated by the General Conference. The location of an extraordinary session shall be decided by the General Conference if the session is summoned by it, or otherwise by the Executive Board.

10. The General Conference shall adopt its own rules of procedure. It shall at each session elect a President and other officers.

11. The General Conference shall set up special and technical committees and such other subordinate bodies as may be necessary for its purposes.

12. The General Conference shall cause arrangements to be made for public access to meetings, subject to such regulations as it shall prescribe.

E. Observers 13. The General Conference, on the recommendation of the Executive Board and by a two-thirds majority may, subject to its rules of procedure, invite as observers at specified sessions of the Conference or of its Commissions representatives of international organizations, such as those referred to in Article XI, paragraph 4.

14. When consultative arrangements have been approved by the Executive Board for such international nongovernmental or semigovernmental organizations in the manner provided in Article XI, paragraph 4, those organizations shall be invited to send observers to sessions of the General Conference and its Commissions.

ARTICLE V—EXECUTIVE BOARD

A. *Composition* 1. The Executive Board shall be elected by the General Conference from among the delegates appointed by the Member States and shall consist of thirty members, each of whom shall represent the Government of the State of which he is a national. The President of the General Conference shall sit *ex officio* in an advisory capacity on the Executive Board.

2. In electing the members of the Executive Board the General Conference shall endeavour to include persons competent in the arts, the humanities, the sciences, education and the diffusion of ideas, and qualified by their experience and capacity to fulfil the administrative and executive duties of the Board. It shall also have regard to the diversity of cultures and a balanced geographical distribution. Not more than one national of any Member State shall serve on the Board at any one time, the President of the Conference excepted.

3. Members of the Board shall serve from the close of the session of the General Conference which elected them until the close of the second ordinary session of the General Conference following that election. They shall be immediately eligible for a second term, but shall not serve consecutively for more than two terms. Half of the members of the Board shall be elected every two years.

4. In the event of the death or resignation of a member of the Executive Board, his replacement for the remainder of his term shall

be appointed by the Executive Board on the nomination of the Government of the State the former member represented. The Government making the nomination and the Executive Board shall have regard to the factors set forth in paragraph 2 of this article.

B. Functions 5. (a) The Executive Board shall prepare the agenda for the General Conference. It shall examine the program of work for the Organization and corresponding budget estimates submitted to it by the Director-General in accordance with paragraph 3 of Article VI and shall submit them with such recommendations as it considers desirable to the General Conference.

(b) The Executive Board, acting under the authority of the General Conference, shall be responsible for the execution of the program adopted by the Conference. In accordance with the decisions of the General Conference and having regard to circumstances arising between two ordinary sessions, the Executive Board shall take all necessary measures to ensure the effective and rational execution of the program by the Director-General.

(c) Between ordinary sessions of the General Conference, the Board may discharge the functions of adviser to the United Nations, set forth in Article IV, paragraph 5, whenever the problem upon which advice is sought has already been dealt with in principle by the Conference, or when the solution is implicit in decisions of the Conference.

6. The Executive Board shall recommend to the General Conference the admission of new Members to the Organization.

7. Subject to decisions of the General Conference, the Executive Board shall adopt its own rules of procedure. It shall elect its officers from among its members.

8. The Executive Board shall meet in regular session at least twice a year and may meet in special session if convoked by the Chairman on his own initiative or upon the request of six members of the Board.

9. The Chairman of the Executive Board shall present, on behalf of the Board, to each ordinary session of the General Conference, with or without comments, the reports on the activities of the Organization which the Director-General is required to prepare in accordance with the provisions of Article VI.3 (b).

10. The Executive Board shall make all necessary arrangements to consult the representatives of international organizations or qualified persons concerned with questions within its competence.

11. Between sessions of the General Conference, the Executive Board may request advisory opinions from the International Court of Justice on legal questions arising within the field of the Organization's activities.

12. Although the members of the Executive Board are representative of their respective Governments they shall exercise the powers delegated to them by the General Conference on behalf of the Conference as a whole.

C. Transitional Provisions 13. At the twelfth session of the General Conference, eighteen members shall be elected to the Executive Board pursuant to the provisions of this article. Three of them shall retire at the close of the thirteenth session of the General Conference, the retiring members being chosen by the drawing of lots. Thereafter, fifteen members shall be elected at each ordinary session of the General Conference.

ARTICLE VI—SECRETARIAT

1. The Secretariat shall consist of a Director-General and such staff as may be required.

2. The Director-General shall be nominated by the Executive Board and appointed by the General Conference for a period of six years under such conditions as the Conference may approve, and shall be eligible for reappointment. He shall be the chief administrative officer of the Organization.

3. (a) The Director-General, or a deputy designated by him, shall participate, without the right to vote, in all meetings of the General Conference, of the Executive Board, and of the Committees of the Organization. He shall formulate proposals for appropriate action by the Conference and the Board, and shall prepare for submission to the Board a draft program of work for the Organization with corresponding budget estimates.

(b) The Director-General shall prepare and communicate to Member States and to the Executive Board periodical reports on the activities of the Organization. The General Conference shall determine the periods to be covered by these reports.

4. The Director-General shall appoint the staff of the Secretariat in accordance with staff regulations to be approved by the General Conference. Subject to the paramount consideration of securing the highest standards of integrity, efficiency and technical competence,

appointment to the staff shall be on as wide a geographical basis as possible.

5. The responsibilities of the Director-General and of the staff shall be exclusively international in character. In the discharge of their duties they shall not seek or receive instructions from any government or from any authority external to the Organization. They shall refrain from any action which might prejudice their position as international officials. Each State Member of the Organization undertakes to respect the international character of the responsibilities of the Director-General and the staff, and not to seek to influence them in the discharge of their duties.

6. Nothing in this Article shall preclude the Organization from entering into special arrangements within the United Nations Organization for common services and staff and for the interchange of personnel.

ARTICLE VII—NATIONAL COOPERATING BODIES

1. Each Member State shall make such arrangements as suit its particular conditions for the purpose of associating its principal bodies interested in educational, scientific and cultural matters with the work of the Organization, preferably by the formation of a National Commission broadly representative of the Government and such bodies.

2. National Commissions or national cooperating bodies, where they exist, shall act in an advisory capacity to their respective delegations to the General Conference and to their Governments in matters relating to the Organization and shall function as agencies of liaison in all matters of interest to it.

3. The Organization may, on the request of a Member State, delegate, either temporarily or permanently, a member of its Secretariat to serve on the National Commission of that State, in order to assist in the development of its work.

ARTICLE VIII—REPORTS BY MEMBER STATES

Each Member State shall report periodically to the Organization, in a manner to be determined by the General Conference, on its laws, regulations and statistics relating to educational, scientific and cultural life and institutions, and on the action taken upon the recommendations and conventions referred to in Article IV, paragraph 4.

ARTICLE IX—BUDGET

1. The budget shall be administered by the Organization.

2. The General Conference shall approve and give final effect to the budget and to the apportionment of financial responsibility among the States Members of the Organization subject to such arrangement with the United Nations as may be provided in the agreement to be entered into pursuant to Article X.

3. The Director-General, with the approval of the Executive Board, may receive gifts, bequests, and subventions directly from governments, public and private institutions, associations and private persons.

ARTICLE X—RELATIONS WITH THE UNITED NATIONS ORGANIZATION

This Organization shall be brought into relation with the United Nations Organization, as soon as practicable, as one of the specialized agencies referred to in Article 57 of the Charter of the United Nations. This relationship shall be effected thru an agreement with the United Nations Organization under Article 63 of the Charter, which agreement shall be subject to the approval of the General Conference of this Organization. The Agreement shall provide for effective cooperation between the two Organizations in the pursuit of their common purposes, and at the same time shall recognize the autonomy of this Organization, within the fields of its competence as defined in this Constitution. Such agreement may, among other matters, provide for the approval and financing of the budget of the Organization by the General Assembly of the United Nations.

ARTICLE XI—RELATIONS WITH OTHER SPECIALIZED INTERNATIONAL ORGANIZATIONS AND AGENCIES

1. This Organization may cooperate with other specialized intergovernmental organizations and agencies whose interests and activities are related to its purposes. To this end the Director-General, acting under the general authority of the Executive Board, may establish effective working relationships with such organizations and

agencies and establish such joint committees as may be necessary to assure effective cooperation. Any formal arrangements entered into with such organizations or agencies shall be subject to the approval of the Executive Board.

2. Whenever the General Conference of this Organization and the competent authorities of any other specialized intergovernmental organizations or agencies whose purposes and functions lie within the competence of this Organization, deem it desirable to effect a transfer of their resources and activities to this Organization, the Director-General, subject to the approval of the Conference, may enter into mutually acceptable arrangements for this purpose.

3. This Organization may make appropriate arrangements with other intergovernmental organizations for reciprocal representation at meetings.

4. The United Nations Educational, Scientific and Cultural Organization may make suitable arrangements for consultation and cooperation with non-governmental international organizations concerned with matters within its competence, and may invite them to undertake specific tasks. Such cooperation may also include appropriate participation by representatives of such organizations on advisory committees set up by the General Conference.

ARTICLE XII—LEGAL STATUS OF THE ORGANIZATION

The provisions of Articles 104 and 105 of the Charter of the United Nations Organization concerning the legal status of that Organization, its privileges and immunities shall apply in the same way to this Organization.

ARTICLE XIII—AMENDMENTS

1. Proposals for amendments to this Constitution shall become effective upon receiving the approval of the General Conference by a two-thirds majority; provided, however, that those amendments which involve fundamental alterations in the aims of the Organization or new obligations for the Member States shall require subsequent acceptance on the part of two-thirds of the Member States before they come into force. The draft texts of proposed amendments shall be communicated by the Director-General to the Member States at least six months in advance of their consideration by the General Conference.

2. The General Conference shall have the power to adopt by a two-thirds majority rules of procedure for carrying out the provisions of this Article.

ARTICLE XIV—INTERPRETATION

1. The English and French texts of this Constitution shall be regarded as equally authoritative.

2. Any question or dispute concerning the interpretation of this Constitution shall be referred for determination to the International Court of Justice or to an arbitral tribunal, as the General Conference may determine under its rules of procedure.

ARTICLE XV—ENTRY INTO FORCE

1. This Constitution shall be subject to acceptance. The instruments of acceptance shall be deposited with the Government of the United Kingdom.

2. This Constitution shall remain open for signature in the archives of the Government of the United Kingdom. Signature may take place either before or after the deposit of the instrument of acceptance. No acceptance shall be valid unless preceded or followed by signature.

3. This Constitution shall come into force when it has been accepted by twenty of its signatories. Subsequent acceptances shall take effect immediately.

4. The Government of the United Kingdom will inform all members of the United Nations of the receipt of all instruments of acceptance and of the date on which the Constitution comes into force in accordance with the preceding paragraph.

In faith whereof, the undersigned, duly authorized to that effect, have signed this Constitution in the English and French languages, both texts being equally authentic.

Done in London the sixteenth day of November, one thousand nine hundred and forty-five, in a single copy, in the English and French languages, of which certified copies will be communicated by the Government of the United Kingdom to the Governments of all the Members of the United Nations.

Universal Declaration of Human Rights

The year 1968 was designated by the United Nations General Assembly as International Year for Human Rights to commemorate the twentieth anniversary of the Universal Declaration of Human Rights.

PREAMBLE

Whereas recognition of the inherent dignity and of the equal and inalienable rights of all members of the human family is the foundation of freedom justice and peace in the world,

Whereas disregard and contempt for human rights have resulted in barbarous acts which have outraged the conscience of mankind, and the advent of a world in which human beings shall enjoy freedom of speech and belief and freedom from fear and want has been proclaimed as the highest aspiration of the common people,

Whereas it is essential, if man is not be be compelled to have recourse, as a last resort, to rebellion against tyranny and oppression, that human rights should be protected by the rule of the law,

Whereas it is essential to promote the development of friendly relations between nations,

Whereas the peoples of the United Nations have in the Charter reaffirmed their faith in fundamental human rights, in the dignity and worth of the human person and in the equal rights of men and women and have determined to promote social progress and better standards of life in larger freedom,

Whereas Member States have pledged themselves to achieve, in co-operation with the United Nations, the promotion of universal respect for and observance of human rights and fundamental freedoms,

Whereas a common understanding of these rights and freedoms is of the greatest importance for the full realization of this pledge,

Now, therefore,
The General Assembly
Proclaims this Universal Declaration of Human Rights as a common standard of achievement for all peoples and all nations, to the end that every individual and every organ of society, keeping this Declaration constantly in mind, shall strive by teaching and education to promote respect for these rights and freedoms and by progressive measures, national and international, to secure their universal and effective recognition and observance, both among the peoples of Member States themselves and among the peoples of territories under their jurisdiction.

ARTICLE I

All human beings are born free and equal in dignity and rights. They are endowed with reason and conscience and should act towards one another in a spirit of brotherhood.

ARTICLE II

Everyone is entitled to all the rights and freedoms set forth in this Declaration, without distinction of any kind, such as race, colour, sex, language, religion, political or other opinion, national or social origin, property, birth or other status.

Furthermore, no distinction shall be made on the basis of the political, jurisdictional or international status of the country or territory to which a person belongs, whether it be independent, trust, non-self-governing or under any other limitation of sovereignty.

ARTICLE III

Everyone has the right to life, liberty and the security of person.

ARTICLE IV

No one shall be held in slavery or servitude; slavery and the slave trade shall be prohibited in all their forms.

ARTICLE V

No one shall be subjected to torture or to cruel, inhuman or degrading treatment or punishment.

ARTICLE VI

Everyone has the right to recognition everywhere as a person before the law.

ARTICLE VII

All are equal before the law and are entitled without any discrimination to equal protection of the law. All are entitled to equal protection against any discrimination in violation of this Declaration and against any incitement to such discrimination.

ARTICLE VIII

Everyone has the right to an effective remedy by the competent national tribunals for acts violating the fundamental rights granted him by the constitution or by law.

ARTICLE IX

No one shall be subjected to arbitrary arrest, detention or exile.

ARTICLE X

Everyone is entitled in full equality to a fair and public hearing by an independent and impartial tribunal, in the determination of his rights and obligations and of any criminal charge against him.

ARTICLE XI

1. Everyone charged with a penal offence has the right to be persuaded innocent until proved guilty according to law in a public trial at which he has had all the guarantees necessary for his defence.

2. No one shall be held guilty of any penal offence on account of any act or omission which did not constitute a penal offence, under national or international law, at the time when it was committed. Nor shall a heavier penalty be imposed than the one that was applicable at the time the penal offence was committed.

ARTICLE XII

No one shall be subjected to arbitrary interference with his privacy, family, home or correspondence, nor to attacks upon his honour and reputation. Everyone has the right to the protection of the law against such interference or attacks.

ARTICLE XIII

1. Everyone has the right to freedom of movement and residence within the borders of each State.

2. Everyone has the right to leave any country, including his own, and to return to his country.

ARTICLE XIV

1. Everyone has the right to seek and to enjoy in other countries asylum from persecution.

2. This right may not be invoked in the case of prosecutions genuinely arising from non-political crimes or from acts contrary to the purposes and principles of the United Nations.

ARTICLE XV

1. Everyone has the right to a nationality.

2. No one shall be arbitrarily deprived of his nationality nor denied the right to change his nationality.

ARTICLE XVI

1. Men and women of full age, without any limitation due to race, nationality or religion, have the right to marry and to found a family. They are entitled to equal rights as to marriage, during marriage and its dissolution.

2. Marriage shall be entered into only with the free and full consent of the intending spouses.

3. The family is the natural and fundamental group unit of society and is entitled to protection by society and the State.

ARTICLE XVII

1. Everyone has the right to own property alone as well as in association with others.

2. No one shall be arbitrarily deprived of his property.

ARTICLE XVIII

Everyone has the right to freedom of thought, conscience and religion; this right includes freedom to change his religion or belief, and freedom, either alone or in community with others and in public or private, to manifest his religion or belief in teaching, practice, worship and observance.

ARTICLE XIX

Everyone has the right to freedom of opinion and expression; this right includes freedom to hold opinions without interference and to seek, receive and impart information and ideas through any media and regardless of frontiers.

ARTICLE XX

1. Everyone has the right to freedom of peaceful assembly and association.

2. No one may be compelled to belong to an association.

ARTICLE XXI

1. Everyone has the right to take part in the government of his country directly or through freely chosen representatives.

2. Everyone has the right of equal access to public service in his country.

3. The will of the people shall be the basis of the authority of government; this will shall be expressed in periodic and genuine elections which shall be by universal and equal suffrage and shall be held by secret vote or by equivalent free voting procedures.

ARTICLE XXII

Everyone, as a member of society has the right to social security and is entitled to realization, through national effort and international co-operation and in accordance with the organization and resources of each State, of the economic, social and cultural rights indispensable for his dignity and the free development of his personality.

ARTICLE XXIII

1. Everyone has the right to work, to free choice of employment,

to just and favourable conditions of work and to protection against unemployment.

2. Everyone, without any discrimination, has the right to equal pay for equal work.

3. Everyone who works has the right to just and favourable remuneration ensuring for himself and his family an existence worthy of human dignity, and supplemented, if necessary, by other means of social protection.

4. Everyone has the right to form and to join trade unions for the protection of his interests.

ARTICLE XXIV

Everyone has the right to rest and leisure including reasonable limitation of working hours and periodic holidays with pay.

ARTICLE XXV

1. Everyone has the right to a standard of living adequate for the health and well-being of himself and of his family, including food, clothing, housing, and medical care and necessary social services, and the right to security in the event of unemployment, sickness, disability, widowhood, old age or other lack of livelihood in circumstances beyond his control.

2. Motherhood and childhood are entitled to special care and assistance. All children, whether born in or out of wedlock, shall enjoy the same social protection.

ARTICLE XXVI

1. Everyone has the right to education. Education shall be free, at least in the elementary and fundamental stages. Elementary education shall be compulsory. Technical and professional education shall be made generally available and higher education shall be equally accessible to all on the basis of merit.

2. Education shall be directed to the full development of the human personality and to the strengthening of respect for human rights and fundamental freedoms. It shall promote understanding, tolerance and friendship among all nations, racial or religious groups,

and shall further the activities of the United Nations for the maintenance of peace.

3. Parents have a prior right to choose the kind of education that shall be given to their children.

ARTICLE XXVII

1. Everyone has the right freely to participate in the cultural life of the community, to enjoy the arts and to share in scientific advancement and its benefits.

2. Everyone has the right to the protection of the moral and material interests resulting from any scientific, literary or artistic production of which he is the author.

ARTICLE XXVIII

Everyone is entitled to a social and international order in which the rights and freedoms set forth in this Declaration can be fully realized.

ARTICLE XXIX

1. Everyone has duties to the community in which alone the free and full development of his personality is possible.

2. In the exercise of his rights and freedoms, everyone shall be subject only to such limitations as are determined by law solely for the purpose of securing due recognition and respect for the rights and freedoms of others and of meeting the just requirements of morality, public order and the general welfare in a democratic society.

3. These rights and freedoms may in no case be exercised contrary to the purposes and principles of the United Nations.

ARTICLE XXX

Nothing in this Declaration may be interpreted as implying for any State, group or person any right to engage in any activity or to perform any act aimed at the destruction of any of the rights and freedoms set forth herein.

Note: December 10 was observed as the second anniversary of the approval by the General Assembly of the United Nations of the Universal Declaration of Human Rights.

TROPICAL PATIO IN THE PAN AMERICAN UNION, WASHINGTON, D.C.

The Pan American Union is the headquarters of the Organization of American States which has as its members 23 American Republics.

PART VI

The Organization of American States

THE ORGANIZATION *of American States unites the 23 republics of the Western Hemisphere for the common purpose of maintaining the peace, ensuring freedom and security, and promoting the welfare of all Americans. The member states are Argentina, Barbados, Bolivia, Brazil, Chile, Colombia, Costa Rica, Cuba, The Dominican Republic, Ecuador, El Salvador, Guatemala, Haiti, Honduras, Mexico, Nicaragua, Panama, Paraguay, Peru, Trinidad and Tobago, United States, Uruguay, and Venezuela.*

In 1890 at the First International Conference of American States held in Washington, the International Union of American Republics was established for the collection and distribution of commercial information. The date of the signing of this agreement, April 14, has since been observed as "Pan American Day." In 1910 the Commercial Bureau was given the name Pan American Union and in 1948, at the Ninth International Conference of American States, a Charter was adopted reorganizing the inter-American system and giving it the name of Organization of American States, with the Pan American Union as its permanent secretariat.

The OAS at Work

THE Organization of American States carries out its objectives by means of several organs, each with its own separate function: [1] The Inter-American Conference determines policies and prescribes the functions of the administrative agencies; [2] the Meeting of Consultation of Ministers of Foreign Affairs is convoked to meet emergencies; [3] the Council sits in permanent session to execute policies and administer the activities of the Organization; [4] the Pan American Union acts as the General Secretariat of the Organization; [5] the Specialized Conferences are called to deal with special technical matters; and [6] the Specialized Organizations are separate intergovernmental bodies established to carry out specific functions of common interest.

The Charter of the OAS describes the Organization as "a regional agency" within the United Nations. In actual fact, the character of agency in the relations of the OAS to the United Nations is limited to the maintenance of peace and the pacific settlement of disputes. There is close cooperation between the two organizations in fields where their common interests run along the same lines, as illustrated in the relations between UNESCO and the Inter-American Cultural Council.

The outstanding achievement of the OAS is its success in creating tested machinery for defending the Western Hemisphere against aggression, and for settling inter-American disputes by peaceful means. However, it seeks to achieve more than the mere absence of war. It is also striving for the economic and social security of the Western Hemisphere. Its activities are conducted in the fields of juridical matters, education and culture, public health, statistics, geography and history, women's rights, child welfare, Indian affairs, science development, and agriculture. For further information write the Pan American Union, Washington, D.C.

PART VII

The Citizen and Law

OUR CONSTITUTION *is not alone the working plan of a great Federation of States under representative government. There is embedded in it also the vital principles of the American system of liberty. That system is based upon certain inalienable freedoms and protections which not even the government may infringe and which we call the Bill of Rights. It does not require a lawyer to interpret those provisions. They are as clear as the Ten Commandments. Among others the freedom of worship, freedom of speech and of the press, the right of peaceable assembly, equality before the law, just trial for crime, freedom from unreasonable search, and security from being deprived of life, liberty, or property without due process of law, are the principles which distinguish our civilization. Herein are the invisible sentinels which guard the door of every home from invasion of coercion, of intimidation and fear. Herein is the expression of the spirit of men who would be forever free.—Herbert Hoover*

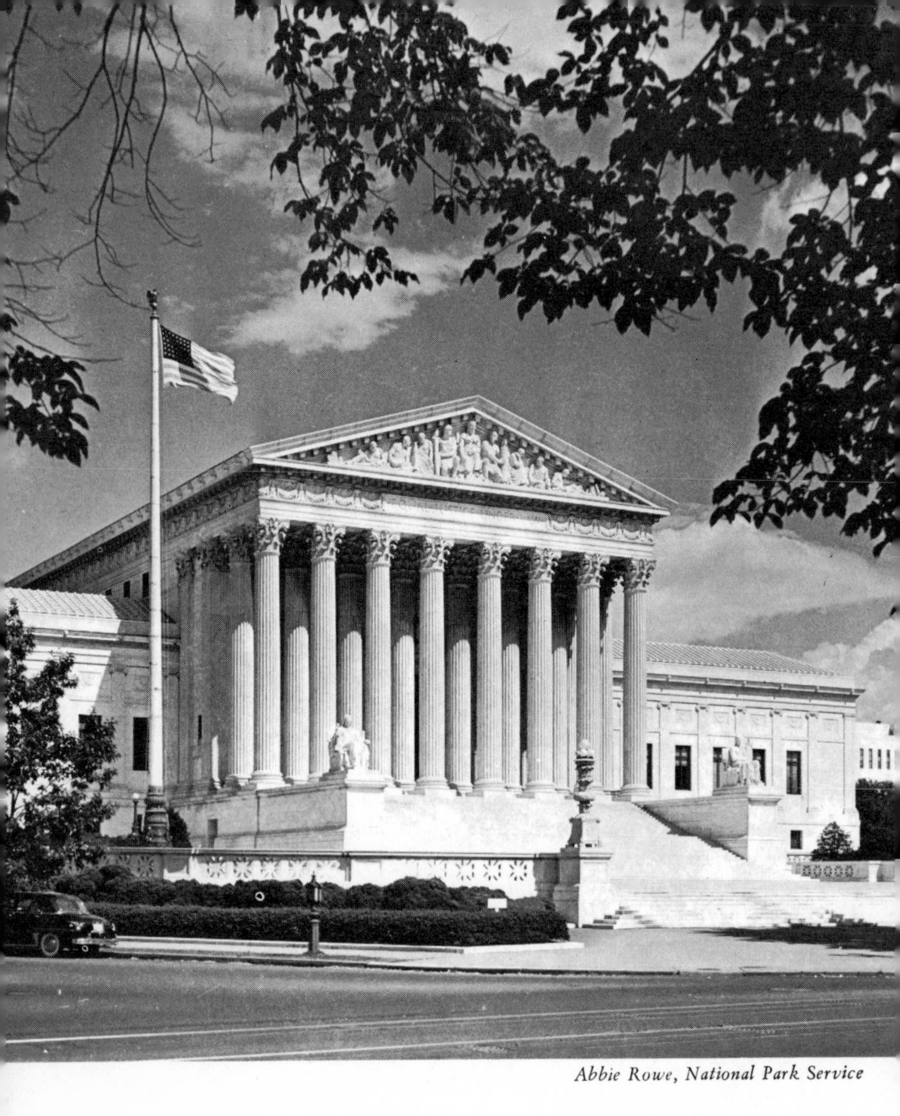

Abbie Rowe, National Park Service

SUPREME COURT BUILDING

The United States Supreme Court Building, adjacent to the Library of Congress on Capitol Hill in Washington, was completed in 1935 at a cost of 10 million dollars. The austere and classic grandeur of the building reflects the solemnity of its purpose. It includes an impressive Court Chamber, offices for the justices, a law library, and conference and reading rooms. Over the outside entrance are inscribed the words: "Equal Justice Under Law."

Law and Our Democratic System

RICHARD L. BRAUN

B.A. Stanford University; J.D. and L.L.M. Georgetown University. Member of California, District of Columbia, and Virginia Bars.

> *"Let reverence for the laws . . . become the political religion of the nation."*
>
> *—Abraham Lincoln*

> *"No man is above the law, and no man is below it."*
>
> *—Theodore Roosevelt*

THE above statements by two great Americans highlight the importance of law in the American way of life. The fact that ours is a government of laws and not of men is a major bulwark of protection for our personal freedom and for our democratic society.

Without the primacy of law in our system of government strong, greedy, or corrupt individuals would have a much greater opportunity to disregard or subvert the Constitution and the many safeguards that it imposes against all kinds of oppression. But a viable system of law requires respect for law on the part of the people so governed. Thus the above plea of President Lincoln, made in another troubled time, emphasizes both the need for law and the necessity that we respect and observe it. Applied evenly and fairly the law is a great instrument for social justice. It allows each of us our "day in court." It

Jon Price

MOUNT RUSHMORE, SHRINE OF DEMOCRACY

Mount Ruhmore Memorial in the Black Hills of South Dakota, honoring George Washington, Thomas Jefferson, Theodore Roosevelt, and Abraham Lincoln, was created by the sculptor Gutzon Borglum.

insures the fact that government must abide by its dictates, *and* that the individual citizen must not transgress the rights of others.

"Equal justice for all" is not an empty slogan. On the other hand, uneven and discriminatory application of the law is fatally destructive of the concept of justice that is so fundamental in the United States. This is the message conveyed in President Roosevelt's statement that no man is above the law and no man is below it.

As George Washington said in his farewell address to the nation at the close of his second term as President:

> "Respect for [the government's] authority, compliance with its law, acquiescence in its measures are duties enjoined by the fundamental manner of true liberty . . . The very idea of the power and the right of the people to establish government presupposes the duty of every individual to obey the established government."

That philosophy has been recognized in this country for generations. It has been taken as an article of faith that is beyond dispute. Yet in recent times there seems to have been more unrest, more disrespect, and more challenge of the law than we have seen since the beginning of the twentieth century.

Some of the disregard for law evidenced by the violence that we have witnessed in recent years undoubtedly has resulted from unfairness in the application of that law. To this extent it may be understandable, even if not justified. But the most distressing aspect of these episodes of violence is that they encourage, not the freedom of a democratic society which is the essence of our legal system, but the development of methods which instead would result eventually in oppression and dictatorship.

Our institutions and our laws can and should be changed to meet the demands of changing times by the orderly procedures already established to accomplish this purpose. The supposed redress of grievance by force and the unlawful assumption of power by professed leaders of the people have too often resulted in cruel and oppressive dictatorships in other countries with this century.

It may well be that a major reason for so much defiance of the law has been an ignorance of our legal system and a failure to comprehend its methods. All American citizens should have a knowledge of the sources of our law and the role played by our courts, and the methods of enforcing the law.

Sources of American Law

The fundamental source of law in this nation is our Constitution. Although prepared by delegates from each of the 13 original states, and ratified by the states, the Constitution itself establishes the principle that the ultimate source of government is the people. Its opening words are, "We *the people* of the United States . . . do ordain and establish this Constitution . . ." (emphasis supplied).

The Constitution created a Federal Government and delegated to it certain powers. The authority of this Federal Government derives solely from the Constitution, and is limited to these specified powers, with such additional implied powers as may be necessary for the execution of its assigned responsibilities. All authority not expressly delegated to the Federal Government was reserved to the states, which thus retain substantial governmental responsibility. Any law or other official action taken by

Federal, state or local agencies of government, including the legislatures, is invalid and of no effect if it violates the Constitution. However, the determination of the question of validity is not a matter of individual interpretation. It is well established that this authority rests in the courts of our country, both state and Federal, with the final responsibility residing in the Supreme Court of the United States.

Always subject to the overriding principles of the Constitution, another major source of law is the common law which has been derived over centuries from court decisions creating and defining certain legal rules or principles. This common law commenced in England during medieval times and upon the establishment of our independence was made applicable to this country except as it might offend the basic tenets of the Constitution. Since this nation was established, the common law has continued to build upon the thousands of court decisions which have been laid down throughout the land.

An example of the body of common law can be found in the development by courts of the law of negligence governing the rights of recovery by one person against another person, or corporate entity for damages suffered as a result of wrongful conduct. Much of the law of contracts has also evolved from, and is still being modified through, our system of court decisions gradually molding the law.

Legislation is a third source of our law. Subsequent to adoption of the Federal Constitution and the creation of constitutions in our various states there has been a continually increasing number of laws enacted by our legislatures. This statutory law has assumed a constantly greater role in creating the rules by which we all must live. Frequently it modifies previously established common law principles. In the 90th session of Congress approximately 21,000 bills were introduced into the Senate and House of Representatives. Only a fraction of these bills will become law, but the large volume of legislative enactments can be appreciated when we remember that each of the 50 states also have legislatures which are producing large numbers of new laws at each session. Furthermore, each city and county has its own ordinances, which are enacted by its governing body.

In addition to the Constitution, legislative enactments, and the common law, much law is now created by executive regulation and by administrative bodies established by our legislatures. Well-known examples of such regulations include rules promulgated by the Internal Revenue Service concerning income taxes; by the Securities and Exchange Commission, concerning stock market transactions; and by state departments of motor vehicles governing the registration and sale of such vehicles. These regulations, when promulgated in accordance with proper statutes, also have the force and effect of law. Frequently their violation results in criminal charges.

The Judicial System

Because of its importance in creating and refining the common law; its vital role in interpreting the rules and standards by which all branches of Federal, state, and local governments operate; and its role as arbitrator of individual disputes, the judicial system of our country is of critical importance in our system of government by law. Thus it merits special attention by those who are interested in understanding and upholding the law. We hear a great deal about the Supreme Court, and the vast importance of its rules cannot be overemphasized. Nevertheless, the great bulk of our lawsuits and court decisions emanate from what are commonly referred to as the "lower courts." These courts generally are organized in a sort of pyramid, with the most numerous being those which handle relatively less important cases, both a criminal and civil nature.

The first level of judicial action occurs in what are frequently called justices of the peace, commissioners or magistrates tribunals. They take their names from the title of the official. In the Federal system the presiding official is a U.S. Commissioner. These tribunals handle cases of a petty nature that may include traffic fines, minor breaches of the peace, or private lawsuits involving small amounts of money. They do not involve jury trials and the decision is normally made promptly without benefit of a written opinion. Many such cases are also handled without the participation of attorneys. If one of the parties wants a jury trial he may ask that the case be transferred to a higher court, and there request a jury trial. Frequently, in criminal matters, an accused person is brought first before a justice of the peace or commissioner to be informed of the charge against him, to be advised of his rights, and to have bail set. The official involved may also determine whether there is probable cause to hold the accused for trial in a higher court. Appeals from the decisions in lower court cases normally proceed to a higher court. However, such appeals are relatively rare.

The first level of formal courts which hold what are

commonly known as trials, with juries where requested, and with more formal proceedings, are known as municipal, city, or county courts. They handle cases which are sufficiently serious to merit more detailed and lengthy fact-finding procedures, with stricter procedural rules. Criminal cases in such courts normally are restricted to misdemeanors, and there is a maximum jurisdiction with respect to financial claims in civil cases. This may vary from a maximum of a few hundred to a few thousand dollars. Proceedings here also are usually somewhere abbreviated but may in certain instances be lengthy, with the employment of teams of lawyers and lengthy written court opinions.

The highest level of trial courts in state systems generally is called a circuit, superior, or district court. In the Federal system, it is called a U.S. District Court. There is one such U. S. District Court in each state. Some states have as many as three. Each district has one or more judges, depending on the volume of work. For example, in the Southern District of New York there are 24 Federal trial judges.

These courts handle serious criminal cases, usually involving felonies, and civil trials involving substantial financial disputes. Often they also hear requests for injunctions or restraining orders or other types of particularized matters such as the probate of wills, or the granting of divorces. Sometimes these special problems are handled by special courts known as probate or surrogate courts or orphans courts. Proceedings in these trial courts of general jurisdiction normally are formal and almost invariably involve the use of attorneys to present and argue the various questions. Trials in these courts may be with or without a jury. Normally a jury will not be empaneled unless one of the parties requests it. In criminal cases, trials are held before a jury if the defendant requests it. If not, the trial is usually held by the judge, although the prosecution can also request a jury trial in some jurisdictions.

Many disputes also are settled by special proceedings. Sometimes a court will appoint a referee or commissioner to hold hearings and ascertain facts. A referee in bankruptcy is a typical example. The Tax Court, Customs Court, and Patent Court are examples of other special Federal tribunals, and many decisions are now made by such administrative agencies as the Federal Trade Commission or the National Labor Relations Board. States and cities have similar such agencies to hear all manner of specialized disputes.

All American judicial systems also provide for appeal. In each state and in the Federal Government there is one court (usually called the supreme court) which serves as a final source for settling appeals of a very serious or important nature within that jurisdiction. However, because of the multitude of cases that now pass through our judicial system it is not possible for either the State or U. S. Supreme Courts to consider all claims of error. Thus disputes from the lower trial courts usually are appealed to the higher circuit or district trial courts. Appeals also may sometimes be taken from these higher trial courts to an intermediate range of appellate courts. These sometimes are called district courts of appeal. In the Federal system they are known as United States Courts of Appeal. There are 11 such Federal courts, each of which presides over an assigned geographic jurisdiction. Appeals from the inter-

CONFERENCE ROOM WHERE THE SUPREME COURT JUSTICES MEET IN SECRECY

During the Court term, the Justices meet in this private conference room to discuss what cases to review and to determine decisions to hand down in cases they have already heard. Each Justice's chair is identified on the back by a metal plate bearing his name. In this picture, a messenger is preparing the room for a conference.

mediate courts of appeal proceed to the state supreme court or in the federal system to the U. S. Supreme Court.

Decisions of the state supreme courts generally are final and cannot be appealed further. However, an appeal can be made from a state supreme court to the United States Supreme Court where there is a substantial claim that the state action violates the United States Constitution or some provision of Federal law. Thus every year the Supreme Court decides many cases involving various questions of Federal statutory or constitutional law, which arise either in the Federal or state judicial systems. Needless to say, the Supreme Court's decision is final. It can be changed only by Congressional enactment governing Federal statutes, or by constitutional amendment with respect to an interpretation of that Document. This has occurred very infrequently. In 1913, after a Supreme Court decision declared a Federal income tax to be invalid, the Sixteenth Amendment was adopted, authorizing Congress to levy such taxes. After the Civil War, the Thirteenth, Fourteenth, and Fifteenth Amendments were adopted abolishing slavery and protecting the rights of former slaves to the full status of citizenship. With a very few exceptions there is no "right" to appeal to the United States Supreme Court. That tribunal determines which appeals it will hear, depending on their importance to the parties involved and to the nation's legal system.

Civil Law

Lawsuits and other disputes involving noncriminal questions are too complex to be outlined in this chapter, and a simplified summary of rights and duties would very probably result in more confusion than benefit. However, where a person feels that his rights have been infringed or that he has been injured by the improper conduct of another, his first step should be to contact an attorney. In the alternative, he may be able to utilize the services of a government agency, many of which have been created recently to give legal assistance to persons who cannot afford an attorney. In addition, many private organizations have created various systems for providing legal services to individuals, and some corporations and unions undertake such assistance.

Frequently a complaint exists with regard to government action of some type for which no specific remedy is provided. For example, vehicle registration offices may not operate properly; sanitary inspections may be lax or offensive; and building codes may not be evenly enforced. To reach such problems, many cities and states have established grievance boards or offices where all such complaints by citizens may be voiced and where improper practices can be corrected.

The importance of seeking the assistance of trained legal specialists *before* the problem grows so acute that it can only be settled in court cannot be overemphasized. Court actions usually are lengthy and expensive and often do not give complete satisfaction to either party.

Crime in the United States

Lawless conduct during recent years has increased at an alarming rate. Basically this lawless conduct can be classified in two varieties, although there is a great deal of overlap between them. One type results from the riots and other types of mob defiance of the law which have occurred in cities and schools on such a large scale recently.

The other may be classified as traditional crime which has been known to the world since civilization began and which consists of violation of the criminal laws by individuals or by small groups of persons. Typical such crimes are murder, robbery, theft, etc.

Between 1960 and 1967 serious crime reported by the Federal Bureau of Investigation increased 88% in volume. This is a rate of increase more than six times that of the population increase during the same period. Arrests of youths in the age bracket of 11-17 have increased nearly 70%. The cost of this type of crime has been estimated at more than 30 billion dollars per year.

The causes of crime are many and varied. A thorough analysis is beyond the province of this brief discussion. One major cause is the great migration of people from rural to urban centers. The crime rate in big cities is approximately three times that of rural areas, and approximately three-fourths of our population now resides in cities or metropolitan areas. Another major cause is the fact that the agencies of criminal justice—police, sheriffs, prosecutors, courts and correction agencies (these include jails, prisons and probation—parole authorities) generally have received inadequate funds. Usually the personnel in these agencies are insufficient in number. They are also underpaid and undertrained. As a result of action being undertaken now by Federal, state and local governments, it is expected that these agencies will be substantially improved in the next decade. This greater concentration on improvement of our methods for fighting crime, along with sociological-economic advances in our society, should go far in arresting and reversing the recent trend toward lawlessness.

Crime and Social Conditions

An excerpt from The Challenge of Crime in a Free Society, *a report by the President's Commission on Law Enforcement and Administration of Justice published in February, 1967. The Commission was established on July 23, 1965 by President Lyndon B. Johnson, who instructed it to inquire into the causes of crime and delinquency and report to him with recommendations for preventing crime and delinquency and improving law enforcement and the administration of criminal justice.*

WHAT appears to be happening throughout the country, in the cities and in the suburbs, among the poor and among the well-to-do, is that parental, and especially paternal, authority over young people is becoming weaker. The community is accustomed to rely upon this force as one guarantee that children will learn to fit themselves into society in an orderly and peaceable manner, that the natural and valuable rebelliousness of young people will not express itself in the form of warring violently on society or any of its members. The programs and activities of almost every kind of social institution with which children come in contact—schools, churches, social-service agencies, youth organizations—are predicated on the assumption that children acquire their fundamental attitudes toward life, their moral standards, in their homes. The social institutions provide children with many opportunities: to learn, to worship, to play, to socialize, to secure expert help in solving a variety of problems. However, offering opportunities is not the same thing as providing moral standards. The community's social institutions have so far not found ways to give young people the motivation to live moral lives; some of them have not even recognized their duty to seek for such ways. Young people who have not received strong and loving parental guidance, or whose experience leads them to believe that all of society is callous at best, or a racket at worst, tend to be unmotivated people, and therefore people with whom the community is most unprepared to cope. Much more to the point, they are people who are unprepared to cope with the many ambiguities and lacks that they find in the community. Boredom corrodes ambition and cynicism corrupts those with ethical sensitivity.

That there are all too many ambiguities and lacks in the community scarcely needs prolonged demonstration. Poverty and racial discrimination, bad housing and commercial exploitation, the enormous gap between American ideals and American achievements, and the many distressing consequences and implications of these conditions are national failings that are widely recognized. Their effects on young people have been greatly aggravated by the technological revolution of the last two decades, which has greatly reduced the market for unskilled labor. A job, earning one's own living, is probably the most important factor in making a person independent and making him responsible. Today education is a prerequisite for all but the most menial jobs; a great deal of education is a prerequisite for really promising ones.

And so there are two continually growing groups of discontented young people: those whose capacity or desire for becoming educated has not been developed by their homes or schools (or both), and who therefore are unemployed or even unemployable; and those whose entry into the adult working world has been delayed by the necessity of continuing their studies long past the point at which they have become physically and psychologically adult. Young people today are sorely discontented in the suburbs and on the campuses as well as in the slums.

However, there is no doubt that they more often express this discontent criminally in the slums. So do older people. It is not hard to understand why. The conditions of life there, economic and social, conspire to make crime not only easy to engage in but easy to invent justifications for. A man who lives in the country or in a small town is likely to be conspicuous, under surveillance by his community so to speak, and therefore under its control. A city man is often almost invisible, socially isolated from his neighborhood and therefore incapable of being controlled by it. He has more opportunities for crime. At the same time in a city, much more than in a small community, he rubs constantly, abrasively, and impersonally against other people; he is likely to live his life unnoticed and unrespected, his hopes unfulfilled. He can fall easily into resentment against his neighbors and against society, into a feeling that he is in a jungle where force and cunning are the only means of survival. There have always been slums in the cities, and they have always been places where there was the most crime. What has made this condition even more menacing in recent years is that the slums, with all their squalor and turbulence, have more and more become ghettos, neighborhoods in which racial minorities are sequestered with little chance of escape. People who, though declared by the law to be equal, are prevented by society from improving their circumstances, even when they have the ability and the desire to do so, are people with extraordinary strains on their respect for the law and society.

It is with the young people and the slum dwellers who have been embittered by these painful social and economic pressures that the criminal justice system preponderantly deals. Society insists that individuals are responsible for their actions, and the criminal process operates on that assumption. However, society has not devised ways for ensuring that all its members have the ability to assume responsibility. It has let too many of them grow up untaught, unmotivated, unwanted. The criminal justice system has a great potential for dealing with individual instances of crime, but it was not designed to eliminate the conditions in which most crime breeds. It needs help. Warring on poverty, inadequate housing and unemployment, is warring on crime. A civil rights law is a law against crime. Money for schools is money against crime. Medical, psychiatric, and family-counseling services are services against crime. More broadly and most importantly every effort to improve life in America's "inner cities" is an effort against crime. A community's most enduring protection against crime is to right the wrongs and cure the illnesses that tempt men to harm their neighbors.

Finally, no system, however well staffed or organized, no level of material well-being for all, will rid a society of crime if there is not a widespread ethical motivation, and a widespread belief that by and large the government and the social order deserve credence, respect and loyalty.

What Everyone Should Know About Law

JOHN SUMNER WOOD, SR.

B.S., Harvard; LL.B., J.D., George Washington University; Member of the Bar of Maryland, of the District of Columbia, of the District Court of the United States for the Eastern District of Virginia, and of the Supreme Court of the United States.

OURS is a government of laws which we, by our vote, have a part in making, and not of men, secret police, bosses, or dictators. The body of our laws was brought over to our country from England, and is called the "Common Law." To these rules of human conduct we have made a number of important additions: the democratic selfgovernment principles of the Mayflower Compact, early customs, the Declaration of Independence, the Constitution of the United States (which you can read in fifteen minutes), the Bill of Rights and subsequent Amendments to our Constitution, various statutes and treaties made by Congress, and the laws made by our states. These traditions and rules are our laws which are interpreted for us by our courts. All men in America are free and equal, but laws are necessary to keep freedom and equality from being crushed by force, whether that force be military, subversive, financial, or administrative. Laws protect the majority from the will of an undemocratic and unfair minority. And they protect the minority from injustice or persecution by the majority.

In our democracy, restrictions on freedom are made by the majority. But they are made within the framework of our Constitution (and particularly the first ten amendments known as the Bill of Rights) that guarantees basic freedoms to each individual. "The will of the majority but the rights of the minority" are phrases of importance to us. Helping to ensure the law's protection for any individual is an obligation for each of us, and insurance for all of us.

We should all know enough about the law to avoid common errors of conduct in our daily life and to recognize a duty or a right or a situation upon which we should seek legal advice. Many of the laws vary from state to state and it is important to obtain professional legal help whenever you have problems involving the law. If you do not have a lawyer, ask the president of your local or state bar association, your minister, your legal aid society, your school superintendent or principal, your banker or other business acquaintance to recommend someone to you. The following is a brief discussion of some of the laws and of our rights and obligations under the law. Keep in mind that timely advice is cheaper than a law suit. A few dollars will often pay for a will, a deed, most contracts, and considerable helpful legal advice.

A lawyer never represents himself, nor does a doctor ever attend any member of his family who is ill, so obviously no layman should attempt to be his own lawyer, no matter how many outlines or books he may have read. The layman should know enough about the law to avoid common errors of conduct in his daily life and to recognize a duty or a right or a situation as to which he should promptly seek legal advice.

Your Rights Under Criminal Law

An act in violation of a criminal law which injures and endangers the community is called a crime and is punished by the state thru its criminal prosecuting officer. You, as an individual, receive protection and redress by complaining under oath of your injury to the District Attorney or State's Attorney, and he, for the state, conducts a criminal proceeding. Insofar as that act damages you as an individual, it is a civil wrong which we call a tort. To receive money damages for a tort, you proceed by a civil action against the person who has violated your rights.

Murder, manslaughter, rape, larceny, robbery, burglary, embezzlement, failure to comply with certain statutes, such as income tax law, certain labor legislation, and health regulations, are crimes punishable by the state. A serious crime which is usually attended by a year or more in prison, or involves moral turpitude, is called a "felony." Any crime less than a "felony" is called a "misdemeanor."

Rights of a Citizen

If you are arrested, the arresting officer must immediately advise you of your rights under the law—you don't have to make a statement and you are entitled to an attorney. Remember, if you do make a statement, it can be used as evidence in court. If you are detained for an unreasonable length of time you obtain your freedom by a writ of habeas corpus. The duration of your detention depends somewhat on the seriousness of the crime committed. If you are detained an undue length of time, the police, who have thus kept you, are themselves probably committing a crime. No man should be kept waiting without being charged with some crime in a warrant and being given an opportunity to obtain counsel and reasonable bail, if the crime is not too serious.

We are protected against unlawful search and seizure or false arrest, and we are entitled to our day in court, an opportunity to defend ourselves and to be represented by counsel, a fair hearing before a jury, the benefit of the services of an impartial judge who presides over the meeting which is called our trial, and who maintains order, rules on the evidence, and tells the jury what the law is. We are entitled to have the jury render a verdict in accordance with the facts, without prejudice, favoritism, or any feeling of anger.

So many safeguards have been set up in our criminal procedure to prevent the conviction of an innocent man that occasionally a guilty man may go free, but this is a necessary evil incident to a free society. It is basic to our whole system of law that a man is innocent until proved guilty.

Torts or Wrongs Committed Against You

Each citizen, as he grows and begins to acquire possessions he values, will be interested in those branches of law known as torts, contracts, and property rights.

A tort is a wrong against you, the individual, and, for damages sustained, you usually receive money from the person doing the wrong. A steals B's ring. A has committed a crime against society and also a wrong or tort against B who may compel A to return the ring or pay for it. It is our duty not to injure our neighbor's right of property, reputation, personal security, privacy, or freedom.

Assault and Battery—Defense of Life or Property

The apparent intent, apparent physical ability, plus an unsuccessful attempt to injure, done so as to put a reasonable man in fear of bodily harm, is an *Assault.* A doubles up his fist and, moving toward B, says "I will knock you down," or "Do not take one step from where you are until you have paid me that debt," or A points a gun at B in a threatening manner, or A strikes at B and misses him. These are examples of an Assault. A completed assault becomes a *Battery,* at the mere offensive touching of the body or clothes of another. There need to be no actual damages because tort law protects the interests of your personal security. Examples of battery are kicking, striking, injuring by throwing an object, or shooting, "smoking out" a tenant, cutting a man's hair, or throwing water on him.

The Right of Self-defense

Self-defense may justify or excuse what might otherwise be an assault or battery, providing it is reasonable and not excessive. Life can only be taken to save a life or in defending your home or person from a criminal attack which might endanger your life. You may evict a trespasser from your property or prevent someone from stealing your property, but force must be sparingly used. You may meet force with like force after all means of retreat or persuasion are exhausted, but the duty is on you not to use more force than is necessary. The policeman, parent, teacher, football player, prize fighter, using excessive force may himself become liable in tort. Self-defense, also known as Self-help, like a strong medicine, has to be given at the proper time in the proper amount and at the peril of the person who is relying upon this type of a right. Mere words, threats, or conduct unaccompanied by an overt act never excuse or justify an assault or a battery. You have no right to strike anyone no matter how abusive and personally offensive his profane language may be to you. In this situation the law provides you with two remedies; namely, a criminal action for the use of profane language and the tort action of slander. Members of a family, husband, wife, child, and probably near relatives, master or servant may defend one another providing they use the same amount and kind of force which the person in danger requires in order to be defended.

Types of Torts

False Imprisonment occurs wherever a person or a policeman without right detains you by force or fear, even if the detention against your will takes place in an open street. Absence of malice or mistake are not excuses for any restraint of the liberty of the person of another. Example: "I will not let you take one step until you have paid that debt"; or A places B in a room from which the only means of escape is unsafe; or locks B in a moving vehicle; or sets B adrift in a boat without oars; or without right touches B, intending to take him into custody, stating that B is under arrest, and B submits.

Malicious Prosecution occurs wherever a criminal judicial proceeding without reasonable or probable cause and actuated by malice has been instituted against you and terminated in your favor.

Malicious Interference with Contract is wherever one maliciously causes another to break his contract with a third person to the injury of said third person, and whether with or without benefit to the wrongdoer at the expense of the third person.

Trespass is a broad term including any wrong committed with force to the person or property of another. Trespass is primarily an abuse of our possession of lands or goods rather than of our ownership. Mere walking upon another's land is a trespass. You must be in actual possession or have the right to take possession, or you must have constructive possession, as where the actual physical possession of your property is in the hands of your agent. Certain trespasses are permitted, in cases of the abatement of nuisance, distress, necessity, private defense, expressed or implied consent, or a special property privilege called an easement, that is, a right to use adjoining land for the benefit of your land.

Conversion is a wrong that occurs wherever one assumes power over property from its true owner irrespective of motive. If a garage or repair man withholds your car as security for more money than you owe him, he has converted your car, and thereby has become liable for its value; and he cannot insist upon returning the property to you at a later date. If A intentionally or unintentionally in good faith sells B's property, without B's authority, to C, both A and C are liable to B for the conversion. Some states give the innocent purchaser a right to return the property to B. If A finds B's property, he can require B to make some reasonable proof of his title, but, if A's demands are excessive, A becomes a converter. Possession, popularly speaking, is nine points of the law? No! Indeed it may be the makings of a law suit for conversion, or even of a crime.

Waste pertains solely to real estate. For example, a tenant cannot remove virgin soil, wrongfully cut timber, or destroy wild life which is natural around the land without the owner's permission.

Nuisance exists where you wrongfully use your property so as to interfere with or annoy another in the enjoyment of his legal rights; with actual injury and damages. Excessive noise, vapors, or smells, may render life and the use of property so unenjoyable as to constitute a nuisance. Under certain circumstances you are allowed to abate a nuisance, if you can do so without a breach of the peace. If a tree on your neighbor's land has branches that overhang your land, you may cut off the parts of branches overhanging your land, but not cut down the tree. You may move an automobile in order to unpark your own car, providing you do so without injury to the car.

Negligence is the thoughtless or careless failure to exercise care which you are under a legal duty to use and which failure proximately causes injury to another. The failure intentionally or otherwise to be as careful as persons in any like particular situation should be is negligence, and such a thoughtless person is liable in damages. If you see the danger or negligent acts of another and do not use reasonable care in your own protection and are injured, then your own contributory negligence bars you, the injured person, from any recovery. Where a person is negligently or wrongfully killed, most states provide that damages can be recovered by the personal representative of the deceased person.

Defamation is the speaking or writing words about a person so as to hurt his good fame. *Slander* consists of acts or words falsely uttered, and *Libel* consists of written or printed false matter published, with malice and of a dis-

Photographs, Architect's Office, Capitol

Pictured here are the chambers where our lawmakers meet in the United States Capitol. Above is the Senate Chamber. Senators sit by seniority from front to rear. Below is the House Chamber which ranks as one of the largest legislative halls in the world.

paraging character, which are heard, seen, or read by a third party and which are calculated to subject a person to public hatred, contempt, or ridicule. The slander or libel may be "privileged," as when given in discharge of a duty, or part of fair criticism and comment. Truth, as to a civil or tort slander or libel is a complete defense, but not so as to a criminal defamation.

Important Facts About Contracts

Where one offers orally or in writing to do or not do a legal act for another at a price, money, promise, or act, i. e., a valuable consideration, in exchange or return, and the offer is accepted by word, act, or writing, we have a contract. When there has been a meeting of the minds, offer and acceptance, completed by word, act, or conduct, and the amount of the money consideration involved is large or the time element long, or it relates to real estate, or sale of personal property, then there should be a written memorandum signed by the parties who are to be bound. For your protection all contracts should be in writing, but as a rule an oral contract can be just as binding, and, too, it is your word of honor. An offer must be accepted without modification or condition. An acceptance differing from the offer may itself be a counter offer which must be accepted "as is" in order to ripen into a contract. Except as to an "option," which is itself a contract consisting of an offer, acceptance, and valuable consideration to hold an offer open for a certain time, any offer can be revoked at any time before acceptance; or it lapses if not accepted within a reasonable time, or upon death or insanity of either party before acceptance. A contract requires a consideration, but in most states no proof of consideration is necessary if the word "Seal" appears with the signature. A promise to do the impossible, or that which you are already bound to do, or where A owes B $100, and B offers to accept $50 as payment in full and A pays the $50, are a few examples of transactions which do not amount to a contract for want of any valuable consideration. A contract may be a nullity because one party is under 21 years of age, insane, drunk, a married woman in some states or is an alien, or because the contract is lacking in real mutual consent, or because there has been a mistake, misrepresentation, fraud, duress or undue influence.

Refrain from making oral contracts because they may become too difficult to prove. Your honor may be of the highest, but how many have a word-perfect memory? Never make an offer to two different people relative to buying or selling one type of property, because both may accept and instead of one contract you will be bound by two contracts. If A makes an offer to B by mail, telegram, or phone and B accepts in identical manner, a contract has been created the instant that the acceptance starts back to the offeror. A telegraphs an offer to B and B accepts by mail, but before the letter reaches A, B receives a revocation. There is no contract. Had B accepted by telegraph a contract would have been made the instant that B sent his telegram. If the offer is by letter and the acceptance by letter, then a contract is created the instant the acceptance is mailed. A revocation to be effective must have reached the offeree before he has posted his acceptance. Keep envelopes because their postmark and date may be vital as evidence in proving a contract. A writing except it be under seal is not the contract, but instead it is evidence of the contract. The contract remains in existence even tho the writing be lost, burnt, or stolen.

It is wise never to sign your name to any writing you do not understand; the law has to presume that you knew what you were signing. Read all small printed matter on front and especially on the back of every paper you sign. Look for carbon paper under page you are signing. The mere signing of your name, mark, or initials is an act of magic—from it a binding or troublesome contract may spring into existence. It is no excuse to sign something and later say that you did not read or understand it. Misrepresentations short of fraud, expressions of opinion, belief, or expectation, as a rule will not afford you any escape. Where there has been a mistake or misrepresentation, broken condition or warranty, fraud, duress, or something irregular, it is wise to consult a lawyer. Delay in acting promptly may get you into serious difficulty. Do not accept any benefits under a contract which you feel is questionable or unfair or shady. It may be wise never to stop paying on an installment debt but go to your Small Claims Court and consult its clerk, or go to a Legal Aid group.

When Contracts Are Unenforceable

A contract may be unenforceable if its object or consideration is illegal or against public policy, or if you have allowed a valid contract to run unperformed for too long a time, usually 3 or 6 years, or 12 or 15 years if under seal. The latter situation usually involves a debt which has not been paid in part or had interest paid on it or been acknowledged in writing within a certain statutory period of time. But with an "open account," as in the case of a doctor's bill, each new professional service rendered keeps the debt alive. If you consult a doctor or attorney or ask a real estate or other salesman to sell your property, the law implies a promise on your part to pay either for professional services rendered or for the bringing to you of a buyer who is ready, willing and able to buy at your price.

Kinds of Contracts

We have *contracts of sale* where the owner of property, being competent, agrees to transfer title for a money consideration or a contract of exchange when the consideration is something other than money. If the amount involved is above a certain figure, there must be a signed written memorandum, or part delivery and acceptance, or part payment, and thus we have deposits or a dollar down to bind the sale. The passing of title does not rest upon delivery or non-delivery but is a matter of intention; it is of great importance in a sales transaction if the property becomes destroyed or damaged. It is wise for the buyer to stipulate that the risk of loss shall remain with the seller until delivery of possession, or in the case of real estate until a deed has been delivered in hand to the buyer. It is also wise for a buyer to put the seller on notice that he is relying upon every representation the seller is making about the quality or condition of the property. In dealing with an agent the buyer as a rule relies at his own peril upon that agent's authority to sell or bind his principal, and often the buyer finds that he has bound himself to a mere offer which does not become a contract until the principal has countersigned; the agent merely signs to make the buyer think he has entered into a contract. Always read and understand before you sign your name to any paper.

A *contract of bailment* consists of the delivery of personal property to a bailee upon certain contract conditions but title remains in you as the owner and bailor. You deliver your automobile to B for repair, at a price, safe keeping, and return, or you may create a gratuitous bailment, or a pledge or pawn as security with power of sale in case of default. The liability of the bailee for negligence depends upon the amount of benefit he is to receive.

A negotiable contract, promissory note, check, or *bill of exchange* transfers its rights to money by delivery and endorsement. An example of a negotiable promissory note is: "I promise for value received upon demand or within a fixed time to pay a fixed sum of money with or without interest to the order of a payee." If A orders B to pay to the order of C, and B accepts, then it is a bill of exchange. Beware of the contract which reads "pay to the order of," because you cannot later escape having to pay this debt if it has passed into the hands of an innocent party. A sells B a radio which is guaranteed to get London, and B gives A a "pay to the order of" paper which A endorses over to C. The radio can not possibly get London, but B must pay C, altho B can sue A on the warranty. You have set in motion a type of "to the order of" contract upon which C has an absolute right to rely. This "pay to the order of" contract with payee's signature on back passes as currency. When you have one of these contracts made to you as payee, and this includes a check, do not sign your name on the back until it is paid, or until you intend to negotiate it to another person, because it can be lost or stolen, and cashed. If you write on the back, pay to the order of B, then only B can use it, and to escape liability you should endorse it: "Pay to the order of B without recourse to me"; a check which you have received and are mailing to your bank should be endorsed "For deposit account of" and your name. Do not sign checks and leave them in your pocket. Refrain from making your checks payable to "Cash."

It may happen that your friend will ask you to sign your name on the back of his note to enable him to borrow money; without realizing it you have become responsible for his debt, if he fails to pay it. Many people have been financially ruined by going on someone's note. Never do it, because if your friend cannot pay his note, he cannot repay you, and all you have may be taken away from you in payment of the note from which you received no benefit. "Neither a lender nor a borrower be"; never endorse another person's note, or become his surety or guarantor unless you have and keep enough money in your bank to pay, if called upon when this friend defaults.

If you make a contract as agent for another person you must sign as agent and disclose your principal's name in order to escape liability on your principal's contract. Certain contracts are often made and later sold to another. This is called an assignment. The original party, the assignor, remains liable unless released for a consideration.

A *contract of marriage* requires free mutual consent between capable unmarried or divorced parties, but once made it can only be dissolved by a formal proceeding. Some divorces are valid only in the state where obtained. Going to some state to get an easy or quick divorce and then immediately returning to your home state may not give you a legal divorce. Each state has its own causes for divorce, rules as to capacity of married women to contract, liability of husband for torts of his wife, dower and curtesy, conveyances of either spouse, liability of husband for wife's contracts and his duty to support his wife and minor children, emancipation of children, rights of parents to earnings of children, and [in a few states] duty of child to support the parent—all of which are beyond the scope of any general brief outline of the law.

Purchasing and Owning Property

Dower unless changed by statute is a one-third right for life which a wife has in her husband's real estate; and curtesy is the right for life which the husband has in his wife's real property, if they have had a child born alive. These rights to use and income only come into full being upon the death of a spouse, but before that time each must sign contract or deed relating to real estate. In most states a husband and wife may contract with one another and convey real estate from one to the other. Dower and curtesy have been abolished in some states. It is important to know the laws of your state concerning right of survivorship.

When you purchase land you contract for a fee simple title good of record and free of encumbrances, but to get the land there must be a conveyance by deed, which must be properly executed, acknowledged before a Notary Public, delivered, and recorded. The contract alone does not convey title to the land. When contracting to purchase land you should obtain the signature of the seller's wife. If two men buy land they usually take title as tenants in common, so that upon the death of one his share goes to his heirs at law. If they hold title as joint tenants with right of survivorship, then upon the death of one, his interest passes to the surviving joint tenant.

When husband and wife buy property they usually hold title as tenants by the entirety, so upon the death of one the land passes to the surviving spouse, and also the creditors of one spouse usually cannot attach the land because the whole belongs to both the husband and the wife. If a man had children by a wife who is deceased; marries and has children by this latter marriage, then he should not hold title as tenants by the entirety, because upon his death his property would pass to his widow and upon her death to his children by the second wife, his children by the prior marriage being disinherited. His surviving wife is protected by her right to dower, if she has not released her dower rights.

Land can be acquired by adverse possession over a period of usually 21 years and an easement can be acquired by adverse use for a statutory period of time. If your neighbor openly, exclusively, and hostilely uses a strip of your land or walks or drives over your land for a sufficient time, he may acquire and claim the land or right to use the land.

If you do not pay your taxes your land is sold, and after a certain period of time a tax deed passes to the purchaser. A tax title is usually an expensive nuisance which blocks you from ever selling or borrowing on the land, and often you may lose it entirely. Do not buy "tax title" land, and do not contract to sell "tax title" land without stating in the contract that you hold title under a tax deed. When paying taxes be sure that your land is properly described and keep the receipted tax bills.

Leases or rent agreements are usually by the month or

year. When the term is up it is your duty to vacate. Some leases provide that you, the tenant or lessee, must give to the owner a thirty days' notice in writing on or prior to a rent date of your intention to vacate, for otherwise you may continue liable for the rent. The owner must give you the same notice if he wants you to move. Any landlord and tenant trouble justifies the obtaining of legal advice.

The Importance of Wills

Everyone who is of legal age and sound mind should have a will and not depend upon the law in effect writing a will for him after he is dead, because the laws of distribution may change, or he may not properly understand what the law of distribution of his estate is in his particular state. By making a will you pass on to your loved ones your life's accumulations according to your own wishes and their particular needs. A will is made by simply writing or typewriting your wishes on paper, such as "date, place of residence. . . . All I have I give to A"; then call in three people and in their presence as they stand and watch the movement of your hand, you sign your name, declaring the piece of paper to be your will, and they in turn sign their respective names as witnesses, in your presence, and in the presence of one another. Tell someone where you are leaving the will so that it can be found after you are gone. You are free to destroy, revoke, or change your will at any time before death merely by executing another will. Do not write any changes on your will.

Renunciation. When a will leaves a spouse less than a statutory share, usually a third, or when a husband dies heavily in debt, then the survivor promptly should consult a lawyer.

A Primer of Parliamentary Law

F. M. GREGG

Author of "Handbook of Parliamentary Law"

WE ATTACH importance to good manners. They enable social life to run smoothly and pleasantly. Good form in the transaction of public business is equally important. Without a common understanding of procedure to be followed, there is likely to be confusion and ill-will. Parliamentary law is a system of procedure. Its four basic principles are: justice and courtesy to all; one thing at a time; the rule of the majority; and the rights of the minority. Procedure for conducting public business goes back at least to the Roman Senate. It came to us by way of the English Parliament. Thomas Jefferson was the pioneer parliamentarian in America. His Manual is still a part of the "Rules of the United States House of Representatives." A knowledge of parliamentary law is necessary to effective participation in important public affairs.

How To Study Parliamentary Law

The best way to master the principles of parliamentary law is thru constant practice in clubs and groups. In addition to the practice gained thru the transaction of the usual business, a period may well be provided at various times to give each member experience in presiding over a meeting, introducing motions, debating them, referring matters to a committee, voting, and the other common procedures. The table which follows is a summary of parliamentary motions discussed in this article. Every club should have a good text on parliamentary law and it is desirable that courses in the subject be included in highschool and college curriculums. This primer is but a simple introduction. You will do well to study, observe, and practice to make yourself a master in the use of parliamentary forms and procedures.

Table of Parliamentary Motions

I. PRINCIPAL MOTIONS

[1] Main Motion
[2] Rescind (or Repeal)
[3] Expunge

II. SUBSIDIARY MOTIONS

[1] Postpone Indefinitely
[2] Amend a Question
[3] Refer to a Committee
[4] Postpone to a Certain Time
[5] Previous Question (Stop Debate)
[6] Lay on or Take from the Table

III. INCIDENTAL MOTIONS

[1] Suspension of Rules
[2] Withdrawal of a Motion or Question
[3] Reading of Papers
[4] Objection to Considering a Question
[5] Point of Order and Appeal
[6] Reconsider the Vote on a Question

IV. PRIVILEGED MOTIONS

[1] Call for the Order of the Day
[2] Question of Privilege
[3] Take a Recess
[4] Adjourn (Unqualified)
[5] Fix Time for Reassembling

Principal Motions or Questions

Principal Motions service to bring new business before the club and may be made only when no other business is under consideration. They include [1] *Main Motions,* which bring new propositions before the club, are open to debate, and require a majority vote to carry them; [2] *To Rescind;* and [3] *To Expunge.* The last two are little used.

Subsidiary Motions or Questions

Subsidiary motions are attached to other questions for one or more of three purposes: To modify them, to delay action on them, or to stop debate on them. It is important to know the order of precedence in dealing with *Subsidiary Motions* or *Questions.*

One of the most frequently used of Subsidiary Motions is that of *Amending.* This means that one may add words to the Main Question, or subtract words, or substitute words, or divide the question. Suppose the question to be "that we hold five meetings this year at Mr. Smith's house." A member addresses the president and says, "I move to amend the question by striking out the word 'five' and inserting the word 'seven.'" If a second is heard, the president says, "It has been proposed to amend the question by striking out . . . etc." When debate is called for, a secondary amendment may be proposed to the primary one, but no more, such as "to strike out the word 'seven' and substitute the word 'nine.'" In voting, the secondary amendment is first voted on, then the primary one, and finally the original question or the question as amended.

Incidental Motions

Sometimes when there are several matters under consideration, things get tangled. At such times some *Incidental Motion* is brought in to keep the business traffic moving properly. Only two or three of these are much used. *Withdrawal of a Motion or Question* may be asked for by the maker and, if no one objects, its withdrawal is allowed. If anyone objects, it is necessary to make a motion to permit its withdrawal. When there has been a parliamentary mistake, a member may make a *Point of Order* calling attention to the matter. If a member disagrees with the president's decision, he may "*Appeal* from the decision of the chair to the judgment of the assembly," which may then vote either to sustain or overrule the chair's decision. An *Appeal* is usually debatable.

Privileged Motions

Privileged Motions, are so important that they may break in at almost any time. Three of these are quite commonly used: [1] *ToTake a Recess* makes all the motions above it in all the lists "stand by," tho it may not be made when anyone is speaking on a question. It is not debatable but may be amended as to length of time for the recess. [2] *To Adjourn* is like the motion *To Take a Recess* but may not be amended. This is true for the simple form only—"I move that we adjourn." However, if a motion *To Adjourn* contains additional words, it at once becomes exactly like a *Main Motion* and is debatable. [3] *To Fix a Time for Reassembling* attempts just what it says and takes precedence over all other motions or questions.

Action by Common Consent

The method of getting business accomplished by "common consent" is one that may well be employed to push business along in cases where there is likely to be general agreement on the matter, or where the group is so small that less formality is required. The chair says, "If there is no objection, such and such will be done." After pausing for objection, "There is no objection and it is so ordered." Suppose, for example, that a number of nominations have been made, and someone now moves that nominations come to a close. Instead of taking a vote on such a matter, the chair may say, "If there are no objections, the nominations will be declared closed." If no objection is made, time is saved and business expedited. If objection is made, the chair will then state the motion and take a vote.

THE LIBERTY BELL, INDEPENDENCE HALL, PHILADELPHIA

Jack Boucher, National Park Service

PART VIII

A Golden Treasury for the Citizen

IT IS IMPORTANT *that people who are to live and work together shall have a common mind—a like heritage of purpose, religious ideals, love of country, beauty, and wisdom to guide and inspire them. This heritage is best acquired during childhood, in home and school. Children should be taught to understand, love and remember the great expressions of truth and beauty upon which our civilization rests. Children grow in spirit and in mental power by what they retain. Learning by heart is essential and can be made delightful. Children love beauty and have a natural feeling for rhythm and rime which grows with cultivation. The material in the following pages includes selections which were chosen by teachers in leading school systems thruout the United States for publication in* Personal Growth Leaflets—Selections for Memorizing—*one for each grade. These leaflets are no longer in print. Each teacher and indeed each pupil may well make up his own list of favorite selections.*

This section is grouped according to the headings below:

Page

Information Office, Library of Congress

LIBRARY OF CONGRESS

The grandiose Italian Renaissance Main building of the Library of Congress is richly decorated inside with mosaic vaulted ceilings, marble inlaid floors, statuary and murals. In the elegant Main Hall many items of historic interest are on permanent display, such as Jefferson's rough draft of the Declaration of Independence and the first message, "What Hath God Wrought," sent by Morse on the original electric telegraph in 1844. The beautiful Main Public Reading room seats about 300 persons. The Library and the nearby Annex contain over 13 million books.

Selections in the Golden Treasury

FROM SACRED WRITINGS

LIFE AND ASPIRATION

HISTORICAL SELECTIONS

THE FLAG OF THE UNITED STATES

SONGS OF AMERICA

THE WORLD OF NATURE

A TREASURY FOR YOUNG CHILDREN

AGE AND IMMORTALITY

PART VIII—SECTION I

From Sacred Writings

THE GREATEST THING IN THE WORLD

THO I SPEAK with the tongues of men and of angels, and have not love, I am become as sounding brass, or a tinkling cymbal. And tho I have the gift of prophecy, and understand all mysteries, and all knowledge; and tho I have all faith, so that I could remove mountains, and have not love, I am nothing. And tho I bestow all my goods to feed the poor, and tho I give my body to be burned, and have not love, it profiteth me nothing. Love suffereth long, and is kind; love envieth not; love vaunteth not itself, is not puffed up, Doth not behave itself unseemly, seeketh not her own, is not easily provoked, thinketh no evil; Rejoiceth not in iniquity, but rejoiceth in the truth; Beareth all things, believeth all things, hopeth all things, endureth all things. Love never faileth: but whether there be prophecies, they shall fail; whether there be tongues, they shall cease; whether there be knowledge, it shall vanish away. For we know in part, and we prophesy in part. But when that which is perfect is come, then that which is in part shall be done away. When I was a child, I spake as a child, I understood as a child, I thought as a child: but when I became a man, I put away childish things. For now we see thru a glass, darkly; but then face to face: now I know in part; but then shall I know even as also I am known. And now abideth faith, hope, love, these three; but the greatest of these is love.—*I Corinthians 13.*

A LIVING SACRIFICE

I BESEECH YOU therefore, brethren, by the mercies of God, that ye present your bodies a living sacrifice, holy, acceptable unto God, which is your reasonable service. And be not conformed to this world: but be ye transformed by the renewing of your mind, that ye may prove what is that good, and acceptable, and perfect, will of God. For I say, thru the grace given unto me, to every man that is among you, not to think of himself more highly than he ought to think; but to think soberly, according as God hath dealt to every man the measure of faith. For as we have many members in one body, and all members have not the same office: So we, being many, are one body in Christ, and every one members one of another. Having then gifts differing according to the grace that is given to us, whether prophecy, let us prophesy according to the proportion of faith; Or ministry, let us wait on our ministering: or he that teacheth, on teaching; Or he that exhorteth, on exhortation: he that giveth, let him do it with simplicity; he that ruleth, with diligence; he that showeth mercy, with cheerfulness. Let love be without dissimulation. Abhor that which is evil; cleave to that which is good. Be kindly affectioned one to another with brotherly love; in honor preferring one another; Not slothful in business; fervent in spirit; serving the Lord; Rejoicing in hope; patient in tribulation; continuing instant in prayer; Distributing to the necessity of saints; given to hospitality. Bless them which persecute you: bless, and curse not. Rejoice with them that do rejoice, and weep with them that weep. Be of the same mind one toward another. Mind not high things, but condescend to men of low estate. Be not wise in your own conceits. Recompense to no man evil for evil. Provide things honest in the sight of all men. If it be possible, as much as lieth in you, live peaceably with all men. Dearly beloved, avenge not yourselves, but rather give place unto wrath: for it is written, Vengeance is mine; I will repay, saith the Lord. Therefore if thine enemy hunger, feed him; if he thirst, give him drink: for in so doing thou shalt heap coals of fire on his head. Be not overcome of evil, but overcome evil with good.—*Romans 12.*

THE TEN COMMANDMENTS

[1] Thou shalt have no other Gods before me.
[2] Thou shalt not make unto thee any graven image.
[3] Thou shalt not take the name of the Lord thy God in vain.
[4] Remember the Sabbath day, to keep it holy.
[5] Honor thy father and thy mother.
[6] Thou shalt not kill.
[7] Thou shalt not commit adultery.
[8] Thou shalt not steal.
[9] Thou shalt not bear false witness against thy neighbor.
[10] Thou shalt not covet anything that is thy neighbor's.

—*Exodus 20:3-17*

THE BEATITUDES

BLESSED are the poor in spirit: for theirs is the kingdom of heaven. Blessed are they that mourn: for they shall be comforted. Blessed are the meek: for they shall inherit the earth. Blessed are they which do hunger and thirst after righteousness: for they shall be filled. Blessed are the merciful: for they shall obtain mercy. Blessed are the pure in heart: for they shall see God. Blessed are the peacemakers: for they shall be called the children of God. Blessed are they which are persecuted for righteousness' sake: for theirs is the kingdom of heaven. Blessed are ye, when men shall revile you, and persecute you, and shall say all manner of evil against you falsely, for my sake. Rejoice, and be exceeding glad: for great is your reward in heaven: for so persecuted they the prophets which were before you.—*Matthew 5:3-12.*

THE LORD'S PRAYER

Our Father who art in heaven,
Hallowed be thy name.
Thy kingdom come.
Thy will be done
In earth, as it is in heaven.
Give us this day
Our daily bread.
And forgive us our debts,
As we forgive our debtors.
And lead us not into temptation,
But deliver us from evil:
For thine is the kingdom,
And the power,
And the glory,
For ever and ever. Amen.

—*Matthew 6:9-13.*

THE GREAT COMMANDMENTS

JESUS said unto him, "Thou shalt love the Lord thy God with all thy heart, and with all thy soul, and with all thy mind. This is the first and great commandment. And the second is like unto it, Thou shalt love thy neighbor as thyself."—*Matthew 22:37-39.*

PROVERBS FROM THE BIBLE

THE FEAR of the Lord is the beginning of knowledge.—*1:7.*

Happy is the man that findeth wisdom, and the man that getteth understanding. For the merchandise of it is better than the merchandise of silver, and the gain thereof than fine gold. She is more precious than rubies: and all the things thou canst desire are not to be compared unto her. Length of days is in her right hand; and in her left hand riches and honor. Her ways are ways of pleasantness, and all her paths are peace. She is a tree of life to them that lay hold upon her: and happy is every one that retaineth her. The Lord by wisdom hath founded the earth; by understanding hath He established the heavens. By His knowledge the depths are broken up, and the clouds drop down the dew.—*3:13-20.*

Wisdom is the principal thing; therefore get wisdom: and with all thy getting get understanding.—*4:7.*

Keep thy heart with all diligence; for out of it are the issues of life. —*4:23.*

Righteousness exalteth a nation: but sin is a reproach to any people. —*14:34.*

A soft answer turneth away wrath; but grievous words stir up anger.—*15:1.*

He that is slow to anger is better than the mighty; and he that ruleth his spirit than he that taketh a city.—*16:32.*

Even a fool, when he holdeth his peace, is counted wise: and he that shutteth his lips is esteemed a man of understanding.—*17:28.*

A man that hath friends must shew himself friendly.—*18:24.*

Wine is a mocker, strong drink is raging: and whosoever is deceived thereby is not wise.—*20:1.*

A good name is rather to be chosen than great riches, and loving favor rather than silver and gold.—*22:1.*

Train up a child in the way he should go; and when he is old, he will not depart from it.—*22:6.*

If thine enemy be hungry, give him bread to eat; and if he be thirsty, give him water to drink: for thou shalt heap coals of fire upon his head, and the Lord shalt reward thee.—*25:21-22.*

Where there is no vision, the people perish; but he that keepeth the law, happy is he.—*39:18.*

THE WISDOM OF THE PSALMS

The Book of Psalms as we know it is a collection of collections, many of them attributed to King David, accumulated over a period of time, according to Edgar J. Goodspeed in his The Story of the Bible. *Here are some favorite quotations:*

Blessed is the man that walketh not in the counsel of the ungodly, nor standeth in the way of sinners, nor sitteth in the seat of the scornful. 1:1.

What is man, that thou art mindful of him? and the son of man, that thou visitest him? 8:4.

For the needy shall not always be forgotten: the expectation of the poor shall not perish forever. 9:18.

The Lord is my rock, and my fortress, and my deliverer; my God, my strength, in whom I will trust; my buckler, and the horn of my salvation, and my high tower. 18:12.

The heavens declare the glory of God; and the firmament sheweth his handiwork. Day unto day uttereth speech, and night unto night sheweth knowledge. 19:1-2.

Let the words of my mouth, and the meditation of my heart, be accepted in thy sight, O Lord, my strength, and my redeemer. 19:14.

The Lord is my shepherd; I shall not want. 23:1.

Who shall ascend into the hill of the Lord? or who shall stand in his holy place? He that hath clean hands, and a pure heart; who hath not lifted up his soul into vanity, nor sworn deceitfully. 24:3-4.

Be of good courage, and he shall strengthen your heart, all ye that hope in the Lord. 31:24.

Keep thy tongue from evil, and thy lips from speaking guile. Depart from evil, and do good; seek peace, and pursue it. 34:13-14.

Blessed is he that considereth the poor; the Lord will deliver him in time of trouble. 41:1.

Create in me a clean heart, O God, and renew a right spirit within me. 51:10.

So teach us to number our days, that we may apply our hearts unto wisdom. 90:12.

And let the beauty of the Lord our God be upon us; and establish thou the work of our hands upon us; yea, the work of our hands, establish thou it. 90:17.

Behold, how good and how pleasant it is for brethren to dwell together in unity! 133:1.

THE WISDOM OF GAUTAMA BUDDHA

Gautama Buddha, 568-488 B. C., founder of Buddhism, left a body of teaching which has profoundly influenced history. Present Buddhist leaders stress its freedom from dogma, its respect for science, and its emphasis on selfreliance. The Buddhist seeks Nirvana—*a state of happiness here and now—thru* Karma—*the law of cause and effect.*

The five commands of uprighteousness are: do not kill, do not steal, do not lie, do not commit adultery, do not become intoxicated at any time.

The Four Noble Truths: All existence involves suffering; all suffering is caused by indulging desires; all suffering will cease with the suppression of desires; to achieve this suppression and to gain *Nirvana* after a suitable number of preparatory existences, one must follow the *Noble Eightfold Path.*

The Eightfold Path teaches the *Eight Rules of Life:* right belief, right resolve, right speech, right behavior, right occupation, right effort, right contemplation, right concentration.

Right belief is the belief that truth is the guide of man.

Right resolve is to be calm all the time and never to do harm to any living creature.

Right speech is never to lie, never to slander anyone, and never to use coarse or harsh language.

Right behavior is never to steal, never to kill, and never to do anything that one may later regret or be ashamed of.

Right occupation is never to choose an occupation that is bad, like forgery, the handling of stolen goods, usury, and the like.

Right effort is always to strive after that which is good, and always to keep away from that which is evil.

Right contemplation is always to be calm and not allow one's thoughts to be mastered by either joy or sorrow.

Right concentration is found when all the other rules of the Eightfold Path have been followed and one has reached the perfect state of peace.

That which one desireth not for himself, do not do unto others.

Let a man overcome anger by love, let him overcome evil by good; let him overcome the greedy by liberality; the liar by truth.

THE WISDOM OF CONFUCIUS

Confucius 551-478 B. C. laid no claim to being more than a man. Yet when he died he was venerated almost as a god, and temples rose to his name in every city of China. He was officially worshiped in China from 195 B. C. to 1912. He lived during a period of cultural decadence, but his teachings and exemplary personal conduct effected a moral and spiritual recovery and a cultural renaissance among the people of China. He emphasized the virtues of sincerity, justice, benevolence, courtesy, respect for older people, and reverence for ancestors. Here are some sayings based on his Analects:

The tendency of man's nature is good.

Faithfulness and sincerity are first principles.

Benevolence is to love all men; knowledge is to know all men.

To see what is right and not to do it, that is cowardice.

A heart set on love can do no wrong.

To hold dear the effort more than the prize may be called love.

The man of perfect virtue, wishing to be established himself, seeks also to establish others; wishing to be enlarged himself, he seeks also to enlarge others.

Recompense injury with justice and recompense kindness with kindness.

The great man is he who does not lose his child's heart.

In matters which he does not understand, the wise man will always reserve judgment.

If order and harmony do not flourish, law and justice will not attain their ends.

What you would not wish done to yourself, do not do unto others.

The man of true distinction is simple, honest, and a lover of justice and duty.

The superior man is watchful over himself when he is alone.

When you know, to know that you know, and when you do not know, to know that you do not know—that is true knowledge.

At *fifteen,* my mind was bent on learning. At *thirty,* I stood firm. At *forty,* I was free from delusions. At *fifty,* I understood the laws of providence. At *sixty,* my ears were attentive to the truth. At *seventy,* I could follow the promptings of my heart.

PROVERBS OF HINDUSTAN

FAITH is the surest guide on the road.

A good man finds all the world friendly.

Every man is the guardian of his own honor.

A one-eyed man is a king among the blind.

Emulation is better than envy.

Pearls are of no value in a desert.

When a house is on fire, whatever can be saved is so much gain.

The thirsty person goes to the well not the well to him.

He that exalteth himself shall be humbled.

The cloud that thunders much, rains little.

Preserve the character of others so that they may preserve yours.

He that digs a pit for another, falls into it himself.

The foolish man speaks, the wise man thinks.

That which is in the mind comes into the mouth.

People become great thru performing their duty.

SAYINGS OF MOHAMMED

NO MAN is a true believer unless he desireth for his brother that which he desireth for himself.

Riches are not from abundance of worldly goods, but from a contented mind.

No man is true in the truest sense of the word but he who is true in word, in deed, and in thought.

Who are the learned? They who practice what they know.

The love of the world is the root of all evil.

Those who earn an honest living are the beloved of God.

Seek knowledge from the cradle to the grave.

Heaven lieth at the feet of mothers.

Be persistent in good actions.

Do not speak ill of the dead.

Acquire knowledge. It enableth its possessor to distinguish right from wrong; it lighteth the way to Heaven; it is our friend in the desert, our society in solitude, our companion when friendless; it guideth us to happiness; it sustaineth us in misery; it is an ornament amongst friends, and an armour against enemies.

THE WISDOM OF BAHA'I

More than one hundred years ago Baha'u'llah, founder of Baha'i (pronounced Ba-ha-ee) World Faith, proclaimed the principle of the oneness of mankind. The purpose of the Baha'i movement is to make possible a true and lasting unity among peoples of different races, classes, interests, character and creeds. Accepting the supreme sanction of universal love, the scientific must associate with the simple and unlearned, the rich with the poor, the white with the colored, the mystic with the literalist, the Christian with the Jew, the Muslim with the Parsee. The Baha'i Scriptures are established in relationship to all scriptures which have gone before, whose unfoldment they are. Here are some selections.

The beginning of all things is the knowledge of God.

The tongue is a smoldering fire and loquacity is a deadly poison. Material fire devours our bodies but the fire of the tongue consumes souls and minds.

Thru affliction hath His light shown and His praise been bright increasingly; this hath been His method thru past ages and bygone times.

Blessed is he who is illumined with the mantle of integrity.

The trainer of the world is justice, for it consists of two pillars: Reward and Retribution.

Union and harmony are the cause of the order of the world and the life of nations.

Ask thou God to strengthen your eyes, and illumine them with a new light; perhaps they may attain to that which is peerless and unique.

Wert thou to observe mercy, then thou wouldst not regard thine own interest, but the interest of all mankind.

Fellowship is the cause of unity, and the source of order in the world.

Close your eyes to racial differences and welcome all with the light of oneness.

Naught shall befall us, save that which God hath decreed unto us.

Appreciate the value of time, for thou shalt never see it again, nor shall thou find a like opportunity.

The poor among you are My trust, therefore guard My trust, and be not wholly occupied with your own ease.

THE WISDOM OF MAHATMA GANDHI

Mahatma Gandhi was born at Porbandar, India October 2, 1869 and died at the hands of an assassin in New Delhi October 30, 1948. Influenced by the teaching of Jesus and the writings of Tolstoy, Ruskin, and Thoreau, he developed a philosophy which is profoundly influencing the whole world. He coined the word satyagraha *or* soul force *to describe his movement. The satyagrahi does three things:* first *deliberately and voluntarily chooses to share the suffering brought on humanity by mammon;* second, *endures that suffering patiently without hate, revenge or violence;* third *endures that suffering redemptively so that thru his love, patience and understanding the oppressed may be freed and the evil of the oppressor changed to goodness. Using this method the Hindus freed themselves from British rule. Here are some of Gandhi's sayings.*

What you think you become.

Truth is the first thing to be sought for and beauty and goodness will then be added unto you.

Man is the maker of his own destiny in the sense that he has freedom of choice as to the manner in which he uses that freedom.

Man cannot live by logic but also needs poetry.

After long study and experience I have come to these conclusions: that all religions are true; all have some error in them.

Education does not mean a knowledge of letters but character building. It means a knowledge of duty.

Forgiveness is the ornament of the brave.

A true lawyer is one who places truth and service in the first place and the emoluments of the profession in the next place only.

Nonviolence requires more bravery than violence; forgiveness is more manly than punishment.

Physical force is nothing compared to moral force. Moral force never fails.

Any secrecy hinders the real spirit of democracy.

Voluntary interdependence is the goal of the world state, a federation of friendly interdependent states.

Whether mankind will consciously follow the law of love, I do not know. But that need not disturb us. The law will work just as the law of gravitation works, whether we accept it or not.

PART VIII—SECTION 2

Life and Aspiration

BE STRONG

Be Strong!
We are not here to play, to dream, to drift;
We have hard work to do, and loads to lift;
Shun not the struggle—face it; 'tis God's gift.
Be Strong!

Say not, "The days are evil. Who's to blame?"
And fold the hands and acquiesce—oh shame!
Stand up, speak out, and bravely, in God's name.
Be Strong!

It matters not how deep intrenched the wrong,
How hard the battle goes, the day how long;
Faint not—fight on! Tomorrow comes the song.

—*Maltbie Davenport Babcock*

WE LIVE IN DEEDS, not years; in thoughts, not breaths; in feelings, not in figures on a dial. We should count time by heart throbs. He most lives who thinks most, feels the noblest, acts the best.—*Philip James Bailey*

BE TRUE

Thou must be true thyself,
If thou the truth wouldst teach;
Thy soul must overflow, if thou
Another's soul wouldst reach!
It needs the overflow of heart
To give the lips full speech.

Think truly, and thy thoughts
Shall the world's famine feed;
Speak truly, and each word of thine
Shall be a fruitful seed;
Live truly, and thy life shall be
A great and noble creed.

—*Horatius Bonar*

THE THINKER

Back of the beating hammer
By which the steel is wrought,
Back of the workshop's clamor
The seeker may find the thought;
The thought that is ever master
Of iron and steam and steel,
That rises above disaster
And tramples it under heel!

The drudge may fret and tinker,
Or labor with lusty blows,
But back of him stands the thinker,
The clear-eyed man who knows;
For into each plow or sabre,
Each piece and part and whole,
Must go the brains of labor
Which give the work a soul!

Back of the motor's humming,
Back of the belts that sing,
Back of the hammer's drumming,
Back of the cranes that swing,
There is the eye which scans them,
Watching thru stress and strain,
There is the mind which plans them;
Back of the brawn, the brain!

Might of the roaring boiler,
Force of the engine's thrust,
Strength of the sweating toiler,
Greatly in these we trust.
But back of them stands the schemer,
The thinker who drives things thru;
Back of the job—the dreamer,
Who's making the dream come true!

—*Berton Braley*

THE HAPPY HEART

Beauty lies within ourselves,
After all, they say;
And be sure, the happy heart
Makes the happy day.

—*Gertrude M. Cannon*

LIFE'S MIRROR

There are loyal hearts, there are spirits brave,
  There are souls that are pure and true;
Then give to the world the best you have,
  And the best will come back to you.

Give love, and love to your life will flow,
  A strength in your utmost need;
Have faith, and a score of hearts will show
  Their faith in your word and deed.

Give truth, and your gift will be paid in kind,
  And honor will honor meet;
And a smile that is sweet will surely find
  A smile that is just as sweet.

For life is the mirror of king and slave;
  'Tis just what we are and do;
Then give to the world the best you have,
  And the best will come back to you.

—*Madeline S. Bridges*

THE NIGHT HAS A THOUSAND EYES

The night has a thousand eyes,
  The day but one;
Yet the light of the bright world dies
  With the dying sun.

The mind has a thousand eyes,
  And the heart but one;
Yet the light of a whole life dies
  When love is done.

—*F. W. Bourdillon*

Build a little fence of trust
  Around today;
Fill the space with loving work
  And therein stay;
Look not between the shelt'ring bars
  Upon tomorrow,
But take whatever comes to thee,
  Of joy or sorrow.

—*Mary E. Butts*

DO YOU FEAR THE FORCE OF THE WIND?

Do you fear the force of the wind,
The slash of the rain?
Go face them and fight them,
Be savage again.
Go hungry and cold like the wolf,
Go wade like the crane:
The palms of your hands will thicken,
The skin of your cheek will tan,
You'll grow ragged and weary and swarthy,
But you'll walk like a man!

—*Hamlin Garland*

MY SYMPHONY

To live content with small means;
To seek elegance rather than luxury, and refinement rather than fashion;
To be worthy, not respectable, and wealthy, not rich;
To listen to stars and birds, babes and sages with open heart;
To study hard;
To think quietly, act frankly, talk gently, await occasions, hurry never;
In a word, to let the spiritual, unbidden and unconscious, grow up thru the common—
This is my symphony.

—*William Henry Channing*

THE DAY'S WORK

The day's work counts—it isn't what
You mean to do a week ahead;
It isn't what you know you'll gain
When all annoyances have fled;
It isn't what you dreamed and planned;
Such hopes are but a phantom land—
The day's work counts.

The day's work counts—it isn't much,
The gain of those few painful hours,
But be content if there is shown
Some product of those sacred powers
Which guide each mind—uphold each hand,
Strive with the best at your command—
The day's work counts.

—*Arthur Chapman*

DON'T GIVE UP

If you've tried and have not won,
  Never stop for crying;
All that's good and great is done
  Just by patient trying.

Tho young birds, in flying, fall,
  Still their wings grow stronger;
And the next time they can keep
  Up a little longer.

Tho the sturdy oak has known
  Many a wind that bowed her,
She has risen again and grown
  Loftier and prouder.

If by easy work you beat,
  Who the more will prize you?
Gaining victory from defeat,
  That's the test that tries you.

—*Phoebe Cary*

MORNING

Will there really be a morning?
  Is there such a thing as day?
Could I see it from the mountains
  If I were as tall as they?

Has it feet like water lilies?
  Has it feathers like a bird?
Is it brought from famous countries
  Of which I have never heard?

Oh, some scholar! Oh, some sailor!
  Oh, some wise man from the skies!
Please to tell a little pilgrim
  Where the place called morning lies!

—*Emily Dickinson*

DUTY

So nigh is grandeur to our dust,
  So near is God to man,
When Duty whispers low, "Thou must,"
  The youth replies, "I can."

—*Ralph Waldo Emerson*

Washington Convention and Visitors Bureau

AN AERIAL VIEW OF THE JEFFERSON MEMORIAL

On the south bank of the Tidal Basin in Washington, D. C. is the Pantheon-style Jefferson Memorial. Within its Ionic columns stands a heroic bronze statue of Jefferson by Rudulph Evans. From the portico may be seen the Washington monument.

THE SAYING OF OMAR IBN AL HALIF

Four things come not back:
The spoken word;
The sped arrow;
Time past;
The neglected opportunity.

EACH IN HIS OWN TONGUE

A fire-mist and a planet,—
  A crystal and a cell,—
A jellyfish and a saurian,
  And caves where the cavemen dwell;
Then a sense of law and beauty,
  And a face turned from the clod,—
Some call it Evolution,
  And others call it God.

A haze on the far horizon,
  The infinite, tender sky,
The ripe, rich tint of the cornfields,
  And the wild geese sailing high,—
And all over upland and lowland
  The charm of the goldenrod,—
Some of us call it Autumn,
  And others call it God.

Like tides on a crescent sea-beach,
  When the moon is new and thin,
Into our hearts high yearnings
  Come welling and surging in,—
Come from the mystic ocean,
  Whose rim no foot has trod,—
Some of us call it Longing,
  And others call it God.

A picket frozen on duty,—
  A mother starved for her brood,—
Socrates drinking the hemlock,
  And Jesus on the rood;
And millions who, humble and nameless,
  The straight, hard pathway plod,—
Some call it Consecration.
  And others call it God.

—*William Herbert Carruth*

THE CALF-PATH

One day, thru the primeval wood,
A calf walked home, as good calves should;
But made a trail all bent askew,
A crooked trail as all calves do.

Since then two hundred years have fled,
And, I infer, the calf is dead.
But still he left behind his trail,
And thereby hangs my moral tale.

The trail was taken up next day
By a lone dog that passed that way;
And then a wise bellwether sheep
Pursued the trail o'er vale and steep,
And drew the flock behind him, too,
As good bellwethers always do.

And from that day, o'er hill and glade,
Thru those old woods a path was made;
And many men wound in and out,
And dodged, and turned, and bent about
And uttered words of righteous wrath
Because 'twas such a crooked path.

But still they followed—do not laugh—
The first migrations of that calf,
And thru this winding wood-way stalked,
Because he wobbled when he walked.

This forest path became a lane,
That bent, and turned, and turned again.
This crooked lane became a road,
Where many a poor horse with his load
Toiled on beneath the burning sun,
And traveled some three miles in one.
And thus a century and a half
They trod the footsteps of that calf.

The years passed on in swiftness fleet,
The road became a village street;
And this, before men were aware,
A city's crowded thorofare;
And soon the central street was this
Of a renowned metropolis;
And men two centuries and a half
Trod in the footsteps of that calf.

Each day a hundred thousand rout
Followed the zigzag calf about;
And o'er his crooked journey went
The traffic of a continent.
A hundred thousand men were led
By one calf near three centuries dead.
They followed still his crooked way,
And lost one hundred years a day;
For thus such reverence is lent
To well-established precedent.

A moral lesson this might teach,
Were I ordained and called to preach;
For men are prone to go it blind
Along the calf-paths of the mind,
And work away from sun to sun
To do what other men have done.

They follow in the beaten track,
And out and in, and forth and back,
And still their devious course pursue,
To keep the path that others do.

But how the wise old woods-gods laugh,
Who saw the first primeval calf!
Ah! many things this tale might teach,—
But I am not ordained to preach.

—*Sam Walter Foss*

THE SPIRIT OF THE WORKER

Life is indeed darkness save when there is urge,
And all urge is blind save when there is knowledge,
And all knowledge is vain save when there is work,
And all work is empty save when there is love;
And when you work with love you bind yourself to yourself, and to one another, and to God.
And what is it to work with love?
It is to weave the cloth with threads drawn from your heart, even as if your beloved were to wear that cloth.
It is to build a house with affection, even as if your beloved were to dwell in that house.
It is to sow seeds with tenderness and reap the harvest with joy, even as if your beloved were to eat the fruit.
It is to charge all things you fashion with a breath of your own spirit.

—From *Kahlil Gibran's* "The Prophet"

BUILDING THE BRIDGE

An old man, going a lone highway,
Came, at evening, cold and gray,
To a chasm, vast, and deep, and wide,
Thru which was flowing a sullen tide.
The old man crossed in the twilight dim:
The sullen stream had no fears to him;
But he turned, when safe on the other side,
And built a bridge to span the tide.
"Old man," said a fellow pilgrim, near,
"You are wasting strength with building here;
Your journey will end with the ending day;
You never again must pass this way;
You have crossed the chasm, deep and wide—
Why build you the bridge at the eventide?"
The builder lifted his old gray head:
"Good friend, in the path I have come," he said,
"There followeth after me today
A youth, whose feet must pass this way.
This chasm, that has been naught to me,
To that fair-haired youth may a pitfall be.
He, too, must cross in the twilight dim;
Good friend, I am building the bridge for *him.*"

—*Will Allen Dromgoole*

Genius is 1 percent inspiration and 99 percent perspiration.

—*Thomas A. Edison*

REST

Rest is not quitting
The busy career;
Rest is the fitting of self
To one's sphere.

'Tis the brook's motion
Clear, without strife
Fleeting to ocean
After its life.

'Tis loving and serving
The highest and best;
'Tis onward unswerving
And this is true Rest.

—Partly paraphrased from *Goethe* by *John Sullivan Dwight*

THE HOUSE BY THE SIDE OF THE ROAD

There are hermit souls that live withdrawn
In the place of their selfcontent;
There are souls like stars, that dwell apart,
In a fellowless firmament;
There are pioneer souls that blaze their paths
Where highways never ran—
But let me live by the side of the road
And be a friend to man.

Let me live in a house by the side of the road
Where the race of men go by—
The men who are good and the men who are bad,
As good and as bad as I.
I would not sit in the scorner's seat
Or hurl the cynic's ban—
Let me live in a house by the side of the road
And be a friend to man.

I see from my house by the side of the road,
By the side of the highway of life,
The men who press with the ardor of hope,
The men who are faint with the strife,
But I turn not away from their smiles nor their tears,
Both parts of an infinite plan—
Let me live in a house by the side of the road
And be a friend to man.

I know there are brook-gladdened meadows ahead,
And mountains of wearisome height;
That the road passes on thru the long afternoon
And stretches away to the night.
And still I rejoice when the travelers rejoice
And weep with the strangers that moan,
Nor live in my house by the side of the road
Like a man who dwells alone.

Let me live in my house by the side of the road,
Where the race of men go by—
They are good, they are bad, they are weak, they are strong,
Wise, foolish—so am I.
Then why should I sit in the scorner's seat,
Or hurl the cynic's ban?
Let me live in a house by the side of the road
And be a friend to man.

—*Sam Walter Foss*

DREAMS

Hold fast to dreams.
For if dreams die,
Life is a broken-winged bird
That cannot fly.

Hold fast to dreams.
For when dreams go,
Life is a barren field
Frozen with snow.

—*Langston Hughes*

THE GREATEST of faults, I should say, is to be conscious of none.—*Thomas Carlyle*

MY MIND TO ME A KINGDOM IS

My mind to me a kingdom is,
  Such present joys therein I find,
That it excels all other bliss
  That earth affords or grows by kind:
Tho much I want which most would have,
Yet still my mind forbids to crave.

Content to live, this is my stay;
  I seek no more than may suffice;
I press to bear no haughty sway;
  Look, what I lack my mind supplies:
Lo, thus I triumph like a king,
Content with that my mind doth bring.

Some have too much, yet still do crave;
  I little have, and seek no more.
They are but poor, tho much they have,
  And I am rich with little store:
They poor, I rich; they beg, I give;
They lack, I leave; they pine, I live.

My wealth is health and perfect ease;
  My conscience clear my chief defense;
I neither seek by bribes to please,
  Nor by deceit to breed offense:
Thus do I live; thus will I die;
Would all did so as well as I!

—*Edward Dyer*

HOLD FAST YOUR DREAMS

Hold fast your dreams!
Within your heart
Keep one still, secret spot
Where dreams may go,
And, sheltered so,
May thrive and grow
Where doubt and fear are not.
O keep a place apart,
Within your heart,
For little dreams to go!

Think still of lovely things that are not true.
Let wish and magic work at will in you.
Be sometimes blind to sorrow. Make believe!
Forget the calm that lies
In disillusioned eyes.
Tho we all know that we must die,
Yet you and I
May walk like Gods and be
Even now at home in immortality.

We see so many ugly things—
Deceits and wrongs and quarrelings;
We know, alas! we know
How quickly fade
The color in the west,
The bloom upon the flower,
The bloom upon the breast
And youth's blind hour.
Yet keep within your heart
A place apart
Where little dreams may go,
May thrive and grow.
Hold fast—hold fast your dreams!

—*Louise Driscoll*

From time to time I meet with a youth in whom I can wish for no alteration or improvement, only I am sorry to see how often his nature makes him quite ready to swim with the stream of time; and it is on this I would always insist that man in his fragile boat has the rudder placed in his hand, just that he may not be at the mercy of the waves, but follow the direction of his own insight.—*Wolfgang von Goethe*

NOT IN VAIN

If I can stop one heart from breaking,
I shall not live in vain:
If I can ease one life from aching,
Or cool one pain,
Or help one fainting robin
Unto his nest again,
I shall not live in vain.

—*Emily Dickinson*

TAKE CARE of the minutes, for the hours will take care of themselves.—*Lord Chesterfield*

FRIENDSHIP improves happiness and abates misery, by doubling our joy and dividing our grief.—*Cicero*

A THING OF BEAUTY

A thing of beauty is a joy forever:
Its loveliness increases; it will never
Pass into nothingness; but still will keep
A bower quiet for us, and a sleep
Full of sweet dreams, and health, and quiet breathing.
Therefore, on every morrow, are we wreathing
A flowery band to bind us to the earth,
Spite of despondence, of the inhuman dearth
Of noble natures, of the gloomy days,
Of all the unhealthy and o'er-darken'd ways
Made for our searching; yes, in spite of all,
Some shape of beauty moves away the pall
From our dark spirits. Such the sun, the moon;
Trees old and young, sprouting a shady boon
For simple sheep; and such are daffodils
With the green world they live in; and clear rills
That for themselves a cooling covert make
'Gainst the hot season; the mid-forest brake,
Rich with a sprinkling of fair musk-rose blooms;
And such too is the grandeur of the dooms
We have imagined for the mighty dead;
All lovely tales that we have heard or read:
An endless fountain of immortal drink,
Pouring unto us from the heaven's brink.

—From *John Keats*' "Endymion"

IF AND AND

If you can think
About your work
As being help
To someone else
You soon will find
That that alone
Will make your task
A happier one.
And if you add
To each task done
Some little touch
That goes beyond
What is required,
Your work becomes
A thing of art
And leads you out
Into a realm
Where pleasure lives
And drudgery dies.
And this domain
Of artistry
Has ample room
For hope and dreams
And spreading wings
And lilting song,
To make the day
Eternal dawn.

—*W. P. King*

THE MOVING FINGER WRITES

The Moving Finger writes; and, having writ,
Moves on: nor all your Piety nor Wit
Shall lure it back to cancel half a Line,
Nor all your Tears wash out a Word of it.

—From the *Rubáiyát of Omar Khayyám;*
Translated by *Edward Fitzgerald*

Truth crushed to earth shall rise again,—
The eternal years of God are hers;
But Error, wounded, writhes in pain,
And dies among his worshipers.

—*William Cullen Bryant*

ABOU BEN ADHEM

Abou Ben Adhem [may his tribe increase!]
Awoke one night from a deep dream of peace,
And saw, within the moonlight in his room,
Making it rich, and like a lily in bloom,
An Angel writing in a book of gold:
Exceeding peace had made Ben Adhem bold,
And to the Presence in the room he said,
"What writest thou?" The Vision raised its head,
And with a look made of all sweet accord
Answered, "The names of those who love the Lord."
"And is mine one?" said Abou. "Nay, not so,"
Replied the Angel. Abou spoke more low,
But cheerily still; and said, "I pray thee, then,
Write me as one that loves his fellowmen."
The Angel wrote, and vanished. The next night
It came again with a great wakening light,
And showed the names whom love of God had blessed,
And lo! Ben Adhem's name led all the rest!

—Leigh Hunt

YOUR AFTERSELF

YOUR FIRST DUTY in life is toward your afterself. So live that the man you ought to be may, in his time, be possible, be actual. Far away in the years he is waiting his turn. His body, his brain, his soul, are in your boyish hands. He cannot help himself. What will you leave for him? Will it be a brain unspoiled by lust or dissipation; a mind trained to think and act; a nervous system true as a dial in its response to the truth about you? Will you, Boy, let him come as a man among men in his time? Or will you throw away his inheritance before he has had the chance to touch it? Will you turn over to him a brain distorted, a mind diseased, a will untrained to action, a spinal cord grown thru and thru with "the devil-grass of wild oats"? Will you let him come and take your place, gaining thru your experience, happy in your friendships, hallowed thru your joys, building on them his own? Or will you fling it all away, decreeing, wanton-like, that the man you might have been shall never be? This is your problem in life—the problem which is vastly more to you than any or all others. How will you meet it, as a man or as a fool? It comes before you today and every day, and the hour of your choice is the crisis in your destiny!—*David Starr Jordan*

He prayeth best, who loveth best
All things both great and small;
For the dear God, who loveth us,
He made and loveth all.

—From *Samuel Taylor Coleridge's* "The Rime of the Ancient Mariner"

IF

If you can keep your head when all about you
Are losing theirs and blaming it on you,
If you can trust yourself when all men doubt you,
But make allowance for their doubting too;
If you can wait and not be tired by waiting,
Or being lied about, don't deal in lies,
Or being hated don't give way to hating,
And yet don't look too good, nor talk too wise:

If you can dream—and not make dreams your master;
If you can think—and not make thoughts your aim,
If you can meet with Triumph and Disaster
And treat those two imposters just the same;
If you can bear to hear the truth you've spoken
Twisted by knaves to make a trap for fools,
Or watch the things you gave your life to, broken,
And stoop and build 'em up with worn-out tools;

If you can make one heap of all your winnings;
And risk it on one turn of pitch-and-toss,
And lose, and start again at your beginnings
And never breathe a word about your loss;
If you can force your heart and nerve and sinew
To serve your turn long after they are gone,
And so hold on when there is nothing in you
Except the Will which says to them: "Hold on!"

If you can talk with crowds and keep your virtue,
Or walk with Kings—nor lose the common touch,
If neither foes nor loving friends can hurt you,
If all men count with you, but none too much;
If you can fill the unforgiving minute
With sixty seconds' worth of distance run,
Yours is the Earth and everything that's in it,
And—which is more—you'll be a Man, my son!

—*Rudyard Kipling*

THE BUILDERS

All are architects of Fate,
Working in these walls of Time;
Some with massive deeds and great,
Some with ornaments of rime.

Nothing useless is or low;
Each thing in its place is best;
And what seems but idle show
Strengthens and supports the rest.

For the structure that we raise,
Time is with materials filled;
Our todays and yesterdays
Are the blocks with which we build.

Truly shape and fashion these;
Leave no yawning gaps between;
Think not, because no man sees,
Such things will remain unseen.

In the elder days of Art,
Builders wrought with greatest care
Each minute and unseen part;
For the gods see everywhere.

Let us do our work as well,
Both the unseen and the seen;
Make the house where gods may dwell
Beautiful, entire, and clean.

Else our lives are incomplete,
Standing in these walls of Time,
Broken stairways, where the feet
Stumble, as they seek to climb.

Build today, then, strong and sure,
With a firm and ample base;
And ascending and secure
Shall tomorrow find its place.

Thus alone can we attain
To those turrets, where the eye
Sees the world as one vast plain,
And one boundless reach of sky.

—*Henry W. Longfellow*

INSPIRATION FOR LIVING

Life is a leaf of paper white
Whereon each one of us may write
His word or two, and then comes night;

Greatly begin! Tho thou hast time
But for a line, be that sublime!
Not failure, but low aim, is crime.

—*James Russell Lowell*

Into each life some rain must fall,
Some days must be dark and dreary.

—*Henry W. Longfellow*

OPPORTUNITY

They do me wrong who say I come no more
When once I knock and fail to find you in;
For every day I stand outside your door
And bid you wake, and rise to fight and win.

Wail not for precious chances passed away!
Weep not for golden ages on the wane!
Each night I burn the records of the day—
At sunrise every soul is born again!

Dost thou behold thy lost youth all aghast?
Dost reel from righteous Retribution's blow?
Then turn from blotted archives of the past
And find the future's pages white as snow.

Art thou a mourner? Rouse thee from thy spell;
Art thou a sinner? Sins may be forgiven;
Each morning gives thee wings to flee from hell,
Each night a star to guide thy feet to heaven.

Laugh like a boy at splendors that have sped,
To vanished joys be blind and deaf and dumb.
My judgments seal the dead past with its dead,
But never bind a moment yet to come.

Tho deep in mire, wring not your hands and weep;
I lend my arm to all who say, "I can!"
No shamefaced outcast ever sank so deep
But yet might rise and be again a man!

—*Walter Malone*

WAVE AND TIDE

On the far reef the breakers
Recoil in shattered foam,
Yet still the sea behind them
Urges its forces home;
Its chant of triumph surges
Thru all the thunderous din—
The wave may break in failure,
But the tide is sure to win!

The reef is strong and cruel;
Upon its jagged wall
One wave—a score—a hundred,
Broken and beaten fall;
Yet in defeat they conquer,
The sea comes flooding in—
Wave upon wave is routed,
But the tide is sure to win!

O mighty sea! thy message
In clanging spray is cast;
Within God's plan of progress
It matters not at last
How wide the shores of evil,
How strong the reefs of sin—
The wave may be defeated,
But the tide is sure to win!

—Priscilla Leonard

THE ARROW AND THE SONG

I shot an arrow into the air,
It fell to earth, I knew not where;
For, so swiftly it flew, the sight
Could not follow it in its flight.

I breathed a song into the air,
It fell to earth, I knew not where;
For who has sight so keen and strong,
That it can follow the flight of song?

Long, long afterward, in an oak
I found the arrow, still unbroke;
And the song, from beginning to end,
I found again in the heart of a friend.

—Henry W. Longfellow

GEMS FROM GRACIAN'S MANUAL

Seventeenth Century Spain

MIND is not enough; spirit is necessary.

Knowledge is long, and life is short, and he who does not know, does not live.

Hard luck is mostly the punishment of foolishness.

Know your chief asset, your greatest talent; cultivate it, and help along the others.

Do not belong so wholly to others that you no longer belong to yourself.

Think, and most about that which is most important.

Of what use is knowledge unless it be made to function?

Do not live at too great pace. To know how to spread out things, is to know how to enjoy them.

A just man stands on the side of truth with such conviction, that neither the passion of a mob, nor the violence of a despot can make him overstep the bounds of reason.

Strive daily to develop yourself in your person, in your calling, until perfection is attained: the fullness of your every gift, of your every faculty. You will know it in the improvement of your taste, in the clarification of your thinking, in the maturity of your judgment, in the control of your will.

THE HOME

A house is built of bricks and stones
Of sills and posts and piers,
But a home is built of loving deeds,
That stand a thousand years.

—*Victor Hugo*

IT'S THE BRAIN THAT COUNTS

YOU CAN GET along with a wooden leg, but you can't get along with a wooden head. It is the brain that counts, but in order that your brain may be kept clear you must keep your body fit and well. That cannot be done if one drinks liquor, which breaks down the command of the individual over his own life and his own destiny.—*Charles Mayo*

HABIT is a cable; we weave a thread of it each day, and it becomes so strong we cannot break it.—*Horace Mann*

There is a destiny that makes us brothers.
None goes his way alone;
All that is sent into the lives of others
Comes back into our own.
—*Edwin Markham*

RECESSIONAL

God of our Fathers, known of old—
Lord of our far-flung battle line—
Beneath whose awful hand we hold
Dominion over palm and pine—
Lord God of Hosts, be with us yet,
Lest we forget—lest we forget!

The tumult and the shouting dies—
The Captains and the Kings depart—
Still stands Thine ancient sacrifice,
An humble and a contrite heart.
Lord God of Hosts, be with us yet,
Lest we forget—lest we forget!

Far-called, our navies melt away—
On dune and headland sinks the fire—
Lo, all our pomp of yesterday
Is one with Nineveh and Tyre!
Judge of the Nations, spare us yet,
Lest we forget—lest we forget!

If, drunk with sight of power, we loose
Wild tongues that have not Thee in awe—
Such boastings as the Gentiles use,
Or lesser breeds without the Law—
Lord God of Hosts, be with us yet,
Lest we forget—lest we forget!

For heathen heart that puts her trust
In reeking tube and iron shard—
All valiant dust that builds on dust,
And guarding calls not Thee to guard,—
For frantic boast and foolish word,
Thy mercy on Thy People, Lord! Amen.
—*Rudyard Kipling*

TODAY

So here hath been dawning
  Another blue day;
Think, wilt thou let it
  Slip useless away?

Out of Eternity
  This new day is born;
Into Eternity,
  At night, will return.

Behold it aforetime
  No eye ever did;
So soon it forever
  From all eyes is hid.

Here hath been dawning
  Another blue day;
Think, wilt thou let it
  Slip useless away?

—*Thomas Carlyle*

ADVICE OF POLONIUS TO HIS SON

SEE THOU character. Give thy thoughts no tongue, Nor any unproportioned thought his act. Be thou familiar, but by no means vulgar. The friends thou hast, and their adoption tried, grapple them to thy soul with hoops of steel; but do not dull thy palm with entertainment of each new-hatch'd, unfledg'd comrade. Beware of entrance to a quarrel, but, being in, bear't that the opposed may beware of thee. Give every man thy ear, but few thy voice; Take each man's censure, but reserve thy judgment. Costly thy habit as thy purse can buy, but not express'd in fancy; rich, not gaudy; for the apparel oft proclaims the man, and they in France of the best rank and station are most select and generous, chief in that. Neither a borrower nor a lender be: for loan oft loses both itself and friend, and borrowing dulls the edge of husbandry. This above all: to thine own self be true, And it must follow, as the night the day, thou canst not then be false to any man. Farewell; my blessing season this in thee.

—From *Shakespeare's* "Hamlet"

GO OFTEN to the house of thy friend, for weeds choke up the unused path.—*Shakespeare*

Cowards die many times before their deaths;
The valiant never taste of death but once.
—From *Shakespeare's* "Julius Caesar"

Men at some time are masters of their fates:
The fault, dear Brutus, is not in our stars,
But in ourselves, that we are underlings.
—From *Shakespeare's* "Julius Caesar"

All the world's a stage,
And all the men and women merely players.
They have their exits and their entrances;
And one man in his time plays many parts.
—From *Shakespeare's* "As You Like It"

THE QUALITY OF MERCY

The quality of mercy is not strain'd,
It droppeth as the gentle rain from heaven
Upon the place beneath. It is twice blest:
It blesseth him that gives and him that takes.
'Tis mightiest in the mightiest: it becomes
The throned monarch better than his crown;
His sceptre shows the force of temporal power,
The attribute to awe and majesty,
Wherein doth sit the dread and fear of kings;
But mercy is above this sceptred sway,
It is enthroned in the hearts of kings,
It is an attribute to God himself;
And earthly power doth then show likest God's,
When mercy seasons justice.
—From *Shakespeare's* "Merchant of Venice"

SWEET ARE THE USES OF ADVERSITY

Sweet are the uses of adversity;
Which, like the toad, ugly and venomous,
Wears yet a precious jewel in his head;
And this our life, exempt from public haunt,
Finds tongues in trees, books in the running brooks,
Sermons in stones, and good in every thing.
—From *Shakespeare's* "As You Like It"

TO BE OR NOT TO BE

To be or not to be; that is the question:
Whether 'tis nobler in the mind to suffer
The slings and arrows of outrageous fortune,
Or to take arms against a sea of troubles,
And by opposing end them? To die: to sleep:
No more; and by a sleep to say we end
The heartache and the thousand natural shocks
That flesh is heir to,—'tis a consummation
Devoutly to be wish'd. To die, to sleep;
To sleep: perchance to dream: ay, there's the rub:
For in that sleep of death what dreams may come,
When we have shuffled off this mortal coil,
Must give us pause: there's the respect
That makes calamity of so long life;
For who would bear the whips and scorns of time,
The oppressor's wrong, the proud man's contumely,
The pangs of dispris'd love, the law's delay,
The insolence of office and the spurns
That patient merit of the unworthy takes,
When he himself might his quietus make
With a bare bodkin? Who would fardels bear
To grunt and sweat under a weary life,
But that the dread of something after death,
The undiscover'd country from whose bourn
No traveller returns, puzzles the will
And makes us rather bear those ills we have
Than fly to others that we know not of?
Thus conscience does make cowards of us all;
And thus the native hue of resolution
Is sicklied o'er with the pale cast of thought,
And enterprises of great pith and moment
With this regard their currents turn away,
And lose the name of action.

—From *Shakespeare's* "Hamlet"

Good name in man and woman, dear my lord,
Is the immediate jewel of their souls:
Who steals my purse steals trash; 'tis something, nothing;
'Twas mine, 'tis his, and has been slave to thousands;
But he that filches from me my good name
Robs me of that which not enriches him
And makes me poor indeed.

—From *Shakespeare's* "Othello"

PREPAREDNESS

For all your days prepare,
And meet them ever alike:
When you are the anvil, bear—
When you are the hammer, strike.

—Edwin Markham

A LITTLE SONG OF LIFE

Glad that I live am I;
That the sky is blue,
Glad for the country lanes,
And the fall of dew.

After the sun the rain,
After the rain the sun;
This is the way of life,
Till the work be done.

All that we need to do,
Be we low or high,
Is to see that we grow
Nearer the sky.

—Lizette Woodworth Reese

OPPORTUNITY

This I beheld, or dreamed it in a dream:
There spread a cloud of dust along a plain;
And underneath the cloud, or in it, raged
A furious battle, and men yelled and swords
Shocked upon swords and shields. A prince's banner
Wavered, then staggered backward, hemmed by foes.
A craven hung along the battle's edge,
And thought, "Had I a sword of keener steel—
That blue blade that the king's son bears—but this
Blunt thing!" He snapped and flung it from his hand,
And lowering crept away and left the field.
Then came the king's son, wounded, sore bestead,
And weaponless, and saw the broken sword,
Hilt-buried in the dry and trodden sand,
And ran and snatched it, and with battle shout
Lifted afresh, he hewed his enemy down,
And saved a great cause that heroic day.

—Edward Rowland Sill

THE WAY OF LIFE

To be honest
To be kind
To earn a little
To spend a little less
To make upon the whole
  A family happier for his presence
To renounce when that shall be necessary
  And not be embittered
To keep a few friends
  But these without capitulation
Above all on the same grim condition
To keep friends with himself
Here is a task for all that a man has
  Of fortitude and delicacy.

—*Robert Louis Stevenson*

LET US LEARN to be content with what we have. Let us get rid of our false estimates, set up all the higher ideals—a quiet home; vines of our own planting; a few books full of the inspiration of genius; a few friends worthy of being loved and able to love us in return; a hundred innocent pleasures that bring no pain or remorse; a devotion to the right that will never swerve; a simple religion empty of all bigotry, full of trust and hope and love—and to such a philosophy this world will give up all the empty joy it has.—*David Swing*

LOOK TO THIS DAY, for it is life; the very life of life. In its brief course lie all the verities and realities of your existence; the bliss of growth, the glory of action, the splendor of beauty. For yesterday is but a dream, and tomorrow is only a vision; but today, well lived, makes every yesterday a dream of happiness and every tomorrow a vision of hope. Look well, therefore, to this day, such is the salutation of the dawn.—From the *Sanscrit*

IDEALS are like stars. You will not succeed in touching them with your hands; but, like the seafaring man, you choose them as your guides, and following them, you will reach your destiny.—*Carl Schurz*

LEADERSHIP

We are all blind until we see
That in the human plan
Nothing is worth the making
If it does not make the man.

Why build these cities glorious,
If man unbuilded goes?
In vain we build the world, unless
The builder also grows.

—*Edwin Markham*

Be ashamed to die until you have won some victory for humanity.
—*Horace Mann*

OUTWITTED

He drew a circle that shut me out—
Heretic, rebel, a thing to flout.
But Love and I had the wit to win:
We drew a circle that took him in!

—*Edwin Markham*

BARTER

Life has loveliness to sell,
  All beautiful and splendid things,
Blue waves whitened on a cliff,
  Soaring fire that sways and sings,
And children's faces looking up
Holding wonder like a cup.

Life has loveliness to sell,
  Music like a curve of gold,
Scent of pine trees in the rain,
  Eyes that love you, arms that hold,
And for your spirit's still delight,
Holy thoughts that star the night.

Spend all you have for loveliness,
  Buy it and never count the cost;
For one white singing hour of peace
  Count many a year of strife well lost,
And for a breath of ecstasy
Give all you have been, or could be.

—*Sara Teasdale*

HOW BIG ARE YOU?

The world stands out on either side
No wider than the heart is wide;
Above the world is stretched the sky,—
No higher than the soul is high.
The heart can push the sea and land
Farther away on either hand;
The soul can split the sky in two,
And let the face of God shine thru.
But East and West will pinch the heart
That cannot keep them pushed apart;
And he whose soul is flat—the sky
Will cave in on him by and by.

—*Edna St. Vincent Millay*

Fame is the scentless sunflower,
  With gaudy crown of gold;
But friendship is the breathing rose,
  With sweets in every fold.

—*Oliver Wendell Holmes*

BUGLE SONG

The splendor falls on castle walls
  And snowy summits old in story:
The long light shakes across the lakes,
  And the wild cataract leaps in glory.
Blow, bugle, blow, set the wild echoes flying,
Blow, bugle; answer, echoes, dying, dying, dying.

O hark, O hear! how thin and clear,
  And thinner, clearer, farther going!
O sweet and far from cliff and scar
  The horns of Elfland faintly blowing!
Blow, let us hear the purple glens replying:
Blow, bugle; answer, echoes, dying, dying, dying.

O love, they die in yon rich sky,
  They faint on hill or field or river:
Our echoes roll from soul to soul,
  And grow for ever and for ever.
Blow, bugle, blow, set the wild echoes flying,
And answer, echoes, answer, dying, dying, dying.

—*Alfred Tennyson*

KEEPING CHRISTMAS

It is a good thing to observe Christmas day. The mere marking of times and seasons, when men agree to stop work and make merry together, is a wise and wholesome custom. It helps one to feel the supremacy of the common life over the individual life. It reminds a man to set his own little watch, now and then, by the great clock of humanity which runs on sun time.

But there is a better thing than the observance of Christmas day and that is keeping Christmas.

Are you willing to forget what you have done for other people and to remember what other people have done for you; to ignore what the world owes you and to think of what you owe the world; to put your rights in the background and your duties in the middle distance and your chances to do a little more than your duty in the foreground; to see that your fellowmen are just as real as you are and try to look behind their faces to their hearts, hungry for joy; to own that probably the only good reason for your existence is not what you are going to get out of life but what you are going to give to life; to close your book of complaints against the management of the universe and look around you for a place where you can sow a few seeds of happiness—are you willing to do these things even for a day? Then you can keep Christmas.

Are you willing to stoop down and consider the needs and the desires of little children; to remember the weakness and loneliness of people who are growing old; to stop asking how much your friends love you and ask yourself whether you love them enough; to bear in mind the things that other people have to bear on their hearts; to try to understand what those who live in the same house with you really want, without waiting for them to tell you; to trim your lamp so that it will give more light and less smoke and to carry it in front so that your shadow will fall behind you; to make a grave for your ugly thoughts and a garden for your kindly feelings, with the gate open—are you willing to do these things even for a day? Then you can keep Christmas.

Are you willing to believe that love is the strongest thing in the world—stronger than hate, stronger than evil, stronger than death—and that the blessed life which began in Bethlehem nineteen hundred years ago is the image and brightness of the Eternal Love? Then you can keep Christmas. And if you keep it for a day, why not always? But you can never keep it alone.—*Henry van Dyke*

THE CHAMBERED NAUTILUS

This is the ship of pearl, which, poets feign,
  Sails the unshadowed main,—
  The venturous bark that flings
On the sweet summer wind its purpled wings
In gulfs enchanted, where the Siren sings,
  And coral reefs lie bare,
Where the cold sea-maids rise to sun their streaming hair.

Its webs of living gauze no more unfurl;
  Wrecked is the ship of pearl!
  And every chambered cell,
Where its dim dreaming life was wont to dwell,
  As the frail tenant shaped his growing shell,
  Before thee lies revealed,—
Its irised ceiling rent, its sunless crypt unsealed!

Year after year beheld the silent toil
  That spread his lustrous coil;
  Still, as the spiral grew,
He left the past year's dwelling for the new,
Stole with soft step its shining archway thru,
  Built up its idle door,
Stretched in his last-found home, and knew the old no more.

Thanks for the heavenly message brought by thee,
  Child of the wandering sea,
  Cast from her lap, forlorn!
From thy dead lips a clearer note is born
Than ever Triton blew from wreathed horn!
  While on mine ear it rings,
Thru the deep caves of thought I hear a voice that sings —

Build thee more stately mansions, O my soul,
  As the swift seasons roll!
  Leave thy low-vaulted past!
Let each new temple, nobler than the last,
Shut thee from heaven with a dome more vast,
  Till thou at length art free,
Leaving thine outgrown shell by life's unresting sea!

—Oliver Wendell Holmes

I WILL govern my life and my thoughts, as if the whole world were to see the one, and to read the other.—*Seneca*

RING OUT, WILD BELLS

Ring out, wild bells, to the wild sky,
  The flying cloud, the frosty light;
  The year is dying in the night;
Ring out, wild bells, and let him die.

Ring out the old, ring in the new,
  Ring, happy bells, across the snow;
  The year is going, let him go;
Ring out the false, ring in the true.

Ring out a slowly dying cause,
  And ancient forms of party strife;
  Ring in the nobler modes of life;
With sweeter manners, purer laws.

Ring out the want, the care, the sin,
  The faithless coldness of the times;
  Ring out, ring out my mournful rimes,
But ring the fuller minstrel in.

Ring out false pride in place and blood,
  The civic slander and the spite;
  Ring in the love of truth and right,
Ring in the common love of good.

—Alfred Tennyson

WORK

Let me but do my work from day to day,
  In field or forest, at the desk or loom,
  In roaring market place or tranquil room;
Let me but find it in my heart to say,
When vagrant wishes beckon me astray,
  "This is my work; my blessing, not my doom;
  Of all who live, I am the one by whom
This work can best be done in the right way."

Then shall I see it not too great, nor small,
  To suit my spirit and to prove my powers;
  Then shall I cheerful greet the laboring hours,
And cheerful turn, when the long shadows fall
At eventide, to play and love and rest,
Because I know for me my work is best.

—Henry van Dyke

FRIENDS

It is my joy in life to find
  At every turning of the road,
The strong arm of a comrade kind
  To help me onward with my load.

And since I have no gold to give,
  And love alone must make amends,
My only prayer is while I live—
  God make me worthy of my friends.

—*Frank D. Sherman*

THE THINGS I PRIZE

These are the things I prize
  And hold of dearest worth:
Light of the sapphire skies,
Peace of the silent hills,
Shelter of the forests,
Comfort of the grass,
Music of the birds, murmur of the rills,
  And, after showers,
  The smell of flowers
And of the good brown earth—
And best of all, along the way, friendship and mirth.

—*Henry van Dyke*

LIFE

Let me but live my life from year to year
  With forward face and unreluctant soul;
  Not hurrying to, nor turning from, the goal;
Not mourning for the things that disappear
In the dim past, nor holding back in fear
  From what the future veils; but with a whole
  And happy heart, that pays its toll
To Youth and Age, and travels on with cheer.
So let the way wind up the hill or down,
  O'er rough or smooth, the journey will be joy;
  Still seeking what I sought when but a boy,
New friendships, high adventure, and a crown,
My heart will keep the courage of the quest,
And hope the road's last turn will be the best.

—*Henry van Dyke*

CHARACTER OF THE HAPPY WARRIOR

Who is the happy Warrior? Who is he
  That every man in arms should wish to be?
It is the generous spirit, who, when brought
  Among the tasks of real life, hath wrought
Upon the plan that pleased his boyish thought:
  Whose high endeavors are an inward light
That makes the path before him always bright:
  Who, with a natural instinct to discern
What knowledge can perform, is diligent to learn;
  Abides by this resolve, and stops not there,
But makes his moral being his prime care;
  Who, doomed to go in company with pain,
And fear, and bloodshed, miserable train!
  Turns his necessity to glorious gain;
In face of these doth exercise a power
  Which is our human nature's highest dower;
Controls them and subdues, transmutes, bereaves
  Of their bad influence, and their good receives:
By objects, which might force the soul to abate
  Her feeling, rendered more compassionate;
Is placable—because occasions rise
  So often that demand such sacrifice;
More skilful in selfknowledge, even more pure,
  As tempted more; more able to endure,
As more exposed to suffering and distress;
  Thence, also, more alive to tenderness.
'Tis he whose law is reason; who depends
  Upon that law as on the best of friends;
Whence, in a state where men are tempted still
  To evil for a guard against worse ill,
And what in quality or act is best
  Doth seldom on a right foundation rest,
He labors good on good to fix, and owes
  To virtue every triumph that he knows:
Who, if he rise to station of command,
  Rises by open means; and there will stand
On honorable terms, or else retire,
  And in himself possess his own desire;
Who comprehends his trust, and to the same
  Keeps faithful with a singleness of aim;
And therefore does not stoop, nor lie in wait
  For wealth, or honors, or for worldly state;

Whom they must follow; on whose head must fall,
  Like showers of manna, if they come at all:
Whose powers shed round him in the common strife,
  Or mild concerns of ordinary life,
A constant influence, a peculiar grace;
  But who, if he be called upon to face
Some awful moment to which Heaven has joined
  Great issues, good or bad for human kind,
Is happy as a lover; and attired
  With sudden brightness, like a man inspired;
And, thru the heat of conflict, keeps the law
  In calmness made, and sees what he foresaw;
Or if an unexpected call succeed,
  Come when it will, is equal to the need:
He who, tho thus endued as with a sense
  And faculty for storm and turbulence,
Is yet a soul whose master-bias leans
  To homefelt pleasures and to gentle scenes;
Sweet images! which, wheresoe'er he be,
  Are at his heart; and such fidelity
It is his darling passion to approve;
  More brave for this, that he hath much to love.
'Tis, finally, the Man, who lifted high,
  Conspicuous object in a Nation's eye,
Or left unthought-of in obscurity,—
  Who, with a toward or untoward lot,
Prosperous or adverse, to his wish or not—
  Plays, in the many games of life, that one
Where what he most doth value must be won:
  Whom neither shape of danger can dismay,
Nor thought of tender happiness betray;
  Who not content that former worth stand fast,
Looks forward, persevering to the last,
  From well to better, daily selfsurpassed:
Who, whether praise of him must walk the earth
  For ever, and to noble deeds give birth,
Or he must fall, to sleep without his fame,
  And leave a dead unprofitable name—
Finds comfort in himself and in his cause;
  And, while the mortal mist is gathering, draws
His breath in confidence of Heaven's applause.
  This is the happy Warrior; this is he
That every man in arms should wish to be.

—*William Wordsworth*

IN SCHOOL-DAYS

Still sits the schoolhouse by the road,
A ragged beggar sunning;
Around it still the sumachs grow,
And blackberry vines are running.

Within, the master's desk is seen,
Deep scarred by raps official;
The warping floor, the battered seats,
The jack-knife's carved initial;

The charcoal frescos on its wall;
Its door's worn sill, betraying
The feet that, creeping slow to school,
Went storming out to playing!

Long years ago a winter sun
Shone over it at setting;
Lit up its western window panes,
And low eaves' icy fretting.

It touched the tangled golden curls,
And brown eyes full of grieving,
Of one who still her steps delayed
When all the school were leaving.

For near her stood the little boy
Her childish favor singled:
His cap pulled low upon a face
Where pride and shame were mingled.

Pushing with restless feet the snow
To right and left, he lingered;—
As restlessly her tiny hands
The blue-checked apron fingered.

He saw her lift her eyes; he felt
The soft hand's light caressing,
And heard the tremble of her voice,
As if a fault confessing.

"I'm sorry that I spelt the word:
I hate to go above you,
Because,"—the brown eyes lower fell,—
"Because, you see, I love you!"

Still memory to a gray-haired man
That sweet child-face is showing.
Dear girl! the grasses on her grave
Have forty years been growing!

He lives to learn, in life's hard school,
How few who pass above him
Lament their triumph and his loss,
Like her,—because they love him.

—*John Greenleaf Whittier*

A PERSIAN PROVERB

He who knows not
And knows not that he knows not
Is a fool. Shun him.

He who knows not
And knows that he knows not
Is a child. Teach him.

He who knows
And knows not that he knows
Is asleep. Waken him.

He who knows
And knows that he knows
Is wise. Follow him.

THE WINDS OF FATE

One ship drives east, another west,
By the selfsame winds that blow.
'Tis the set of the sail, and not the gale,
That determines the way they go.
Like the winds of the sea are the ways of Fate
As we voyage along thru life.
'Tis the set of the soul that decides its goal,
And not the calm or the strife.

—*Ella Wheeler Wilcox*

'Tis easy enough to be pleasant
When life flows along like a song,
But the man worthwhile is the man who will smile
When everything goes dead wrong.

—*Ella Wheeler Wilcox*

IT COULDN'T BE DONE

Somebody said that it couldn't be done
But he with a chuckle replied
That "maybe it couldn't," but he would be one
Who wouldn't say so till he'd tried.
So he buckled right in with the trace of a grin
On his face. If he worried he hid it.
He started to sing as he tackled the thing
That couldn't be done, and he did it.

Somebody scoffed: "Oh, you'll never do that;
At least no one ever has done it";
But he took off his coat and he took off his hat,
And the first thing we knew he'd begun it.
With a lift of his chin and a bit of a grin,
Without any doubting or quiddit,
He started to sing as he tackled the thing
That couldn't be done and he did it.

There are thousands to tell you it cannot be done,
There are thousands to prophesy failure;
There are thousands to point out to you one by one
The dangers that wait to assail you.
But just buckle in with a bit of a grin,
Just take off your coat and go to it;
Just start to sing as you tackle the thing
That "cannot be done," and you'll do it.

—*Edgar A. Guest*

NO THOUGHTFUL MAN ever came to the end of his life, and had time and a little space of calm from which to look back upon it, who did not know and acknowledge that it was what he had done unselfishly and for others, and nothing else, that satisfied him in the retrospect and made him feel that he had played the man.—*Woodrow Wilson*

OUR GENERATION KNOWS, as no generation before it has ever known, that peace must be made. If we mean when we talk of peace that nothing this time will stop us from making peace—that neither lies nor deceptions nor tricks nor our own weariness will prevent us—if we mean this we can speak of peace to the living and dead without shame. For nothing is true or honest in the talk of peace but our own purpose. And the choice is ours.—*Archibald MacLeish*

FORGET AND REMEMBER

Forget each kindness that you do
  As soon as you have done it;
Forget the praise that falls to you
  The moment you have won it.
Forget the slander that you hear
  Before you can repeat it;
Forget each slight, each spite, each sneer,
  Wherever you may meet it.

Remember every kindness done
  To you, whate'er its measure;
Remember praise by others won,
  And pass it on with pleasure;
Remember every promise made,
  And keep it to the letter;
Remember those who lend you aid,
  And be a grateful debtor.

—Author Unknown

L'ENVOI

When Earth's last picture is painted, and the tubes are twisted and dried,
When the oldest colors have faded, and the youngest critic has died,
We shall rest, and, faith, we shall need it—lie down for an eon or two,
Till the Master of All Good Workmen shall set us to work anew!

And those that were good shall be happy: they shall sit in a golden chair;
They shall splash at a ten-league canvas with brushes of comets' hair;
They shall find real saints to draw from—Magdalene, Peter, and Paul;
They shall work for an age at a sitting and never be tired at all!

And only the Master shall praise us, and only the Master shall blame;
And no one shall work for money, and no one shall work for fame;
But each for the joy of working, and each, in his separate star
Shall draw the Thing as he sees It for the God of Things as They Are!

—Rudyard Kipling

THOUGHT FOR THE DAY

This day is mine to mar or make,
 God keep us strong and true;
Let me no erring bypath take,
 No doubtful action do.

Grant me, when the setting sun
 This fleeting day shall end,
I may rejoice o'er something done,
 Be richer by a friend.

Let all I meet along the way
 Speak well of me tonight,
I would not have the humblest say
 I'd hurt him by a slight.

Let me be patient and serene,
 Gentle and kind and fair,
Help me to keep my record clean
 Thru all that I must bear.

Grant that because I live today,
 And to my thoughts give voice,
O'er something he shall hear me say
 Another shall rejoice.

Let there be something true and fine
 When night slips down, to tell
That I have lived this day of mine
 Not selfishly, but well.

—Edgar A. Guest

SAYINGS OF THE PEOPLE

GOD HELPS THEM that help themselves.

Diligence is the mother of good luck.

It is easier to prevent bad habits than to break them.

Genius without education is like silver in a mine.

A good traffic rule is: When you meet temptation on the road of life, turn to the right.

Some people grow under responsibility: others only swell.

Politeness is to do and to say the kindest thing in the kindest way.

A wise old owl lived in an oak. The more he saw the less he spoke. The less he spoke the more he heard: Why can't we all be like that bird?

THE ONLY WAY to have a friend is to be one. A friend is a person with whom I may be sincere. Before him I may think aloud. Happy is the house that shelters a friend. Let the soul be assured that somewhere in the universe it should rejoin its friend, and it would be content and cheerful alone for a thousand years.—*Ralph Waldo Emerson*

IT IS EASY in the world to live after the world's opinion; it is easy in solitude to live after our own; but the great man is he who in the midst of the crowd keeps with perfect sweetness the independence of solitude.—*Ralph Waldo Emerson*

A FOOLISH CONSISTENCY is the hobgoblin of little minds, adored by little statesmen and philosophers and divines.—*Ralph Waldo Emerson*

IF A MAN can write a better book, preach a better sermon, or make a better mousetrap, than his neighbor, tho he builds his house in the woods, the world will make a beaten path to his door.—*Ralph Waldo Emerson*

OUR STRENGTH grows out of our weakness. When man is pushed, tormented, defeated, he has a chance to learn something; he has been put on his wits, on his manhood; he has gained facts; learns his ignorance; is cured of the insanity of conceit; has got moderation and real skill.—*Ralph Waldo Emerson*

WHAT MAKES A SAINT?

Why were the saints saints?

Because they were cheerful when it was difficult to be cheerful; patient when it was difficult to be patient;

And because they pushed on when they wanted to stand still; and kept silent when they wanted to talk; and were agreeable when they wanted to be disagreeable.

That was all.

It was quite simple, and always will be.

—*Author Unknown*

INVICTUS

Out of the night that covers me,
  Black as the pit from pole to pole,
I thank whatever gods may be
  For my unconquerable soul.

In the fell clutch of circumstance
  I have not winced nor cried aloud.
Under the bludgeonings of chance
  My head is bloody, but unbowed.

Beyond this place of wrath and tears
  Looms but the Horror of the shade,
And yet the menace of the years
  Finds, and shall find, me unafraid.

It matters not how strait the gate,
  How charged with punishments the scroll,
I am the master of my fate:
  I am the captain of my soul.

—*William Ernest Henley*

Not what we give, but what we share,
For the gift without the giver is bare.

—*James Russell Lowell*

HOW DO I LOVE THEE?

How do I love thee? Let me count the ways.
I love thee to the depth and breadth and height
My soul can reach, when feeling out of sight
For the ends of being and ideal grace.
I love thee to the level of everyday's
Most quiet need, by sun and candlelight.
I love thee freely, as men strive for right;
I love thee purely, as they turn from praise.
I love thee with the passion put to use
In my old griefs, and with my childhood's faith.
I love thee with a love I seemed to lose
With my lost saints,—I love thee with the breath,
Smiles, tears, of all my life!—and, if God choose,
I shall but love thee better after death.

—*Elizabeth Barrett Browning*

A COLLECT FOR ALL WOMEN

KEEP US, O God, from pettiness: let us be large in thought, in word, in deed. Let us be done with faultfinding and leave off selfseeking. May we put away all pretense and meet each other face to face, without selfpity and without prejudice. May we never be hasty in judgment and always generous. Let us take time for all things: make us to grow calm, serene, gentle. Teach us to put into action our better impulses, straightforward and unafraid. Grant that we may realize it is the little things that create differences: that in the big things of life we are at one. And may we strive to touch and to know the great common human heart of us all: and, O Lord God, let us forget not to be kind!—*Mary Stewart*

THE QUITTER

It's easy to cry that you're beaten and die,
It's easy to crawfish and crawl,
But to fight and to fight when hope's out of sight,
Why, that's the best game of them all;
And tho you come out of each grueling bout
All broken and beaten and scarred—
Just have one more try. It's dead easy to die,
It's the keeping on living that's hard.

—*Robert W. Service*

ON HIS BLINDNESS

When I consider how my light is spent
Ere half my days in this dark world and wide,
And that one talent, which is death to hide,
Lodged with me useless, thou my soul more bent
To serve therewith my Maker, and present
My true account, lest He returning chide;
"Doth God exact day-labor, light denied?"
I fondly ask. But Patience, to prevent
That murmur, soon replies, "God doth not need
Either man's work or his own gifts; who best
Bear his mild yoke, they serve him best; his state
Is kingly; thousands at his bidding speed,
And post o'er land and ocean without rest;
They also serve who only stand and wait."

—*John Milton*

HAPPINESS

Who seeks afar for happiness
Will find it not.
It stands a guest unheeded at thy very door today,
Open thine eyes to see,
Thine ears to hear,
Thy heart to feel,
The call for touch of human sympathy;
In answering this there enters
And close beside thee sits
The guest thou soughtest in vain afar.

—*Caroline S. Woodruff*

FOUR THINGS

Four things a man must learn to do
If he would make his record true:
To think without confusion clearly;
To love his fellowmen sincerely;
To act from honest motives purely;
To trust in God and Heaven securely.

Henry van Dyke

INTIMATIONS OF IMMORTALITY

Our birth is but a sleep and a forgetting;
The Soul that rises with us, our life's Star,
  Hath had elsewhere its setting,
    And cometh from afar;
  Not in entire forgetfulness,
  And not in utter nakedness,
But trailing clouds of glory do we come
    From God, who is our home:
Heaven lies about us in our infancy!
Shades of the prison-house begin to close
    Upon the growing Boy,
But he beholds the light, and whence it flows,
    He sees it in his joy;
The Youth, who daily farther from the east
  Must travel, still is Nature's priest
    And by the vision splendid
    Is on his way attended;
At length the Man perceives it die away,
And fade into the light of common day.

—*William Wordsworth*

MY CREED

I would be true,
For there are those who trust me;
I would be pure,
For there are those who care;
I would be strong,
For there is much to suffer;
I would be brave,
For there is much to dare;
I would be friend
To all—the foe—the friendless;
I would be giving,
And forget the gift;
I would be humble,
For I know my weakness;
I would look up—
And laugh and love and lift.

—*Howard Arnold Walter*

Kiwanis International has erected 30 Boundary Peace Tablets along the United States-Canadian border to express the friendly relations which have existed between the two nations for over a century.

THE TOUCH OF A HAND

It's the human touch in this world that counts
The touch of your hand and mine
That means far more to the fainting heart
Than shelter or bread or wine
For shelter is gone when the night is o'er
And bread lasts only a day
But the touch of a hand and the sound of a voice
Sing on in the soul alway.

—*Author Unknown*

THOUGHTS ON BOOKS AND READING

THAT IS A GOOD BOOK which is opened with expectation and closed with profit.—*A. Bronson Alcott*

READING maketh a full man; conference a ready man; and writing an exact man.—*Francis Bacon*

SOME BOOKS are to be tasted, others to be swallowed, and some few to be chewed and digested.—*Francis Bacon*

A LITTLE LIBRARY, growing larger every year, is an honorable part of a man's possessions. A library is not a luxury. It is one of the necessities of a full life.—*Henry Ward Beecher*

IDEAS are the mightiest influence on earth. One great thought breathed into a man may regenerate him.—*W. H. Channing*

There is no frigate like a book
To take us lands away,
Nor any courser like a page
Of prancing poetry.

—*Emily Dickinson*

FOR BOOKS are more than books, they are the life, the very heart and core of ages past, the reason why men lived and worked and died, the essence and quintessence of their lives.—*Amy Lowell*

A little learning is a dangerous thing;
Drink deep, or taste not the Pierian Spring.

—*Alexander Pope*

PART VIII—SECTION 3

World Brotherhood

The time will come when men
Will be as free and equal as the waves,
That seem to jostle, but that never jar.
—*Alfred J. Austin*

PEACE

Lord, make me an instrument of your peace!
Where there is hatred, let me sow love;
Where there is injury, pardon;
Where there is doubt, faith;
Where there is despair, hope;
Where there is darkness, light;
Where there is sadness, joy.

O Divine Master, grant that I may not so much seek
To be consoled, as to console;
To be understood, as to understand;
To be loved, as to love.
For it is in giving that we receive;
It is in pardoning that we are pardoned;
It is in dying that we are born to eternal life.
—*St. Francis of Assisi*

JUSTICE is as strictly due between neighbor nations as between neighbor citizens. A highwayman is as much a robber when he plunders in a gang as when single; and a nation that makes an unjust war is only a *great gang*.—*Benjamin Franklin*

DISARM THE HEART

In hearts too young for enmity
There lies the way to make men free.
When children's friendships are worldwide,
New ages will be glorified.
Let child love child and wars will cease
Disarm the heart—for that is peace.
—*Ethel Blair Jordan*

THE PARLIAMENT OF MAN

For I dipt into the future,
  Far as human eye can see,
Saw the Vision of the world,
  And all the wonder that would be;
Saw the heavens fill with commerce,
  Argosies of magic sails,
Pilots of the purple twilight,
  Dropping down with costly bales;
Heard the heavens fill with shouting,
  And there rained a ghastly dew
From the nations' airy navies
  Grappling in the central blue;
Far along the worldwide whisper
  Of the southwind rushing warm,
With the standards of the peoples
  Plunging thru the thunderstorm;
Till the war-drum throbbed no longer,
  And the battleflags were furled
In the Parliament of man, the
  Federation of the world.
There the common sense of most
  Shall hold a fretful realm in awe,
And the kindly earth shall slumber,
  Lapped in universal law.

—From *Alfred Tennyson's* "Locksley Hall"

Lord, let war's tempests cease,
Fold the whole world in peace
  Under Thy wings.
Make all the nations one,
All hearts beneath the sun,
Till Thou shalt reign alone,
  Great King of Kings.

—*Henry W. Longfellow*

Were half the power that fills the world with terror,
  Were half the wealth bestowed on camps and courts,
Given to redeem the human mind from error,
  There were no need of arsenals and forts. . . .

—From *Henry W. Longfellow's*
"The Arsenal at Springfield"

Mel Chamowitz

THE PAGEANT OF PEACE AND THE NATIONAL CHRISTMAS TREE WITH THE WASHINGTON MONUMENT IN THE BACKGROUND

AMERICA FIRST

Not merely in matters material, but in things of the spirit.
Not merely in science, inventions, motors, and skyscrapers, but also in ideals, principles, character.
Not merely in the calm assertion of rights, but in the glad assumption of duties.
Not flaunting her strength as a giant, but bending in helpfulness over a sick and wounded world like a Good Samaritan.
Not in splendid isolation, but in courageous cooperation.
Not in pride, arrogance, and disdain of other races and peoples, but in sympathy, love, and understanding.
Not in treading again the old, worn, bloody pathway which ends inevitably in chaos and disaster, but in blazing *a new trail,* along which, please God, *other nations will follow,* into the new Jerusalem where wars shall be no more.
Some day some nation must take that path—unless we are to lapse once again into utter barbarism—and that honor I covet for my beloved America.
And so, in that spirit and with these hopes, I say with all my heart and soul, "*America First.*"

—*Bishop G. Ashton Oldham*

First Battalion, Third Infantry, U. S. Army

TOMB OF THE UNKNOWN SOLDIER,
ARLINGTON NATIONAL CEMETERY.

THE YOUNG DEAD SOLDIERS

The young dead soldiers do not speak.
Nevertheless they are heard in the still houses.
[Who has not heard them?]
They have a silence that speaks for them at night
And when the clock counts.
They say,
We were young. We have died. Remember us.
They say,
We have done what we could
But until it is finished it is not done.
They say,
We have given our lives
But until it is finished no one can know what our lives gave.
They say,
Our deaths are not ours,
They are yours,
They will mean what you make them.
They say,
Whether our lives and our deaths were for peace and a new hope
Or for nothing
We cannot say.

It is you who must say this.
They say,
We leave you our deaths.
Give them their meaning.
Give them an end to the war and a true peace,
Give them a victory that ends the war and a peace afterwards,
Give them their meaning.

We were young, they say.
We have died.
Remember us.

—*Archibald MacLeish*
[*Poem dedicated to Richard Myers*]

YOUTH ANSWERS

We speak to you, young dead soldiers.
We have heard you above the riotous noises.
[Do you not hear us?]
Our hearts and our voices call to you across the black chasms of war
And the bright fields of peace.
We say,
We are young. We live. We remember you.
We say,
As you have given in death,
So shall we give in life—gladly, unstintedly.
We say,
We dedicate ourselves
To those high principles which you died to preserve.
We say,
Your deaths are ours.
We shall give them meaning,
You were our brothers, our friends, our countrymen;
We shall not forget you.
We say,
We shall live your democracy, not dream it.
We shall promote tolerance and justice.
We shall keep peace on the earth.
Your mission shall be ours, God helping us.
We are young, we say.
We live.
We remember you.

[*Composite class poem, Arsenal Technical Schools of Indianapolis, Indiana, in reply to "The Young Dead Soldiers" by Archibald MacLeish*]

If everyone else were just like me,
What kind of a world would our world be?

—Author Unknown

THESE ARE THE TIMES that try men's souls. The summer soldier and the sunshine patriot will, in this crisis, shrink from the service of their country; but he that stands it *now*, deserves the love and thanks of men and women. Tyranny, like hell, is not easily conquered; yet we have this consolation with us, that the harder the conflict, the more glorious the triumph.

—Thomas Paine

Unless within my heart I hold
Abiding peace,
No league of nations can succeed
Nor will strife cease.

If I myself see every fault
In kin and friend,
The world may never see the day
When war will end.

—Eugenia T. Finn

BETWEEN MIDNIGHT AND MORNING

You that have faith to look with fearless eyes
Upon the tragedy of a world at strife,
And know, that out of night and death shall rise
The dawn of ampler life:

Rejoice! whatever anguish rend your heart,
That God hath given you this priceless dower,
To live in these great times and have your part
In Freedom's crowning hour;

That you may tell your sons, who see the light
High in the heavens, their heritage to take:—
"I saw the powers of darkness put to flight!
I saw the morning break!"

—Owen Seaman

PRAYER

God of the free, we pledge our hearts and lives today to the cause of all free mankind.

Grant us victory over the tyrants who would enslave all free men and nations.

Grant us faith and understanding to cherish all those who fight for freedom as if they were our brothers. Grant us brotherhood in hope and union, not only for the space of this bitter war, but for the days to come which shall and must unite all the children of earth.

Our earth is but a small star in the great universe. Yet of it we can make, if we choose, a planet unvexed by war, untroubled by hunger or fear, undivided by senseless distinctions of race, color, or theory. Grant us that courage and foreseeing to begin this task today that our children and our children's children may be proud of the name of man.

The spirit of man has awakened and the soul of men has gone forth. Grant us the wisdom and the vision to comprehend the greatness of man's spirit, that suffers and endures so hugely for a goal beyond his own brief span. Grant us honor for the dead who died in the faith, honor for our living who work and strive for the faith, redemption and security for all captive lands and peoples. Grant us patience with the deluded and pity for the betrayed. And grant us the skill and the valor that shall cleanse the world of oppression and the old base doctrine that the strong must eat the weak because they are strong.

Yet most of all grant us brotherhood, not only for this day but for all our years—a brotherhood not of words but of acts and deeds. We are all of us children of earth—grant us that simple knowledge. If our brothers are oppressed, then we are oppressed. If they hunger, we hunger. If their freedom is taken away, our freedom is not secure. Grant us a common faith that man shall know bread and peace, that he shall know justice and righteousness, freedom and security, an equal chance to do his best, not only in our own lands, but thruout the world. And in the faith let us march toward the clean world our hands can make. Amen.

—*Stephen Vincent Benét*

[*Read by President Roosevelt at United Nations Day Ceremony, White House, June 15, 1942.*]

FOREIGN?

I thought that foreign children
  Lived far across the sea
Until I got a letter
  From a boy in Italy.

"Dear little foreign friend," it said
  As plainly as could be.
Now I wonder which is "foreign,"
  The other child or me.

—*Ethel Blair Jordan*

TODAY

To be alive in such an age!
With every year a lightning page
Turned in the world's great wonder-book
Whereon the leaning nations look,
When men speak strong for brotherhood
For peace and universal good;
When miracles are everywhere
And every inch of common air throbs a tremendous prophecy
Of greater marvels yet to be.
O, Thrilling Age!
O, Willing Age!
When steel and stone and rail and rod
Become the utterance of God
A trump to shout His thunder thru,
Proclaiming all that man may do.

To be alive in such an age!
To live to it! To give to it!
Rise, soul, from thy despairing knees,
What if thy lips have drunk the lees?
Fling forth thy sorrow to the wind
And link thy hope with humankind:
The passion of a larger claim
Will put thy puny grief to shame.
Breathe the world-thought, do the world-deed,
Think hugely of thy brother's need.
Give thanks with all thy flaming heart,
Crave but to have in it a part—
Give thanks and clasp thy heritage—
To be alive in such an age!

—*Angela Morgan*

PART VIII—SECTION 4

Creeds, Pledges, and Codes

THE AMERICAN'S CREED

I BELIEVE in the United States of America as a government of the people, by the people, for the people, whose just powers are derived from the consent of the governed; a democarcy in a republic; a sovereign nation of many sovereign states; a perfect union, one and inseparable, established upon those principles of freedom, equality, justice, and humanity for which American patriots sacrificed their lives and fortunes.

I therefore believe it is my duty to my country to love it, to support its Constitution, to obey its laws, to respect its flag, and to defend it against all enemies.—*William Tyler Page,* Clerk of the House of Representatives, in 1917. Accepted by the House on behalf of the American people April 3, 1918. See also Congressional Record for April 13, 1918.

[*The Pledge to the Flag appears on page 423.*]

OATH OF THE AMERICAN BOY SCOUT

ON MY HONOR I will do my best—[1] To do my duty to God and my country, and to obey the Scout Law. [2] To help other people at all times. [3] To keep myself physically strong, mentally awake, and morally straight.

THE SCOUT LAW

[1] A Scout is trustworthy
[2] A Scout is loyal
[3] A Scout is helpful
[4] A Scout is friendly
[5] A Scout is courteous
[6] A Scout is kind
[7] A Scout is obedient
[8] A Scout is cheerful
[9] A Scout is thrifty
[10] A Scout is brave
[11] A Scout is clean
[12] A Scout is reverent

THE COUNTRY BOY'S CREED

I BELIEVE that the Country which God made is more beautiful than the City which man made; that life out-of-doors and in touch with the earth is the natural life of man. I believe that work is work wherever we find it, but that work with Nature is more inspiring than work with the most intricate machinery. I believe that the dignity of labor depends not on what you do, but on how you do it; that opportunity comes to a boy on the farm as often as to a boy in the city, that life is larger and freer and happier on the farm than in town, that my success depends not upon my location, but upon myself—not upon my dreams, but upon what I actually do, not upon luck but upon pluck. I believe in working when you work and in playing when you play and in giving and demanding a square deal in every act of life.—*Edwin Osgood Grover*

FUTURE FARMERS OF AMERICA CREED

I BELIEVE in the future of farming, with a faith born not of words but of deeds—achievements won by the present and past generations of farmers; in the promise of better days thru better ways, even as the better things we now enjoy have come up to us from the struggles of former years.

I believe that to live and work on a good farm is pleasant as well as challenging; for I know the joys and discomforts of farm life and hold an inborn fondness for those associations which, even in hours of discouragement, I cannot deny.

I believe in leadership from ourselves and respect from others. I believe in my own ability to work efficiently and think clearly, with such knowledge and skill as I can secure, and in the ability of organized farmers to serve our own and the public interest in marketing the product of our toil. I believe we can safeguard those rights against practices and policies that are unfair.

I believe in less dependence on begging and more power in bargaining; in the life abundant and enough honest wealth to help make it so —for others as well as myself; in less need for charity and more of it when needed; in being happy myself and playing square with those whose happiness depends upon me.

I believe that rural America can and will hold true to the best traditions in our national life and that I can exert an influence in my home and community which will stand solid for my part in that inspiring task.

A COUNTRY GIRL'S CREED

I AM GLAD I live in the country. I love its beauty and its spirit. I rejoice in the things I can do as a country girl for my home and my neighborhood.

I believe I can share in the beauty around me—in the fragrance of the orchards in spring, in the weight of the ripe wheat at harvest, in the morning song of birds, and in the glow of the sunset on the far horizon. I want to express this beauty in my life as naturally and happily as the wild rose blooms by the roadside.

I believe I can have a part in the courageous spirit of the country. This spirit has entered into the brook in our pasture. The stones placed in its way call forth its strength and add to its strength a song. It swells in the tender plants as they burst the seed cases that imprison them and push thru the dark earth to the light. It sounds in the nesting notes of the meadowlark. With this courageous spirit I, too, can face the hard things of life with gladness.

I believe there is much I can do in my country home. Thru studying the best way to do my everyday work I find joy in common tasks done well. Thru loving comradeship I can help bring into my home the happiness and peace that are always so near us in God's out-of-door world. Thru such a hope I can help make real to all who pass that way their highest ideal of country life.

I believe my love and loyalty for my country home should reach out in service to that larger home that we call our neighborhood. I would join with people who live there in true friendliness. I would wholeheartedly give my best to further all that is being done for a better community. I would have all that I think and say and do help to unite country people near and far in the great Kingdom of Love for Neighbors.—*Jessie Field*

OATH OF THE ATHENIAN YOUNG MAN

WE WILL never bring disgrace to this our city, by any act of dishonesty or cowardice; we will fight for our ideals and sacred things of the city, both alone and with many; we will revere and obey the city's laws and do our best to incite a like respect and reverence in those about us; we will strive unceasingly to quicken the public's sense of civic duty; and thus in all these ways we will strive to transmit this city not only not less but greater, better, and more beautiful than it was transmitted to us.

FUTURE TEACHERS OF AMERICA PLEDGE

THE GOOD TEACHER requires:

Physical vitality. I will keep my body well and strong.

Mental vigor. I will study daily to keep my mind active and alert.

Moral discrimination. I will seek to know the right and to live by it.

Wholesome personality. I will cultivate in myself goodwill, friendliness, poise, upright bearing, and careful speech.

Helpfulness. I will learn the art of helping others by doing helpful things daily in home and school.

Knowledge. I will fill my mind with worthy thoughts by observing all that is beautiful in the world around me, by reading the best books, and by associating with the best companions.

Leadership. I will make my influence count on the side of right, avoiding habits that weaken and destroy.

These Things Will I Do Now that I May Be Worthy the High Office of Teacher.

Written by Joy Elmer Morgan, founder of Future Teachers of America

THE GIRL SCOUT PROMISE

On my honor, I will try:
To do my duty to God and my country,
To help other people at all times,
To obey the Girl Scout laws.

THE GIRL SCOUT LAW

1. A Girl Scout's honor is to be trusted.
2. A Girl Scout is loyal.
3. A Girl Scout's duty is to be useful and to help others.
4. A Girl Scout is a friend to all and a sister to every other Girl Scout.
5. A Girl Scout is courteous.
6. A Girl Scout is a friend to animals.
7. A Girl Scout obeys orders.
8. A Girl Scout is cheerful.
9. A Girl Scout is thrifty.
10. A Girl Scout is clean in thought, word and deed.

THE NATIONAL 4-H CLUB PLEDGE AND EMBLEM

I Pledge

My Head to clearer thinking,
My Heart to greater loyalty,
My Hands to larger service, and
My Health to better living, for
My Club, my Community, and My
Country.

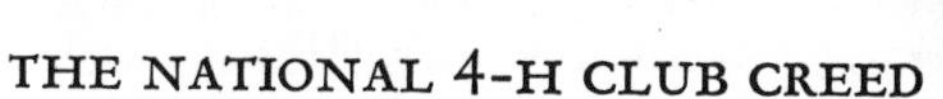

THE NATIONAL 4-H CLUB CREED

I believe in 4–H Club work for the opportunity it will give me to become a useful citizen.

I believe in the training of my HEAD for the power it will give me to think, to plan, and to reason.

I believe in the training of my HEART for the nobleness it will give me to become kind, sympathetic, and true.

I believe in the training of my HANDS for the ability it will give me to be helpful, useful, and skillful.

I believe in the training of my HEALTH for the strength it will give me to enjoy life, to resist disease, and to work efficiently.

I believe in my country, my State, and my community, and in my responsibility for their development.

In all these things I believe, and I am willing to dedicate my efforts to their fulfillment.

THE NATIONAL 4-H CLUB CITIZENSHIP PLEDGE

We, individually and collectively, pledge our efforts from day to day to fight for the ideals of this Nation.

We will never allow tyranny and injustice to become enthroned in this, our country, thru indifference to our duties as citizens.

We will strive for intellectual honesty and exercise it thru our power of franchise. We will obey the laws of our land and endeavor increasingly to quicken the sense of public duty among our fellow men.

We will strive for individual perfection and for social betterment. We will devote our talents to the improvement of our homes and our communities in their recreational, social, and spiritual needs.

We will endeavor to transmit this Nation to posterity not merely as we found it, but freer, happier, and more beautiful than when it was transmitted to us.

THE CODE OF THE GOOD AMERICAN

The Code of the Good American, originally known as The Children's Morality Code, grew out of a nationwide movement for character education led by the Character Education Institution of Washington, D. C., Dr. Milton Fairchild, Chairman. In 1916 the Institution sponsored a National Morality Code Competition with a prize of $5,000. The prize was awarded to William J. Hutchins. The judges were Professor George Trumbull Ladd of Yale University; Justice Mahlen Pitney of the Supreme Court of the United States; and Mrs. Phillip North More of the National Council of Women. All states participated and the code was revised to include the best points from the 51 other codes submitted and checked against a list of 650 childhood morality acts. Under the title, The Code of the Good American, it was published serially in chart form in the Journal of the National Education Association *during 1946 and 1947. These posters were reprinted and widely distributed to schools.*

THE CODE

Citizens who are good Americans try to become strong and useful, worthy of their nation, that our country may become ever greater and better. Therefore, they obey the laws of right living which the best Americans have always obeyed.

[1] *The Law of Selfcontrol*

The Good American Controls Himself. Those who best control themselves can best serve their country.

I will control my *tongue,* and will not allow it to speak mean, vulgar, or profane words. I will think before I speak. I will tell the truth and nothing but the truth.

I will control my *temper,* and will not get angry when people or things displease me. Even when indignant against wrong and contradicting falsehood, I will keep my selfcontrol.

I will control my *thoughts,* and will not allow a foolish wish to spoil a wise purpose.

I will control my *actions.* I will be careful and thrifty, and insist on doing right.

I will not ridicule nor defile the character of another; I will keep my selfrespect, and help others to keep theirs.

[2] *The Law of Good Health*

The Good American Tries to Gain and Keep Good Health. The welfare of our country depends upon those who are physically fit for their daily work. Therefore:

I will try to take such food, sleep, and exercise as will keep me always in good health.

I will keep my clothes, my body, and my mind clean.

I will avoid those habits which would harm me, and will make and never break those habits which will help me.

I will protect the health of others, and guard their safety as well as my own.

I will grow strong and skilful.

[3] *The Law of Kindness*

The Good American Is Kind. In America those who are different must live in the same communities. We are of many different sorts, but we are one great people. Every unkindness hurts the common life; every kindness helps. Therefore:

I will be kind in all my thoughts. I will bear no spites or grudges. I will never despise anybody.

I will be kind in all my speech. I will never gossip nor will I speak unkindly of anyone. Words may wound or heal.

I will be kind in my acts. I will not selfishly insist on having my own way. I will be polite: rude people are not good Americans. I will not make unnecessary trouble for those who work for me, nor forget to be grateful. I will be careful of other people's things. I will do my best to prevent cruelty, and will give help to those in need.

[4] *The Law of Sportsmanship*

The Good American Plays Fair. Clean play increases and trains one's strength and courage, and helps one to be more useful to one's country. Sportsmanship helps one to be a gentleman, a lady. Therefore:

I will not cheat, nor will I play for keeps or for money. If I should not play fair, the loser would lose the fun of the game, the winner would lose his selfrespect, and the game itself would become a mean and often cruel business.

I will treat my opponents with courtesy, and trust them if they deserve it. I will be friendly.

If I play in a group game, I will play not for my own glory, but for the success of my team and the fun of the game.

I will be a good loser or a generous winner.

And in my work as well as in my play, I will be sportsmanlike—generous, fair, honorable.

[5] *The Law of Selfreliance*

The Good American Is Selfreliant. Selfconceit is silly, but self-reliance is necessary to citizens who would be strong and useful.

I will gladly listen to the advice of older and wiser people; I will reverence the wishes of those who love and care for me, and who know life and me better than I. I will develop independence and wisdom to think for myself, choose for myself, act for myself, according to what seems right and fair and wise.

I will not be afraid of being laughed at when I am right. I will not be afraid of doing right when the crowd does wrong.

When in danger, trouble, or pain, I will be brave. A coward does not make a good American.

[6] *The Law of Duty*

The Good American Does His Duty. The shirker and the willing idler live upon others, and burden fellow-citizens with work unfairly. They do not do their share, for their country's good.

I will try to find out what my duty is as a good American, and my duty I will do, whether it is easy or hard. What it is my duty to do I can do.

[7] *The Law of Reliability*

The Good American Is Reliable. Our country grows great and good as her citizens are able more fully to trust each other. Therefore:

I will be honest, in word and in act. I will not lie, sneak, or pretend.

I will not do wrong in the hope of not being found out. I cannot hide the truth from myself and cannot often hide it from others. Nor will I injure the property of others.

I will not take without permission what does not belong to me. A thief is a menace to me and others.

I will do promptly what I have promised to do. If I have made a foolish promise, I will at once confess my mistake, and I will try to make good any harm which my mistake may have caused. I will so speak and act that people will find it easier to trust each other.

[8] *The Law of Truth*

The Good American Is True. I will be slow to believe suspicions lest I do injustice; I will avoid hasty opinions lest I be mistaken as to facts.

I will stand by the truth regardless of my likes and dislikes, and scorn the temptation to lie for myself or friends; nor will I keep the truth from those who have a right to it.

I will hunt for proof, and be accurate as to what I see and hear; I will learn to think, that I may discover new truth.

[9] *The Law of Good Workmanship*

The Good American Tries to Do the Right Thing in the Right Way. The welfare of our country depends upon those who have learned to do in the right way the work that makes civilization possible. Therefore:

I will get the best possible education, and learn all that I can as a preparation for the time when I am grown up and at my life work. I will invent and make things better if I can.

I will take real interest in work, and will not be satisfied to do slipshod, lazy, and merely passable work. I will form the habit of good work and keep alert; mistakes and blunders cause hardships, sometimes disaster, and spoil success.

I will make the right thing in the right way to give it value and beauty, even when no one else sees or praises me. But when I have done my best, I will not envy those who have done better, or have received larger reward. Envy spoils the work and the worker.

[10] *The Law of Teamwork*

The Good American Works in Friendly Cooperation with Fellow-Workers. One alone could not build a city or a great railroad. One alone would find it hard to build a bridge. That I may have bread, people have made plows and threshers, have built mills and mined coal, made stoves and kept stores. As we learn better how to work together, the welfare of our country is advanced.

In whatever work I do with others, I will do my part and encourage others to do their part, promptly, quickly.

I will help to keep in order the things which we use in our work. When things are out of place, they are often in the way, and sometimes they are hard to find.

In all my work with others, I will be cheerful. Cheerlessness depresses all the workers and injures all the work.

When I have received money for my work, I will be neither a miser nor a spendthrift. I will save or spend as one of the friendly workers of America.

[11] *The Law of Loyalty*

The Good American Is Loyal. If our America is to become ever greater and better, her citizens must be loyal, devotedly faithful in every relation of life; full of courage and regardful of their honor.

I will be loyal to my family. In loyalty I will gladly obey my parents or those who are in their place, and show them gratitude. I will do my best to help each member of my family to strength and usefulness.

I will be loyal to my school. In loyalty I will obey and help other pupils to obey those rules which further the good of all.

I will be loyal to my town, my state, my country. In loyalty I will respect and help others to respect their laws and their courts of justice.

I will be loyal to humanity and civilization. In loyalty I will do my best to help the friendly relations of our country with every other country, and to give to everyone in every land the best possible chance. I will seek truth and wisdom; I will work, and achieve if I can, some good for the civilization into which I have been born.

If I try simply to be loyal to my family, I may be disloyal to my school. If I try simply to be loyal to my school, I may be disloyal to my town, my state, and my country. If I try simply to be loyal to my town, state and country, I may be disloyal to humanity. I will try above all things else to be loyal to humanity; then I shall surely be loyal to my country, my state, and my town, to my school, and to my family. And this loyalty to humanity will keep me faithful to civilization.

He who obeys the law of loyalty obeys all of the other ten laws of the Good American.

Loyalty is *the willing and practical and thorogoing devotion of a person to a cause.* A man is loyal when, first he has some *cause* to which he is loyal; when, secondly, he *willingly* and *thoroly* devotes himself to this cause; and when, thirdly, he expresses his devotion in some *sustained and practical way,* by acting steadily in the service of his cause.—From *The Philosophy of Loyalty* by Josiah Royce. Macmillian Company. New York, 1909. Page 16-17.

PART VIII—SECTION 5

Love of Country

DEMOCRACY IS A TRUST

LET US SAY this much to ourselves, not only with our lips but in our hearts. Let us say this: I myself am a part of democracy—I myself must accept responsibilities. Democracy is not merely a privilege to be enjoyed—it is a trust to keep and maintain. I am an American. I intend to remain an American. I will do my best to wipe from my heart hate, rancor, and political prejudice. I will sustain my government. And thru good days or bad I will try to serve my country.—*Stephen Vincent Benét*

FREE SPEECH

WITHOUT free speech no search for truth is possible; without free speech no discovery of truth is useful; without free speech progress is checked and the nations no longer march forward toward the nobler life which the future holds for man. Better a thousandfold abuse of free speech than denial of free speech. The abuse dies in a day, but the denial slays the life of the people, and entombs the hope of the race. —*Bradlaugh*

TAXES

I've paid my taxes, I'm proud to say
I bought some civilization today
I helped build a bridge and a highway, too
I bought my three children a park and a zoo
When I paid my taxes.

I helped build a library and paid for more books
I paid for having the streets cleaned, improving their looks
I helped put drinking founts in my own home town
I paid for new street lights in the same old town
When I paid my taxes.

I helped hire a doctor and fireman's crew
I paid for a nurse and some policemen, too
I helped buy a young man a very fine job,
I helped buy a bathing beach for my Dorothy and Bob
When I paid my taxes.

I helped build a school and hire teachers, too
I helped buy a golf course for my son to play thru
I helped build a museum of music and art
Now, friends, don't you think I really was smart
When I paid my taxes?

C. C. Clinton
[*In* Childhood Education, *December 1941*]

LIBERTY will not descend to a people, a people must raise themselves to liberty; it is a blessing that must be earned before it can be enjoyed.—*Charles Caleb Colton*

THE BETTER WAY

Who serves his country best?
Not he who, for a brief and stormy space,
Leads forth her armies to the fierce affray.
Short is the time of turmoil and unrest,
Long years of peace succeed it and replace:
There is a better way.

Who serves his country best?
Not he who guides her senates in debate,
And makes the laws which are her prop and stay;
Not he who wears the poet's purple vest
And sings her songs of love and grief and fate:
There is a better way.

He serves his country best
Who joins the tide that lifts her nobly on;
For speech has myriad tongues for every day,
And song but one; and law within the breast
Is stronger than graven law on stone:
This is a better way.

He serves his country best
Who lives pure life, and doeth righteous deed,
And walks straight paths, however others stray.
And leaves his sons as uttermost bequest
A stainless record which all men may read:
This is the better way.

No drop but serves the slowly lifting tide,
No dew but has an errand to some flower,
No smallest star but sheds some helpful ray,
And man by man, each giving to all the rest,
Makes the firm bulwark of the country's power:
There is no better way.

—*Susan Coolidge*

Architect's Office, U. S. Capitol

STATUE OF FREEDOM

The 19½-foot, 7½-ton statue atop the Capitol dome was designed by the sculptor, Thomas Crawford.

DEAR LAND OF ALL MY LOVE

Long as thine Art shall love true love,
Long as thy Science truth shall know,
Long as thine Eagle harms no Dove,
Long as thy Law by law shall grow,
Long as thy God is God above,
Thy brother every man below,
So long, dear Land of all my love,
Thy name shall shine, thy fame shall glow!

—*Sidney Lanier*

THIS LAND IS OURS

This land is ours; its golden grains,
Its mountain peaks, and fruited plains.

This land is ours to have and hold;
Its wells of oil, its veins of gold.

Its sturdy schools, its churches fine;
Its forest plots of spruce and pine.

Its waterfalls, its caps of snow;
Its ferns and moss where brooklets flow!

Its surfaced roads on which we ride
Stretch miles across the countryside.

This land is ours; its sun and shade,
Where democratic codes are made.

This land is ours; its fields of corn
Where gentlemen of strength are born.

This land is ours to love and cherish,
To guard, that freedom does not perish!

—*Nona Keen Duffy*

WHAT CONSTITUTES A STATE?

What constitutes a State?
Not high-raised battlement or labored mound,
Thick wall or moated gate;
Not cities proud with spires and turrets crowned;
Not bays and broad-armed ports,
Where, laughing at the storm, rich navies ride;
Not starred and spangled courts,
Where low-browed baseness wafts perfume to pride.
No:—Men! high-minded men
With powers as far above dull brutes endued
In forests, brake, or den,
As beasts excel cold rocks and brambles rude—
Men who their duties know,
But know their rights, and knowing, dare maintain,
Prevent the long-aimed blow,
And crush the tyrant while they rend the chain:
These constitute a State. . . .

—*William Jones*

THE MAN AMERICA NEEDS

Of no use are the men who study to do exactly as was done before, who can never understand that today is a new day. There never was such a combination as this of ours, and the rules to meet it are not set down in any history. We want men of original perception and original action, who can open their eyes wider than to a nationality—namely, to consideration of benefit to the human race—can act in the interest of civilization; men of elastic, men of normal mind, who can live in the moment and take a step forward.—*Ralph Waldo Emerson*

BARS FIGHT

August 'twas the twenty fifth
Seventeen hundred forty-six
The Indians did in ambush lay
Some very valient men to slay
The names of whom I'll not leave out
Samuel Allen like a hero fout
And though he was so brave and bold
His face no more shall we behold.
Eleazer Hawks was killed outright
Before he had time to fight
Before he did the Indians see
Was shot and killed immediately.
Oliver Amsden he was slain
Which caused his friends much grief and pain.
Samuel Amsden they found dead
Not many rods off from his head.
Adonijah Gillet we do hear
Did lose his life which was so dear.
John Saddler fled across the water
And so excaped the dreadful slaughter.
Eunice Allen see the Indians comeing
And hoped to save herself by running
And had not her petticoats stopt her
The awful creatures had not cotched her
And tommyhawked her on the head
And left her on the ground for dead.
Young Samuel Allen, Oh! lack a-day
Was taken and carried to Canada.

—*Written in 1746 by Lucy Terry, a slave*

THE BALLOT

A weapon that comes down as still
  As snowflakes fall upon the sod;
But executes a freeman's will,
  As lightning does the will of God.

—John Pierpont

MY NATIVE LAND

Breathes there the man with soul so dead
Who never to himself hath said:
  This is my own, my native land?
Whose heart hath ne'er within him burned
As home his footsteps he hath turned,
  From wandering on a foreign strand?
If such there breathe, go, mark him well!
For him no minstrel raptures swell;
High tho his titles, proud his name,
Boundless his wealth as wish can claim,
Despite those titles, power, and pelf,
The wretch concentred all in self,
Living, shall forfeit fair renown,
And, doubly dying, shall go down
To the vile dust from whence he sprung,
Unwept, unhonored, and unsung.

—Sir Walter Scott

GOD GIVE US MEN

God give us men! A time like this demands
Strong minds, great hearts, true faith, and ready hands,
Men whom the lust of office does not kill;
  Men whom the spoils of office cannot buy;
Men who possess opinions and a will;
  Men who have honor; men who will not lie;
Men who can stand before a demagogue
  And damn his treacherous flatteries without winking;
Tall men, sun-crowned, who live above the fog
  In public duty and in private thinking;
For while the rabble with their thumb-worn creeds
Their large profession and their little deeds
Mingle in selfish strife, lo! Freedom weeps,
Wrong rules the land, and waiting Justice sleeps.

—Josiah Gilbert Holland

I HEAR AMERICA SINGING

I hear America singing, the varied carols I hear,
Those of mechanics, each one singing his as it should be blithe and strong,
The carpenter singing his as he measures his plank or beam,
The mason singing his as he makes ready for work, or leaves off work,
The boatman singing what belongs to him in his boat, the deckhand singing on the steamboat deck,
The shoemaker singing as he sits on his bench, the hatter singing as he stands,
The woodcutter's song, the plowboy's on his way in the morning, or at noon intermission or at sundown,
The delicious singing of the mother, or of the young wife at work, or of the girl sewing or washing,
Each singing what belongs to him or her and to none else,
The day what belongs to the day—at night the party of young fellows, robust, friendly,
Singing with open mouths their strong melodious songs.

—*Walt Whitman*

You and I are America. Unless we change, America will not change. Unless we are willing to experiment boldly with the application of absolute honesty, absolute purity, absolute unselfishness, and absolute love in our lives and in our relationships and responsibilities, America, the land of the free, may lose her freedom because she no longer has the moral and spiritual values to maintain it.—*J. Herbert Smith*

REVERENCE FOR LAW

Let reverence for the laws be breathed by every American mother to the lisping babe that prattles on her lap; let it be taught in schools, in seminaries, and in colleges; let it be written in primers, spelling-books, and in almanacs; let it be preached from the pulpit, proclaimed in legislative halls, and enforced in courts of justice. And, in short, let it become the political religion of the nation; and let the old and the young, the rich and the poor, the grave and the gay of all sexes and tongues and colors and conditions, sacrifice unceasingly upon its altars.—*Abraham Lincoln*

THE SHIP OF DEMOCRACY

Sail, Sail thy best, ship of Democracy!
Of value is thy freight, 'tis not the Present only,
The Past is also stored in thee;
Thou holdest not the venture of thyself alone, not of the western continent alone,
Earth's résumé entire floats on thy keel, O ship, is steadied by thy spars,
With thee Time voyages in trust, the antecedent nations sink or swim with thee,
With all their ancient struggles, martyrs, heroes, epics, wars, thou bear'st the other continents,
Theirs, theirs as much as thine, the destination—port triumphant;
Steer then with good strong hand and wary eye, O helmsman, thou carriest great companions,
Venerable priestly Asia sails this day with thee,
And royal feudal Europe sails with thee.

—*Walt Whitman*

CREDO

I believe
That there are greater things in life
Than life itself;
I believe
In climbing upward
Even when the spent and broken thing
I call my body
Cries "Halt!"
I believe
To the last breath
In the truths
Which God permits me to see.

I believe
In fighting for them;
In drawing,
If need be,
Not the bloody sword of man
Brutal with conquest
And drunk with power,
But the white sword of God,
Flaming with His truth
And healing while it slays.

I believe
In my country and her destiny,
In the great dream of her founders,
In her place among the nations,
In her ideals;
I believe
That her democracy must be protected,
Her privileges cherished,
Her freedom defended.
I believe
That, humbly before the Almighty,
But proudly before all mankind,
We must safeguard her standards,
The vision of her Washington,
The martyrdom of her Lincoln,
With the patriotic ardor
Of the minute men
And the boys in blue
Of her glorious past.
I believe
In loyalty to my country
Utter, irrevocable, inviolate.
Thou, in whose sight
A thousand years are but as yesterday
And as a watch in the night,
Help me
In my frailty
To make real
What I believe.

—*Elias Lieberman*

ON THE FIRING LINE

For glory? For good? For fortune or for fame?
Why, ho, for the front when the battle is on!
Leave the rear to the dolt, the lazy, the lame;
Go forward as ever the valiant have done.
Whether city or field, whether mountain or mine,
Go forward, right on for the firing line!

Whether newsboy or plowboy or cowboy or clerk,
Fight forward; be ready, be steady, be first;
Be fairest, be bravest, be best at your work;
Exult and be glad; dare to hunger, to thirst.
As David, as Alfred—let dog skulk and whine—
There is room but for men on the firing line.

Aye, the one place to fight and the one place to fall—
As fall we must all, in God's good time—
It is where the manliest man is the wall,
Where boys are as men in their pride and prime,
Where glory gleams brightest, where brightest eyes shine—
Far out on the roaring red firing line!

—Joaquin Miller

AMERICA FOR ME

'Tis fine to see the Old World, and travel up and down
Among the famous palaces and cities of renown,
To admire the crumbly castles and the statues of the kings—
But now I think I've had enough of antiquated things.

So it's home again, and home again, America for me!
My heart is turning home again, and there I long to be,
In the land of youth and freedom beyond the ocean bars,
Where the air is full of sunlight and the flag is full of stars.

Oh, London is a man's town, there's power in the air;
And Paris is a woman's town, with flowers in her hair;
And it's sweet to dream in Venice, and it's great to study Rome;
But when it comes to living, there is no place like home.

I like the German fir-woods, in green battalions drilled;
I like the gardens of Versailles with flashing fountains filled;
But oh, to take your hand, my dear, and ramble for a day
In the friendly western woodland where Nature has her way!

I know that Europe's wonderful, yet something seems to lack:
The Past is too much with her, and the people looking back.
But the glory of the Present is to make the Future free—
We love our land for what she is and what she is to be.

Oh, it's home again, and home again, America for me!
I want a ship that's westward bound to plow the rolling sea,
To the blessed Land of Room Enough beyond the ocean bars,
Where the air is full of sunlight and the flag is full of stars.

—Henry van Dyke

THOSE who expect to reap the blessings of freedom, must, like men, undergo the fatigue of supporting it.—*Thomas Paine*

YOUNG AMERICA

I'm proud of this America
 In which I had my birth;
To me it is the finest land
 Of any on this earth.
I'm proud to know the stars and stripes
 Floats over great and small,
And gives, regardless of their race,
 Security to all.
And, for the blessed privilege
 Of being safe and free,
I'll try my very best to make
 My country proud of me.

—*Anna M. Priestly*

WHAT DOES IT MEAN TO BE AMERICAN?

What does it mean? I look across the years . . .
I see them come, but thru a mist of tears,
Our gallant forebears, full of hopes and fears.

I see them leave behind for conscience' sake,
The homes they loved, the ties so hard to break
Their questing, wondering, westward way to take.

I see them face and fight the wilderness,
Undaunted by its dangers, its duress,
And from its wildness, wrest and win success.

I see them take their living from the soil,
The men and women joined in homely toil—
Where they then planted, now our heart-roots coil.

I see them build their homes, their house of prayer,
And when its bell rings out upon the air,
I see them kneel in simple worship there.

I hear the drums of war's alarum beat,
I see them seize their arms, rise to their feet
Their enemies—and liberty's—to meet.

I see them face and conquer every foe,
I see their cities rise, a nation grow,
To whose broad breast earth's eager pilgrims go.

To be American is to be one
In whom these brave inheritances run,
A worthy daughter, or a noble son. . . .

—*Roselle Mercier Montgomery*

Louis Checkman

JOHN F. KENNEDY CENTER FOR THE PERFORMING ARTS, WASHINGTON, D. C. (ARCHITECT'S MODEL)

. . . I would emphasize the importance, in teaching students about public affairs, of avoiding the confusion of national patriotism with national mythology. Instillation of a sense of patriotism, of national pride, of awareness and gratitude for the liberties and opportunities that are ours as Americans—these are precepts which, of course, it is hoped every student shall grasp.

But at the same time let us recognize the necessity of clearing away these false axioms and myths which, however comforting to our sense of security or appealing to our sense of patriotism, impair a realistic view of our nation's role in the world. I refer to those myths, among others, that are based upon the untouchability of national sovereignty; the existence of inherently good, bad, or backward nations; or the emphasis of governmental economy over national security.

Many Americans persist in the myth that a democratic way of life, inasmuch as it is the best way, will inevitably be the victor in any struggle with an alien power; that the United States can never lose a war. Many still hold to the belief that our allies owe homage and gratitude to the United States and to all of its views at all times.

There are those who oppose assistance to or cooperation with our allies, those who reject bargaining or diplomatic pressure as a method of dealing with international disputes. Education for citizenship, for increased participation in American political life, must dispel these myths. . . . *John Fitzgerald Kennedy Speech before the American Association of School Administrators, Atlantic City, 1957*

LIBERTY AND PEACE

Lo! freedom comes. Th' prescient muse foretold,
All eyes th' accomplish'd prophecy behold:
Her port describ'd, "She moves divinely fair,
Olive and laurel bind her golden hair."
She, the bright progeny of Heaven, descends,
And every grace her sovereign step attends;
For now kind Heaven, indulgent to our prayer,
In smiling peace resolves the din of war.
Fix'd in Columbia her illustrious line,
And bids in thee her future councils shine.
To every realm her portals open'd wide,
Receives from each the full commercial tide.
Each art and science now with rising charms,
Th' expanding heart with emulation warms.
E'en great Britannia sees with dread surprise,
And from the dazzling splendors turns her eyes.
Britain, whose navies swept th' Atlantic o'er,
And thunder sent to every distant shore;
E'en thou, in manners cruel as thou art,
The sword resign'd, resume the friendly part.
For Gallia's power espous'd Columbia's cause,
And new-born Rome shall give Britannia laws,
Nor unremember'd in the grateful strain,
Shall princely Louis' friendly deed remain;
The generous prince th' impending vengeance eyes,
Sees the fierce wrong and to the rescue flies.
Perish that thirst of boundless power, that drew
On Albion's head the curse to tyrants due.
But thou appeas'd submit to Heaven's decree,
That bids this realm of freedom rival thee.
Now sheathe the sword that bade the brave atone
With guiltless blood for madness not their own.
Sent from th' enjoyment of their native shore,
Ill-fated—never to behold her more.
From every kingdom on Europa's coast
Throng'd various troops, their glory, strength, and boast.
With heart-felt pity fair Hibernia saw
Columbia menac'd by the Tyrant's law:
On hostile fields fraternal arms engage,
And mutual deaths, all dealt with mutual rage:
The muse's ear hears mother earth deplore

Her ample surface smoke with kindred gore:
The hostile field destroys the social ties,
And everlasting slumber seals their eyes.
Columbia mourns, the haughty foes deride,
Her treasures plunder'd and her towns destroy'd:
Witness how Charlestown's curling smokes arise,
In sable columns to the clouded skies.
The ample dome, high-wrought with curious toil,
In one sad hour the savage troops despoil.
Descending peace the power of war confounds;
From every tongue celestial peace resounds:
As from the east th' illustrious king of day,
With rising radiance drives the shades away,
So freedom comes array'd with charms divine,
And in her train commerce and plenty shine.
Britannia owns her independent reign,
Hibernia, Scotia, and the realms of Spain;
And great Germania's ample coast admires
The generous spirit that Columbia fires.
Auspicious Heaven shall fill with fav'ring gales,
Where'er Columbia spreads her swelling sails:
To every realm shall peace her charms display,
And heavenly freedom spread her golden ray.

—*Written in 1784 by Phillis Wheatley, a slave*

THE POOR VOTER ON ELECTION DAY

The proudest now is but my peer,
The highest not more high;
Today, of all the weary year,
A king of men am I.
Today, alike are great and small,
The nameless and the known;
My palace is the people's hall,
The ballot box my throne!

Who serves today upon the list
Beside the served shall stand;
Alike the brown and wrinkled fist,
The gloved and dainty hand!
The rich is level with the poor,
The weak is strong today;
And sleekest broadcloth counts no more
Than homespun frock of gray.

Today let pomp and vain pretence
My stubborn right abide;
I set a plain man's common sense
Against the pedant's pride.
Today shall simple manhood try
The strength of gold and land;
The wide world has not wealth to buy
The power in my right hand!

While there's a grief to seek redress,
Or balance to adjust,
Where weighs our living manhood less
Than Mammon's vilest dust—
While there's a right to need my vote,
A wrong to sweep away,
Up! clouted knee and ragged coat!
A man's a man today!

—*John Greenleaf Whittier*

THE SHIP OF STATE

Thou, too, sail on, O Ship of State!
Sail on, O Union, strong and great!
Humanity with all its fears,
With all the hopes of future years,
Is hanging breathless on thy fate!
We know what Master laid thy keel,
What Workmen wrought thy ribs of steel,
Who made each mast, and sail, and rope,
What anvils rang, what hammers beat,
In what a forge and what a heat
Were shaped the anchors of thy hope!
Fear not each sudden sound and shock,
'Tis of the wave and not the rock;
'Tis but the flapping of the sail,
And not a rent made by the gale!
In spite of rock and tempest's roar,
In spite of false lights on the shore,
Sail on, nor fear to breast the sea!
Our hearts, our hopes, are all with thee,
Our hearts, our hopes, our prayers, our tears,
Our faith triumphant o'er our fears,
Are all with thee—are all with thee!

—*Henry W. Longfellow*

THE LAND WHERE HATE SHOULD DIE

This is the land where hate should die—
No feuds of faith, no spleen of race,
No darkly brooding fear should try
Beneath our flag to find a place.
Lo! every people here has sent
Its sons to answer freedom's call;
Their lifeblood is the strong cement
That builds and binds the nation's wall.

This is the land where hate should die—
Tho dear to me my faith and shrine,
I serve my country well when I
Respect beliefs that are not mine.
He little loves his land who'd cast
Upon his neighbor's word a doubt,
Or cite the wrongs of ages past
From present rights to bar him out.

This is the land where hate should die—
This is the land where strife should cease,
Where foul, suspicious fear should fly
Before our flag of light and peace.
Then let us purge from poisoned thought
That service to the State we give,
And so be worthy as we ought
Of this great Land in which we live!

—Denis A. McCarthy

Where is the true man's fatherland?
Is it where he by chance is born?
Doth not the yearning spirit scorn
In such scant borders to be spanned?
Oh, yes! his fatherland must be
As the blue heaven wide and free!

—James Russell Lowell

PART VIII—SECTION 6

Historical Selections

LINCOLN, THE MAN OF THE PEOPLE

When the Norn Mother saw the Whirlwind Hour
Greatening and darkening as it hurried on,
She left the Heaven of Heroes and came down
To make a man to meet the mortal need.
She took the tried clay of the common road—
Clay warm yet with the genial heat of Earth,
Dasht thru it all a strain of prophecy;
Tempered the heap with thrill of human tears;
Then mixt a laughter with the serious stuff.
Into the shape she breathed a flame to light
That tender, tragic, ever-changing face;
And laid on him a sense of the Mystic Powers,
Moving—all husht—behind the mortal veil.
Here was a man to hold against the world,
A man to match the mountains and the sea.
The color of the ground was in him, the red earth;
The smack and tang of elemental things;
The rectitude and patience of the cliff;
The good-will of the rain that loves all leaves;
The friendly welcome of the wayside well;
The courage of the bird that dares the sea;
The gladness of the wind that shakes the corn;
The pity of the snow that hides all scars;
The secrecy of streams that make their way
Under the mountain to the rifted rock;
The tolerance and equity of light
That gives as freely to the shrinking flower
As to the great oak flaring to the wind—
To the grave's low hill as to the Matterhorn
That shoulders out the sky. Sprung from the West,
He drank the valorous youth of a new world.
The strength of virgin forests braced his mind,
The hush of spacious prairies stilled his soul.
His words were oaks in acorns; and his thoughts
Were roots that firmly gript the granite truth.

Abbie Rowe, National Park Service

THE LINCOLN MEMORIAL

Up from log cabin to the Capitol,
One fire was on his spirit, one resolve—
To send the keen ax to the root of wrong,
Clearing a free way for the feet of God,
The eyes of conscience testing every stroke,
To make his deed the measure of a man.
He built the rail-pile as he built the State,
Pouring his splendid strength thru every blow:
The grip that swung the ax in Illinois
Was on the pen that set a people free.

So came the Captain with the mighty heart;
And when the judgment thunders split the house,
Wrenching the rafters from their ancient rest,
He held the ridgepole up, and spikt again
The rafters of the Home. He held his place—
Held the long purpose like a growing tree—
Held on thru blame and faltered not at praise.
And when he fell in whirlwind, he went down
As when a lordly cedar, green with boughs,
Goes down with a great shout upon the hills,
And leaves a lonesome place against the sky.

—*Edwin Markham*

[*As revised for the dedication of the Lincoln Memorial, 1922*]

LANDING OF THE PILGRIM FATHERS

November 1620

The breaking waves dashed high
  On a stern and rock-bound coast,
And the woods, against a stormy sky,
  Their giant branches tossed;

And the heavy night hung dark
  The hills and waters o'er,
When a band of exiles moored their bark
  On the wild New England shore.

Not as the conqueror comes,
  They, the true-hearted, came:
Not with the roll of the stirring drums,
  And the trumpet that sings of fame;

Not as the flying come,
  In silence and in fear—
They shook the depths of the desert's gloom
  With their hymns of lofty cheer.

Amidst the storm they sang,
  And the stars heard, and the sea;
And the sounding aisles of the dim woods rang
  To the anthem of the free!

The ocean eagle soared
  From his nest by the white wave's foam,
And the rocking pines of the forest roared:
  This was their welcome home!

There were men with hoary hair
  Amidst that pilgrim band;
Why had they come to wither there,
  Away from their childhood's land?

There was woman's fearless eye,
  Lit by her deep love's truth;
There was manhood's brow, serenely high,
  And the fiery heart of youth.

What sought they thus afar?
  Bright jewels of the mine?
The wealth of seas, the spoils of war?—
  They sought a faith's pure shrine!

Aye, call it holy ground,
  The soil where first they trod!
They have left unstained what there they found—
  Freedom to worship God!

—Felicia Dorothea Hemans

THE WAR INEVITABLE, MARCH 1775

THEY TELL US, Sir, that we are weak—unable to cope with so formidable an adversary. But when shall we be stronger? Will it be the next week, or the next year? Will it be when we are totally disarmed, and when a British guard shall be stationed in every house? Shall we gather strength by irresolution and inaction? Shall we acquire the means of effectual resistance by lying supinely on our backs, and hugging the delusive phantom of hope, until our enemies shall have bound us hand and foot? Sir, we are not weak, if we make a proper use of those means which the God of nature hath placed in our power.

Three millions of people, armed in the holy cause of liberty, and in such a country as that which we possess, are invincible by any force which our enemy can send against us. Besides, Sir, we shall not fight our battles alone. There is a just God who presides over the destinies of nations, and who will raise up friends to fight our battles for us. The battle, Sir, is not to the strong alone; it is to the vigilant, the active, the brave. Besides, Sir, we have no election. If we were base enough to desire it, it is now too late to retire from the contest. There is no retreat but in submission and slavery! Our chains are forged! their clanking may be heard on the plains of Boston! The war is inevitable —and let it come! I repeat, Sir, let it come!

It is in vain, Sir, to extenuate the matter. Gentlemen may cry, Peace, Peace!—but there is no peace. The war is actually begun! The next gale that sweeps from the North will bring to our ears the clash of resounding arms! Our brethren are already in the field! Why stand we here idle? What is it that gentlemen wish? What would they have? Is life so dear, or peace so sweet, as to be purchased at the price of chains and slavery? Forbid it, Almighty God! I know not what course others may take; but as for me, give me liberty or give me death!

—Patrick Henry

Washington Convention and Visitors Bureau

ARLINGTON HOUSE, HOME OF ROBERT E. LEE

The Mansion was built by George Washington Custis, grandson of Martha Washington. His daughter, Mary, married Lt. Robert E. Lee and it was their home for 30 years. During the Civil War, the Lee family was forced to flee from the home; the grounds became a soldiers' cemetery; and later the United States acquired the property and restored it as a national museum. In the sarcophagus in front of the mansion is buried Pierre L'Enfant, designer of the Capital City.

ROBERT E. LEE

A gallant foeman in the fight,
A brother when the fight was o'er,
The hand that led the host with might
The blessed torch of learning bore.

No shriek of shells nor roll of drums,
No challenge fierce, resounding far,
When reconciling Wisdom comes
To heal the cruel wounds of war.

Thought may the minds of men divide,
Love makes the heart of nations one,
And so, thy soldier grave beside,
We honor thee, Virginia's son.

—*Julia Ward Howe*

COLUMBUS

Behind him lay the gray Azores,
Behind the Gates of Hercules;
Before him not the ghost of shores,
Before him only shoreless seas.
The good mate said: "Now must we pray,
For lo! the very stars are gone.
Brave Admiral, speak, what shall I say?"
"Why, say, 'Sail on! sail on! and on!' "

"My men grow mutinous day by day;
My men grow ghastly wan and weak."
The stout mate thought of home; a spray
Of salt wave washed his swarthy cheek.
"What shall I say, brave Admiral, say,
If we sight naught but seas at dawn?"
"Why, you shall say at break of day,
'Sail on! sail on! sail on! and on!' "

They sailed and sailed, as winds might blow,
Until at last the blanched mate said:
"Why, now not even God would know
Should I and all my men fall dead.
These very winds forget their way,
For God from these dread seas is gone.
Now speak, brave Admiral, speak and say"—
He said: "Sail on! sail on! and on!"

They sailed. They sailed. Then spake the mate:
"This mad sea shows his teeth tonight.
He curls his lip, he lies in wait,
He lifts his teeth, as if to bite!
Brave Admiral, say but one good word:
What shall we do when hope is gone?"
The words leapt like a leaping sword:
"Sail on! sail on! sail on! and on!"

Then, pale and worn, he paced his deck,
And peered thru darkness. Ah, that night
Of all dark nights! And then a speck—
A light! a light! at last a light!
It grew, a starlit flag unfurled!
It grew to be Time's burst of dawn.
He gained a world; he gave that world
Its grandest lesson: "On! sail on!"

—*Joaquin Miller*

ABRAHAM LINCOLN WALKS AT MIDNIGHT

[*In Springfield, Illinois*]

It is portentous, and a thing of state
That here at midnight, in our little town,
A mourning figure walks, and will not rest,
Near the old court-house pacing up and down,

Or by his homestead, or in shadowed yards
He lingers where his children used to play;
Or thru the market, on the well-worn stones
He stalks until the dawn-stars burn away.

A bronzed, lank man! His suit of ancient black,
A famous high top-hat and plain worn shawl
Make him the quaint great figure that men love,
The prairie-lawyer, master of us all.

He cannot sleep upon his hillside now.
He is among us:—as in times before!
And we who toss and lie awake for long
Breathe deep, and start, to see him pass the door.

His head is bowed. He thinks on men and kings.
Yea, when the sick world cries, how can he sleep?
Too many peasants fight, they know not why,
Too many homesteads in black terror weep.

The sins of all the war-lords burn his heart.
He sees the dreadnaughts scouring every main.
He carries on his shawl-wrapped shoulders now
The bitterness, the folly and the pain.

He cannot rest until a spirit-dawn
Shall come;—the shining hope of Europe free:
The league of sober folk, the Workers' Earth
Bringing long peace to Cornland, Alp, and Sea.

It breaks his heart that kings must murder still,
That all his hours of travail here for men
Seem yet in vain. And who will bring white peace
That he may sleep upon his hill again?

—*Vachel Lindsay*

OLD IRONSIDES

Aye, tear her tattered ensign down!
  Long has it waved on high,
And many an eye has danced to see
  That banner in the sky;
Beneath it rung the battle shout,
  And burst the cannon's roar;—
The meteor of the ocean air
  Shall sweep the clouds no more.

Her deck, once red with heroes' blood,
  Where knelt the vanquished foe,
When winds were hurrying o'er the flood,
  And waves were white below,
No more shall feel the victor's tread,
  Or know the conquered knee;—
The harpies of the shore shall pluck
  The eagle of the sea!

Oh, better that her shattered hulk
  Should sink beneath the wave;
Her thunders shook the mighty deep,
  And there should be her grave;
Nail to the mast her holy flag,
  Set every threadbare sail,
And give her to the God of storms,
  The lightning and the gale!

—Oliver Wendell Holmes

[*The Constitution, or Old Ironsides as it is best known, was one of the first and most famous vessels in the American Navy. Following her launching in 1797, she had a successful career including a brilliant encounter during the War of 1812 with the British frigate Guerriere which greatly improved the prestige and morale of the American navy. It was condemned in 1830 as unseaworthy, but because of this poem, published in the Boston Advertiser, and the public clamor it aroused, Old Ironsides was rebuilt instead of abandoned.*]

PART VIII—SECTION 7

The Flag of the United States

THE PLEDGE TO THE FLAG

I PLEDGE allegiance to the Flag of the United States of America and to the Republic for which it stands; one nation under God, indivisible, with liberty and justice for all.

[ACCORDING to Congressional resolution, December 22, 1942, the pledge of allegiance should "be rendered by standing with the right hand over the heart. However, civilians will always show full respect to the flag when the pledge is given by merely standing at attention, men removing the headdress. Persons in uniform shall render the military salute."]

AMERICA, I LOVE YOU!

PROUDLY I salute the flag of these United States of America, and treasure the ideals for which it stands: Liberty and justice for all. Gladly I respond to every call for loyalty to the American way of life, in thought and deed; to make our country strong, and to keep our country united. Willingly would I give all that I am, and all that I have, by the grace of God, to preserve our precious America for ourselves; and to transmit it ever more glorious, for our children to enjoy, pure and untainted, in the way our Fathers have bequeathed it to us. *America, I love you!—Aaron Metchik*

WHAT THE FLAG MEANS

THIS FLAG means more than association and reward. It is the symbol of our national unity, our national endeavor, our national aspiration. It tells you of the struggle for independence, of union preserved, of liberty and union one and inseparable, of the sacrifices of brave men and women to whom the ideals and honor of this nation have been dearer than life.

It means America first; it means an undivided allegiance . . . It means that you cannot be saved by the valor and devotion of your ancestors; that to each generation comes its patriotic duty; and that upon your willingness to sacrifice and endure as those before you have sacrificed and endured rests the national hope.

It speaks of equal rights; of the inspiration of free institutions exemplified and vindicated; of liberty under law intelligently conceived and impartially administered. There is not a thread in it but scorns selfindulgence, weakness, and rapacity. It is eloquent of our common destiny.—*Charles Evans Hughes.*

A SONG FOR FLAG DAY

Your flag and my flag,
And how it flies today
In your land and my land
And half a world away!
Rose-red and blood-red,
The stripes for ever gleam;
Snow-white and soul-white—
The good forefathers' dream;

Sky-blue and true blue, with stars to gleam aright—
The gloried guidon of the day; a shelter thru the night.

Your flag and my flag!
And, oh, how much it holds—
Your land and my land—
Secure within its folds!
Your heart and my heart
Beat quicker at the sight;
Sun-kissed and wind-tossed—
Red and blue and white.

The one flag—the great flag—the flag for me and you—
Glorified all else beside—the red and white and blue!

Your flag and my flag!
To every star and stripe
The drums beat as hearts beat
And fifers shrilly pipe!
Your flag and my flag—
A blessing in the sky;
Your hope and my hope—
It never hid a lie!

Home land and far land and half the world around,
Old Glory hears our glad salute and ripples to the sound!

—*Wilbur D. Nesbit*

THE FLAG GOES BY

Hats off!
Along the street there comes
A blare of bugles, a ruffle of drums,
A flash of color beneath the sky:
Hats off!
The flag is passing by!

Blue and crimson and white it shines,
Over the steel-tipped, ordered lines.
Hats off!
The colors before us fly;
But more than the flag is passing by:

Sea-fights and land-fights, grim and great,
Fought to make and to save the State:
Weary marches and sinking ships;
Cheers of victory on dying lips;

Days of plenty and years of peace;
March of a strong land's swift increase;
Equal justice, right, and law,
Stately honor and reverent awe;

Sign of a nation, great and strong
To ward her people from foreign wrong:
Pride and glory and honor—all
Live in the colors to stand or fall.

Hats off!
Along the street there comes
A blare of bugles, a ruffle of drums;
And loyal hearts are beating high:
Hats off!
The flag is passing by!

—Henry Holcomb Bennett

UNION AND LIBERTY

Flag of the heroes who left us their glory,
Borne thru their battle-fields' thunder and flame,
Blazoned in song and illumined in story,
Wave o'er us all who inherit their fame!
Up with our banner bright,
Sprinkled with starry light,
Spread its fair emblems from mountains to shore,

While thru the sounding sky
Loud rings the nation's cry,—
Union and Liberty! One evermore!

Light of our firmament, guide of our nation,
Pride of her children, and honored afar,
Let the wide beams of thy full constellation
Scatter each cloud that would darken a star!

Empire unsceptred! what foe shall assail thee,
Bearing the standard of Liberty's van?
Think not the God of thy fathers shall fail thee,
Striving with men for the birthright of man!

Yet if, by madness and treachery blighted,
Dawns the dark hour when the sword thou must draw,
Then with the arms of thy millions united,
Smite the bold traitors to Freedom and Law!

Lord of the Universe! shield us and guide us,
Trusting Thee always, thru shadow and sun!
Thou hast united us, who shall divide us!
Keep us, O keep us the *many in one!*
Up with our banner bright,
Sprinkled with starry light,
Spread its fair emblems from mountain to shore,
While thru the sounding sky
Loud rings the nation's cry,—
Union and Liberty! One evermore!

—*Oliver Wendell Holmes*

THE AMERICAN FLAG

I

When Freedom, from her mountain-height,
Unfurled her standard to the air,
She tore the azure robe of night,
And set the stars of glory there.
She mingled with its gorgeous dyes
The milky baldric of the skies,
And striped its pure, celestial white
With streakings of the morning light;
Then, from his mansion in the sun,
She called her eagle bearer down,
And gave into his mighty hand,
The symbol of her chosen land.

II

Majestic monarch of the cloud!
  Who rear'st aloft thy regal form,
To hear the tempest-trumpings loud,
And see the lightning lances driven,
  When strive the warriors of the storm,
And rolls the thunder-drum of heaven—
Child of the sun! to thee 'tis given
To guard the banner of the free,
To hover in the sulphur smoke,
To ward away the battle-stroke,
And bid its blendings shine afar,
Like rainbows on the cloud of war,
  The harbingers of victory!

III

Flag of the brave! thy folds shall fly,
The sign of hope and triumph high,
When speaks the signal-trumpet tone,
And the long line comes gleaming on:
Ere yet the life-blood, warm and wet,
Has dimmed the glistening bayonet,
Each soldier eye shall brightly turn
Where thy sky-born glories burn,
And, as his springing steps advance,
Catch war and vengeance from the glance;
And when the cannon-mouthings loud
Heave in wild wreaths the battle-shroud,
And gory sabres rise and fall,
Like shoots of flame on midnight's pall;
  Then shall thy meteor-glances glow,
And cowering foes shall sink beneath
  Each gallant arm that strikes below
That lovely messenger of death.

IV

Flag of the seas! on ocean wave
Thy stars shall glitter o'er the brave;
When death, careering on the gale,
Sweeps darkly round the bellied sail,
And frighted waves rush wildly back
Before the broadside's reeling rack,
Each dying wanderer of the sea
Shall look at once to heaven and thee,

And smile to see thy splendors fly
In triumph o'er his closing eye.

V

Flag of the free heart's hope and home,
  By angel hands to valor given;
Thy stars have lit the welkin dome,
  And all thy hues were born in heaven.
Forever float that standard sheet!
  Where breathes the foe but falls before us,
With Freedom's soil beneath our feet,
  And Freedom's banner streaming o'er us?

—*Joseph Rodman Drake*

THERE ARE MANY FLAGS

There are many flags in many lands;
  There are flags of every hue;
But there is no flag, however grand,
  Like our own Red, White, and Blue.

I know where the prettiest colors are;
  And I'm sure, if I only knew
How to get them here, I could make a flag
  Of glorious red, white, and blue.

I would cut a piece from the evening sky
  When the stars were shining thru,
And use it, just as it was on high,
  For my stars and field of blue.

Then I'd take a part of a fleecy cloud,
  And some red from a rainbow, bright,
And put them together, side by side,
  For my stripes of red and white.

We shall always love the Stars and Stripes,
  And we mean to be ever true
To this land of ours, and the dear old flag,
  The Red, the White, and the Blue.

Then hurrah for the flag! our country's flag!
  Its stripes, and white stars, too!
There is no flag in any land
  Like our own Red, White, and Blue!

—*Mary Howlister*

MAKERS OF THE FLAG

THIS MORNING as I passed into the Land Office, the Flag dropped me a most cordial salutation, and from its rippling folds I heard it say, "Good morning, Mr. Flag-maker."

"I beg your pardon, Old Glory," I said, "aren't you mistaken? I am not the President of the United States, nor a member of Congress, nor even a general in the army. I am only a government clerk."

"I greet you again, Mr. Flag-maker," replied the gay voice. "I know you well. You are the man who worked in the swelter of yesterday straightening out the tangle of that farmer's homestead in Idaho; or perhaps you found the mistake in that Indian contract in Oklahoma; or helped to clear that patent for the hopeful inventor in New York, or pushed the opening of that new ditch in Colorado, or made that mine in Illinois more safe, or brought relief to the old soldier in Wyoming. No matter; whichever one of these beneficent individuals you may happen to be, I give you greeting, Mr. Flag-maker."

I was about to pass on when the Flag stopped me with these words:

"Yesterday the President spoke a word that made happier the future of ten million peons in Mexico; but that act looms no larger on the Flag than the struggle which the boy in Georgia is making to win the Corn Club prize this summer.

"Yesterday the Congress spoke a word which will open the door of Alaska; but a mother in Michigan worked from sunrise until far into the night to give her boy an education. She, too, is making the Flag.

"Yesterday we made a new law to prevent financial panics, and yesterday, maybe, a schoolteacher in Ohio taught his first letters to a boy who will one day write a song that will give cheer to the millions of our race. We are all making the Flag."

"But," I said impatiently, "these people were only working!"

Then came a great shout from the Flag: "The work that we do is the making of the Flag. I am not the Flag; not at all. I am but its shadow.

"I am whatever you make me, nothing more.

"I am your belief in yourself, your dream of what a people may become.

"I live a changing life, a life of moods and passions, of heartbreaks and tired muscles.

"Sometimes I am strong with pride when men do an honest work, fitting the rails together truly. Sometimes I droop, for then purpose has gone from me, and cynically I play the coward. Sometimes, I am loud, garish, and full of that ego that blasts judgment.

"But always I am all that you hope to be and have the courage to try for.

"I am song and fear, struggle and panic and ennobling hope.

"I am the day's work of the weakest man and the largest dream of the most daring.

"I am the Constitution and the courts, statutes and the statute makers, soldier and dreadnaught, drayman and street sweep, cook, counselor, and clerk.

"I am the battle of yesterday and the mistake of tomorrow.

"I am the mystery of the men who do without knowing why.

"I am the clutch of an idea and the reasoned purpose of resolution.

"I am no more than what you believe me to be, and I am all that you believe I can be.

"I am what you make me, nothing more.

"I swing before your eyes as a bright gleam of color, a symbol of yourself, the pictured suggestion of that big thing which makes this nation.

"My stars and stripes are your dreams and your labors. They are bright with cheer, brilliant with courage, firm with faith because you have made them so out of your hearts. For you are the makers of the Flag, and it is well that you glory in the making."

[*From an address before the employes of the Department of the Interior by Secretary Franklin K. Lane on Flag Day, 1914*]

THE NAME OF OLD GLORY

Old Glory! say, who,
By the ships and the crew,
And the long, blended ranks of the gray and the blue—
Who gave you, Old Glory, the name that you bear
With such pride everywhere
As you cast yourself free to the rapturous air
And leap out full-length, as we're wanting you to?—
Who gave you that name, with the ring of the same,
And the honor and fame so becoming to you?—
Your stripes stroked in ripples of white and of red,
With your stars at the glittering best overhead—
By day or by night

Their delightfulest light
Laughing down from their little square heaven of blue.
Who gave you the name of Old Glory?—say, who—
Who gave you the name of Old Glory?

The old banner lifted, and faltering then,
In vague lisps and whispers fell silent again.

Old Glory: the story we're wanting to hear
Is what the plain facts of your christening were—
For your name—just to hear it,
Repeat it, and cheer it, 's a tang to the spirit
As salt as a tear;
And seeing you fly, and the boys marching by,
There's a shout in the throat and a blur in the eye
And an aching to live for you always—or die,
If, dying, we still keep you waving on high.
And so, by our love
For you, floating above,
And the scars of all wars and the sorrows thereof,
Who gave you the name of Old Glory, and why
Are we thrilled at the name of Old Glory?

Then the old banner leaped, like a sail in the blast,
And fluttered an audible answer at last.

And it spake, with a shake of the voice, and it said:—
"By the driven snow white and the living blood red
Of my bars, and their heaven of stars overhead—
By the symbol conjoined of them all, skyward cast,
As I float from the steeple, or flap at the mast,
Or droop o'er the sod where the long grasses nod—
My name is as old as the Glory of God.
So I came by the name of Old Glory."

—James Whitcomb Riley

OUR FLAG

I love to see the starry flag
That floats above my head.
I love to see its waving folds
With stripes of white and red.
"Be brave," say the red stripes,
"Be pure," say the white.
"Be true," say the bright stars,
"And stand for the right."

—Author Unknown

THIS LAND AND FLAG

WHAT is the love of country for which our flag stands? Maybe it begins with love of the land itself. It is the fog rolling in with the tide at Eastport, or thru the Golden Gate and among the towers of San Francisco. It is the sun coming up behind the White Mountains, over the Green, throwing a shining glory on Lake Champlain and above the Adirondacks. It is the storied Mississippi rolling swift and muddy past St. Louis, rolling past Cairo, pouring down past the levees of New Orleans. It is lazy noontide in the pines of Carolina, it is a sea of wheat rippling in Western Kansas, it is the San Francisco peaks far north across the glowing nakedness of Arizona, it is the Grand Canyon and a little stream coming down out of a New England ridge, in which are trout.

It is men at work. It is the storm-tossed fishermen coming into Gloucester and Provincetown and Astoria. It is the farmer riding his great machine in the dust of harvest, the dairyman going to the barn before sunrise, the lineman mending the broken wire, the miner drilling for the blast. It is the servants of fire in the murky splendor of Pittsburgh, between the Allegheny and the Monongahela, the trucks rumbling thru the night, the locomotive engineer bringing the train in on time, the pilot in the clouds, the riveter running along the beam a hundred feet in air. It is the clerk in the office, the housewife doing the dishes and sending the children off to school. It is the teacher, doctor, and parson tending and helping, body and soul, for small reward.

It is small things remembered, the little corners of the land, the houses, the people that each one loves. We love our country because there was a little tree on a hill, and grass thereon, and a sweet valley below; because the hurdy-gurdy man came along on a sunny morning in a city street; because a beach or a farm or a lane or a house that might not seem much to others were once, for each of us, made magic. It is voices that are remembered only, no longer heard. It is parents, friends, the lazy chat of street and store and office, and the ease of mind that makes life tranquil. It is summer and winter, rain and sun and storm. These are flesh of our flesh, bone of our bone, blood of our blood, a lasting part of what we are, each of us and all of us together.

It is stories told. It is the Pilgrims dying in their first dreadful winter. It is the Minute Man standing his ground at Concord Bridge, and dying there. It is the army in rags, sick, freezing, starving at Valley Forge. It is the wagons and the men on foot going westward over Cumberland Gap, floating down the great rivers, rolling over the great plains. It is the settler hacking fiercely at the primeval forest on his new, his own lands. It is Thoreau at Walden Pond, Lincoln at Cooper Union, and Lee riding home from Appomattox. It is corruption and disgrace, answered always by men who would not let the flag lie in the dust, who have stood up in every generation to fight for the old ideals and the old rights, at risk of ruin or of life itself.

It is a great multitude of people on pilgrimage, common and ordinary people, charged with the usual human failings, yet filled with such a hope as never caught the imaginations and the hearts of any nation on earth before. The hope of liberty. The hope of justice. The hope of a land in which a man can stand straight, without fear, without rancor.

The land and the people and the flag—the land a continent, the people of every race, the flag a symbol of what humanity may aspire to when the wars are over and the barriers are down; to these each generation must be dedicated and consecrated anew, to defend with life itself, if need be, but, above all, in friendliness, in hope, in courage, to live for.—*The New York Times*

WE AMERICANS are natives of all the world, gathered here under one flag in the name of liberty. There is no race or creed or culture that has a monopoly on Americanism—except the human race, the creed of friendship and good will, and the culture of free speech and free opportunity.—*David Cushman Coyle*

A THOUGHTFUL MIND, when it sees a nation's flag, sees not the flag only, but the nation itself; and . . . he reads chiefly in the flag the government, the principles, the truths, the history which belongs to the nation that set it forth.—*Henry Ward Beecher*

THE UNITED STATES FLAG CODE

On June 14, 1777, a year after the signing of the Declaration of Independence, the Continental Congress in Philadelphia adopted this resolution: "That the flag of the United States be thirteen stripes, alternate red and white; that the union be thirteen stars, white in a blue field representing a new constellation." In 1916 President Woodrow Wilson proclaimed June 14 as Flag Day, which is annually observed thruout America by celebrations in the schools and public observances. The stripes of the flag represent the thirteen original states, which had a population of some 3 million people. In the stars is recorded the growth of the American nation. With the addition in 1959 of Alaska and Hawaii, the stars in the flag reached fifty. The fifty-star flag became official July 4, 1960. Flags in use before that day may be utilized until unserviceable.

In response to the need for uniformity in the use of the Flag, a National Flag Conference was held in Washington, D. C., on June 14, 1923, to adopt a code for displaying the Flag. A year later the code was revised by the Second National Flag Conference. On June 22, 1942, Congress codified and emphasized existing rules and customs pertaining to the display and use of the Flag—in a joint resolution, Public Law 623. On December 22, 1942, this was amended by Public Law 829.

Laws in most states require local schoolboards to use school funds to purchase flags and flagstaffs. Promotion of respect for the Flag and knowledge about it is required in most states, usually thru flag exercises, programs, or instruction. However, the U. S. Supreme Court on June 14, 1943, ruled [West Virginia State Board of Education v. Barnette et. al.] that state boards of education or local schoolboards cannot make the flag salute compulsory.

How To Display the Flag

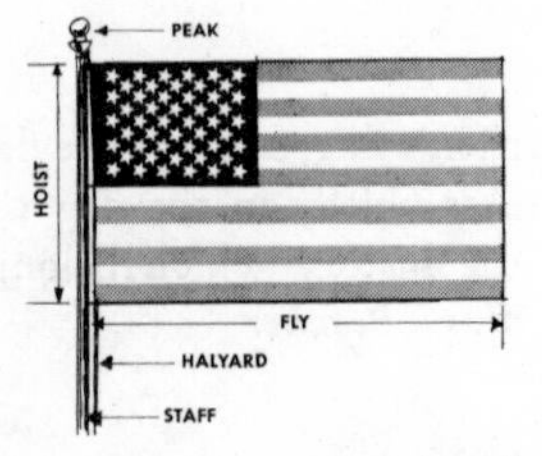

THE FLAG OF THE UNITED STATES OF AMERICA HAS 13 horizontal stripes —7 red and 6 white, alternating—and a union of white stars of 5 points on a blue field in the upper quarter next the staff and extending to the lower edge of the fourth red stripe from the top. The union or canton now contains fifty stars arranged in 9 horizontal rows, five of which have 6 stars each and 4 of which have 5 stars. Each star has one point upward. The proportions of the Flag as prescribed by Executive Order of President Eisenhower, August 21, 1959, are:

Hoist [width] of Flag	1.
Fly [length] of Flag	1.9
Hoist [width] of union	7/13
Fly [length] of union	0.76
Width of each stripe	1/13
Diameter of each star [i.e. of circle in which it is drawn]	.0616

It is the custom to display the flag only from sunrise to sunset on buildings and stationary flagstaffs in the open, but it may be displayed at night on special occasions for patriotic effect. Weather permitting, it should be displayed every day, especially national and state holidays and historic occasions; daily on or near administration building of every public institution; in or near every polling place on election days; during school days in or near every schoolhouse. Hoist briskly; lower ceremoniously.

When carried in a procession with another flag or flags, the Flag of the United States of America should be either on the marching right [the Flag's own right, which is the observer's left], or when there is a line of other flags, the Flag may be in front of the center of that line.

WHEN DISPLAYED WITH ANOTHER FLAG AGAINST A WALL FROM CROSSED STAFFS, the Flag of the United States of America should be on the right, the Flag's own right, and its staff should be in front of the staff of the other flag.

WHEN A NUMBER OF FLAGS ARE GROUPED AND DISPLAYED FROM STAFFS, the Flag of the United States of America should be at the center or at the highest point of the group.

WHEN FLAGS OF STATES OR CITIES OR PENNANTS OF SOCIETIES are flown on the same halyard with the Flag of the United States of America, the latter should always be at the peak. When flown from adjacent staffs, the Flag should be on the right of the line [the observer's left]. The Flag should be hoisted first, lowered last. No flag should be placed above or to right of the Flag, except in church services conducted by naval chaplains at sea, when church pennant may be flown above.

WHEN FLAGS OF TWO OR MORE NATIONS ARE DISPLAYED, they should be flown from separate staffs of the same height, and the flags should be of approximately equal size. International usage forbids the display of the flag of one nation above that of another nation in time of peace.

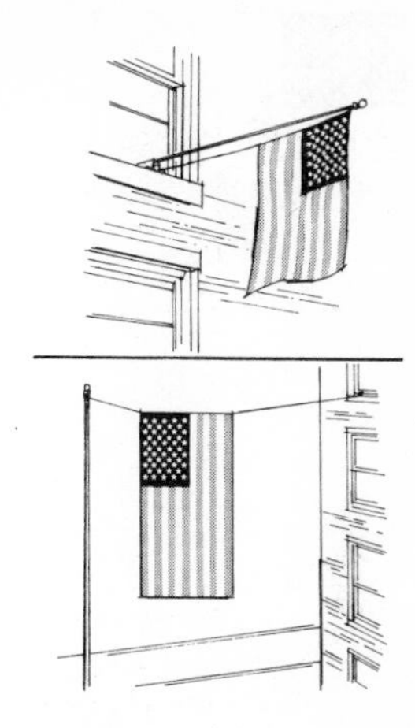

When the flag is displayed from a staff projecting horizontally or at an angle from a window-sill, balcony, or the front of a building, the union of the Flag should go clear to the peak of the staff unless the Flag is at half-mast. When suspended over a sidewalk from a rope, extending from a house to a pole at the edge of the sidewalk, the Flag should be hoisted out from the building, union first.

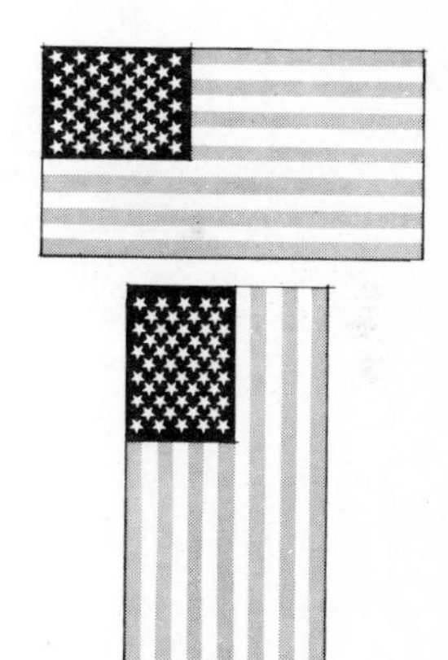

When the flag is displayed in a manner other than by being flown from a staff, it should be displayed flat, whether indoors or out, or so suspended that its folds fall as free as tho the flag were staffed. The Flag should never be used as drapery of any sort whatsoever. When rosettes or drapings of blue, white, and red, are desired, bunting should be used, with the blue above, the white in the middle, and the red below.

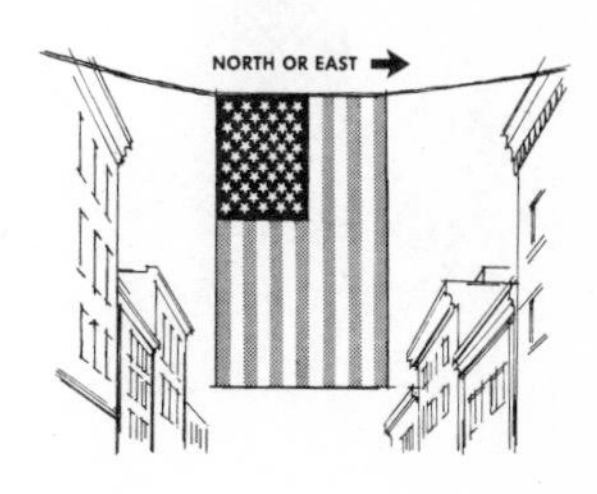

When displayed over the middle of the street, as between buildings, the Flag of the United States of America should be suspended vertically with the union to the north in an east and west street or to the east in a north and south street.

When used on a speaker's platform, the Flag, if displayed flat, should be displayed above and behind the speaker.

When displayed from a staff in a church or public auditorium, if it is displayed in the chancel of a church or on the speaker's platform in a public auditorium, the Flag should occupy the position of honor and be placed at the clergyman's or speaker's right as he faces the congregation or audience. Any other flag so displayed in the chancel or on the platform should be placed at the clergyman's or speaker's left as he faces the congregation or audience. But when the Flag is displayed from a staff in a church or public auditorium elsewhere than in the chancel or on the platform it shall be placed in the position of honor at the right of the congregation or audience as they face the chancel or platform. Any other flag so displayed should be placed on the left of the congregation or audience as they face the chancel or platform.

When used in connection with the unveiling of a statue or monument, the Flag forms a distinctive feature of the ceremony. The Flag itself should never be used as covering for the statue.

FLAGS FLOWN FROM FIXED STAFFS are placed at half-staff to indicate mourning. When flown at half-staff, the Flag should be hoisted to the peak for an instant and then lowered to the half-staff position; but before lowering the Flag for the day, it is raised again to the peak. By half-staff or half-mast is meant lowering the Flag to one-half the distance between top and bottom of the staff. On Memorial Day, May 30, the Flag is displayed at half-staff from sunrise until noon and at full-staff from noon until sunset.

WHEN THE FLAG IS DISPLAYED on a small staff, as when carried in a parade, mourning is indicated by attaching two streamers of black crepe to the spearhead, allowing the streamers to fall naturally. Crepe is used on the flagstaff only by order of the President of the United States.

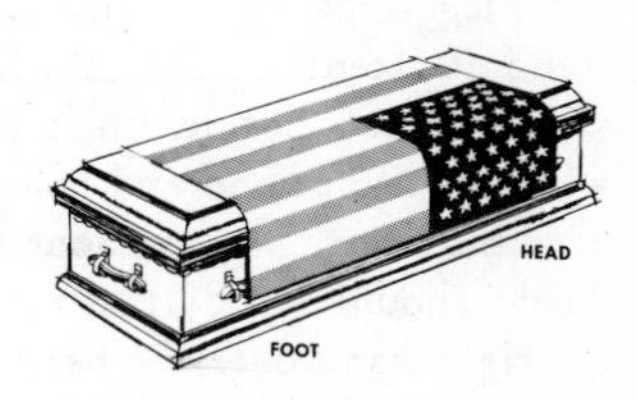

WHEN USED TO COVER A CASKET, the Flag should be placed so that the union is at the head and over the left shoulder. The Flag should not be lowered into the grave or allowed to touch the ground.

Cautions in Displaying the Flag

[1] Do not display or store the Flag in such manner that it will be soiled or damaged. When no longer in condition for use, the Flag should be destroyed in a dignified way, preferably by burning.

[2] Do not let the Flag touch anything beneath it, such as ground, floor, water.

[3] Do not display the Flag on a float in a parade except from a staff.

[4] Do not drape the Flag over the hood, top, sides, or back of a vehicle, railroad train, or boat. When displayed on a motor car, the flagstaff should be affixed firmly to chassis, or clamped to radiator cap.

[5] Do not use the Flag as a portion of a costume or athletic uniform. Do not embroider it on cushions, handkerchiefs, or put on paper napkins, boxes, or the like.

[6] Do not use the Flag as receptacle for receiving, holding, or delivering anything.

[7] Do not put any lettering, insignia, or design upon the Flag.

[8] Never carry the flag flat or horizontally, but always aloft and free.

[9] Do not use Flag for covering ceiling.

[10] Never dip the Flag to any person or thing; regimental colors, state flags, and organizations or institutional flags are to be dipped as a mark of honor.

[11] Do not use the Flag in any form of advertising or fasten an advertising sign to a pole from which the Flag is flown.

[12] Do not display with union down save as a signal of dire distress.

Saluting the Flag

During the ceremony of hoisting or lowering the Flag, or when the Flag is passing in parade or review, all present face the Flag, stand at attention, and salute. Those in uniform render the military salute. When not in uniform, men should remove the head-dress with the right hand and hold it at the left shoulder, the hand being over the heart. Men without hats should salute in the same manner. Aliens should stand at attention. Women should salute by placing the right hand over the heart. The salute to the Flag in the moving column should be rendered at the moment the Flag passes.

When "The Star-Spangled Banner"—adopted by Congress in 1931 as the national anthem—is played and no flag is displayed, all present should stand and face toward the music. Those in uniform salute at the first note of the anthem, retaining this position until the last note. All others stand at attention, men removing their head-dress. When the Flag is displayed, all face the Flag and salute. Words of the national anthem are on page 442 of this HANDBOOK.

PART VIII—SECTION 8

Songs of America

AMERICA

My country, 'tis of thee,
Sweet land of liberty,
Of thee I sing.
Land where my fathers died!
Land of the Pilgrim's pride!
From every mountain side,
Let freedom ring!

My native country, thee,
Land of the noble free,
Thy name I love.
I love thy rocks and rills,
Thy woods and templed hills;
My heart with rapture thrills
Like that above.

Let music swell the breeze,
And ring from all the trees
Sweet freedom's song.
Let mortal tongues awake;
Let all that breathe partake;
Let rocks their silence break,
The sound prolong.

Our fathers' God, to Thee,
Author of liberty,
To Thee we sing.
Long may our land be bright
With freedom's holy light;
Protect us by Thy might,
Great God, our King!

—*Samuel Francis Smith*

THE STAR-SPANGLED BANNER

Oh, say! can you see by the dawn's early light,
What so proudly we hailed at the twilight's last gleaming,
Whose broad stripes and bright stars, thru the perilous fight,
O'er the ramparts we watched were so gallantly streaming?
And the rocket's red glare, the bombs bursting in air,
Gave proof thru the night that our flag was still there.
Oh, say, does that Star-Spangled Banner yet wave
O'er the land of the free and the home of the brave?

On the shore, dimly seen thru the mists of the deep,
Where the foe's haughty host in dread silence reposes,
What is that which the breeze, o'er the towering steep,
As it fitfully blows, half conceals, half discloses?
Now it catches the gleam of the morning's first beam,
In full glory reflected now shines on the stream.
'Tis the Star-Spangled Banner, oh, long may it wave
O'er the land of the free and the home of the brave!

Oh, thus be it ever when free men shall stand
Between their loved homes and the war's desolation!
Blest with vict'ry and peace, may the heav'n-rescued land
Praise the Pow'r that hath made and preserved us a nation!
Then conquer we must, when our cause it is just,
And this be our motto: "In God is our Trust."
And the Star-Spangled Banner in triumph shall wave
O'er the land of the free and the home of the brave.

—*Francis Scott Key*

What was originally the third stanza, now rarely used, is as follows:

And where is that band who so vauntingly swore
That the havoc of war and the battle's confusion
A home and a country should leave us no more?
Their blood has washed out their foul footstep's pollution.
No refuge could save the hireling and slave
From the terror of flight, or the gloom of the grave;
And the Star-Spangled Banner in triumph doth wave
O'er the land of the free, and the home of the brave.

AMERICA THE BEAUTIFUL

O beautiful for spacious skies,
  For amber waves of grain,
For purple mountain majesties
  Above the fruited plain.
America! America!
  God shed his grace on thee,
And crown thy good with brotherhood,
  From sea to shining sea!

O beautiful for pilgrim feet,
  Whose stern impassioned stress
A thoroughfare for freedom beat
  Across the wilderness.
America! America!
  God mend thine every flaw,
Confirm thy soul in self-control,
  Thy liberty in law!

O beautiful for heroes proved
  In liberating strife,
Who more than self their country loved,
  And mercy more than life.
America! America!
  May God thy gold refine
Till all success be nobleness,
  And every gain divine!

O beautiful for patriot dream
  That sees beyond the years
Thine alabaster cities gleam
  Undimmed by human tears.
America! America!
  God shed his grace on thee,
And crown thy good with brotherhood,
From sea to shining sea!

—*Katharine Lee Bates*

Katharine Lee Bates, Wellesley College professor, was so inspired by her first trip to Pikes Peak in 1893 that she said, "As I was looking out over the sea-like expanse of fertile country spreading away so far under those ample skies, the opening lines of the hymn floated into my mind."

COLUMBIA, THE GEM OF THE OCEAN

O Columbia, the gem of the ocean,
  The home of the brave and the free,
The shrine of each patriot's devotion,
  A world offers homage to thee.
Thy mandates make heroes assemble,
  When Liberty's form stands in view;
Thy banners make tyranny tremble,
  When borne by the red, white, and blue!
When borne by the red, white, and blue!
  When borne by the red, white, and blue!
Thy banners make tyranny tremble,
  When borne by the red, white, and blue!

When war wing'd its wide desolation,
  And threatened the land to deform,
The ark then of freedom's foundation,
  Columbia rode safe thru the storm:
With her garlands of vict'ry around her,
  When so proudly she bore her brave crew;
With her flag proudly floating before her,
  The boast of the red, white, and blue!
The boast of the red, white, and blue!
  The boast of the red, white, and blue!
With her flag proudly floating before her,
  The boast of the red, white, and blue!

The Star-Spangled Banner bring hither,
  O'er Columbia's true sons let it wave;
May the wreaths they have won never wither,
  Nor its stars cease to shine on the brave:
May thy service, united ne'er sever,
  But hold to their colors so true;
The army and navy forever,
  Three cheers for the red, white, and blue!
Three cheers for the red, white, and blue!
  Three cheers for the red, white, and blue!
The army and navy forever,
  Three cheers for the red, white, and blue!

—*Thomas à Becket*

BATTLE-HYMN OF THE REPUBLIC

Mine eyes have seen the glory of the coming of the Lord;
He is trampling out the vintage where the grapes of wrath are stored;
He hath loosed the fateful lightning of His terrible swift sword;
His truth is marching on.

I have seen Him in the watch-fires of a hundred circling camps;
They have builded Him an altar in the evening dews and damps;
I can read his righteous sentence by the dim and flaring lamps;
His day is marching on.

I have read His fiery gospel, writ in burnished rows of steel:
"As ye deal with my contemners, so with you my grace shall deal!"
Let the Hero, born of woman, crush the serpent with His heel,
Since God is marching on.

He has sounded forth the trumpet that shall never call retreat;
He is sifting out the hearts of men before His judgment-seat:
Oh, be swift, my soul, to answer Him! be jubilant, my feet!
Our God is marching on.

In the beauty of the lilies Christ was born across the sea,
With a glory in His bosom that transfigures you and me;
As He died to make men holy, let us die to make men free,
While God is marching on.

—Julia Ward Howe

GOD BLESS AMERICA

God bless America,
Land that I love,
Stand beside her and guide her
Thru the night with a light from above;
From the mountains, to the prairies,
To the oceans white with foam,
God bless America
My home sweet home.

—Irving Berlin

DIXIE

I wish I was in de land ob cotton,
Old times dar am not forgotten,
Look away, look away, look away, Dixie Land!
In Dixie Land whar I was born in,
Early on one frosty mornin',
Look away! Look away! Look away, Dixie Land!

Den I wish I was in Dixie, Hoo-ray! Hoo-ray!
In Dixie's Land I'll take my stand to lib and die in Dixie;
Away, away, away down south in Dixie,
Away, away, away down south in Dixie!

Old Missus marry Will-de-weaber,
Willium was a gay deceaber;
Look away! etc.
But when he put his arm around 'er
He smiled as fierce as a forty-pounder,
Look away! etc.

His face was sharp as a butcher's cleaber,
But dat did not seem to greab 'er;
Look away! etc.
Old Missus acted the foolish part,
And died for a man dat broke her heart,
Look away! etc.

Now here's a health to the next old Missus,
And all de gals dat want to kiss us;
Look away! etc.
But if you want to drive 'way sorrow,
Come and hear dis song tomorrow,
Look away! etc.

Dar's buckwheat cakes an' Ingen batter,
Makes you fat or a little fatter;
Look away! etc.
Den hoe it down and scratch your grabble,
To Dixie Land I'm bound to trabble,
Look away! etc.

—*Daniel Decatur Emmett*

MY OLD KENTUCKY HOME

The sun shines bright in the old Kentucky home;
'Tis summer, the darkies are gay;
The corn-top's ripe, and the meadow's in the bloom,
While the birds make music all the day.
The young folks roll on the little cabin floor,
All merry, all happy and bright;
By'n by hard times comes a-knocking at the door—
Then my old Kentucky home, good-night!

Weep no more, my lady,
O, weep no more today!
We will sing one song for the old Kentucky home,
For the Old Kentucky home, far away.

They hunt no more for the possum and the coon,
On the meadow, the hill, and the shore;
They sing no more by the glimmer of the moon,
On the bench by the old cabin door.
The day goes by like a shadow o'er the heart,
With sorrow, where all was delight;
The time has come when the darkies have to part—
Then my old Kentucky home, good-night!

The head must bow, and the back will have to bend,
Wherever the darkey may go;
A few more days and the troubles all will end,
In the field where the sugar-canes grow.
A few more days for to tote the weary load—
No matter, 'twill never be light;
A few more days till we totter on the road—
Then my old Kentucky home, good-night!

Weep no more, my lady,
O, weep no more today!
We will sing one song for the old Kentucky home,
For the old Kentucky home, far away.

—*Stephen Collins Foster*

HOME, SWEET HOME!

Mid pleasures and palaces tho we may roam,
Be it ever so humble, there's no place like home;
A charm from the sky seems to hallow us there,
Which, seek thru the world, is ne'er met with elsewhere.
Home, Home! sweet, sweet Home!
There's no place like Home! there's no place like Home!

How sweet 'tis to sit 'neath a fond father's smile,
And the cares of a mother to soothe and beguile!
Let others delight mid new pleasures to roam,
But give me, oh, give me, the pleasures of home!
Home, Home! sweet, sweet Home!
There's no place like Home! there's no place like Home!

To thee I'll return, overburdened with care;
The heart's dearest solace will smile on me there;
No more from that cottage again will I roam;
Be it ever so humble, there's no place like home.
Home, Home! sweet, sweet Home!
There's no place like Home! there's no place like Home!

—*John Howard Payne*

CONCORD HYMN

By the rude bridge that arched the flood,
Their flag to April's breeze unfurled,
Here once the embattled farmers stood,
And fired the shot heard round the world.

The foe long since in silence slept;
Alike the conqueror silent sleeps;
And Time the ruined bridge has swept
Down the dark stream which seaward creeps.

On this green bank, by this soft stream,
We set today a votive stone;
That memory may their deed redeem,
When, like our sires, our sons are gone.

Spirit, that made those heroes dare
To die, and leave their children free,
Bid Time and Nature gently spare
The shaft we raise to them and thee.

—*Ralph Waldo Emerson*

[*Sung at the completion of the Battle Monument, April 19, 1836*]

PART VIII—SECTION 9

Our Faith in Education

THE WHOLE PEOPLE must take upon themselves the education of the whole people and be willing to bear the expense of it.—*John Adams*

THE FUTURE of the world is left to highly educated races who alone can handle the scientific apparatus necessary for preeminence in peace or survival in war. I hope our education will become broader and more liberal.—*Winston Churchill*

WHAT THE BEST and wisest parent wants for his own child, that must the community want for all its children.—*John Dewey*

THE GOOD EDUCATION of youth has been esteemed by wise men in all ages as the surest foundation of the happiness both of private families and of commonwealths.—*Benjamin Franklin*

WHOM, then, do I call educated? First, those who control circumstances instead of being mastered by them, those who meet all occasions manfully and act in accordance with intelligent thinking, those who are honorable in all dealings, who treat good naturedly persons and things that are disagreeable, and furthermore, those who hold their pleasures under control and are not overcome by misfortune, finally those who are not spoiled by success.—*Isocrates*

IF A NATION expects to be ignorant and free in a state of civilization, it expects what never was and never will be.—*Thomas Jefferson*

IN OUR COUNTRY, and in our times, no man is worthy the honored name of statesman, who does not include the highest practicable education of the people in all his plans of administration.—*Horace Mann*

TWO TEMPLES

A builder builded a temple,
He wrought it with grace and skill;
Pillars and groins and arches
All fashioned to work his will.
Men said as they saw its beauty,
"It shall never know decay.
Great is thy skill, O builder:
Thy fame shall endure for aye."

A mother [teacher] builded a temple
With loving and infinite care,
Planning each arch with patience,
Laying each stone with prayer.
None praised her unceasing efforts
None knew of her wondrous plan,
For the temple the mother [teacher] builded
Was unseen by the eyes of man.

Gone is the builder's temple,
Crumbled into the dust;
Low lies each stately pillar,
Food for consuming rust.
But the temple the mother [teacher] builded
Will last while the ages roll,
For that beautiful unseen temple
Is a child's immortal soul.

—*Hattie Vose Hall*

I VIEW education as the most important subject we as a people can be engaged in.—*Abraham Lincoln*

A POPULAR GOVERNMENT without popular information or the means of acquiring it is but the prolog to a farce or a tragedy, or perhaps both.—*James Madison*

RELIGION, morality and knowledge being necessary to good government and the happiness of mankind, schools and the means of education shall forever be encouraged.—From the *Ordinance of 1787*

WE HAVE FAITH in education as the foundation of democratic government.—*Franklin Delano Roosevelt*

WHAT OUR schools do may prove in the long run to be more decisive than any other factor in preserving the form of government we cherish.—*Franklin Delano Roosevelt*

I SING the praise of the unknown teacher. Famous educators plan new systems of pedagogy, but it is the unknown teacher who delivers and guides the young. He lives in obscurity and contends with hardship. He keeps the watch along the borders of darkness and makes the attack on the trenches of ignorance and folly. Patient in his daily duty he strives to conquer the evil powers which are the enemies of youth. He awakens sleeping spirits. He quickens the indolent, encourages the eager, and steadies the unstable. He communicates his own joy in learning and shares with boys and girls the best treasures of his mind. He lights many candles which, in later years, will shine back to cheer him. This is his reward. Knowledge may be gained from books; but the love of knowledge is transmitted only by personal contact. No one has deserved better of the republic than the unknown teacher.—*Henry van Dyke*

IF EVER THERE was a cause, if ever there can be a cause, worthy to be upheld by all the toil or sacrifice that the human heart can endure, it is the cause of education.—*Horace Mann*

LET US SET the child in our midst as our greatest wealth and our most challenging responsibility. Let us exalt him above industry, above business, above politics, above all the petty and selfish things that weaken and destroy a people. Let us know that the race moves forward thru its children and, by the grace of Almighty God, setting our faces toward the morning, dedicate ourselves anew to the welfare of childhood.—*Joy Elmer Morgan*

WITHOUT POPULAR EDUCATION no government which rests on popular action can long endure; the people must be schooled in the knowledge and if possible in the virtues upon which the maintenance and success of free institutions depend.—*Woodrow Wilson*

THE NEXT TIME you pass a school pause a moment to think what that school means to humanity. Recall the long dark centuries when the masses were kept in ignorance—when greed and oppression ruled the world with an iron hand. From the very beginning of man's struggle for knowledge, selfrespect, and the recognition of his inalienable rights, the school has been his greatest ally. We refer to the school as "common" because it belongs to us all; it is ourselves working together in the education of our children. But it is a most uncommon institution. It is relatively new. It is democracy's greatest gift to civilization. Thruout the world, among upward struggling peoples, wherever parents share in the aspirations of their children, the American common school is being copied. Let us cherish and improve our schools.—*Joy Elmer Morgan*

PROMOTE, then, as an object of primary importance, institutions for the general diffusion of knowledge. In proportion as the structure of a government gives force to public opinion, it is essential that public opinion should be enlightened.—*George Washington*

CIVILIZATION is a race between education and catastrophe.—*H. G. Wells*

THE TEACHER, whether mother, priest, or schoolmaster, is the real maker of history.—*H. G. Wells*

OUR CIVILIZATION cannot survive materially unless it be redeemed spiritually.—*Woodrow Wilson*

THE COMMON SCHOOL is the greatest discovery ever made by man. In two grand, characteristic attributes, it is supereminent over all others: first, in its universality—for it is capacious enough to receive and cherish in its parental bosom every child that comes into the world; and second, in the timeliness of the aid it proffers—its early, seasonable supplies of counsel and guidance making security antedate danger. Other social organizations are curative and remedial; this is a preventive and an antidote; they come to heal diseases and wounds; this, to make the physical and moral frame invulnerable to them. Let the common school be expanded to its capabilities, let it be worked with the efficiency of which it is susceptible, and nine-tenths of the crimes in the penal code would become obsolete; the long catalog of human ills would be abridged; property, life, and character held by a stronger tenure; all rational hopes respecting the future brightened.—*Horace Mann*

A TRIBUTE TO THE TEACHER

The teacher is a *prophet;* He lays the foundations of tomorrow.

The teacher is an *artist;* He works with the precious clay of unfolding personality.

The teacher is a *friend;* His heart responds to the faith and devotion of his students.

The teacher is a *citizen;* He is selected and licensed for the improvement of society.

The teacher is an *interpreter;* Out of his maturer and wider life he seeks to guide the young.

The teacher is a *builder;* He works with the higher and finer values of civilization.

The teacher is a *culture-bearer;* He leads the way toward worthier tastes, saner attitudes, more gracious manners, higher intelligence.

The teacher is a *planner;* He sees the young lives before him as a part of a great system which shall grow stronger in the light of truth.

The teacher is a *pioneer;* He is always attempting the impossible and winning out.

The teacher is a *reformer;* He seeks to remove the handicaps that weaken and destroy life.

The teacher is a *believer;* He has abiding faith in the improvability of the race.

—*Joy Elmer Morgan*

THE HOPE OF TOMORROW

Somewhere in a schoolroom today under the care of an unknown teacher is a child who in his own time, grown to maturity, will lead the world away from war and toward peace. The affection planted in that child's life by wise guidance; the sense of right values with which he is constantly surrounded; the integrity and initiative that are fostered in his unfolding life will come to fruition in a mighty service to the human race. It is a wise providence that no one can tell which of the two million babies born in our country each year is to be this savior of tomorrow. We are done with king-children and their pampered training to maintain a class system. We want the children of the people, of all the people—rich and poor of every race and creed—to have their chance. And when through honest growth, proved merit, and wise leadership the pilots of tomorrow take their places at the helm, we want them to be surrounded and supported by their fellows likewise schooled in the simple and abiding principles of democracy. With this purpose and in this faith, the teachers of America carry on. This faith was good enough for the founding fathers who launched this ship of state in even more troubled seas than we now face. This faith has been good enough for the teachers and prophets of all ages who have understood the power of human aspiration and growth. It is the faith of Jesus—the Golden Rule and the brotherhood of man. It is the faith that for 1900 years has held aloft through good times and bad the torch of eternal truth. As we come this year to the Christmas season, let us renew our faith in this destiny of the individual human soul lifted by true teaching through the leavening power of God's grace to nobility and wisdom. This faith of the teacher—your faith and mine as we look into the eager faces of youth—is the hope of tomorrow, a hope that cannot fail. It is bigger than all the fears and partisanships of our time. Let us renew and deepen our faith as we celebrate Christmas.

—*Joy Elmer Morgan*

A TEACHER'S PRAYER

O Lord of all learners and all teachers:

Help us to reexamine our loyalties by the light of thy teaching and to square them with eternal truth.

Help us to dedicate ourselves anew to the children; for of such is the kingdom of heaven.

Help us to dedicate ourselves anew to the free public school; for it is the bulwark of our personal rights, our political liberties, and our representative institutions.

Help us to dedicate ourselves anew to our chosen goal of a united profession of teachers; for in it we shall find our larger selfhood.

Help us to dedicate ourselves anew to the democratic ideals of our country; for it is the last best hope of earth.

Help us to dedicate ourselves anew to the universal brotherhood of humanity; for we are all members one of another.

Grant, O Lord, that we may hold high the torch of truth, goodness, and beauty, that we may be worthy the high office of teacher.

For thine is the kingdom and the power and glory forever.

—*Joy Elmer Morgan*

PART VIII—SECTION 10

The World of Nature

MEMORY

My mind lets go a thousand things,
Like dates of wars and deaths of kings,
And yet recalls the very hour—
'Twas noon by yonder village tower,
And on the last blue noon in May—
The wind came briskly up this way,
Crisping the brook beside the road;
Then, pausing here, set down its load
Of pine-scents, and shook listlessly
Two petals from that wild-rose tree.

—*Thomas Bailey Aldrich*

WHAT DO WE PLANT

What do we plant when we plant the tree?
We plant the ship, which will cross the sea.
We plant the mast to carry the sails;
We plant the planks to withstand the gales—
The keel, the keelson, the beam, the knee;
We plant the ship when we plant the tree.

What do we plant when we plant the tree?
We plant the houses for you and me.
We plant the rafters, the shingles, the floors,
We plant the studding, the lath, the doors,
The beams and siding, all parts that be;
We plant the house when we plant the tree.

What do we plant when we plant the tree?
A thousand things that we daily see;
We plant the spire that out-towers the crag,
We plant the staff for our country's flag,
We plant the shade, from the hot sun free;
We plant all of these when we plant the tree.

—*Henry Abbey*

FIRST SNOW

Snow makes whiteness where it falls,
The bushes look like popcorn balls,
And places where I always play,
Look like somewhere else today.

—*Marie Louise Allen*

PIPPA'S SONG

The year's at the spring;
The day's at the morn;
Morning's at seven;
The hillside's dew-pearled;
The lark's on the wing;
The snail's on the thorn;
God's in His Heaven—
All's right with the world!

—*Robert Browning*

THE SEA

There is a pleasure in the pathless woods,
There is a rapture on the lonely shore,
There is society where none intrudes
By the deep Sea, and music in its roar;
I love not Man the less, but Nature more,
From these our interviews, in which I steal
From all I may be, or have been before,
To mingle with the Universe, and feel
What I can ne'er express, yet can not all conceal.

Roll on, thou deep and dark blue Ocean, roll!
Ten thousand fleets sweep over thee in vain;
Man marks the earth with ruin, his control
Stops with the shore; upon the watery plain
The wrecks are all thy deed, nor doth remain
A shadow of man's ravage, save his own,
When, for a moment, like a drop of rain,
He sinks into thy depths with bubbling groan,
Without a grave, unknelled, uncoffined, and unknown.

—From *George Gordon Byron's*
"Childe Harold's Pilgrimage"

TO A WATERFOWL

Whither, midst falling dew,
While glow the heavens with the last steps of day,
Far, thru their rosy depths, dost thou pursue
Thy solitary way?

Vainly the fowler's eye
Might mark thy distant flight to do thee wrong,
As, darkly painted on the crimson sky,
Thy figure floats along.

Seek'st thou the plashy brink
Of weedy lake, or marge of river wide,
Or where the rocking billows rise and sink
On the chafed ocean-side?

There is a Power whose care
Teaches thy way along that pathless coast,—
The desert and illimitable air,—
Lone wandering, but not lost.

All day thy wings have fanned
At that far height, the cold, thin atmosphere,
Yet stoop not, weary, to the welcome land,
Tho the dark night is near.

And soon that toil shall end;
Soon shalt thou find a summer home, and rest,
And scream among thy fellows; reeds shall bend,
Soon, o'er thy sheltered nest.

Thou'rt gone, the abyss of heaven
Hath swallowed up thy form; yet, on my heart
Deeply hath sunk the lesson thou hast given,
And shall not soon depart.

He who, from zone to zone,
Guides thru the boundless sky thy certain flight,
In the long way that I must tread alone,
Will lead my steps aright.

—*William Cullen Bryant*

Wild flowers and birds—
Enjoy, but do not destroy.

CLOUDS

Over the hill the clouds race by
Playing tag in a blue, blue sky;
Some are fat and some are thin
And one old cloud has a double-chin;

One is a girl with up-turned nose
And one wears slippers with pointed toes;
There's a puppy-dog too with a bumpety tail
And a farmer boy with his milking pail.

Sometimes they jumble all in a mass
And get tangled up with others that pass
As over the hill they go racing by
Playing tag in a blue, blue sky.

—*Helen Wing*

PUSSY WILLOWS

I have some dainty pussies here
All dressed in soft gray fur,
But you might listen all day long
And not once hear them purr.

Nor do they run and frisk about,—
These pretty living things,
But closely round a slender twig
Each tiny pussy clings.

All thru the winter's storms and cold,
These furry babies swung,
In cradle beds of shining brown,
On willow branches hung.

But by and by the sunbeams warm
Peeped into each small bed,
And said: "Come, Pussies, waken now,
For winter days are fled."

So bravely come the pussies forth,
Tho still the cold wind blows,
And up and down the long, brown stems
They cling in shining rows.

But when the days grow long and bright,
And breezes not so cold,
They'll change their dress of silver fur
For robes of green and gold.

—*Mary E. Plummer*

Library of Congress Collections

ROBERT FROST

STOPPING BY WOODS ON A SNOWY EVENING

Whose woods these are I think I know.
His house is in the village tho;
He will not see me stopping here.
To watch his woods fill up with snow.

My little horse must think it queer
To stop without a farmhouse near
Between the woods and frozen lake
The darkest evening of the year.

He gives his harness bells a shake
To ask if there is some mistake.
The only other sound's the sweep
Of easy wind and downy flake.

The woods are lovely, dark and deep,
But I have promises to keep,
And miles to go before I sleep
And miles to go before I sleep.

—*Robert Frost*

Abbie Rowe, National Park Service

THE WASHINGTON MONUMENT

DAFFODILS

I wandered lonely as a cloud
That floats on high o'er vales and hills,
When all at once I saw a crowd,
A host, of golden daffodils;
Beside the lake, beneath the trees,
Fluttering and dancing in the breeze.

Continuous as the stars that shine
And twinkle in the milky way,
They stretched in never-ending line
Along the margin of a bay:
Ten thousand saw I at a glance,
Tossing their heads in sprightly dance.

The waves beside them danced; but they
Outdid the sparkling waves in glee:
A poet could not but be gay,
In such a jocund company:
I gazed—and gazed—but little thought
What wealth the show to me had brought:

For oft, when on my couch I lie
In vacant or in pensive mood,
They flash upon that inward eye
Which is the bliss of solitude;
And then my heart with pleasure fills,
And dances with the daffodils.

—*William Wordsworth*

MAKING A GARDEN

Man plows and plants and digs and weeds
He works with hoe and spade;
God sends the sun and rain and air,
And thus a garden's made.

He must be proud who tills the soil
And turns the heavy sod;
How wonderful a thing to be
In partnership with God.

—*Ida M. Thomas*

HAIKU

The Haiku is a Japanese verse form containing three lines of seventeen syllables grouped five-seven-five. Each Haiku should denote a season of the year. A Haiku never rhymes.

Wild martial music:
Wind beats time with pine branches;
Winter marches in.

Cold dark winter rain:
Yesterday's merry snowman
This pile of gray slush.

Snowflakes, like white moths,
Flutter in the golden glare
Of sudden street lights.

Waves try to escape,
But the sea pulls them back to
Its bottomless maw.

—*Truth Mary Fowler*

SILVER

Slowly, silently, now the moon
Walks the night in her silver shoon;
This way, and that, she peers, and sees
Silver fruit upon silver trees;
One by one the casements catch
Her beams beneath the silvery thatch;
Couched in his kennel, like a log,
With paws of silver sleeps the dog;
From their shadowy cote the white breasts peep
Of doves in a silver-feathered sleep;
A harvest mouse goes scampering by,
With silver claws and silver eye;
And moveless fish in the water gleam,
By silver reeds in a silver stream.

—*Walter De La Mare*

WIND IS A CAT

Wind is a cat
  That prowls at night,
Now in a valley,
  Now on a height,

Pouncing on houses
  Till folks in their beds
Draw all the covers
  Over their heads.

It sings to the moon,
  It scratches at doors;
It lashes its tail
  Around chimneys and roars.

It claws at the clouds
  Till it fringes their silk,
It laps up the dawn
  Like a saucer of milk;

Then, chasing the stars
  To the tops of the firs,
Curls down for a nap
  And purrs and purrs.

—Ethel Romig Fuller

TREES

I think that I shall never see
A poem lovely as a tree.

A tree whose hungry mouth is pressed
Against the earth's sweet flowing breast;

A tree that looks at God all day
And lifts her leafy arms to pray;

A tree that may in summer wear
A nest of robins in her hair;

Upon whose bosom snow has lain;
Who intimately lives with rain.

Poems are made by fools like me,
But only God can make a tree.

—Joyce Kilmer

THE WONDERFUL WORLD

Great, wide, beautiful, wonderful World,
With the wonderful water round you curled,
And the wonderful grass upon your breast,
World, you are beautifully dressed.

The wonderful air is over me,
And the wonderful wind is shaking the tree—
It walks on the water, and whirls the mills,
And talks to itself on the tops of the hills.

You friendly Earth, how far do you go,
With the wheat-fields that nod and the rivers that flow,
With cities and gardens, and cliffs and isles,
And people upon you for thousands of miles?

Ah! you are so great, and I am so small,
I tremble to think of you, World, at all;
And yet, when I said my prayers to-day,
A whisper inside me seemed to say,
"You are more than the Earth, tho you are such a dot:
You can love and think, and the Earth cannot!"

—*William Brighty Rands*

PLANT A TREE

He who plants a tree
  Plants a hope.
  Rootlets up thru fibres blindly grope;
Leaves unfold into horizons free.
  So man's life must climb
  From the clods of time
  Unto heavens sublime,
Canst thou prophesy, thou little tree,
What the glory of thy boughs shall be?

He who plants a tree
  Plants a joy;
  Plants a comfort that will never cloy;
Every day a fresh reality,
  Beautiful and strong,
  To whose shelter throng
  Creatures blithe with song.
If thou couldst but know, thou happy tree,
Of the bliss that shall inhabit thee!

He who plants a tree,—
He plants peace.
Under its green curtains jargons cease.
Leaf and zephyr murmur soothingly;
Shadows soft with sleep
Down tired eyelids creep,
Balm of slumber deep.
Never hast thou dreamed, thou blessed tree,
Of the benediction thou shalt be.

He who plants a tree,—
He plants youth;
Vigor won for centuries in sooth;
Life of time, that hints eternity!
Boughs their strength uprear;
New shoots, every year,
On old growths appear;
Thou shalt teach the ages, sturdy tree,
Youth of soul is immortality.

He who plants a tree,—
He plants love,
Tents of coolness spreading out above
Wayfarers he may not live to see.
Gifts that grow are best;
Hands that bless are blest;
Plant! life does the rest!
Heaven and earth help him who plants a tree,
And his work its own reward shall be.

—Lucy Larcom

THE CLOUD

I bring fresh showers for the thirsting flowers
From the seas and the streams;
I bear light shade for the leaves when laid
In their noonday dreams.
From my wings are shaken the dews that waken
The sweet buds every one,
When rocked to rest on their mother's breast,
As she dances about the sun.
I wield the flail of the lashing hail,
And whiten the green plains under;
And then again I dissolve it in rain,
And laugh as I pass in thunder.

—Percy Bysshe Shelley

RAIN

The rain is raining all around,
It falls on field and tree,
It rains on the umbrellas here,
And on the ships at sea.

—Robert Louis Stevenson

OCTOBER'S BRIGHT BLUE WEATHER

O suns and skies and clouds of June,
And flowers of June together,
Ye cannot rival for one hour
October's bright blue weather,

When loud the bumble-bee makes haste,
Belated, thriftless vagrant,
And goldenrod is dying fast,
And lanes with grapes are fragrant;

When gentians roll their fringes tight
To save them for the morning,
And chestnuts fall from satin burrs
Without a sound of warning;

When on the ground red applies lie
In piles like jewels shining,
And redder still on old stone walls
Are leaves of woodbine twining;

When all the lovely wayside things
Their white-winged seeds are sowing,
And in the fields, still green and fair,
Late aftermaths are growing;

When springs run low, and on the brooks,
In idle golden freighting,
Bright leaves sink noiseless in the hush
Of woods for winter waiting;

When comrades seek sweet country haunts.
By twos and twos together,
And count like misers hour by hour
October's bright blue weather.

O suns and skies and flowers of June,
Count all your boasts together,
Love loveth best of all the year
October's bright blue weather.

Helen Hunt Jackson

FOG

The fog comes
on little cat feet.
It sits looking
over harbor and city
on silent haunches
and then moves on.

—*Carl Sandburg*

THE SANDPIPER

Across the narrow beach we flit,
One little sandpiper and I,
And fast I gather, bit by bit,
The scattered driftwood bleached and dry.
The wild waves reach their hands for it,
The wild wind raves, the tide runs high,
As up and down the beach we flit,—
One little sandpiper and I.

Above our heads the sullen clouds
Scud black and swift across the sky;
Like silent ghosts in misty shrouds
Stand out the white lighthouses high.
Almost as far as eye can reach
I see the close-reefed vessels fly,
As fast we flit along the beach,—
One little sandpiper and I.

I watch him as he skims along,
Uttering his sweet and mournful cry.
He starts not at my fitful song,
Or flash of fluttering drapery.
He has no thought of any wrong;
He scans me with a fearless eye.
Staunch friends are we, well tried and strong,
The little sandpiper and I.

Comrade, where wilt thou be tonight
When the loosed storm breaks furiously?
My driftwood fire will burn so bright!
To what warm shelter canst thou fly?
I do not fear for thee, tho wroth
The tempest rushes thru the sky:
For are we not God's children both,
Thou, little sandpiper, and I?

—*Celia Thaxter*

WHO HAS SEEN THE WIND?

Who has seen the wind?
Neither I nor you:
But when the leaves hang trembling
The wind is passing thru.

Who has seen the wind?
Neither you nor I:
But when the trees bow down their heads
The wind is passing by.

—*Christina Georgina Rossetti*

MY HEART LEAPS UP

My heart leaps up when I behold
A rainbow in the sky:
So was it when my life began;
So is it now I am a man;
So be it when I shall grow old,
Or let me die!
The Child is father of the Man;
And I could wish my days to be
Bound each to each by natural piety.

—*William Wordsworth*

BEAUTY IN COMMON THINGS

Seek not far for beauty. Lo! It glows
In dew-wet grasses all about thy feet;
In birds, in sunshine, childish faces sweet,
In stars, and mountain summits topped with snows.

Go not abroad for happiness. For, see,
It is a flower that blossoms at thy door!
Bring love and justice home, and then no more
Thou'lt wonder in what dwellings joy may be.

Dream not of noble service elsewhere wrought;
The simple duty that awaits thy hand
Is God's voice uttering a divine command;
Life's common duties build all that saints have thought.

In wonder-workings or some bush aflame,
Men look for God, and fancy Him concealed;
But in earth's common things He stands revealed,
While grass and stars and flowers spell out His name.

—*Minot J. Savage*

BROADCASTING

Last night the thunder began to roll
And I began to cry,
Then Daddy said, "That's broadcasting, child,
From Station SKY!

'A storm is coming,' the thunder says,
So step inside real quick,
We'll watch the lightning's fireworks play
And hear the wind's music."

I'll not be frightened at all next year
When March comes blowing by
And Daddy and I tune in again
With Station SKY!

From *Mildred D. Shacklett's*
"The Golden Flute," by permission.

A DAY IN JUNE

And what is so rare as a day in June?
  Then, if ever, come perfect days;
Then Heaven tries earth if it be in tune,
  And over it softly her warm ear lays;
Whether we look, or whether we listen,
We hear life murmur, or see it glisten;
Every clod feels a stir of might,
  An instinct within it that reaches and towers,
And, groping blindly above it for light,
  Climbs to a soul in grass and flowers;
The flush of life may well be seen
  Thrilling back over hills and valleys;
The cowslip startles in meadows green,
  The buttercup catches the sun in its chalice,
And there's never a leaf nor a blade too mean
  To be some happy creature's palace;
The little bird sits at his door in the sun,
  Atilt like a blossom among the leaves,
And lets his illumined being o'errun
  With the deluge of summer it receives;
His mate feels the eggs beneath her wings,
And the heart in her dumb breast flutters and sings;
He sings to the wide world and she to her nest,—
In the nice ear of Nature which song is the best?

—From *James Russell Lowell's*
"The Vision of Sir Launfal"

A BOY'S SONG

Where the pools are bright and deep,
Where the gray trout lies asleep,
Up the river and o'er the lea,
That's the way for Billy and me.

Where the blackbird sings the latest,
Where the hawthorn blooms the sweetest,
Where the nestlings chirp and flee,
That's the way for Billy and me.

Where the mowers mow the cleanest,
Where the hay lies thick and greenest,
There to track the homeward bee,
That's the way for Billy and me.

Where the hazel bank is steepest,
Where the shadow falls the deepest,
Where the clustering nuts fall free,
That's the way for Billy and me.

—*James Hogg*

TIT FOR TAT

I often pass a gracious tree
Whose name I can't identify,
But still I bow, in courtesy
It waves a bough, in kind reply.

I do not know your name, O tree
[Are you a hemlock or a pine?]
But why should that embarrass me?
Quite probably you don't know mine.

—*Christopher Morley*

WHEN THE FROST IS ON THE PUNKIN

When the frost is on the punkin and the fodder's in the shock,
And you hear the kyouck and gobble of the struttin' turkey-cock,
And the clackin' of the guineys, and the cluckin' of the hens,
And the rooster's hallylooyer as he tiptoes on the fence;
O, it's then's the times a feller is a-feelin' at his best,
With the risin' sun to greet him from a night of peaceful rest,
As he leaves the house, bareheaded, and goes out to feed the stock,
When the frost is on the punkin and the fodder's in the shock.

—*James Whitcomb Riley*

THE PEAR TREE

In this squalid, dirty dooryard,
Where the chickens scratch and run,
White, incredible, the pear tree
Stands apart and takes the sun,
Mindful of the eyes upon it,
Vain of its new holiness,
Like the waste-man's little daughter
In her first communion dress.

—*Edna St. Vincent Millay*

The snow had begun in the gloaming,
And busily all the night
Had been heaping field and highway
With a silence deep and white.

Every pine and fir and hemlock
Wore ermine too dear for an earl,
And the poorest twig on the elm-tree
Was ridged inch deep with pearl.

—From *James Russell Lowell's*
"The First Snow-Fall"

APRIL RAIN

It is not raining rain to me,
It's raining daffodils;
In every dimpled drop I see
Wild flowers on the hills;

The clouds of gray engulf the day
And overwhelm the town;
It is not raining rain to me,
It's raining roses down.

It is not raining rain to me,
But fields of clover bloom,
Where any buccaneering bee
Can find a bed and room.

A health unto the happy,
A fig for him who frets!
It is not raining rain to me,
It's raining violets.

—*Robert Loveman*

FOUR-LEAF CLOVER

I know a place where the sun is like gold,
  And the cherry blossoms burst like snow,
And down underneath is the loveliest nook,
  Where the four-leaf clovers grow.

One leaf is for hope, and one is for faith,
  And one is for love, you know,
And God put another one in for luck—
  If you search, you will find where they grow.

But you must have hope, and you must have faith,
  You must love and be strong—and so,
If you work, if you wait, you will find the place
  Where the four-leaf clovers grow.

—Ella Higginson

The world is too much with us; late and soon,
Getting and spending, we lay waste our powers:
Little we see in Nature that is ours;
We have given our hearts away, a sordid boon!
This sea that bares her bosom to the moon,
The winds that will be howling at all hours,
And are up-gathered now like sleeping flowers;
For this, for everything, we are out of tune;
It moves us not.—Great God! I'd rather be
A Pagan suckled in a creed outworn;
So might I, standing on this pleasant lea,
Have glimpses that would make me less forlorn;
Have sight of Proteus rising from the sea;
Or hear old Triton blow his wreathed horn.

—William Wordsworth

FLOWER IN THE CRANNIED WALL

Flower in the crannied wall
I pluck you out of the crannies,
I hold you here, root and all, in my hand,
Little flower—but *if* I could understand
What you are, root and all, and all in all,
I should know what God and man is.

—Alfred Tennyson

PART VIII—SECTION 11

A Treasury for Young Children

ALL THINGS BRIGHT AND BEAUTIFUL

All things bright and beautiful,
All creatures great and small,
All things wise and wonderful,
The Lord God made them all.

Each little flower that opens,
Each little bird that sings,
He made their glowing colors,
He made their tiny wings.

The purple-headed mountain,
The river running by,
The sunset, and the morning,
That brightens up the sky,
The cold wind in the winter,
The pleasant summer sun,
The ripe fruits in the garden,
He made them every one;

He gave us eyes to see them,
And lips that we might tell
How great is God Almighty,
Who has made all things well.

—Cecil F. Alexander

SINGING VERSE

I like a little verse that sings,
Reminding me of pleasant things:
A garden gate, a misty lane,
A robin singing in the rain;
Teacups white or trimmed with blue,
Perhaps a little rocker, too;
A cheery fire, a friendly talk,
An open path where I may walk
To see the stars when twilight comes.
I like a little verse that hums.

—Annamae Kelly

THE LITTLE ELF

I met a little elf-man, once,
Down where the lilies blow.
I asked him why he was so small,
And why he didn't grow.

He slightly frowned, and with his eye
He looked me thru and thru.
"I'm quite as big for me," said he,
"As you are big for you."

—*John Kendrick Bangs*

THANKSGIVING DAY

Over the river and thru the wood,
To grandfather's house we go;
The horse knows the way
To carry the sleigh
Thru the white and drifted snow.

Over the river and thru the wood—
Oh, how the wind does blow!
It stings the toes
And bites the nose
As over the ground we go.

Over the river and thru the wood,
To have a first-rate play.
Hear the bells ring,
"Ting-a-ling-ding!"
Hurrah for Thanksgiving Day!

Over the river and thru the wood,
And straight thru the barnyard gate,
We seem to go
Extremely slow,
It is so hard to wait!

Over the river and thru the wood—
Now grandmother's cap I spy!
Hurrah for the fun!
Is the pudding done?
Hurrah for the pumpkin pie!

—*Lydia Maria Child*

STOP-LOOK-LISTEN

Stop! Look! Listen!
Before you cross the street.
Use your eyes!
Use your ears!
And then use your feet.

—*Florence Slown Hyde*

THE OWL AND THE PUSSY-CAT

The Owl and the Pussy-Cat went to sea
In a beautiful pea-green boat.
They took some honey, and plenty of money
Wrapped up in a five-pound note.
The Owl looked up to the moon above,
And sang to a small guitar,

"O lovely Pussy! O Pussy, my love!
What a beautiful Pussy you are,—
You are;
What a beautiful Pussy you are!"

Pussy said to the Owl, "You elegant fowl,
How charmingly sweet you sing!
O let us be married,—too long we have tarried,—
But what shall we do for a ring?"

They sailed away for a year and a day
To the land where the Bong-tree grows.
And there in the wood, a piggy-wig stood
With a ring in the end of his nose,—
His nose;
With a ring in the end of his nose.

"Dear Pig, are you willing to sell for one shilling
Your ring?" Said the piggy, "I will."
So they took it away, and were married next day
By the turkey who lives on the hill.
They dined upon mince and slices of quince,
Which they ate with a runcible spoon,
And hand in hand, on the edge of the sand,
They danced by the light of the moon,—
The moon;
They danced by the light of the moon.

—*Edward Lear*

MORNING PRAYER

Be with me, Lord, as here I pray,
And keep me by Thy side today.
Please make me gentle, pure, and true
And kind in all I say and do,
Honest in every word and deed,
And quick to help when others need. Amen.

A CHILD'S GRACE

Thank you for the world so sweet.
Thank you for the food we eat.
Thank you for the birds that sing.
Thank you, God, for everything.

—*Author Unknown*

GOLDEN KEYS

A bunch of golden keys is mine
To make each day with gladness shine.

"Good morning" is the golden key
That unlocks every day for me.

When at the table, "If you please"
I take from off my bunch of keys.

When friends give anything to me
I use my little "Thank you" key.

"Excuse me"—"Beg your pardon" too
If by some mistake some harm I do.

When evening comes, "Goodnight," I say
And close the door of each glad day.

With a golden ring these keys I bind
This motto—"Be ye kind."

I'll often use each golden key
And then a child polite I'll be.

—*Author Unknown*

LITTLE THINGS COUNT

Little drops of water,
Little grains of sand,
Make the mighty ocean
And the pleasant land.

Little deeds of kindness,
Little words of love,
Help to make earth happy
Like the Heaven above.

—Ebenezer Cofham Brewer

THE CHILD'S GOLDEN RULE

Be you to others kind and true,
As you'd have others be to you.

—New England Primer

WHICH LOVED BEST?

"I love you, mother," said little John,
Then forgetting his work, his cap went on,
And he was off to the garden swing,
Leaving his mother the wood to bring.

"I love you, mother," said little Nell,
"I love you better than tongue can tell."
Then she teased and pouted half the day,
Till mother rejoiced when she went to play.

"I love you, mother," said little Fan.
"Today I'll help you all I can."
To the cradle then she did softly creep,
And rocked the baby till it fell asleep.

Then stepping softly, she took the broom,
And swept the floor and dusted the room;
Busy and happy all day was she,
Helpful and cheerful as child could be.

"I love you, mother," again they said,—
Three little children, going to bed.
How do you think that mother guessed
Which of them really loved her best?

—Joy Allison

Library of Congress Collections

CHARCOAL DRAWING OF ROBERT LOUIS STEVENSON

MY SHADOW

I have a little shadow that goes in and out with me,
And what can be the use of him is more than I can see.
He is very, very like me from the heels up to the head;
And I see him jump before me, when I jump into my bed.

The funniest thing about him is the way he likes to grow—
Not at all like proper children, which is always very slow;
For he sometimes shoots up taller like an India-rubber ball,
And he sometimes gets so little that there's none of him at all.

He hasn't got a notion of how children ought to play,
And can only make a fool of me in every sort of way.
He stays so close beside me, he's a coward you can see;
I'd think shame to stick to nursie as that shadow sticks to me!

One morning, very early, before the sun was up,
I rose and found the shining dew on every buttercup;
But my lazy little shadow, like an arrant sleepy-head,
Had stayed at home behind me and was fast asleep in bed.

—*Robert Louis Stevenson*

GOOD NIGHT!

Good night! Good night!
Far flies the light;
But still God's love
Shall flame above,
Making all bright.
Good night! Good night!

—Victor Hugo

A MORNING PRAYER FOR THE WORLD'S CHILDREN

Our Father, You are sending me
So much of love and joy today,
That I am thinking love and joy
To other children far away.
Whatever they are doing now
Happy or tired with work or play
Yellow or brown or black or white
Our Father, bless them all today.

—Author Unknown

THE LIGHT-HEARTED FAIRY

Oh, who is so merry, so merry, heigh ho!
As the light-hearted fairy? heigh ho!
    Heigh ho!
  He dances and sings
  To the sound of his wings,
With a hey and a heigh and a ho!

Oh, who is so merry, so airy, heigh ho!
As the light-hearted fairy? heigh ho!
    Heigh ho!
  His nectar he sips
  From the primroses' lips
With a hey and a heigh and a ho!

Oh, who is so merry, so merry, heigh ho!
As the light-hearted fairy? heigh ho!
    Heigh ho!
  The night is his noon
  And his sun is the moon,
With a hey and a heigh and a ho!

—Author Unknown

THE ZIG-ZAG BOY AND GIRL

I know a little zig-zag boy,
  Who goes this way and that;
He never knows just where he puts
  His coat or shoes or hat.

I know a little zig-zag girl,
  Who flutters here and there;
She never knows jut where to find
  Her brush to fix her hair.

If you are not a zig-zag child,
  You'll have no cause to say
That you forgot, for you will know
  Where things are put away.

—Author Unknown

THE BILL OF FARE

Pies of pumpkin, apples, mince,
Jams and jellies, peaches, quince,
Purple grapes, and apples red,
Cakes and nuts and gingerbread—
  That's Thanksgiving.

Turkey! Oh, a great big fellow!
Fruits all ripe and rich and mellow,
Everything that's nice to eat,
More than I can now repeat—
  That's Thanksgiving.

Lots and lots of jolly fun,
Games to play and races run,
All as happy as can be—
For this happiness, you can see,
  Makes Thanksgiving.

We must thank the One who gave
All the good things that we have;
That is why we keep the day
Set aside, our mamas say,
  For Thanksgiving.

—Eugene Field

National Park Service

NATURE WALK ON THEODORE ROOSEVELT ISLAND, WASHINGTON, D. C.

FATHER IN HEAVEN, WE THANK THEE

For flowers that bloom about our feet,
For tender grass so fresh, so sweet,
For song of bird and hum of bee,
For all things fair we hear or see,
Father in Heaven, we thank Thee!

For blue of stream and blue of sky,
For pleasant shade of branches high,
For fragrant air and cooling breeze,
For beauty of the blooming trees,
Father in Heaven, we thank Thee!

For mother-love and father-care,
For brothers strong and sisters fair,
For love at home and here each day,
For guidance lest we go astray,
Father in Heaven, we thank Thee!

For this new morning with its light,
For rest and shelter of the night,
For health and food, for love and friends,
For ev'rything His goodness sends,
Father in Heaven, we thank Thee!

—*Author Unknown*

KINDNESS GARDEN

Kind hearts are the gardens.
  Kind thoughts are the roots.
Kind words are the blossoms.
  Kind deeds are the fruits.

Love is sweet sunshine
  That warms into life,
For only in darkness
  Grow hatred and strife.

—*Author Unknown*

WE THANK THEE

For peace and plenty, for freedom, for rest,
For joy in the land, from the east to the west;
For the dear starry flag with its red, white, and blue.
We thank Thee from hearts that are honest and true.

For sowing and reaping, for cold and for heat,
For the sweet of the flowers and the gold of the wheat;
For the ships in the harbor, for sails on the sea,
O Father in heaven, our songs rise to Thee.

For waking and sleeping, for blessings to be,
We children would offer our praises to Thee!
For God is our Father and bends from above,
To keep the round world in the smile of his love.

—*Margaret E. Sangster*

GRATITUDE

I thank Thee, Lord, for quiet rest,
And for Thy care of me,
Oh, let me thru this day be blest
And kept from harm by Thee.

Oh, let me thank Thee, kind Thou art,
To children such as I,
Give me a gentle, loving heart,
Be Thou my friend on high.

Help me to please my parents dear,
And do whate'er they tell,
Bless all my friends both far and near,
And keep them safe and well.

—*Mary L. Duncan*

Abbie Rowe, National Park Service

POETRY IN SCULPTURE

The aluminum Navy-Marine Memorial on Columbia Island by Ernesto Begni del Piatti shows a flight of seven sea gulls wing-tip to wing-tip rising from the crest of a breaking wave. In the background may be seen the Washington Monument.

CHILDREN'S PRAYER

When at night I go to sleep,
Fourteen angels watch do keep,
Two my head are guarding,
Two my feet are guiding,
Two are on my right hand,
Two are on my left hand,
Two who warmly cover,
Two who o'er me hover,
Two to whom 'tis given
To guide my steps to Heaven.

—*From Engelbert Humperdinck's*
"Hansel and Gretel"

THE STAR

Twinkle, twinkle, little star,
How I wonder what you are,
Up above the world so high,
Like a diamond in the sky.

When the blazing sun is set,
And the grass with dew is wet,
Then you show your little light,
Twinkle, twinkle, all the night.

Then the traveller in the dark
Thanks you for your tiny spark,
He could not see where to go
If you did not twinkle so.

In the dark blue sky you keep,
And often thru my curtains peep,
For you never shut your eye
Till the sun is in the sky.

As your bright and tiny spark
Lights the traveller in the dark,
Tho I know not what you are,
Twinkle, twinkle, little star.

—*Jane Taylor*

Happy in work,
Happy in play,
That is the way
To be helpful each day.

If a task is once begun,
Never leave it till it's done;
Be the labor great or small,
Do it well, or not at all.

THIS IS THE WAY

This is the way we wash our clothes,
Wash our clothes, wash our clothes;
This is the way we wash our clothes,
So early Monday morning.

This is the way we iron our clothes,
Iron our clothes, iron our clothes;
This is the way we iron our clothes,
So early Tuesday morning.

This is the way we mend our shoes,
Mend our shoes, mend our shoes;
This is the way we mend our shoes,
So early Wednesday morning.

This is the way we visit our friends,
Visit our friends, visit our friends;
This is the way we visit our friends,
So early Thursday morning.

This is the way we sweep the house,
Sweep the house, sweep the house;
This is the way we sweep the house,
So early Friday morning.

This is the way we bake our cake,
Bake our cake, bake our cake;
This is the way we bake our cake,
So early Saturday morning.

This is the way we go to church,
Go to church, go to church;
This is the way we go to church,
So early Sunday morning.

If wisdom's ways you'd wisely seek,
Five things observe with care:
Of whom you speak,
To whom you speak,
And how and when and where.

—*Author Unknown*

He who would live in peace and rest
Must hear, and see, and say the best.

Little loving thoughts
Are tiny little seeds
From which bud and blossom
Little loving deeds.

One, two, buckle my shoe;
Three, four, knock at the door;
Five, six, pick up sticks;
Seven, eight, lay them straight;
Nine, ten, a big fat hen.

Once I saw a little bird
Come hop, hop, hop!
So I cried, "Little bird
Will you stop, stop, stop?"
And was going to the window
To say, "How do you do,"
But he shook his little tail,
And far away he flew.

Thirty days hath September,
April, June, and November;
All the rest have thirty-one
Save February, which alone
Has twenty-eight; but one day more
We add to it one year in four.

Work while you work,
Play while you play;
That is the way
To be happy and gay.

THE SWING

How do you like to go up in a swing,
Up in the air so blue?
Oh, I do think it the pleasantest thing
Ever a child can do!

Up in the air and over the wall,
Till I can see so wide,
Rivers and trees and cattle and all
Over the countryside—

Till I look down on the garden green,
Down on the roof so brown—
Up in the air I go flying again,
Up in the air and down!

—*Robert Louis Stevenson*

QUESTIONS FROM A THOUGHTFUL CHILD

Our Father, Who art in Heaven,
Up above the world so high,
Where is Heaven?
Where is up?
Where is high?

What is a realm?
And what does yours include?
Twinkling atmosphere?
Black, weightless space?
An astronaut's suit?

I also wonder about down-under
Your globe-shaped world,
In places like New Zealand;
Is their up down,
When their sun sets?

Do Australian children pray,
"Our Father, Who art in Heaven
Down below the world so low?"
Our Father, Who art in Heaven,
Where are You?

—*Truth Mary Fowler*

Ralph H. Anderson, National Park Service

GIANT SEQUOIAS, YOSEMITE NATIONAL PARK, CALIFORNIA

PART VIII—SECTION 12

Age and Immortality

Grow old along with me!
The best is yet to be,
The last of life, for which the first was made.
Our times are in his hand
Who saith, "A whole I planned;
Youth shows but half. Trust God; see all, nor be afraid!"

—From *Robert Browning's* "Rabbi Ben Ezra"

CROSSING THE BAR

Sunset and evening star,
  And one clear call for me!
And may there be no moaning of the bar,
  When I put out to sea,

But such a tide as moving seems asleep,
  Too full for sound and foam,
When that which drew from out the boundless deep
  Turns again home.

Twilight and evening bell,
  And after that the dark!
And may there be no sadness of farewell,
  When I embark;

For tho from out our bourne of Time and Place
  The flood may bear me far,
I hope to see my Pilot face to face
  When I have crossed the bar.

—*Alfred Tennyson*

REQUIEM

Under the wide and starry sky,
Dig the grave and let me lie.
Glad did I live and gladly die,
  And I laid me down with a will.
This be the verse you grave for me:
Here he lies where he longed to be;
Home is the sailor, home from sea,
  And the hunter home from the hill.

—*Robert Louis Stevenson*

THANATOPSIS

To him who in the love of Nature holds
Communion with her visible forms, she speaks
A various language; for his gayer hours
She has a voice of gladness, and a smile
And eloquence of beauty, and she glides
Into his darker musings, with a mild
And healing sympathy, that steals away
Their sharpness, ere he is aware. When thoughts
Of the last bitter hour come like a blight
Over thy spirit, and sad images
Of the stern agony, and shroud, and pall,
And breathless darkness, and the narrow house,
Make thee to shudder, and grow sick at heart;—
Go forth, under the open sky, and list
To Nature's teachings, while from all around—
Earth and her waters, and the depths of air—
Comes a still voice:—
Yet a few days, and thee
The all-beholding sun shall see no more
In all his course; nor yet in the cold ground,
Where thy pale form was laid, with many tears,
Nor in the embrace of ocean, shall exist
Thy image. Earth, that nourished thee, shall claim
Thy growth, to be resolved to earth again,
And, lost each human trace, surrendering up
Thine individual being, shalt thou go
To mix forever with the elements,
To be a brother to the insensible rock
And to the sluggish clod, which the rude swain
Turns with his share, and treads upon. The oak
Shall send his roots abroad, and pierce thy mold.
Yet not to thine eternal resting-place
Shalt thou retire alone, nor couldst thou wish
Couch more magnificent. Thou shalt lie down
With patriarchs of the infant world—with kings,
The powerful of the earth—the wise, the good,
Fair forms, and hoary seers of ages past,
All in one mighty sepulcher. The hills
Rock-ribbed and ancient as the sun,—the vales
Stretching in pensive quietness between;
The venerable woods—rivers that move
In majesty, and the complaining brooks

That make the meadows green; and, poured round all,
Old Ocean's gray and melancholy waste,—
Are but the solemn decorations all
Of the great tomb of man. The golden sun,
The planets, all the infinite host of heaven,
Are shining on the sad abodes of death
Thru the still lapse of ages. All that tread
The globe are but a handful to the tribes
That slumber in its bosom.—Take the wings
Of morning, pierce the Barcan wilderness,
Or lose thyself in the continuous woods
Where rolls the Oregon, and hears no sound,
Save his own dashings—yet the dead are there:
And millions in those solitudes, since first
The flight of years began, have laid them down
In their last sleep—the dead reign there alone.
So shalt thou rest, and what if thou withdraw
In silence from the living, and no friend
Take note of thy departure? All that breathe
Will share thy destiny. The gay will laugh
When thou art gone, the solemn brood of care
Plod on, and each one as before will chase
His favorite phantom; yet all these shall leave
Their mirth and their employments, and shall come
And make their bed with thee. As the long train
Of ages glides away, the sons of men—
The youth in life's fresh spring, and he who goes
In the full strength of years, matron and maid,
The speechless babe, and the gray-headed man—
Shall one by one be gathered to thy side,
By those, who in their turn shall follow them.

So live, that when thy summons comes to join
The innumerable caravan, which moves
To that mysterious realm, where each shall take
His chamber in the silent halls of death,
Thou go not, like the quarry-slave at night,
Scourged to his dungeon, but, sustained and soothed
By an unfaltering trust, approach thy grave
Like one who wraps the drapery of his couch
About him, and lies down to pleasant dreams.

—*William Cullen Bryant*

DEATH?

We watch the liner in the distance glide
Out from the sheltered waters of the bay,
    Into the arms of ocean's vastness won.
Enfolded in infinity of tide
    We lose it, and the last faint smoke line gray
    Merges into the sunset and is gone.

Vanished from sight and lost, art thou, at sea,
Swallowed in ocean's blue immensity?
    Ah, no. Tho trackless be the deep, and wide,
Thy pilot shall bring thee triumphantly
    Into the harbor on the other side.

—*Edith E. McGee*

SINCE our little daughter afforded all our senses the sweetest and most charming pleasure, so ought we to cherish her memory, which will in many ways conduce more to our joy than grief. . . . Moreover, I would have you endeavor to call often to mind that time when our daughter was not as yet born to us, then we had no cause to complain of fortune. Then, joining that time with this, argue thus with yourself, that we are in the same condition as then. Otherwise, dear wife, we shall seem discontented at the birth of our little daughter if we own that our circumstances were better before her birth. But the two years of her life are . . . to be numbered among our blessings. —From *Plutarch's* consolatory letter to his wife on the death of their child.

As a fond mother, when the day is o'er,
    Leads by the hand her little child to bed,
    Half willing, half reluctant to be led,
    And leave his broken playthings on the floor,
Still gazing at them thru the open door,
    Nor wholly reassured and comforted
    By promises of others in their stead,
    Which, tho more splendid, may not please him more;
So Nature deals with us, and takes away
    Our playthings one by one, and by the hand
    Leads us to rest so gently, that we go
Scarce knowing if we wish to go or stay,
    Being too full of sleep to understand
    How far the unknown transcends the what we know.

—*Henry W. Longfellow*

MORITURI SALUTAMUS

The following is abridged from a much longer poem which was read at Bowdoin College on the occasion of the 50th anniversary of Longfellow's graduation.

But why, you ask me, should this tale be told
To men grown old, or who are growing old?
It is too late! Ah, nothing is too late
Till the tired heart shall cease to palpitate.
Cato learned Greek at eighty; Sophocles
Wrote his grand Oedipus, and Simonides
Bore off the prize of verse from his compeers,
When each had numbered more than fourscore years,
And Theophrastus, at fourscore and ten,
Had but begun his Characters of Men.
Chaucer, at Woodstock with the nightingales,
At sixty wrote the Canterbury Tales;
Goethe at Weimar, toiling to the last,
Completed Faust when eighty years were past.
These are indeed exceptions; but they show
How far the gulfstream of our youth may flow
Into the arctic regions of our lives,
Where little else than life itself survives.

As the barometer foretells the storm
While still the skies are clear, the weather warm,
So something in us, as old age draws near,
Betrays the pressure of the atmosphere.
The nimble mercury, ere we are aware,
Descends the elastic ladder of the air;
The telltale blood in artery and vein
Sinks from its higher levels in the brain;
Whatever poet, orator, or sage
May say of it, old age is still old age.
It is the waning, not the crescent moon;
The dusk of evening, not the blaze of noon;
It is not strength, but weakness; not desire,
But its surcease; not the fierce heat of fire,
The burning and consuming element,
But that of ashes and of embers spent,
In which some living sparks we still discern,
Enough to warm, but not enough to burn.

What then? Shall we sit idly down and say
The night hath come; it is no longer day?
The night hath not yet come; we are not quite
Cut off from labor by the failing light;
Somethings remains for us to do or dare;
Even the oldest tree some fruit may bear;
Not Oedipus Coloneus, or greek Ode,
Or tales of Pilgrims that one morning rode
Out of the gateway of the Tabard Inn,
But other something, would we but begin;
For age is opportunity no less
Than youth itself, tho in another dress,
And as the evening twilight fades away
The sky is filled with stars, invisible by day.

—*Henry W. Longfellow*

THE NEVER-OLD

They who can smile when others hate
Nor bind the heart with frosts of fate,
Their feet will go with laughter bold
The green roads of the Never-Old.

They who can let the spirit shine
And keep the heart a lighted shrine,
Their feet will glide with fire-of-gold
The bright roads of the Never-Old.

They who can put the self aside
And in Love's saddle leap and ride,
Their eyes will see the gates unfold
To glad roads of the Never-Old.

—*Edwin Markham*

Preparation for retirement is fully as important as preparation for a career . . . If the mind and body are allowed to remain inactive, the result is a rapid deterioration of their function. —From *The Retirement Handbook* by Joseph C. Buckley.

ESSAY ON YOUTH

[From a volume of poems by Samuel Ullman, entitled *From a Summit of Years, Four Score,* privately printed in 1920 in honor of his 80th birthday. He died in 1924, age 84, in Birmingham, Alabama.]

Youth is not a time of life;
it is a state of mind;
it is not a matter of rosy cheeks, red lips and supple knees;
it is a matter of the will,
a quality of the imagination,
a vigor of the emotions;
it is the freshness of the deep springs of life.

Youth means the temperamental predominance of courage over timidity of the appetite, for adventure over the love of ease.
This often exists in a man of 60 more than a boy of 20.
Nobody grows old merely by a number of years.
We grow old by deserting our ideals.

Years may wrinkle the skin,
but to give up enthusiasm wrinkles the soul.
Worry, fear, selfdistrust
bows the heart
and turns the spirit back to dust.

Whether 60 or 16,
there is in every human being's heart
the lure of wonder,
the unfailing childlike appetite of what's next,
and the joy of the game of living.
In the center of your heart and my heart there is a wireless station;
so long as it receives messages of beauty, hope, cheer, courage and power from men and from the infinite,
so long are you young.

When the aerials are down
and your spirit is covered with snows of cynicism and the ice of pessimism,
then you are grown old, even at 20,
but as long as your aerials are up, to catch waves of optimism,
there is hope you may die young at 80.

—*By Samuel Ullman*

EVERY OLDER PERSON NEEDS

Someone to care for him and to love him.

A purpose that gives direction and significance to his life.

A place to live in wholesome surroundings with fresh air, sun and quiet.

Community responsibilities and activities that bring out his best.

An opportunity to learn new things and keep flexible in mind and spirit.

A diet that meets his individual requirements.

A combination of exercise and rest that suits his condition.

Medical care to maintain health and wellbeing at his highest possible level.

A sufficient variety in life to add interest and keep him mentally alert.

A triumphant religious faith or philosophy to give serenity and peace of mind.

These are universal and growing needs. They have their roots in childhood. To satisfy them adequately requires the effort and achievement of a lifetime. But even if there has been neglect during the earlier years, it is always possible to begin anew if one has the purpose and will to do so.

—*Joy Elmer Morgan in* Senior Citizen, *March 1959*

BREAK, BREAK, BREAK

Break, break, break,
On thy cold gray stones, O sea!
And I would that my tongue could utter
The thoughts that arise in me.

O well for the fisherman's boy
That he shouts with his sister at play!
O well for the sailor lad
That he sings in his boat on the bay!

And the stately ships go on,
To the haven under the hill;
But O for the touch of a vanished hand,
And the sound of a voice that is still!

Break, break, break,
At the foot of thy crags, O sea!
But the tender grace of a day that is dead
Will never come back to me.

—*Alfred Tennyson*

PART IX

The United States of America

THE AMERICAN *dream has grown thru the years as our nation has risen from a handful of colonists to a mighty people made up of all the races of the world. The huge and empty land has been filled with homes, roads, railways, schools, colleges, hospitals, and all the comforts of the most advanced material civilization. The mere physical tasks have been stupendous and unparalleled.*

It has been a great epic and a great dream. What now, of the future? If we are to have a rich and full life in which all are to share and play their parts, if the American dream is to be a reality, those on top, financially, intellectually, or otherwise, have got to devote themselves to the "Great Society," and those who are below in the scale have got to strive to rise, not merely economically, but culturally. We cannot become a great democracy by giving ourselves up as individuals to selfishness, physical comfort, and cheap amusements. The very foundation of the American dream of a better and richer life for all is that all, in varying degrees, shall be capable of wanting to share in it.—Adapted from The Epic of America *(1931) by James Truslow Adams.*

Presidents of the United States

No.	*Name*	*Politics*	*Native State*	*Date of Birth*	*Inaugurated*	*Date of Death*
1	George Washington	F	Va.	Feb 22, 1732	1789	Dec 14, 1799
2	John Adams	F	Mass.	Oct 30, 1735	1797	July 4, 1826
3	Thomas Jefferson	RD	Va.	Apr 13, 1743	1801	July 4, 1826
4	James Madison	RD	Va.	Mar 16, 1751	1809	June 28, 1836
5	James Monroe	RD	Va.	Apr 28, 1758	1817	July 4, 1831
6	John Quincy Adams	RD	Mass.	July 11, 1767	1825	Feb 23, 1848
7	Andrew Jackson	D	S. C.	Mar 15, 1767	1829	June 8, 1845
8	Martin Van Buren	D	N. Y.	Dec 5, 1782	1837	July 24, 1862
9	Wm. Henry Harrison	W	Va.	Feb 9, 1773	1841	Apr 4, 1841
10	John Tyler	W	Va.	Mar 29, 1790	1841	Jan 17, 1862
11	James Knox Polk	D	N. C.	Nov 2, 1795	1845	June 15, 1849
12	Zachary Taylor	W	Va.	Nov 24, 1784	1849	July 9, 1850
13	Millard Fillmore	W	N. Y.	Jan 7, 1800	1850	Mar 8, 1874
14	Franklin Pierce	D	N. H.	Nov 23, 1804	1853	Oct 8, 1869
15	James Buchanan	D	Pa.	Apr 23, 1791	1857	June 1, 1868
16	Abraham Lincoln	R	Ky.	Feb 12, 1809	1861	Apr 15, 1865
17	Andrew Johnson	D	N. C.	Dec 29, 1808	1865	July 31, 1875
18	Ulysses S. Grant	R	Ohio	Apr 27, 1822	1869	July 23, 1885
19	Rutherford B. Hayes	R	Ohio	Oct 4, 1822	1877	Jan 17, 1893
20	James A. Garfield	R	Ohio	Nov 19, 1831	1881	Sept 19, 1881
21	Chester A. Arthur	R	Vt.	Oct 5, 1830	1881	Nov 18, 1886
22	Grover Cleveland	D	N. J.	Mar 18, 1837	1885	June 24, 1908
23	Benjamin Harrison	R	Ohio	Aug 20, 1833	1889	Mar 13, 1901
24	Grover Cleveland	D	N. J.	Mar 18, 1837	1893	June 24, 1908
25	William McKinley	R	Ohio	Jan 28, 1843	1897	Sept 14, 1901
26	Theodore Roosevelt	R	N. Y.	Oct 27, 1858	1901	Jan 6, 1919
27	William Howard Taft	R	Ohio	Sept 15, 1857	1909	Mar 8, 1930
28	Woodrow Wilson	D	Va.	Dec 28, 1856	1913	Feb 3, 1924
29	Warren G. Harding	R	Ohio	Nov 2, 1865	1921	Aug 2, 1923
30	Calvin Coolidge	R	Vt.	July 4, 1872	1923	Jan 5, 1933
31	Herbert C. Hoover	R	Iowa	Aug 10, 1874	1929	Oct 20, 1964
32	Franklin D. Roosevelt	D	N. Y.	Jan 30, 1882	1933	Apr 12, 1945
33	Harry S. Truman	D	Mo.	May 8, 1884	1945	
34	Dwight D. Eisenhower	R	Kansas	Oct 14, 1890	1953	
35	John F. Kennedy	D	Mass.	May 29, 1917	1961	Nov 22, 1963
36	Lyndon Baines Johnson	D	Texas	Aug 27, 1908	1963	

F—Federalist
RD—Republican-Democrat
W—Whig
D—Democrat
R—Republican

The Fifty States

Following the Revolution, the thirteen colonies became the original states. To the west and south these colonies were surrounded by undeveloped wilderness from which other states would eventually be created and admitted to the union. Following is a list of the fifty states with the date of their entry into the union, the last to be admitted being Hawaii which officially became a state on August 21, 1959.

State	Date	State	Date
Alabama	December 14, 1819	Montana	November 8, 1889
Alaska	January 3, 1959	Nebraska	March 1, 1867
Arizona	February 14, 1912	Nevada	October 31, 1864
Arkansas	June 15, 1836	New Hampshire	June 21, 1788
California	September 9, 1850	New Jersey	December 18, 1787
Colorado	August 1, 1876	New Mexico	January 6, 1912
Connecticut	January 9, 1788	New York	July 26, 1788
Delaware	December 7, 1787	North Carolina	November 21, 1789
Florida	March 3, 1845	North Dakota	November 2, 1889
Georgia	January 2, 1788	Ohio	March 1, 1803
Hawaii	August 21, 1959	Oklahoma	November 16, 1907
Idaho	July 3, 1890	Oregon	February 14, 1859
Illinois	December 3, 1818	Pennsylvania	December 12, 1787
Indiana	December 11, 1816	Rhode Island	May 29, 1790
Iowa	December 28, 1846	South Carolina	May 23, 1788
Kansas	January 29, 1861	South Dakota	November 2, 1889
Kentucky	June 1, 1792	Tennessee	June 1, 1796
Louisiana	April 30, 1812	Texas	December 29, 1845
Maine	March 15, 1820	Utah	January 4, 1896
Maryland	April 28, 1788	Vermont	March 4, 1791
Massachusetts	February 6, 1788	Virginia	June 25, 1788
Michigan	January 26, 1837	Washington	November 11, 1889
Minnesota	May 11, 1858	West Virginia	June 20, 1863
Mississippi	December 10, 1817	Wisconsin	May 29, 1848
Missouri	August 10, 1821	Wyoming	July 10, 1890

Roll Call of the States

ALABAMA

Alabama is one of the states of the Old South, located on the Gulf of Mexico between Georgia and Mississippi. De Soto explored the region in 1540 which was later acquired by the Spanish as a part of West Florida. During the years 1783 to 1813 the territory became part of the U. S. and was admitted to the Union in 1819. Chief industries are cotton, iron, and lumber. Nitrate plants of the federal government are at Muscle Shoals. Alabama is known as the "Yellowhammer State." The state flower is the Camellia. State motto: We Dare Defend Our Rights. State bird: Yellowhammer.

Alabama has an area of 51,060 square miles; 67 counties. Population of the state and largest cities in 1960: State 3,266,740; Birmingham 340,887; Mobile 202,779; Montgomery [capital] 134,393; Tuscaloosa 63,370; Gadsden 50,088; Pritchard 47,371; Bessemer 33,054; Anniston 33,657. United States Representatives: 8.

ALASKA

Alaska, which became the 49th state in 1959 was discovered by Vitus Bering, a Dane employed by Russia in 1741. In 1867 it was purchased by the United States from Russia for $7,200,000. In 1896 gold was discovered in Klondike and has been a source of wealth many times the original purchase price. Alaska is the largest state in the union, being larger than Texas, California, and Montana combined. Because of its vast spaces and limited highways, air transportation is especially important in Alaska. Principal income is from fisheries, minerals, timber and wood products, and furs. The official state bird is the Willow Ptarmigan. The official state flower is the Forget-Me-Not.

Alaska has an area of 571,065 square miles. Population of the state and largest cities in 1960: State 226,167; Anchorage 44,237; Fairbanks 13,311; Spenard 9,074; Juneau [capital] 6,797; Ketchikan 6,483; Sitka 3,237. United States Representatives: 1.

ARIZONA

Arizona is situated in Southwestern United States. Originally part of Mexico, Arizona was ceded to the United States with New Mexico in 1848 and was admitted to the Union in 1912. Mining is a chief industry. Thru irrigation projects such as Hoover Dam, Davis Dam, and Roosevelt Dam, much semi-arid land has become highly productive. Grand Canyon, 217 miles long, is a scenic wonder of the world. Arizona is called the "Grand Canyon State." Its flower is the Saguaro Cactus and its bird is the Cactus Wren. Its motto as shown on the state seal is *Ditat Deus* (God Enriches).

Arizona has an area of 113,575 square miles; 14 counties. Population of the state and largest cities in 1960: State 1,302,161; Phoenix [capital] 439,170; Tucson 212,892; Mesa 33,772; Tempe 24,897; Yuma 23,974; Flagstaff 18,214. United States Representatives: 3.

ARKANSAS

Arkansas is of the Old South, an inland state in the South-Central group. It was admitted to the Union in 1836. About one-fourth of the state is mountainous; the Ozark Mountains are in the west. The Mississippi River forms the entire eastern boundary. Agriculture, forestry, and minerals are chief sources of wealth. Arkansas's hot springs, of which there are 47, are included in Hot Springs National Park. The springs and land surrounding them were set aside by Congress in 1832 for the enjoyment of the people. Arkansas is called "The Land of Opportunity." Its flower is the apple blossom; its motto: *Regnat Populus* (The People Rule); its bird, the Mockingbird.

Arkansas has an area of 52,499 square miles; 75 counties. Population of the state and largest cities in 1960: State 1,786,272; Little Rock [capital] 107,813; North Little Rock 58,665; Fort Smith 52,-991; Pine Bluff 44,037; Hot Springs 28,337; El Dorado City 25,292; Jonesboro 21,418; Blytheville 20,797. United States Representatives: 4.

CALIFORNIA

California occupies more than one-half the Pacific coastline of the U. S. Acquired from Mexican control in 1846, California was admitted to the Union in 1850. The gold rush, following discovery of gold in 1848, was one of the greatest ever known. Output of gold is still considerable. California is a leading state in irrigation; fruit and vegetable growing and canning are chief industries. Scenic attractions: the giant redwood trees; Lick Observatory; the Hollywood movie industry; and four national parks including Yosemite with 1189 square miles. California is called the "Golden State." Its flower is the golden poppy; its motto: *Eureka* (I Have Found It); its bird, the California valley quail.

California has an area of 156,573 square miles; 58 counties. Population of the state and largest cities in 1960: State 15,717,204; Los Angeles 2,479,015; San Francisco 740,316; San Diego 573,224; Oakland 367,548; Long Beach 344,168; San Jose 204,196; Sacramento [capital] 191,667; Fresno 133,929. United States Representatives: 38.

COLORADO

Colorado, one of the Mountain States, near the center of the western half of the U. S., was admitted to the Union in 1876. Its territory was made up partly from the Louisiana Purchase of 1803, the annexation of Texas in 1845, and from Mexican cessions in 1848. There are 14 national forests in the state, comprising 20 percent of its area. Big game is still abundant. Irrigation is extensive. Chief industries are agriculture, stock-raising, dairying, mining. Highest peak in Rocky Mountain National Parks is 14,255 feet above sea level. It is called the "Centennial State" (having entered the Union 100 years after the Declaration of Independence). State flower: Rocky Mountain columbine. Motto: *Nil Sine Numine* (Nothing Without the Deity). State bird: lark bunting.

Colorado has an area of 103,884 square miles; 63 counties. Population of the state and largest cities in 1960: State 1,753,947; Denver [capital] 493,887; Pueblo 91,181; Colorado Springs 70,194; Aurora 48,548; Boulder 37,718. United States Representatives: 4.

CONNECTICUT

Connecticut, one of the Thirteen Original States, located in New England, is called the "Constitution State," having framed in 1639 the first written constitution in America. A charter was later obtained from Charles II in England establishing Connecticut as an independent colony under its constitution. Charter Oak Place in Hartford marks the site where the charter was said to have been concealed in 1687 when a royal governor demanded its surrender. Manufacturing is the chief industry, including machinery, clocks, textiles, and hardware. The Berkshire Hills are a scenic attraction. State flower: mountain laurel. Motto: *Qui Transtulit Sustinet* (He Who Transplanted Continues To Sustain). State bird: robin.

Connecticut has an area of 4,899 square miles; 8 counties. Population of state and largest cities in 1960: State 2,535,234; Hartford [capital] 162,178; Bridgeport 156,748; New Haven 152,048; Waterbury 107,130; Stamford 92,713. United States Representatives: 6.

DELAWARE

Delaware, one of the thirteen original states (ratified the Constitution on December 7, 1787), lies in the South Atlantic group. From 1631 to 1776 three nations, for different periods, claimed sovereignty over Delaware: the Netherlands, Sweden, and Great Britain. Much of the state is low-lying, being part of the Atlantic Coastal plain and is an immense market garden and orchard for the North. Fresh water lakes and the Delaware River and Bay provide a large fishing industry. At Wilmington and vicinity is an important industrial center where explosives, chemical and lumber products, and machinery are manufactured. Delaware is nicknamed "Diamond State." Its flower is the peach blossom. The state motto is: Liberty and Independence. State bird: blue hen chicken.

Delaware has an area of 1,978 square miles; 3 counties. Population of state and largest cities in 1960: State 446,292; Wilmington 95,827; Newark 11,404; Elsmere 7,319; Dover [capital] 7,250. United States Representatives: 1.

FLORIDA

Florida, a South Atlantic State, was discovered Easter Sunday 1513 by the Spaniard Ponce de Leon, in his search for the "fountain of youth." Today the state is a favored health and pleasure resort. Called the "Sunshine State," Florida's coastline, excluding islands, is 1145 miles, 470 on the Atlantic Ocean. The central part contains 30,000 lakes. In the southern part are vast swamps, the Everglades, home of the Seminole Indians. Over five million acres of the Everglades are being drained for agriculture. Fisheries, lumber, and fruits and vegetables are chief industries. The state flower is the orange blossom. Motto: In God We Trust. Bird: mockingbird.

Florida has an area of 54,252 square miles; 67 counties. Population of state and largest cities in 1960: State 4,951,560; Miami 291,688; Tampa 274,970; Jacksonville 201,030; Saint Petersburg 181,298; Orlando 88,135; Fort Lauderdale 83,648; Hialeah 66,972; Miami Beach 63,145; Pensacola 56,752; West Palm Beach 56,208; Tallahassee [capital] 48,174. United States Representatives: 12.

GEORGIA

Georgia, of the South Atlantic group and one of the thirteen original states, ratified the United States Constitution January 2, 1788. It was visited by De Soto in 1540 and was settled in 1733 by English colonists under James Oglethorpe who founded it as a refuge for debtors from England. It is the largest state east of the Mississippi River. Savannah is its chief port. Cotton, sugar cane, resin, and turpentine are major products. At Warm Springs is a famous sanatorium for treatment of infantile paralysis. Nickname: "The Empire State of the South." Flower: Cherokee rose. Motto: Wisdom, Justice and Moderation. Bird: brown thrasher.

Georgia has an area of 58,274 square miles; 159 counties. Population of state and largest cities in 1960: State 3,943,116; Atlanta [capital] 487,455; Savannah 149,245; Columbus 116,779; Augusta 70,626; Macon 69,764; Albany 55,890; East Point 35,633; Rome 32,226; Athens 31,355; Valdosta 30,652; Marietta 25,565; La Grange 23,632. United States Representatives: 10.

HAWAII

The Hawaiian Islands were annexed to the United States by a vote of Congress July 7, 1898. The territory was established June 14, 1900. President Eisenhower on August 21, 1959 proclaimed Hawaii the 50th state and ordered a 50-star flag effective July 4, 1960. Hawaii consists of twenty islands, eight of which are inhabited. The islands are volcanic in origin, the highest point is Mauna Kea an extinct volcano 13,784 feet above sea level. Its twin is Mauna Loa, 13,680 feet, largest active volcano in the world. The climate is mild, making this a favorite vacation spot. The population is mixed including native Hawaiians, Japanese, Caucasian, Filipinos, Chinese, Koreans and Puerto Ricans. The state is noted for its excellent schools. Nickname: The Aloha State. Motto: Ua Mau Ke Ea O Ka Aina I Ka Pono (The Life of the Land is Perpetuated in Righteousness). Flower: hibiscus.

Hawaii has an area of 6,415 square miles; 5 counties. Population of state and largest cities in 1960: State 632,772; [Honolulu] 294,-194; Hilo 25,966; Kailua, Lanikai 25,622; Wahiawa 15,512; Kaneohe 14,414. United States Representatives: 2.

IDAHO

Idaho, a Mountain State, is located west of the Rockies in the Pacific Coast region. It is bounded on the north by British Columbia. Lewis and Clark were early explorers in this region. With discovery of gold in 1860 and silver in 1884, settlement was rapid. The territory of Idaho was admitted to the Union in 1890. Visitors to Idaho today follow the old Oregon Trail, the famous route of covered-wagon migration. Idaho is mountainous; altitudes range from 700 feet to Mount Borah, 12,665 feet. Lake Pend Oreille is one of the largest freshwater lakes wholly within U. S. boundaries. Agriculture and stock raising are important industries and are aided by numerous irrigation projects. Nickname: "Gem State." Motto: *Esto Perpetua* (Mayest Thou Endure Forever). Flower: syringa. Bird: mountain bluebird.

Idaho has an area of 82,708 square miles; 44 counties. Population of state and largest cities in 1960: State 632,772, Boise [capital] 34,481; Idaho Falls 33,161. United States Representatives: 2.

ILLINOIS

Illinois, the great "Prairie State," lies in the East North-Central group, its northeastern corner touching Lake Michigan. It was admitted to the Union in 1818. Chicago is one of the greatest air and rail traffic centers in the world. Springfield, the capital, was the scene of the Lincoln-Douglas debates and other events associated with Abraham Lincoln. Flower: violet. Motto: State Sovereignty—National Union. Bird: cardinal.

Meat packing, steel, foundries, petroleum refining, agricultural implements, printing, and publishing are among the chief industries in Illinois. Corn, wheat, oats, barley, and rye are leading crops. The state ranks third in bituminous coal output.

Illinois has an area of 55,930 square miles; 102 counties. Population of state and largest cities in 1960: State 10,081,158: Chicago 3,550,404; Rockford 128,075; Peoria 103,162; Springfield [capital] 83,271; East St. Louis 81,712; Evanston 79,283; Decatur 78,004; Cicero 69,130; Joliet 66,780; Aurora 63,715. United States Representatives: 24.

INDIANA

Indiana, the "Hoosier State," is bounded on the north by Michigan, on the east by Ohio, on the south by Kentucky, and on the west by Illinois. French traders reached Indiana in the early 18th century. Following the Revolution, settlers came into the state from the south and east. Indiana became a state in 1816. Indiana enshrines the birthplaces of James Whitcomb Riley and Lew Wallace. Peony is the state flower. Motto: The Crossroads of America. Bird: cardinal.

Indiana's industry is diversified. Her steel mills in the Calumet region are some of the world's largest. Tho she is predominately a manufacturing state, agriculture is important. Corn is her big crop.

Indiana has an area of 36,185 square miles; 92 counties. Population of state and largest cities in 1960: State 4,662,498; Indianapolis [capital] 476,258; Gary 178,320; Fort Wayne 161,776; Evansville 141,543; South Bend 132,445; Hammond 111,698; Terre Haute 72,500; Muncie 68,603. United States Representatives: 11.

IOWA

Iowa, in the Middle West, is a rolling prairie with soil of great fertility. Ninety-six percent of this state's acres, 34,359,152, are farms. Diversity of crops is unexcelled by any state. Marquette and Joliet were early explorers in this territory which was included in the Louisiana Purchase of 1803 and admitted to the Union in 1846. Iowa is nicknamed the "Hawk-eye State." The wild rose is the state flower. The motto: Our Liberties We Prize and Our Rights We Will Maintain. Bird: goldfinch.

In addition to her agricultural yield, Iowa mines coal and produces gypsum plaster, building stone, clay products, cement, sand and gravel. Processing of agricultural products and handling of grain and livestock are important industries. Among her varied manufactures are: farm implements, washing machines, fountain pens, and railroad equipment.

Iowa has an area of 56,032 square miles; 99 counties. Population of state and largest cities in 1960: State 2,757,537; Des Moines [capital] 208,982; Cedar Rapids 92,035; Sioux City 89,159; Davenport 88,981; Waterloo 71,755; Dubuque 56,606; Council Bluffs 55,641; Ottumwa 33,871; Clinton 33,589; Iowa City 33,443. United States Representatives: 7.

KANSAS

Kansas, the "Sunflower State," includes the geographical center of the United States. Included in the Louisiana Purchase it became a state in 1861. Agriculture is extensive, especially wheat, corn, and potatoes. Kansas City has the country's largest grain elevator. The state ranks high in coal, oil, and natural gas production. State flower: sunflower. Motto: *Ad Astra per Aspera* (To the Stars thru Difficulties). Bird: meadowlark.

Kansas has an area of 82,048 square miles; 105 counties. Population of state and largest cities in 1960: State 2,178,611; Wichita 254,698; Kansas City 121,901; Topeka [capital] 119,484; Salina 43,202; Hutchinson 37,574; Lawrence 32,858; Prairie Village 25,356; Manhattan 22,993; Leavenworth 22,052; Overland Park 21,110; United States Representatives: 5.

KENTUCKY

Kentucky, the "Blue Grass State," was originally part of Virginia, which in 1786 gave consent to its organization as a separate state and it was admitted to the Union in 1792. The population is largely engaged in agriculture. Livestock is an important industry. The state has long been noted for its fine horses. Tourist attractions are Cumberland Gap and Mammoth Cave National Park. The birthplace of Abraham Lincoln is preserved as a national historic shrine. Goldenrod is the state flower. Motto: United We Stand, Divided We Fall. Bird: cardinal.

Kentucky has an area of 39,863 square miles; 120 counties. Population of state and largest cities in 1960: State 3,038,156; Louisville 390,639; Lexington 62,810; Covington 60,376; Owensboro 42,471; Paducah 34,479; Ashland 31,283; Newport 30,070; Bowling Green 28,338; Hopkinsville 19,465; Frankfort [capital] 18,365. United States Representatives: 7.

LOUISIANA

Louisiana is situated in the South-Central region, on the Gulf of Mexico, at the mouth of the Mississippi River. The territory was sold by Napoleon's orders in 1803 to Thomas Jefferson for the United States. The Cabildo, historic government building in New Orleans where the transfer took place, is preserved as a state museum. The territory became a state in 1812. Louisiana leads in the production of sugar cane. Other important crops are corn, sweet potatoes, pecans, cotton. There are rich sulphur mines in the state; also four of the largest salt mines in the world. The colorful New Orleans Mardi Gras, held annually, attracts many tourists. "Pelican State" is Louisiana's nickname. The magnolia is the state flower. Capital: Baton Rouge. Motto: Union, Justice, Confidence. Bird: eastern brown pelican.

Louisiana has an area of 45,106 square miles; 64 Parishes. Population of state and largest cities in 1960: State 3,257,022; New Orleans 627,525; Shreveport 164,372; Baton Rouge [capital] 152,-419; Lake Charles 63,392; Monroe 52,219; Lafayette 40,400. United States Representatives: 8.

MAINE

Maine, the "Pine Tree State," in New England, is bounded on the north and east by Canada, on the south by the Atlantic, and on the west by New Hampshire and Quebec. West Quoddy Head is the extreme eastern point of the U. S. Maine came into the Union in 1820. The state is heavily wooded and mountainous; highest peak is Mt. Katahdin, 5273 feet. Woods, lakes, and streams of Maine are favored vacation spots. Fish and game are plentiful. Chief crop is the potato; as many as 55 million bushels are grown some years. Lumber, fisheries, and pulp and paper production are important. On Mt. Desert Island is Acadia National Park. Flower: pine cone. Motto: *Dirigo* (I Guide). Bird: chickadee.

Maine has an area of 31,012 square miles; 16 counties. Population of state and largest cities in 1960: State 969,265; Portland 72,566; Lewiston 40,804; Bangor 38,912; Auburn 24,449; South Portland 22,788; Augusta [capital] 21,680. United States Representatives: 2.

MARYLAND

Maryland, a Middle Atlantic border state, is one of the original thirteen. The colonial charter was granted in 1632 to Lord Baltimore. On April 28, 1788 the colony ratified the U. S. Constitution. At Annapolis, state capital, is the U. S. Naval Academy. It was during an attack on Baltimore and Fort McHenry, now a national shrine, that Francis Scott Key wrote the "Star-Spangled Banner." Baltimore on Chesapeake Bay is a great seaport and the nation's sixth largest city. Maryland produces pig iron and coal; tobacco, wheat, and corn. Nickname: "Old Line State." Flower: blackeyed Susan; Motto: *Scuto Bonae Voluntatis Tuae Coronasti Nos* (With the Shield of Thy Goodwill Thou Hast Covered Us). Bird: Baltimore oriole.

Maryland has an area of 9,874 square miles; 23 counties. Population of state and largest cities in 1960: State 3,100,689; Baltimore 939,024; Dundalk 82,428; Silver Spring 66,348; Bethesda 56,527; Wheaton 54,635; Cantonsville 37,372; Hagerstown 36,660; Essex 35,205; Cumberland 33,415; Parkville-Carney 27,236; Rockville 26,090; Annapolis [capital] 23,385. United States Representatives: 8.

MASSACHUSETTS

Early history of Massachusetts, one of the thirteen original states, is in large part the early history of America. Historic landmarks abound: Provincetown at the tip of Cape Cod; Plymouth Rock where the Pilgrims landed in 1620; Boston, "cradle of culture," where Faneuil Hall and Bunker Hill recall Revolutionary days. Bounded on the east by the Atlantic, Massachusetts is a leading industrial and manufacturing state. Boston is a great seaport. Like all New England states, Massachusetts is a popular vacation spot. State flower of the "Bay State" is the mayflower. Motto: *Ense Petit Placidam Sub Libertate Quietem* (By the Sword We Seek Peace but Peace Only Under Liberty). Bird: chickadee.

Massachusetts has an area of 7,867 square miles; 14 counties. Population of state and largest cities in 1960: State 5,148,578; Boston [capital] 697,197; Worchester 186,587; Springfield 174,463; New Bedford 102,477; Cambridge 107,716; Fall River 99,942; Somerville 94,697; Lynn 94,478; Newton 92,384; Quincy 87,409; Lawrence 70,933. United States Representatives: 12.

MICHIGAN

Michigan, the "Wolverine State," is in the heart of the Great Lakes Region along the Canadian border. It was in the territory covered by the Ordinance of 1787 and became a state in 1837. Its extensive islands, lakes, and forests are not only important industrially but attract thousands of vacationists. Isle Royale in Lake Superior is a national park. Manufacturing and mining are chief industries. Michigan leads in automobile production. The apple blossom is the state flower. Motto: *Si Quaeris Peninsulam Amoenam Circumspice* (If You Seek a Pleasant Peninsula, Look Around You). Bird: robin.

Michigan has an area of 57,019 square miles; 83 counties. Population of state and largest cities in 1960: State 7,823,194; Detroit 1,670,144; Grand Rapids 197,913; Flint 196,940; Lansing [capital] 113,058; Dearborn 112,007; Saginaw 98,265; Warren 89,246; Pontiac 82,233; Kalamazoo 82,089; Royal Oak 80,612; Ann Arbor 67,-340. United States Representatives: 19.

MINNESOTA

Minnesota contains the headwaters of three great river systems. The state is an ideal recreational area for it has over 10,000 lakes, many state parks, and state and national forests. In the middle of the 17th century, French explorers established forts and fur trading posts in the region. The British then dominated until after the War of 1812 when the U. S. acquired the land and organized a territorial government. Minnesota became a state in 1858. Wheat, corn, dairying, and iron ore are the chief products. State flower of the "North Star State" is the pink and white lady's-slipper. Motto: *L'Etoile du Nord* (Star of the North). Bird: common loon.

Minnesota has an area of 80,009 square miles; 87 counties. Population of state and largest cities in 1960: State 3,413,864; Minneapolis 482,872; St. Paul [capital] 313,411; Duluth 106,884; Bloomington 50,498; St. Louis Park 43,310; Richfield 42,523; Rochester 40,663; St. Cloud 33,815; Edina 28,501; Austin 27,908. United States Representatives: 8.

MISSISSIPPI

Mississippi, the "Magnolia State," in the East South-Central group on the Gulf of Mexico, was admitted to the Union in 1817. The climate is subtropical. Agriculture, especially cotton, is the chief interest. At Vicksburg, now a national military park, the Confederates made their last stand during the Civil War for control of the lower Mississippi River, the highway to the sea for the Union forces. With the fall of Vicksburg, the "fate of the Confederacy was sealed." The magnolia is the state flower. The motto: *Virtute et Armis* (By Valor and Arms). Bird: mockingbird. Pilgrimages to the beautiful gardens and old colonial homes at Natchez attract thousands of visitors each spring.

Mississippi has an area of 47,223 square miles; 82 counties. Population of state and largest cities in 1960: State 2,178,141; Jackson [capital] 144,422; Meridian 49,374; Biloxi 44,053; Greenville 41,502; Hattiesburg 34,989; Gulfport 30,204; Vicksburg 29,130; Laurel 27,889; Columbus 24,771; Natchez 23,791. United States Representatives: 5.

MISSOURI

Missouri, in Midwest United States, has over a thousand miles of navigable waterways on the Mississippi and Missouri Rivers. St. Louis is the gateway for north and south travel. The territory was part of the Louisiana Purchase of 1803 and became a state in 1821. Chief industries: corn, wheat, meat-packing, minerals. Missouri's vacation center is in the Ozark Mountains. Nickname of Missouri: "Show-Me State"; flower: hawthorn; motto: *Salus Populi Suprema Lex Esto* (Let the Welfare of the People Be the Supreme Law). Bird: bluebird.

Missouri has an area of 69,138 square miles; 114 counties. Population of state and largest cities in 1960: State 4,319,813; St. Louis 750,-026; Kansas City 475,539; Springfield 95,865; St. Joseph 79,673; Independence 62,328; University City 51,249; Joplin 38,958; Florissant 38,166; Columbia 36,650; Kirkwood 29,421; Webster Groves 28,990; Jefferson City [capital] 28,288; Cape Girardeau 24,947. United States Representatives: 10.

MONTANA

Montana, the "Treasure State" in Western U. S., has mountain scenery unsurpassed for lofty grandeur. Glacier Park, on the U. S.-Canadian line, is a vast public preserve of 1537 square miles. Lewis and Clark visited the Montana region in 1805. Discovery of gold in 1850 and the influx of settlers caused frequent clashes with the Indians. At Big Horn River in 1876 General Custer and all his men were massacred by Indians. Montana was admitted to the Union in 1889. Irrigation projects, including the largest dirt dam in the world at Fort Peck, have increased wheat and fruit production. Flower: bitterroot. Motto: *Oro y Plata* (Gold and Silver). Bird: meadowlark.

Montana has an area of 145,736 square miles; 56 counties. Population of state and largest cities in 1960: State 674,767; Great Falls 55,-357; Billings 52,851; Butte 27,877; Missoula 27,090; Helena [capital] 20,227; Bozeman 13,361; Anaconda 12,054; Havre 10,740; Kalispell 10,151. United States Representatives: 2.

NEBRASKA

Nebraska, a North-Central state, is in the center of a fertile plain stretching from Hudson Bay to the Gulf of Mexico. It is one of the great agricultural states of the Union. Originally a treeless prairie, the state has planted almost two million acres in trees. By act of its legislature in 1895 Nebraska was designated the "Tree Planters State." In Nebraska City is Arbor Lodge with a memorial to J. Sterling Morton, founder of Arbor Day. Nebraska entered the Union in 1867. In Lincoln is one of the country's most beautiful capitol buildings. In 1934 the state adopted the unicameral, or single chamber legislature of 43 members elected without party designation. State flower: goldenrod. Motto: Equality Before the Law. Nickname: The Cornhusker State. Bird: western meadowlark.

Nebraska has an area of 76,612 square miles; 93 counties. Population of state and largest cities in 1960: State 1,411,330; Omaha 301,598; Lincoln [capital] 128,521; Grand Island 25,742; Hastings 21,412; Fremont 19,698. United States Representatives: 3.

NEVADA

Nevada is from the Spanish meaning "snow-covered." One of the mountain states, seventh in size in the nation, Nevada was admitted to the Union in 1864. It has great stretches of sagebrush and sandy wastes, bounded by mountain ranges. Irrigation is increasing agricultural production. Mining is a chief industry. The Comstock Lode, richest deposit of precious metals ever found in the world, was discovered in 1859. From it has come approximately one billion dollars in gold and silver. Tourist connected industries make up the largest employment category. Nickname: The Silver State. Flower: Sagebrush. Motto: All for Our Country. Bird: Mountain bluebird.

Nevada has an area of 109,788 square miles; 17 counties. Population of state and largest cities in 1960: State 285,278; Las Vegas 64,405; Reno 51,470; North Las Vegas 18,422; Sparks 16,618; Henderson 12,525; Carson City [capital] 5,163; Boulder City 4,059; Elko 4,018. United States Representatives: 1.

NEW HAMPSHIRE

New Hampshire, the "Granite State," one of the original thirteen (ratified the U. S. Constitution June 21, 1788) is in New England. It was settled in 1623 at Dover and Portsmouth, three years after the Pilgrims' landing in Massachusetts. New Hampshire is bounded on the north by Canada and on the east by Maine and the Atlantic. Its surface is rugged and picturesque with high mountains, large forests, fertile valleys, and numerous lakes. The White Mountains and the forest reservations and parks are popular vacation resorts in summer and in winter during the ski season. Manufacturing, recreational resorts, agriculture, and mining are chief sources of income. Lilac is the state flower. Motto: Live Free or Die. Bird: purple finch.

New Hampshire has an area of 9,014 square miles; 10 counties. Population of state and largest cities in 1960: State 606,921; Manchester 88,282; Nashua 39,096; Concord [capital] 28,991; Portsmouth 25,-833; Dover 19,131; Berlin 17,821; Keene 17,562; Rochester 15,927; Laconia 15,288. United States Representatives: 2.

NEW JERSEY

New Jersey, one of the original thirteen (ratified the U. S. Constitution December 18, 1787), is bounded on the north and east by New York and the Atlantic Ocean and on the south and west by Delaware and Pennsylvania. Diversity of soils and climate make New Jersey the "Garden State," which produces great quantities of fruits and vegetables. Newark is an important manufacturing center. Winter sports are enjoyed on the lakes and hills in the north. State flower: violet. Motto: Liberty and Prosperity. Bird: Eastern goldfinch.

New Jersey has an area of 7,531 square miles; 21 counties. Population of state and largest cities in 1960: State 6,066,782; Newark 405,-220; Jersey City 276,101; Paterson 143,663; Camden 117,159; Trenton [capital] 114,167; Elizabeth 107,698; Clifton 82,084; East Orange 77,259; Woodbridge 78,846; Irvington 59,739; Atlantic City 59,544. United States Representatives: 15.

NEW MEXICO

New Mexico, in Southwestern U. S., was the 47th state admitted to the Union (1912). Agriculture, cattle-raising, and mining are chief industries. Rich coal fields still await development. For generations the region was the home of the Pueblo Indians whose community villages attract scientists and tourists. At Carlsbad Caverns, a national park, are some of the largest underground caverns man has yet explored. Nickname: "The Land of Enchantment." Flower: yucca. Motto: *Crescit Eundo* (It Grows as It Goes). Bird: road runner.

New Mexico has an area of 121,510 square miles; 32 counties. Population of state and largest cities in 1960: State 951,023; Albuquerque 201,189; Roswell 39,593; Sante Fe [capital] 33,394; Las Cruces 29,367; Hobbs 26,275; Carlsbad 25,541; Farmington 23,786; Clovis 23,713; Alamogordo 21,723; Gallup 14,089. United States Representatives: 2.

NEW YORK

New York, "Empire State" and most populous in the Union, is one of the original thirteen. On July 26, 1788 it ratified the U. S. Constitution. George Washington was inaugurated first president of the U. S. in New York City in 1789. Having over 800 miles of navigable waterways, New York leads in manufacturing and commerce. New York City, a seaport handling the bulk of tonnage coming to the U. S., is the nation's chief city and one of the world's largest. Among the state's noted vacation spots: Lake Placid, famous for its bobsled run and ski jumps; Lake George; Niagara Falls; the Thousand Islands; the Palisades; and a splendid system of more than 70 state parks. Flower: rose. Motto: *Excelsior* (Higher).

New York has an area of 47,939 square miles; 62 counties. Population of state and largest cities in 1960: State 16,782,304; New York City 7,781,984; Buffalo 532,759; Rochester 318,611; Syracuse 216,038; Yonkers 190,634; Albany [capital] 129,726; Niagara Falls 102,394; Utica 100,410; Schenectady 81,682; Binghamton 75,941. United States Representatives: 41.

NORTH CAROLINA

Half in North Carolina and half in Tennessee are the Great Smoky Mountains, made a national park in 1930, comprising 687 square miles of wooded mountain beauty. North Carolina was twelfth of the thirteen original states to ratify the U. S. Constitution (It ratified on November 21, 1789). At Roanoke Island, in the colony established by Sir Walter Raleigh, was born in 1587 Virginia Dare, first white child of English parentage born in the New World. Primarily an agricultural state, North Carolina "fills every blank in the census of farm products, yielding all crops grown in both northern and southern U. S." Nickname: "Tarheel State." Flower: dogwood. Motto: *Esse Quam Videri* (To Be Rather Than To Seem).

North Carolina has an area of 49,067 square miles; 100 counties. Population of the state and largest cities in 1960: State 4,556,155; Charlotte 201,564; Greensboro 119,574; Winston-Salem 111,135; Raleigh [capital] 93,931; Durham 78,302; High Point 62,063; Asheville 60,192; Fayetteville 47,106; Wilmington 44,013; Gastonia 37,-276. United States Representatives: 11.

NORTH DAKOTA

North Dakota, the "Flickertail State," is in the center of the great western wheat belt. It was organized as a territory during the struggle over slavery. Its territorial motto—Liberty and Union, Now and Forever, One and Inseparable—from a speech by Daniel Webster, was taken over when it became a state in 1889. North Dakota's economy is based on agriculture and mining. Flower, Wild Prairie Rose; bird, Western Meadowlark.

North Dakota has an area of 69,457 square miles; 53 counties. Population of the state and largest cities in 1960: State 632,446; Fargo 46,662; Grand Forks 34,451; Minot 30,604; Bismarck [capital] 27,-670; Jamestown 15,163; Williston 11,866; Mandan 10,525; Dickinson 9,971. United States Representatives: 2.

OHIO

The name Ohio is from the Iroquois meaning great river—the Ohio touching 436 miles of the state's border, to which are added 230 miles along Lake Erie, giving the state a navigable water front of over 650 miles. Ohio was the first state of the vast Northwest Territory to be admitted to the Union under the Congressional Enabling Act of 1802. Fertile soil and rich mineral resources are nature's gift to the "Buckeye State." In the Steubenville-Cleveland-Youngstown triangle is an inland empire of steel and iron. Flower: scarlet carnation. Motto: With God, All Things Are Possible. Bird: cardinal.

Ohio has an area of 40,972 square miles; 88 counties. Population of state and largest cities in 1960: State 9,706,397; Cleveland 876,-050; Cincinnati 502,550; Columbus [capital] 471,316; Toledo 318,-003; Akron 290,351; Dayton 262,332; Youngstown 166,689; Canton 113,631; Parma 82,845; Springfield 82,723; Hamilton 72,354; Lorain 66,932; Cleveland Heights 61,813; Warren 59,648. United States Representatives: 24.

OKLAHOMA

Oklahoma, in the West South-Central group, is a vast rolling plain. The territory was organized in 1834 as Indian territory and white settlers were barred. The area in the central part was opened to the public by the U. S. on April 22, 1889, in the historic "Land Rush." More than 50,000 persons entered in one day. Oklahoma was admitted to the Union in 1907. Oil discovered in the 1900's on land owned by Indians made many of them rich. Oklahoma is primarily agricultural. Nickname: "Sooner State." Flower: mistletoe. Motto: *Labor Omnia Vincit* (Labor Conquers All Things). Bird: scissor-tailed flycatcher.

Oklahoma has an area of 68,887 square miles; 77 counties. Population of state and largest cities in 1960: State 2,328,284; Oklahoma City [capital] 324,253; Tulsa 261,685; Lawton 61,697; Enid 38,-859; Muskogee 38,059; Midwest City 36,058; Norman 33,412; Bartlesville 27,893; Ponca City 24,411; Shawnee 24,326; Stillwater 23,965; Altus 21,225. United States Representatives: 6.

OREGON

Oregon, the "Beaver State," shows some mighty scenery—the broad Columbia River, snow-topped Mt. Hood, Multnomah Falls on the famous Columbia Highway. Within the state are many national forests, extensively used for recreation. The state shares in the revenue from lumber sold off these reserves and from grazing privileges. Agriculture, lumbering, fish canning (of famous Columbia River salmon), and mining, are chief industries. The great Oregon country was explored by the Lewis and Clark expedition in 1805; it became a state in 1859. Flower: Oregon grape. Motto: The Union. Bird: western meadowlark.

Oregon has an area of 96,248 square miles; 36 counties. Population of state and largest cities in 1960: State 1,768,687; Portland 372,676; Eugene 50,977; Salem [capital] 49,142; Medford 24,425; Corvallis 20,669; Springfield 19,616; Klamath Falls 16,949; Pendleton 14,434; Albany 12,926; Bend 11,936; Roseburg 11,467; Astoria 11,239. United States Representatives: 4.

PENNSYLVANIA

Pennsylvania, called the "Keystone State" because it occupied the center of the arch formed by the thirteen original states, is in the Middle Atlantic area. It was named for William Penn, founder of the colony and a leader in selfgovernment. In Philadelphia were adopted the Articles of Confederation; the Declaration of Independence; the Treaty of Peace ending the Revolution; and the U. S. Constitution, which Pennsylvania ratified December 12, 1787. Many tourists come to see historic Valley Forge and Gettysburg. Pennsylvania is one of the great iron and steel producing states. Flower: mountain laurel. Motto: Virtue, Liberty, and Independence. Bird: ruffed grouse.

Pennsylvania has an area of 45,007 square miles; 67 counties. Population of state and largest cities in 1960: State 11,319,366; Philadelphia 2,002,512; Pittsburgh 604,332; Erie 138,440; Scranton 111,443; Allentown 108,347; Reading 98,177; Upper Darby 93,158; Harrisburg [capital] 79,697; Bethlehem 75,408; Altoona 69,407; Chester 63,658; Wilkes Barre 63,551; Lancaster 61,055; Lower Merion 59,-420; York 54,504. United States Representatives: 27.

RHODE ISLAND

Rhode Island, one of the original thirteen, ratified the U. S. Constitution on May 29, 1790. Southern gateway of New England, it is the smallest state in the Union, but the most densely populated. The official name since 1776 has been "State of Rhode Island and Providence Plantations." The first settlement in Rhode Island was made in 1636 by Roger Williams who was banished from Massachusetts for his liberal political and religious ideas. Major industries are textiles, jewelry and silverware manufacture, metals, machinery and rubber and plastics. Nickname: "Little Rhody." Flower: violet. State motto: Hope.

Rhode Island has an area of 1,058 square miles; 5 counties. Population of state and largest cities in 1960: State 859,488; Providence [capital] 207,498; Pawtucket 81,001; Warwick 68,504; Cranston 66,766; Woonsocket 47,080; Newport 47,049; East Providence 41,955; West Warwick 21,414. United States Representatives: 2.

SOUTH CAROLINA

South Carolina, a South Atlantic state, was one of the original thirteen. On May 23, 1788 it ratified the United States Constitution. Fifty percent of the state's acres are in cotton and the manufacture of textiles is an important industry. Principal minerals are phosphate, granite, and clay products. Among the state's scenic attractions are the beautiful magnolia gardens at Charleston visited each year around Easter time by thousands of tourists. Nickname: "Palmetto State." Flower: Yellow jessamine. Motto: *Animis Opibusque Parati* (Prepared in Soul and Resources). Bird: Carolina wren.

South Carolina has an area of 30,272 square miles; 46 counties. Population of state and largest cities in 1960: State 2,382,594; Columbia [capital] 97,433; Greenville 66,188; Charleston 65,925; Spartanburg 44,352; Anderson 41,316; Rock Hill 29,404; Florence 24,722; Sumter 23,062; Greenwood 16,644; Orangeburg 13,852. United States Representatives: 6.

SOUTH DAKOTA

South Dakota, a North-Central state, formed the southern half of the original Dakota Territory organized in 1861 and named after the Dakota Indians. The Territory was divided into North and South by Congress in 1889. Except for the Black Hills, the state is a broad, rolling plain. Most of the population is engaged in agriculture or industries connected with it. The Black Hills area has a diversity of scenic wonders: Wind Cave National Park; five national monuments; one state park; two national forests; and Mt. Rushmore. Nickname: "Coyote State." Flower: pasque flower. Motto: Under God the People Rule. Bird: ringnecked pheasant.

South Dakota has an area of 76,378 square miles; 67 counties. Population of state and largest cities in 1960: State 680,514; Sioux Falls 65,466; Rapid City 42,399; Aberdeen 23,073; Huron 14,180; Watertown 14,077; Mitchell 12,555; Brookings 10,558; Pierre [capital] 10,088; Yankton 9,279; Lead 6,211. United States Representatives: 2.

TENNESSEE

A large part of Tennessee is in the area of the Tennessee Valley Authority, created by Congress in 1933 to conserve and develop the natural resources of the region, which also takes in portions of six other states. The TVA experiment includes control of soil erosion, provision of cheap electric power thru a unified system of dams, and social-economic planning of the region as a whole. Tennessee's great scenic attractions are mountains: Lookout, where the Battle of Chattanooga in the Civil War was fought, and the Great Smokies, now a national park. Flower: iris. Motto: Agriculture and Commerce. Bird: mockingbird.

Tennessee has an area of 41,762 square miles; 95 counties. Population of state and largest cities in 1960: State 3,567,089; Memphis 497,524; Nashville [capital] 170,874; Chattanooga 130,009; Knoxville 111,827; Jackson 34,376; Johnson City 31,187; Oak Ridge 27,169; Inglewood 26,527; Kingsport 26,314; Clarksville 22,021; Morristown 21,267; East Ridge 19,570; Columbia 17,624; Bristol 17,582; Donelson 17,195. United States Representatives: 9.

TEXAS

Texas, in South-Central U. S., second largest state in the Union, grows more cotton than any other state and furnishes much crude oil. It supports millions of cattle. Texans are proud of their history: the winning of their independence from Mexico at the Battle of the Alamo and at San Jacinto under Sam Houston; their status as an independent republic from 1836 to 1845 when they joined the Union. The "Lone Star" flag of their republic is now the state flag. Flower: bluebonnet. Motto: Friendship. Bird: Mockingbird.

Texas has an area of 262,840 square miles; 254 counties. Population of state and largest cities in 1960: State 9,579,677; Houston 938,219; Dallas 679,684; San Antonio 587,718; Fort Worth 356,268; El Paso 276,687; Austin [capital] 186,545; Corpus Christi 167,690; Amarillo 137,969; Lubbock 128,691; Beaumont 119,175; Wichita Falls 101,724; Waco 97,808; Abilene 90,368; Odessa 80,338; Galveston 67,175; Port Arthur 66,676; Midland 62,625; Laredo 60,678. United States Representatives: 23.

UTAH

Utah, in the far West, takes its name from an Indian tribe of Utes or Yutas. Known as the "Beehive State," Utah was settled in 1847 by Mormons who fled, under the leadership of John Smith and Brigham Young, from religious persecution in the Midwest. Utah came into the Union in 1896. The nation was spanned by rail in 1869 when a golden spike was driven at Promontory Point near Great Salt Lake on May 10. Scenic attractions are Utah's two national parks: Zion Canyon with its huge sandstone cliffs, and Bryce Canyon, famous for its Pink Cliffs, brilliantly colored rock pinnacles cut out by weathering along the edge of an 8,000-ft. plateau. Flower: sego lily. Motto: Industry. Bird: seagull.

Utah has an area of 82,339 square miles; 29 counties. Population of state and largest cities in 1960: State 890,627; Salt Lake City [capital] 189,454; Ogden 70,197; Provo 36,047; Logan 18,731; Orem 18,394; Kearns 17,172. United States Representatives: 2.

VERMONT

Vermont, New England's only inland state, was the 14th to join the Union (1791). Lake Champlain forms most of the western boundary. The Green Mountains run north and south thru the state. More than 300 lakes and several state and national forests make this a recreation mecca. Hardly a section is without facilities for winter sports. Preeminently a dairy state, Vermont leads in production of maple syrup. In 1775 at the start of the Revolution, the "Green Mountain Boys" under Ethan Allen captured Fort Ticonderoga—an important victory for the colonies. Nickname: Green Mountain State. Flower: red clover. Motto: Freedom and Unity. Bird: hermit thrush.

Vermont has an area of 9,276 square miles; 14 counties. Population of state and largest cities in 1960: State 389,881; Burlington 35,531; Rutland 18,325; Barre 10,387; Brattleboro 9,315; St. Albans 8,806; Montpelier [capital] 8,782. United States Representatives: 1.

VIRGINIA

Virginia, a Middle Atlantic state, shares with Massachusetts the heritage of America's early history. At Jamestown in 1607 the first permanent English settlement was made. In 1619 at Jamestown was held the first representative assembly of the new world. At Yorktown the Revolution ended (1781) with surrender of a British army. The Civil War closed with surrender of General Lee's army April 1865 at Appomattox Court House. Principal shrines in Virginia: the Colonial National Historic Park including restored Williamsburg; Mount Vernon, Washington's home; Monticello, near Charlottesville, Jefferson's home; and Arlington, home of Lee. Virginia is the "Old Dominion." Flower: dogwood. Motto: *Sic Semper Tyrannis* (Thus Always to Tyrants). Bird: Cardinal.

Virginia has an area of 39,838 square miles; 96 counties. Population of state and largest cities in 1960: State 3,966,949; Norfolk 304,869; Richmond [capital] 219,958; Portsmouth 144,773; Newport News 113,662; Roanoke 97,110; Alexandria 91,023; Hampton 89,258; Lynchburg 54,790. United States Representatives: 10.

WASHINGTON

Washington, "the Evergreen State" on the Pacific Coast, includes 40,000 square miles of forested land. Over the waters and cities of Puget Sound, presides snow-covered Mount Rainier, third highest in the U. S. The state is noted for its apples, lumber products, and canned salmon. Growth of this region has been phenomenal since 1884, with the advent of the first railroad. Seattle is a leading seaport. Washington became a state in 1889. Flower: rhododendron. Motto: *Alki* (settlers at Alki, now Seattle, called the camp "New York of the Pacific," adding *Alki,* which is Indian for "By and By.") Bird: willow goldfinch.

Washington has an area of 66,709 square miles; 39 counties. Population of state and largest cities in 1960: State 2,853,214; Seattle 557,-087; Spokane 181,608; Tacoma 147,979; Yakima 43,284; Everett 40,304; Bellingham 34,688; Vancouver 32,464; Bremerton 28,922; Walla Walla 24,536; Richland 23,548; Longview 23,349; Aberdeen 18,741 Olympia [capital] 18,273. United States Representatives: 7.

WEST VIRGINIA

When Virginia seceded from the Union at the outbreak of the Civil War, the western counties opposed and set up West Virginia, which was admitted to the Union in 1863. The state looks westward from a high plateau which slopes to the Ohio River. There are four geographic regions: Ohio Valley, Cumberland Plateau, Allegheny Highland, and Potomac Valley. Coal, oil, gas, and bromine are among the richest resources; mineral springs abound. About 74 percent of the total area is in timber lands. Flower: rhododendron. Motto: *Montani Semper Liberi* (Mountaineers Are Always Freemen). Bird: Cardinal.

West Virginia has an area of 24,079 square miles; 55 counties. Population of state and largest cities in 1960: State 1,860,421; Charleston [capital] 85,796; Huntington 83,627; Wheeling 53,400; Parkersburg 44,797; Weirton 28,201; Fairmont 27,477; Morgantown 22,-487; Bluefield 19,256; South Charleston 19,180; Beckley 18,642. United States Representatives: 5.

WISCONSIN

Wisconsin, the "Badger State," in the East North-Central group, came into the Union in 1848. It is also called "Copper State" because of the copper in the soil and rocks which gives several rivers their unusual color. Geologists are attracted by the peculiar rock formations as seen in the Dells. Tourists enjoy Devils Lake in Sauk County, which is set between huge quartzite bluffs. The state is a leader in dairying. Agriculture in all phases is important. At Madison, the capital, is the U. S. Department of Agriculture's Forest Products Laboratory, said to be unique in the world. Wisconsin has pioneered in social legislation: its unemployment compensation act was the first adopted by any state. Flower: violet. Motto: Forward. Bird: robin.

Wisconsin has an area of 54,705 square miles; 72 counties. Population of state and largest cities in 1960: State 3,951,777; Milwaukee 741,324; Madison [capital] 126,706; Racine 89,144; West Allis 68,157; Kenosha 67,899; Green Bay 62,888; Wauwatosa 56,923; Appleton 48,411; La Crosse 47,575; Sheboygan 45,747; Oshkosh 45,110. United States Representatives: 10.

WYOMING

Wyoming, in the Western Mountain region, is called "Equality State," because it was the first to grant suffrage to women (1869). It was admitted to the Union in 1890. The state is rich in scenic beauty. In Yellowstone, oldest and best known of the national parks, are Yellowstone Falls, higher than Niagara, and Old Faithful Geyser, greatest single attraction in U. S. parks. Also in Wyoming: Grand Teton National Park; Thermopolis Hot Springs; Devils Tower and Shoshone Cavern. Ranch life still retains Old West flavor. Wyoming is one of the great cattle-raising states. Flower: Indian paintbrush. Motto: *Cedant Arma Togae* (Let Arms Yield to the Gown). Bird: Meadowlark.

Wyoming has an area of 97,411 square miles; 23 counties. Population of state and largest cities in 1960: State 330,066; Cheyenne [capital] 43,505; Casper 38,930; Laramie 17,520; Sheridan 11,651; Rock Springs 10,371. United States Representatives: 1.

OFF SHORE AREAS UNDER JURISDICTION OR ADMINISTRATION OF THE UNITED STATES

AMERICAN SAMOA. An unincorporated territory, which came under U.S. ownership by a treaty with the United Kingdom and Germany in 1899, it is administered by the Department of Interior.

CANAL ZONE AND PANAMA CANAL. The Canal Zone Government and the Panama Canal Company, the two operating agencies of the United States government, are both headed by an individual who acts as Governor of the Canal Zone and President of the Company. The governor is appointed by the President of the U. S. As governor he reports directly to the Secretary of the Army. As president of the company he reports to the board of directors, appointed by the Secretary of the Army.

CAROLINE, MARIANA, AND MARSHALL ISLANDS. The Trust Territory of these Pacific Islands, with the exception of Guam, came under the jurisdiction of the U. S. in 1951 by an agreement with the Security Council of the United Nations. They are under administration of the Department of Interior.

GUAM. Ceded to the U. S. by Spain in 1898, Guam is now an organized and unincorporated territory under the jurisdiction of the Department of Interior.

PUERTO RICO. The constitution of the Commonwealth of Puerto Rico was approved in 1952 and the island is now wholly autonomous in all matters of local government, and is voluntarily associated with the United States.

RYUKU ISLANDS. Okinawa, largest of the group was taken by U. S. troops in 1945. Administration of the islands, which was vested in U. S. by the Japanese peace treaty in 1951, is carried out by a High Commissioner responsible to the U. S. Secretary of Defense.

VIRGIN ISLANDS. The islands, which were purchased from Denmark in 1917 for defense purposes, are an organized and unincorporated territory administered by the Department of Interior.

WAKE AND MIDWAY ISLANDS. U. S. took formal possession of Wake Island in 1899. It is administered by the Federal Aviation Administration. Midway Islands, acquired in 1867, are administered by the Navy Department.

PART X

The Heart of the Nation

As we look down upon Washington from the air, as pictured on the opposite page, we see that the nation's capital is not laid out in the familiar checkerboard pattern of most cities. Instead it is shaped around the mall, or "great garden," which extends from the Capitol in the center of the picture, to the Washington Monument, and thence to the Lincoln Memorial on its commanding site near the Potomac River. Behind the Lincoln Memorial may be seen the Arlington Bridge linking Washington with Virginia.

From the Capitol radiate broad, tree-lined avenues. Most famous are Pennsylvania and Constitution Avenues at the intersection of which may be seen the Federal Triangle Buildings, the "workshops of democracy." To the right behind the Capitol going clockwise are the Senate Office Buildings, the Supreme Court, Library of Congress, Senate and House Office Buildings, and many others.

Photo, Washington Convention and Visitors Bureau

A VISIT TO WASHINGTON, D.C.

Since most visitors have a limited time to enjoy Washington, they will find it helpful to study in advance guidebooks of the city. One of the most complete is the 1968 edition of *Washington, D. C.—A Guide to the Nation's Capital*, edited by Randall Bond Truett (Hastings House, N. Y.). Following are some of the outstanding points of interest and beauty. Many are discussed in this chapter and many are pictured in this book.

Capitol Hill

The Capitol
House Office Buildings
Senate Office Buildings
Library of Congress
Folger Shakespeare Library
Museum of African Arts
Supreme Court
Union Station
Government Printing Office

President's Square and Seventeenth Street

White House
Blair House
St. John's Episcopal Church
Lafayette Square—Historic Houses
Executive Office Building
Memorial Continental Hall
Corcoran Gallery of Art
Pan American Union

Downtown

Ford's Theatre
Nat'l Collection of Fine Arts
Nat'l Portrait Gallery

The Mall and Fourteenth Street

History & Technology Museum
Natural History Museum
National Gallery of Art
Army Medical Museum
Smithsonian Building
Arts & Industries Building
Air and Space Building
Freer Gallery of Art
Washington Monument
Lincoln Memorial
Bureau, Printing & Engraving
Thomas Jefferson Memorial

Federal Triangle

National Archives
Dept. of Justice and the FBI
Other Government Buildings

Nearby Virginia

Arlington Cemetery
Tomb of the Unknown Soldier
Lee Mansion
Iwo Jima Monument
Pentagon
Alexandria and Mt. Vernon

Other

Woodrow Wilson House
Embassies
Phillips Gallery
Washington Gallery of Modern Art
Kennedy Center for Performing Arts
U. S. Naval Observatory
Islamic Center
National Zoological Park
National Arboretum
Theodore Roosevelt Island
Dumbarton Oaks (Georgetown)
Washington Cathedral
Nat'l Shrine of the Immaculate Conception

Washington
Our Many-Splendored City

WILLADENE PRICE

IN 1798 George Washington predicted that this country would produce "on the banks of the Potomack" a city "inferior to few others in Europe." Eight years earlier, after having narrowed the area for a permanent seat of government to an 80-mile stretch along the Potomac, Congress authorized Washington to select the exact site for the capital, which he did. Almost immediately Washington and Thomas Jefferson, his Secretary of State, chose a young artist of great vision, 37-year-old Major Pierre Charles L'Enfant, a French engineer officer who had fought for American independence, to lay out the plan for the new Federal City.

The admirable location of the Capitol and the White House, which now serve as hubs from which emanate broad avenues with circles and squares reserved for monuments to national heroes, was due to L'Enfant's brilliant planning.

On September 18, 1793, President Washington laid the cornerstone for the Capitol building which had been designed by his friend, Dr. William Thornton, a physician and amateur architect, who was awarded a $500 prize for his plan. Later other architects, including Benjamin Latrobe and Charles Bulfinch, worked on the Capitol. The first section of the building, the small flat-roofed wing, adjoining the rotunda area to the north was completed in 1800 but Washington did not live to see his government convened in its permanent home. He died in December 1799, and it was not until May of 1800 that the offices of the government, which for ten years had been in Philadelphia, were removed to the Federal City. George Washington, who gave so much loving attention to the building of an executive's house, is the only president not to live in the White House.

In November 1800, Congress met for the first time in the Federal City, which was not a city at all but a miserable mudhole of a village with fewer than 500 houses, a tavern or two, a hotel, one department building—Treasury—a plain two-story brick building of 30 rooms, and a President's house with no water supply and with the plaster on the walls still wet. Even so, President John Adams told the Congress, "You will consider it as the capital of a great nation, advancing with unexampled rapidity in arts, in commerce, in wealth, and in population."

But the city did not advance with "unexampled rapidity." It remained dreary and desolate, and there was continued agitation for removal of the government to some established place. In 1814 when the British left Washington charred and blackened, the cry for removal of the Capital rose to a high pitch. A wise Congress borrowed half a million dollars and restored the Capitol building.

Fifty years after John Adams had spoken, the Mall was still bordered by a canal that served as an open sewer and pigs, cows, and chickens roamed the city without restraint. However, by the 1850's so many new states had been admitted to the Union that it became necessary to add a wing on either side of the Capitol to house the Senate and the House of Representatives.

While there were many refinements by the time President and Mrs. Lincoln moved to the White House, Mr. Lincoln and the Congress, meeting under the unfinished dome of the Capitol, were more absorbed in the fate of the Union than they were in the beauty of Washington. The unsightly stump of the partially completed Washington Monument was of little concern to a citizenry struggling day and night to feed and care for soldiers.

Actually, there were no great changes until President Grant's administration when Alexander Robey Shepherd, the energetic head of Public Works, initiated a whirlwind program of civic improvement and ran up an illegal public debt of 12 million dollars to finance paving the miles of mud streets and planting thousands of shade trees along them, laying the water lines, and digging sewers, thus putting an end to Washington's notorious stench. Following a Senate investigation, Shepherd left Washington in disgrace, but in 1909 a grateful public erected a bronze statue of the "Boss" which today stands in front of the District Building on Pennsylvania Avenue.

At the turn of the century, while Chicago and all America were still basking in the glory of the success of the World's Columbian Exposition, Congress appointed a commission of illustrious architects and artists to develop a pattern of growth for the city. There was a new awareness of the L'Enfant plan. Americans throughout the land began to recognize that Washington was their city, and there was an ever-growing urge on the part of the citizenry for the creation of a more beautiful Capital City.

Washington of today is the product of a continuing desire on the part of an artistically awakened populace to make our Capital City the most beautiful national showcase of monuments, museums, art galleries, government buildings, and libraries in the world. Today Washington is clean and green and quietly dignified. It has but two major businesses, the government of the United States and tourism. Speed and ease of travel make it possible for seven million Americans from the 50 states and territories to visit Washington each year to see and enjoy their many national treasures. A circumferential highway encircling Washington facilitates entry from any direction. Following is a brief glimpse of our many-splendored Washington—the only city in the United States that belongs to all Americans.

True, Washington, like every other modern city, is suffering from growing pains—expanding traffic, slum poverty, and other problems inherent in a city with a rapidly expanding population. But nothing can change its air of American history or its majestic monuments to freedom.

The city is lovely any time of the year. Even in the winter her great old trees, glistening with snow, transform the many parks and tree-lined streets into a white wonderland. During the Christmas holidays on the Ellipse, an open area near the White House, the President lights a giant community tree thus signaling the opening of the annual Pageant of Peace. Once every four years there is a special attraction on January 20, when a quarter of a million visitors jam the city to take part in the historic event of inaugurating a president. In the spring, the annual Cherry Blossom Festival, usually held during the first ten days of April, is a main attraction.

Throughout the summer, visitors and natives enjoy free outdoor concerts and festivals. Especially thrilling is the spectacular display of fireworks from the base of the Washington Monument on the Fourth of July. Also in the summer there are conducted tours along the Chesapeake and Ohio Canal via an old time mule-drawn barge. On weekends, from June through October, one may take a ferry to explore a small island in the Potomac River opposite Washington and near Georgetown. This island, known as Theodore Roosevelt Island, is a living memorial to the great conservationist.

A Bird's-Eye View of the City

The Washington Monument, along with the Capitol dome, has become a symbol of the city and no matter what the season, is a good starting place for a tour. Designed by Robert Mills, whose original plan called for a Greek peristyle temple around the base, the clean serene obelisk has a stormy history with tales of theft and destruction. In 1848, using the same trowel which Washington had used when he laid the cornerstone for the Capitol, Benjamin French, uncle of Daniel Chester French who years later gave us the magnificent Lincoln for the Lincoln Memorial, laid the cornerstone for the Washington Monument. Seven years later the Monument had reached a height of only 152 feet and it was so beset with problems of finance and controversy that for over 20 years it remained a miserable stump. The Monument's 3,300-pound capstone with a 100-ounce aluminum tip was set in place in a raging gale 36 years after it was started, a delay which is as one writer says "memorialized by a difference in the shading in the stones."

Now, in a minute and a quarter via high-speed elevator, one is transported to the top of the tallest masonry structure in the world to a height of 555 feet and a breathtaking view of the entire city and parts of Maryland and Virginia. From here it is easy to follow the Potomac or the Anacostia River or the lazy course of Rock Creek through miles of magnificent scenery. One can watch the flight of planes at nearby Washington National Airport, see the National Cathedral and the spires of Georgetown University and the Masonic National Memorial to George Washington in Alexandria, Virginia.

Below, in the immediate vicinity, is the Mall, a parkland 1500 feet wide stretching from the Capitol to the Lincoln Memorial with the Washington Monument in the center. The White House to the north of the Monument is at the end of a similar park forming a cross axis which continues south to the Jefferson Memorial.

The Jefferson Memorial

There is a sense of historical continuity in going from the Monument to our first president to the Memorial to Thomas Jefferson, the drafter of the Declaration of Independence, a champion of the Bill of Rights, and our third president. In the early Spring, the bronze Thomas Jefferson, by sculptor Rudulph Evans, standing in a magnificent white Georgia marble temple, looks out over the placid Tidal Basin at the pink flowering Japanese Cherry trees.

The Lincoln Memorial

Of all the national shrines, perhaps the most inspiring, especially when viewed at night is the Lincoln Memorial,

M. Woodridge Williams, National Park Service

STAGE, FORD THEATRE
(Flag-draped President's box to the right)

a classic Greek parthenon designed by Henry Bacon. On a moonlight night, it is an unforgettable experience to walk up the great flight of steps toward the high white temple and gradually approach the majestic statue of Abraham Lincoln seated within its Doric columns. There is strength in the great hands—one sculptured from a life cast of Lincoln's own hand, is clenched as if to show power and tension. The other, gently relaxed over the arm of the curule chair, and fashioned after a cast of the sculptor's own hand, expresses a feeling of calm.

Lincoln, portrayed by the sculptor Daniel Chester French, is tired and worn from the long civil conflict and yet there is a spiritual grandeur that shines through the rugged likeness and imparts to the viewer a feeling of warmth and peace and hope for the future.

Newest of the Lincoln shrines is the recently restored Ford's theatre in downtown Washington where Lincoln was shot.

Washington Convention and Visitors Bureau

THE SMITHSONIAN ADMINISTRATION BUILDING

The Mall and the Smithsonian

Connecting the Lincoln Memorial and the Washington Monument is the famous reflecting pool. Beyond, toward the Capitol, the Mall is lined with museums and galleries. The adjacent territory is dotted with public buildings including the nearby offices of Health, Education and Welfare where one may visit the Voice of America studios, and also the popular Bureau of Engraving and Printing.

Dominating the Mall is the Smithsonian complex. The Smithsonian owes its beginning to a scientist, James Smithson, illegitimate son of an English aristocrat, who bequeathed half a million dollars to the United States Government "to found at Washington, under the name of the Smithsonian Institution, an establishment for the increase and diffusion of knowledge among men."

The original building, a huge red brick castle with towers and turrets, now houses the administrative offices. The tomb of James Smithson is also in this building. Since its completion in 1855, the Smithsonian has grown to include many galleries and museums and is actively engaged in scientific research and cultural development. It even operates within the city a fine zoo.

On the Independence Avenue side of the Mall, there's the Freer Gallery with its collections of oriental art objects, the Arts and Industries Building, and the Air and Space Building.

Across the Mall is the new Museum of History and Technology and the Museum of Natural History. On down the Mall toward the Capitol is the magnificent National Gallery of Art with its priceless collection of great art works, including the only Leonardo da Vinci painting in the United States.

The Smithsonian's two newest art galleries, The National Collection of Fine Arts and The National Portrait Gallery, are located in another area in one of the city's fine Greek revival buildings, the mammoth old Patent Office.

Capitol Hill

High on a hilltop, ever dominating the Washington scene, is the white-domed nation's Capitol. The nine-million pound cast iron dome took shape over the rotunda during the Civil War. The bronze Statue of Freedom, a woman clad in flowing drapes and wearing a helmet surmounted by a crest composed of an eagle's head and an arrangement of feathers, took her place atop on December 2, 1863.

Throughout its marble halls the Capitol is so profusely decorated that Mark Twain suggested here was to be found "the delirium tremens of art." Mark Twain, notwithstanding, there are many great artists represented and much of beauty to be seen among the building's 750 works of art, including portraits, historical paintings, statues, mantles, clocks and stained glass windows.

Of special interest to visitors is Statuary Hall in the Old House Chamber. In 1864 each state was invited to furnish two statues of distinguished deceased favorite sons to be placed in National Statuary Hall. All but a few states contributed at least one statue and due to structural conditions in 1933 it was decided that only one statue from each state would be placed in the Hall and the others would be located elsewhere in the building.

When Congress is in session, those who wish to see and hear our lawmakers carry out their duties under the Constitution may do so by securing, from the office of one of their senators or representatives, a card of admittance to the Visitors gallery of the respective Chambers.

Senate offices are housed in two buildings on Constitution avenue to the north of the Capitol while the three House office buildings are to the south on Independence avenue. The newest and most elaborate of the House office buildings is the Rayburn Building.

Within the grandiose Main Library of Congress, which faces the Capitol, and the five story annex behind it, are some 414 miles of shelves filled with books, pamphlets, manuscripts, maps, music, pictures, and reels of newspapers on microfilm. In a listening room in a corner of the basement one may hear authentic folk music or such famed poets as Robert Frost, Carl Sandburg, or T. S. Eliot reading their poetry. Records may also be purchased there or by mail.

The Folger Shakespeare Library and museum which houses a fabulous collection of Shakespeareana is but a few steps from the Library of Congress Annex.

Nearby is the Museum of African Arts housing, among other things, African musical instruments and a panorama of Afro-American history. The museum is in the first Washington home of Frederick Douglass, a former slave, American statesman, and foremost Negro exponent for equal rights in the nineteenth century.

From the day it first met in New York City in 1790 until 1935, when the Justices occupied the magnificent new marble Supreme Court building near the Capitol, our highest court had had no real home. For the 75 years prior to 1935, it had met in the Old Senate Chamber in the Capitol. Today our Supreme Court meets in a stately chamber befitting its high position. When the opening session of court at 10 A.M. is announced impressively by a crier, the black-robed justices file in and solemnly take their places in the leather chairs behind a high mahogany bench. The drama and the dignity of the proceedings in this courtroom are long to be remembered by the visitor.

Capitol Hill also has its share of Washington's many statues. One of the most impressive, located to the west of the Capitol, is the Grant memorial, the largest and most expensive statuary grouping in the city.

Several blocks from the Capitol, near the Roman Classic Union Station and City Post Office, both designed by Daniel H. Burnham, famed architect and director of works for the Columbian Exposition, is the largest printing plant in the world, The Government Printing Office. It occupies four buildings within whose walls the visitor may get a complete view of bookmaking from manuscript to finished publication.

No other mile of American roadway is so rich in American history as the stretch of Pennsylvania Avenue from the Capitol to the White House. The inaugural parade of every president since Jefferson and the funeral processions of the Presidents who died in office have followed this route.

A huge public buildings program has carried forward the development of the Triangle Plan along Pennsylvania and Constitution Avenues and now the red tile roofs of these buildings form an almost unbroken line of color along the nine blocks of the triangle. Here is located the imposing Archives, designed by John Russell Pope, where one may view the original copies of the Declaration of Independence, Constitution and Bill of Rights.

Young and old alike are fascinated to watch the technicians at work at the business of solving crime at the Federal Bureau of Investigation in the Department of Justice. Other workshops of democracy in the Federal Triangle include the Commerce Department with its huge Census Clock that records the population increase, by minutes and days, through births, deaths, immigration and emigration. There is also a fine aquarium in the lower level of the Commerce Department. Near there, on Pennsylvania Avenue, is the Post Office Department where one may enjoy an exhibition of rare stamps.

White House and Environs

Although the White House, located at 1600 Pennsylvania Avenue, has been enlarged and modified over the years, basically it retains much of the original design of James Hoban, who, like Thornton for his Capitol design, received a prize of $500. Incidentally, years later it was discovered that Thomas Jefferson anonymously submitted one of the rejected designs for the President's house.

Washington Convention and Visitors Bureau

THE WHITE HOUSE

Years ago uninvited visitors, most of them with grievances, wandered at will through the White House. Today the visiting citizens who come by the thousands to see and admire this lovely home are welcomed at certain times only, usually on Tuesday through Saturday mornings. On these days, long lines begin to form early in the morning at the East Gate to enter at ten o'clock. The most famous room shown to the public is the resplendent white and gold reception room known as the East Room. Here bodies of Presidents who die in office are laid in state; here is where Mrs. John Adams hung her wash; and where Teddy Roosevelt staged a wrestling match.

Directly across from the White House is historic Lafayette Park. Among the statues in the park is Clark Mills' Andrew Jackson, the first equestrian statue to be erected in Washington.

Many famous houses are in the vicinity of the park including Dolley Madison House where the widowed

Dolley lived and ruled Washington Society, and the Georgian Decatur House, home of the naval hero Stephen Decatur. Blair House, a guest house for foreign dignitaries on state visits, is also here.

Proclaimed by President Truman as "the greatest monstrosity in America" the old State Building next door to the White House is a baroque masterpiece of the gilded age—inside and outside. This architectural curio which formerly housed the State, War and Navy Departments now contains offices associated with the Executive Office.

Going south, on down Seventeenth Street, the visitor to Washington will find a variety of interesting places. There is the Corcoran Art Gallery, which emphasizes works of American artists, but also has among its original collections over 100 Antoine Barye bronzes of animals. Nearby is the complex of buildings of the National Society, Daughters of the American Revolution: famed Constitution Hall; Memorial Continental Hall housing 28 period rooms and a Museum of Revolutionary relics. There is also the Pan American Union with its elaborate skylit patio, and the huge Interior Department Building which has a fine Museum of Indian and pioneer materials.

Other Points of Interest

Among the many colorful drives in the city is that along Embassy Row out Massachusetts Avenue to view a few of the hundred or so embassies located in Washington.

Close by, in an area known as Kalorama, is the home of President Woodrow Wilson, now a public museum.

Also on Massachusetts Avenue is the spectacular Islamic Center or Mosque, a joint undertaking of the Moslem countries with diplomatic missions here.

One of the newest and most exciting museums in Washington is the National Geographic Society's Explorer's Hall.

Georgetown

Before the Capital City was born Georgetown was a thriving tobacco and wheat port and when the city of Washington was in its infancy many of the government officials chose to live in Georgetown and travel by stagecoach each day to the Capital. It is the same today. High ranking statesmen and others who can afford the luxury of this delightful village, reminiscent of the Federal and Georgian period, reside here. People from everywhere enjoy browsing through the myriad of tiny stores in Georgetown's unique shopping district.

Among the few mansions open to the public in Georgetown is Dumbarton Oaks and its exquisite gardens.

Foggy Bottom

Foggy Bottom, an area southeast of Georgetown, was but a few years past a shabby brewery district. Today it boasts many fine new buildings including the very unusual Pan American Health Organization of Uruguayan design. Here also is the new home of the State Department. By making advance reservation, one may visit its attractive oak-paneled International Conference Suite and beautifully appointed diplomatic rooms. Here, too, along the Potomac, as a living memorial to President John F. Kennedy, is being built the city's first cultural center.

Nearby Virginia

The circular drive around the Lincoln Memorial leads to the Arlington Memorial Bridge Plaza where four mon-

National Park Service

RAISING THE FLAG ON IWO JIMA
U. S. MARINE CORPS WAR MEMORIAL

umental bronze equestrian statues surfaced with pure gold, a gift from the people of Italy, mark the entrance to two bridges. One bridge leads to the Rock Creek and Potomac Parkway and the other to Virginia and the Arlington National Cemetery. If one looks carefully when crossing the Arlington Memorial bridge, he can see the flickering eternal flame at the grave of John F. Kennedy. The first year following his death, seven million persons came to stand at the grave of the young President on the slope in front of the Custis-Lee Mansion. Only one other president is buried there, William Howard Taft.

The simple Tomb of the Unknown Soldier, which is flanked by the resting places of the Unknown Serviceman of World War II, and the Unknown Serviceman of the Korean War, on the plaza of the Arlington Memorial Amphitheater, is a cherished shrine for all Americans. Day and night, 365 days of the year, a solitary honor guard keeps vigil over the monument and every hour on the hour there is a silent changing of the guard.

Near the cemetery, on Arlington Ridge Road, is perhaps the nation's most famous war memorial—Felix de Weldon's bronze Iwo Jima Statue inspired by the photograph taken by Joe Rosenthal when a group of Marines raised the United States flag on Mount Suribachi.

Going out Mount Vernon Memorial Highway, which extends from Arlington bridge to Mt. Vernon, George Washington's home, one crosses an arched bridge connecting a narrow island with the mainland. On this island, known as Columbia, is a striking memorial honoring men who in the Navy and Merchant Marine "had given life or still offer it in the performance of heroic deeds." The statue, designed by Ernesto Begni del Piatti, and cast in aluminum, is a dramatic composition of seven sea gulls in flight rising from the crest of a wave.

Enroute to Mt. Vernon one may stop off at the Pentagon, headquarters for the Department of Defense, and with the aid of a floor plan wander around its 17½ miles of corridor.

Following a visit to Mt. Vernon and its beautiful grounds, a stopover in George Washington's hometown, Alexandria, can be a rewarding experience. The Tourist Council, housed in the reconstructed Ramsey House, known as Alexandria's oldest house, will help you plan a

Washington Convention and Visitors Bureau

THE PENTAGON

tour of the city. Among the many places familiar to George Washington are: historic Gadsby's Tavern, where Washington received his first commission and where he celebrated his last birthday; the Stabler-Leadbeater Apothecary Shop, second oldest drug store in the United States; the *Alexandria Gazette,* oldest continuous daily newspaper in the nation; Friendship Veterans Fire Engine Company, organized by Washington; Carlyle House, built in 1752; an authentic replica of Washington's Town House built on the original site by Gov. and Mrs. Richard Barrett Lowe; Christ Church, attended by both the Washington and the Lee families.

Alexandria was the boyhood home of Robert E. Lee and his home and many other places associated with him remain much as they were 150 years ago. One of Alexandria's newest museums and restored historical sites is Fort Ward, a part of the ring of Civil War defenses around Washington.

PART XI

Democracy in Faith and Practice

★ ★ ★ ★

Democracy as a Great Social Faith

The following material is taken from The Education of Free Men in American Democracy, *published by the National Education Association in 1941. The Educational Policies Commission, appointed by the National Education Association and the American Association of School Administrators, prepared a series of influential reports and* The Education of Free Men *is one of the most outstanding.*

DEMOCRACY is more than institutions and ways of life. It is a great social faith which, in response to the yearnings and struggles of many races and peoples, has been developing thru the centuries. It is a bold and positive faith which, now as in other times, calls men to battle for the defense and realization of noble and lofty conceptions of the nature and destiny of men. It is the finest of all the social faiths that mankind has fashioned and followed during the thousands of years of human history. It is incomparably finer than the totalitarian rivals with which it is engaged in struggle for survival today. It is a social faith that, in spite of the darkness which now seems to be settling over much of the world, will in the course of time conquer the earth. And it will conquer, not by force of arms and the use of terror, but by the power of its ideas and its hopes. It will conquer because it is the only social faith that can bring justice and mercy to all men.

The articles of the democratic faith have never been codified. They are recorded in the carefully preserved sayings and writings of the great prophets and seers of mankind, even as they may be found in the fugitive utterances and letters of ordinary men and women, in the songs and lamentations of the oppressed. They are embodied in customs and institutions—in the public school, the Bill of Rights, courts of justice, representative legislatures, systems of law, and ethical codes. Altho the boundaries of this faith are elastic and changing, the following articles, related and interwoven, must be included:

First, the individual human being is of surpassing worth
Second, the earth and human culture belong to all men
Third, men can and should rule themselves
Fourth, the human mind can be trusted and should be set free
Fifth, the method of peace is superior to that of war
Sixth, racial, cultural, and political minorities should be tolerated, respected, and valued.

According to the first and most basic of the articles of the democratic faith, an article which embraces or at least provides the foundation for all the rest, the individual human being is of surpassing worth. Here is a bold and liberating conception, holding within itself a perpetual challenge to every form of oppression. Individual men are more precious than the earth on which they live, more precious than the food and clothing which sustains and warms them, more precious than the farms and factories and ships by which they gain their livelihood, more precious than the paintings and statuary and symphonies and all the great works of art by which they are inspired. Individual men are more precious than states and principalities, more precious than customs and institutions, more precious than science and technology, more precious than philosophies and systems of thought, more precious than power and fame and glory. Even the Sabbath, symbol of so much that is sacred in the Christian tradition, was said by the founder of this religion to have been made for man. Individual men are not beasts of burden, nor slaves, nor serfs. Neither are they cannon fodder nor a commodity to be bought and sold in the market. Save only for the conditions of life which set them free and the great ideas and hopes which give them nobility, for which they should be ready to die if need be, men are the most precious things on the earth.

The second article of the democratic faith is implicit in the first; the material earth and human culture belong to all men. Whatever may be the appropriate institutional arrangements, the earth with its resources of soil, water, climate, flora, fauna, and minerals, with its continents and islands, its oceans and seas, its lakes and rivers, its mountains and valleys and plains, the earth which makes physical existence possible for man is regarded as the exclusive possession of no "superior" race, or people, or class. Likewise human culture, the social heritage bequeathed to each new generation by all preceding generations of men, the social heritage of tools, machines, and buildings, of habits, customs, and folkways, of knowledges, appreciations, and values, of ideas, philosophies, and institutions, the social heritage whose nurture raises individual man above the brute and bestows upon him the gift of humanity, is looked upon as the monopoly of no privileged order of men. This second article of the democratic faith repeats the affirmation of the great Judaic-Christian ethic that all men are brothers; it repeats the affirmation of the Declaration of Independence that all men are created equal.

The first and second articles of the democratic faith, if taken by themselves, might conceivably be acceptable to a benevolent despotism; the third lays the political foundation of a society of free men. It declares that men can and should rule themselves. This article, be it noted, contains not one but two affirmations, both equally daring and precious. It affirms not only that men *should* but also that they *can* rule themselves. Unequivocally rejecting autocracy in every form, however humane, it proclaims the doctrine that all men can and should be free, that, both as individuals and as members of society, they should share in framing the purposes for which they are to live. It repudiates as tyranny the ancient division of men into the rulers and the ruled. How daring, also how precious, this article is, the American people of the present generation, because of their long experience with political liberty, can scarcely comprehend. It must suffice to say that, from the standpoint of past ages and the totalitarian world of today, the very thought that "hewers of wood and drawers of water" should raise their voices in the councils of the nation is a form of treason—nay, a species of blasphemy.

Whatever else a democracy may be it is first of all a society of free men.

The fourth article of the democratic faith is a corollary of the third; it states without equivocation that the hu-

man mind can be trusted and should be set free. It implies that in the process of rule men should trust their own minds and be eternally vigilant in the guarding of those opportunities and liberties thru which their minds are matured and rendered competent. It implies further that they should resist every effort on the part of any class or group to keep them in leading strings, to shape their opinions for them, to narrow their access to knowledge, to restrict their freedom to inquire and to learn. This fourth article of faith also represents a recognition of the superiority of the judgment of many over the judgment of one, a frank acceptance of the scientific method as the only dependable guide to knowledge about the affairs of men and society, and a clear recognition of the fact that the only trustworthy guardian of freedom is an informed and disciplined mind.

The fifth article of the democratic faith affirms the immeasurable superiority of the method of peace over the method of war in the adjustment of differences and disputes among men. Democracy looks upon resort to brute force as a barbaric survival from the past and works unceasingly for the day when war will be forever banished from the earth. It regards peace, moreover, as one of the great goods of life and knows that military habits and virtues are profoundly hostile to its own spirit. Wherever democracy goes it strives to substitute the method of peace for the method of force. The introduction into society of the process of free discussion, criticism, and decision by secret ballot as a way of rule constitutes one of the supreme achievements of civilized man, or rather perhaps as an achievement marking the appearance of civilized man. It must be evident of course that this fifth article of faith can be operative only in those spheres and in those relationships where all parties to controversy are loyal to its principles and are prepared to abide by judgments achieved by its procedures. As long as there exists in society a party or in the world a state that rejects the method of peace, democracy must be ready to meet force with force. While always working for a universal acceptance of its faith, it must not neglect its own defenses.

Finally, democracy believes that racial, cultural, and political minorities should be tolerated, respected, and valued. It rejects completely the totalitarian theory that the health of a society is to be measured in terms of the extent of conformity and acquiescence. On the one hand, it realizes that the human values which it prizes most highly, personal integrity and charity, are destroyed by the passions aroused in the persecution and suppression of minorities. Bigotry and intolerance are the deadliest enemies of human freedom. On the other hand, democracy sees in the minority, in the dissident individual or group, a major creative force in society, an instrument of social discovery, invention, and advance. Even here, however, there must be a limit to tolerance. Whenever any minority employs the liberties of democracy to undermine and eventually to corrupt or destroy those liberties, it forfeits the guarantees of a free society. While vigilante and mob action in such cases should be prevented at all costs, the forces of public opinion, of social approval and disapproval, and in the last resort of the police power should be brought into full play. If democracy permits loyalty to its forms to sap its essential spirit it will be unable to triumph in its struggle with despotism.

"The Only Thing We Have To Fear Is Fear Itself"

Franklin Delano Roosevelt's First Inaugural Address, delivered on March 4, 1933, at a time when the Nation was in the grip of its greatest economic depression.

I AM certain that my fellow Americans expect that on my induction into the Presidency I will address them with a candor and a decision which the present situation of our Nation impels. This is preeminently the time to speak the truth, the whole truth, frankly and boldly. Nor need we shrink from honestly facing conditions in our country today. This great Nation will endure as it has endured, will revive and will prosper. So, first of all, let me assert my firm belief that the only thing we have to fear is fear itself—nameless, unreasoning, unjustified terror which paralyzes needed efforts to convert retreat into advance. In every dark hour of our national life a leadership of frankness and vigor has met with that understanding and support of the people themselves which is essential to victory. I am convinced that you will again give that support to leadership in these critical days.

In such a spirit on my part and on yours we face our common difficulties. They concern, thank God, only material things. Values have shrunken to fantastic levels; taxes have risen; our ability to pay has fallen; government of all kinds is faced by serious curtailment of income; the means of exchange are frozen in the currents of trade;

the withered leaves of industrial enterprise lie on every side; farmers find no markets for their produce; the savings of many years in thousands of families are gone.

More important, a host of unemployed citizens face the grim problem of existence, and an equally great number toil with little return. Only a foolish optimist can deny the dark realities of the moment.

Yet our distress comes from no failure of substance. We are stricken by no plague of locusts. Compared with the perils which our forefathers conquered because they believed and were not afraid, we have still much to be thankful for. Nature still offers her bounty and human efforts have multiplied it. Plenty is at our doorstep, but a generous use of it languishes in the very sight of the supply. Primarily this is because rulers of the exchange of mankind's goods have failed through their own stubbornness and their own incompetence, have admitted their failure, and have abdicated. Practices of the unscrupulous moneychangers stand indicted in the court of public opinion, rejected by the hearts and minds of men.

True they have tried, but their efforts have been cast in the pattern of an outworn tradition. Faced by failure of credit they have proposed only the lending of more money. Stripped of the lure of profit by which to induce our people to follow their false leadership, they have resorted to exhortations, pleading tearfully for restored confidence. They know only the rules of a generation of selfseekers. They have no vision, and when there is no vision the people perish.

The moneychangers have fled from their high seats in the temple of our civilization. We may now restore that temple to the ancient truths. The measure of the restora-

Library of Congress Collections

PRESIDENT FRANKLIN ROOSEVELT AND WINSTON CHURCHILL CONFER AT CASABLANCA IN 1943

tion lies in the extent to which we apply social values more noble than mere monetary profit.

Happiness lies not in the mere possession of money; it lies in the joy of achievement, in the thrill of creative effort. The joy and moral stimulation of work no longer must be forgotten in the mad chase of evanescent profits. These dark days will be worth all they cost us if they teach us that our true destiny is not to be ministered unto but to minister to ourselves and to our fellow men.

Recognition of the falsity of material wealth as the standard of success goes hand in hand with the abandonment of the false belief that public office and high political position are to be valued only by the standards of pride of place and personal profit; and there must be an end to a conduct in banking and in business which too often has given to a sacred trust the likeness of callous and selfish wrongdoing. Small wonder that confidence languishes, for it thrives only on honesty, on honor, on the sacredness of obligations, on faithful protection, on unselfish performance; without them it cannot live.

Restoration calls, however, not for changes in ethics alone. This Nation asks for action, and action now.

Our greatest primary task is to put people to work. This is no unsolvable problem if we face it wisely and courageously. It can be accomplished in part by direct recruiting by the Government itself, treating the task as we would treat the emergency of a war, but at the same time, through this employment, accomplishing greatly needed projects to stimulate and reorganize the use of our natural resources.

Hand in hand with this we must frankly recognize the overbalance of population in our industrial centers and, by engaging on a national scale in a redistribution, endeavor to provide a better use of the land for those best fitted for the land. The task can be helped by definite efforts to raise the values of agricultural products and, with this, the power to purchase the output of our cities. It can be helped by preventing realistically the tragedy of the growing loss through foreclosure of our small homes and our farms. It can be helped by insistence that the Federal, State, and local governments act forthwith on the demand that their cost be drastically reduced. It can be helped by the unifying of relief activities which today are often scattered, uneconomical, and unequal. It can be helped by national planning for and supervision of all forms of transportation and of communications and other utilities which have a definitely public character. There are many ways in which it can be helped, but it can never be helped merely by talking about it. We must act and act quickly.

Finally, in our progress toward a resumption of work we require two safeguards against a return of the evils of the old order: there must be a strict supervision of all banking and credits and investments, so that there will be an end to speculation with other people's money; and there must be provisions for an adequate but sound currency.

These are the lines of attack. I shall presently urge upon a new Congress, in special session, detailed measures for their fulfillment, and I shall seek the immediate assistance of the several States.

Thru this program of action we address ourselves to putting our own national house in order and making income balance outgo. Our international trade relations, though vastly important, are in point of time and necessity secondary to the establishment of a sound national economy. I favor as a practical policy the putting of first things first. I shall spare no effort to restore world trade by international economic readjustment, but the emergency at home cannot wait on that accomplishment.

The basic thought that guides these specific means of national recovery is not narrowly nationalistic. It is the insistence, as a first consideration, upon the interdependence of the various elements in and parts of the United States—a recognition of the old and permanently important manifestation of the American spirit of the pioneer. It is the way to recovery. It is the immediate way. It is the strongest assurance that the recovery will endure.

In the field of world policy I would dedicate this Nation to the policy of the good neighbor—the neighbor who resolutely respects himself and, because he does so, respects the rights of others—the neighbor who respects his obligations and respects the sanctity of his agreements in and with a world of neighbors.

If I read the temper of our people correctly, we now realize as we have never realized before our interdependence on each other; that we cannot merely take but we must give as well; that if we are to go forward, we must move as a trained and loyal army willing to sacrifice for the good of a common discipline, because without such discipline no progress is made, no leadership becomes effective. We are, I know, ready and willing to submit our lives and property to such discipline, because it makes possible a leadership which aims at a larger good. This I propose to offer, pledging that the larger purposes will bind upon us all as a sacred obligation with a unity of duty hitherto evoked only in time of armed strife.

With this pledge taken, I assume unhesitatingly the leadership of this great army of our people dedicated to a disciplined attack upon our common problems.

Action in this image and to this end is feasible under the form of government which we have inherited from our ancestors. Our Constitution is so simple and practical that it is possible always to meet extraordinary needs by changes in emphasis and arrangements without loss of essential form. That is why our constitutional system has proved itself the most superbly enduring political mechanism the modern world has produced. It has met every stress of vast expansion of territory, of foreign wars, of bitter internal strife, of world relations.

It is to be hoped that the normal balance of Executive and legislative authority may be wholly adequate to meet the unprecedented task before us. But it may be that an unprecedented demand and need for undelayed action may call for temporary departure from that normal balance of public procedure.

I am prepared under my constitutional duty to recommend the measures that a stricken Nation in the midst of a stricken world may require. These measures, or such other measures as the Congress may build out of its experience and wisdom, I shall seek, within my constitutional authority, to bring to speedy adoption.

But in the event that the Congress shall fail to take one of these two courses, and in the event that the national emergency is still critical, I shall not evade the clear course of duty that will then confront me. I shall ask the Congress for the one remaining instrument to meet the crisis —broad Executive power to wage a war against the emergency, as great as the power that would be given to me if we were in fact invaded by a foreign foe.

For the trust reposed in me I will return the courage and the devotion that befit the time. I can do no less.

We face the arduous days that lie before us in the warm courage of national unity; with the clear consciousness of seeking old and precious moral values; with the clear satisfaction that comes from the stern performance of duty by old and young alike. We aim at the assurance of a rounded and permanent national life.

We do not distrust the future of essential democracy. The people of the United States have not failed. In their need they have registered a mandate that they want direct, vigorous action. They have asked for discipline and direction under leadership. They have made me the present instrument of their wishes. In the spirit of the gift I take it.

In this dedication of a Nation we humbly ask the blessing of God. May He protect each and every one of us. May He guide me in the days to come.

President Kennedy's Inaugural Address
January 20, 1961

John Fitzgerald Kennedy, thirty-fifth President of the United States, was born May 29, 1917, in Brookline, Massachusetts, and was assassinated on November 22, 1963. Following his service in the Navy during World War II he was representative in Congress from Massachusetts 1947-53, and was elected to the United States Senate in 1952 where he served until he resigned to become President.

MY FELLOW CITIZENS: We observe today not a victory of party but a celebration of freedom—symbolizing an end as well as a beginning—signifying renewal as well as change. For I have sworn before you and Almighty God the same solemn oath our forebears prescribed nearly a century and three-quarters ago.

The world is very different now. For man holds in his mortal hands the power to abolish all forms of human poverty and all forms of human life. And yet the same revolutionary beliefs for which our forebears fought are still at issue around the globe—the belief that the rights of man come not from the generosity of the state but from the hand of God.

We dare not forget today that we are the heirs of that first revolution. Let the word go forth from this time and place, to friend and foe alike, that the torch has been passed to a new generation of Americans—born in this century, tempered by war, disciplined by a hard and bitter peace, proud of our ancient heritage—and unwilling to witness or permit the slow undoing of those human rights to which this nation has always been committed, and to which we are committed today at home and around the world.

Let every nation know, whether it wishes us well or ill, that we shall pay any price, bear any burden, meet any hardship, support any friend, oppose any foe to assure the survival and the success of liberty.

This much we pledge—and more.

To those old allies whose cultural and spiritual origins we share, we pledge the loyalty of faithful friends. United, there is little we cannot do in a host of co-operative ventures. Divided, there is little we can do—for we dare not meet a powerful challenge at odds and split asunder.

To those new states whom we welcome to the ranks of the free, we pledge our word that one form of colonial control shall not have passed away merely to be replaced by a far more iron tyranny. We shall not always expect to find them supporting our view. But we shall always hope to find them strongly supporting their own freedom—and to remember that, in the past, those who foolishly sought power by riding the back of the tiger ended up inside.

To those peoples in the huts and villages of half the globe struggling to break the bonds of mass misery, we pledge our best efforts to help them help themselves, for whatever period is required—not because the Communists may be doing it, not because we seek their votes, but because it is right. If a free society cannot help the many who are poor, it cannot save the few who are rich.

To our sister republics south of our border, we offer a special pledge—to convert our good words into good deeds—in a new alliance for progress—to assist free men and free governments in casting off the chains of poverty. But this peaceful revolution of hope cannot become the prey of hostile powers. Let all our neighbors know that we shall join with them to oppose aggression or subversion anywhere in the Americas. And let every other power know that this hemisphere intends to remain the master of its own house.

To that world assembly of sovereign states, the United Nations, our last best hope in an age where the instruments of war have far outpaced the instruments of peace, we renew our pledge of support—to prevent it from becoming merely a forum for invective—to strengthen its shield of the new and the weak—and to enlarge the area in which its writ may run.

Finally, to those nations who would make themselves our adversary, we offer not a pledge but a request: that both sides begin anew the quest for peace, before the dark powers of destruction unleashed by science engulf all humanity in planned or accidental self-destruction.

We dare not tempt them with weakness. For only when our arms are sufficient beyond doubt can we be certain beyond doubt that they will never be employed.

But neither can two great and powerful groups of nations take comfort from our present course—both sides overburdened by the cost of modern weapons, both rightly alarmed by the steady spread of the deadly atom, yet both racing to alter that uncertain balance of terror that stays the hand of mankind's final war.

So let us begin anew—remembering on both sides that

civility is not a sign of weakness, and sincerity is always subject to proof. Let us never negotiate out of fear. But let us never fear to negotiate.

Let both sides explore what problems unite us instead of belaboring those problems which divide us.

Let both sides, for the first time, formulate serious and precise proposals for the inspection and control of arms—and bring the absolute power to destroy other nations under the absolute control of all nations.

Let both sides seek to invoke the wonders of science instead of its terrors. Together let us explore the stars, conquer the deserts, eradicate disease, tap the ocean depths and encourage the arts and commerce.

Let both sides unite to heed in all corners of the earth the command of Isaiah—to "undo the heavy burdens . . . (and) let the oppressed go free."

And if a beachhead of co-operation may push back the jungles of suspicion, let both sides join in creating a new endeavor—not a new balance of power, but a new world of law, where the strong are just and the weak secure and the peace preserved.

All this will not be finished in the first one hundred days. Nor will it be finished in the first one thousand days, nor in the life of this Administration, nor even perhaps in our lifetime on this planet. But let us begin.

In your hands, my fellow citizens, more than mine, will rest the final success or failure of our course. Since this country was founded, each generation of Americans has been summoned to give testimony to its national loyalty. The graves of young Americans who answered the call to service surround the globe.

Now the trumpet summons us again—not as a call to

bear arms, though arms we need—not as a call to battle, though embattled we are—but a call to bear the burden of a long twilight struggle, year in and year out, "rejoicing in hope, patient in tribulation"—a struggle against the common enemies of man: tyranny, poverty, disease and war itself.

Can we forge against these enemies a grand and global alliance, north and south, east and west, that can assure a more fruitful life for all mankind? Will you join in that historic effort?

In the long history of the world, only a few generations have been granted the role of defending freedom in its hour of maximum danger. I do not shrink from this responsibility—I welcome it. I do not believe that any of us would exchange places with any other people or any other generation. The energy, the faith, the devotion which we bring to this endeavor will light our country and all who serve it—and the glow from that fire can truly light the world.

And so, my fellow Americans: Ask not what your country can do for you—ask what you can do for your country.

My fellow citizens of the world: Ask not what America will do for you, but what together we can do for the freedom of man.

Finally, whether you are citizens of America or citizens of the world, ask of us here the same high standards of strength and sacrifice which we ask of you. With a good conscience our only sure reward, with history the final judge of our deeds, let us go forth to lead the land we love, asking His blessing and His help, but knowing that here on earth God's work must truly be our own.

"I Have a Dream"

MARTIN LUTHER KING, JR.

More than 200,000 Americans heard Doctor Martin Luther King, Jr. deliver the following address from the steps of the Lincoln Memorial on August 28, 1963 on the occasion of the Civil Rights March on Washington thru which Negro leaders attempted to dramatize the scope of Negro discontent and the tremendous appeal of an open desegregated society. It has been hailed as the greatest of many eloquent addresses delivered by Dr. King during his brief lifetime. Dr. King was born in Atlanta, Georgia, January 15, 1929 and was assassinated in Memphis, Tennessee, April 4, 1968. He was highly schooled in philosophy and theology and, like his father, a Baptist minister. Married to a woman—Coretta Scott—who shared his ideals and purposes and inspired by the philosophy and achievements of Mahatma Gandhi, he lead nonviolent campaigns for civil rights for Negroes and became president of the Southern Christian Leadership Conference. His brilliant and sacrificial leadership and the worldwide interest which it brought to his cause won him the Nobel Peace Prize in 1964. Like Abraham Lincoln, he is regarded by many thruout the world as one of the great liberators of mankind.

FIVE SCORE years ago, a great American, in whose symbolic shadow we stand, signed the Emancipation Proclamation. This momentous decree came as a great beacon light of hope to millions of Negro slaves who had been seared in the flames of withering injustice. It came as a joyous daybreak to end the long night of captivity.

But one hundred years later, we must face the tragic fact that the Negro is still not free. One hundred years later, the life of the Negro is still sadly crippled by the manacles of segregation and the chains of discrimination. One hundred years later, the Negro lives on a lonely island of poverty in the midst of a vast ocean of material prosperity. One hundred years later, the Negro is still languished in the corners of American society and finds himself an exile in his own land. So we have come here today to dramatize an appalling condition.

In a sense we have come to our nation's Capital to cash a check. When the architects of our republic wrote the magnificent words of the Constitution and the Declaration of Independence, they were signing a promissory note to which every American was to fall heir. This note was a promise that all men would be guaranteed the unalienable rights of life, liberty, and the pursuit of happiness.

It is obvious today that America has defaulted on this promissory note insofar as her citizens of color are concerned. Instead of honoring this sacred obligation, America has given the Negro people a bad check; a check which has come back marked "insufficient funds." But we refuse to believe that the bank of justice is bankrupt. We refuse to believe that there are insufficient funds in the great vaults of opportunity of this nation. So we have come to cash this check—a check that will give us upon demand the riches of freedom and the security of justice. We have also come to this hallowed spot to remind America of the fierce urgency of *now*. This is no time to engage in the luxury of cooling off or to take the tranquilizing drug of gradualism. *Now* is the time to make real the promises of Democracy. *Now* is the time to rise from the dark and desolate valley of segregation to the sunlit path of racial justice. *Now* is the time to open the doors of opportunity to all of God's children. *Now* is the time to lift our nation from the quicksands of racial injustice to the solid rock of brotherhood.

It would be fatal for the nation to overlook the urgency of the moment and to underestimate the determination of the Negro. This sweltering summer of the Negro's legitimate discontent will not pass until there is an invigorating autumn of freedom and equality. 1963 is not an end, but a beginning. Those who hope that the Negro needed to blow off steam and will now be content will have a rude awakening if the nation returns to business as usual. There will be neither rest nor tranquillity in America until the Negro is granted his citizenship rights. The whirlwinds of revolt will continue to shake the foundations of our nation until the bright day of justice emerges.

But there is something that I must say to my people who stand on the warm threshold which leads into the palace of justice. In the process of gaining our rightful place we must not be guilty of wrongful deeds. Let us not seek to satisfy our thirst for freedom by drinking from the cup of bitterness and hatred. We must forever conduct our struggle on the high plane of dignity and discipline. We must not allow our creative protest to degenerate into physical violence. Again and again we must rise to the majestic heights of meeting physical force with soul force. The marvelous new militancy which has engulfed the Negro community must not lead us to a distrust of all white people, for many of our white brothers, as evidenced by their presence here today, have come to realize that their destiny is tied up with our destiny and their freedom is inextricably bound to our freedom. We cannot walk alone.

And as we walk, we must make the pledge that we shall march ahead. We cannot turn back. There are those who are asking the devotees of civil rights, "When will you be satisfied?" We can never be satisfied as long as the Negro is the victim of the unspeakable horrors of police brutality. We can never be satisfied as long as our bodies, heavy with the fatigue of travel, cannot gain lodging in the motels of the highways and the hotels of the cities. We cannot be satisfied as long as the Negro's basic mobility is from a smaller ghetto to a larger one. We can never be satisfied as long as a Negro in Mississippi cannot vote and a Negro in New York believes he has nothing for which to vote. No, no, we are not satisfied, and we will not be satisfied until justice rolls down like waters and righteousness like a mighty stream.

I am not unmindful that some of you have come here out of great trials and tribulations. Some of you have come fresh from narrow jail cells. Some of you have come from areas where your quest for freedom left you battered by the storms of persecution and staggered by the winds of police brutality. You have been the veterans of creative suffering. Continue to work with the faith that unearned suffering is redemptive.

Go back to Mississippi, go back to Alabama, go back to South Carolina, go back to Georgia, go back to Louisiana, go back to the slums and ghettos of our northern cities, knowing that somehow this situation can and will be changed. Let us not wallow in the valley of despair.

I say to you today, my friends, that in spite of the difficulties and frustrations of the moment I still have a dream. It is a dream deeply rooted in the American dream.

I have a dream that one day this nation will rise up and

live out the true meaning of its creed: "We hold these truths to be self-evident; that all men are created equal."

I have a dream that one day on the red hills of Georgia the sons of former slaves and the sons of former slave-owners will be able to sit down together at the table of brotherhood.

I have a dream that one day even the state of Mississippi, a desert state sweltering with the heat of injustice and oppression, will be transformed into an oasis of freedom and justice.

I have a dream that my four little children will one day live in a nation where they will not be judged by the color of their skin but by the content of their character.

I have a dream today.

I have a dream that one day the state of Alabama, whose governor's lips are presently dripping with the words of interposition and nullification, will be transformed into a situation where little black boys and black girls will be able to join hands with little white boys and white girls and walk together as sisters and brothers.

I have a dream today.

I have a dream that one day every valley shall be exalted, every hill and mountain shall be made low, the rough places will be made plains, and the crooked places will be made straight, and the glory of the Lord shall be revealed, and all flesh shall see it together.

This is our hope. This is the faith with which I return to the South. With this faith we will be able to hew out of the mountain of despair a stone of hope. With this faith we will be able to transform the jangling discords of our nation into a beautiful symphony of brotherhood. With this faith we will be able to work together, to pray together, to struggle together, to go to jail together, to stand up for freedom together, knowing that we will be free one day.

This will be the day when all of God's children will be able to sing with new meaning

My country, 'tis of thee,
Sweet land of liberty,
Of thee I sing:
Land where my fathers died,
Land of the pilgrims' pride,
From every mountain-side
Let freedom ring.

And if America is to be a great nation this must become true. So let freedom ring from the prodigious hilltops of New Hampshire. Let freedom ring from the mighty mountains of New York. Let freedom ring from the heightening Alleghenies of Pennsylvania!

Let freedom ring from the snowcapped Rockies of Colorado!

Let freedom ring from the curvacious peaks of California!

But not only that; let freedom ring from Stone Mountain of Georgia!

Let freedom ring from Lookout Mountain of Tennessee!

Let freedom ring from every hill and molehill of Mississippi. From every mountainside, let freedom ring.

When we let freedom ring, when we let it ring from every village and every hamlet, from every state and every city, we will be able to speed up that day when all of God's children, black men and white men, Jews and Gentiles, Protestants and Catholics, will be able to join hands and sing in the words of the old Negro spiritual, "Free at last! free at last! thank God Almighty, we are free at last!"

PART XII

Goals for Americans

THE REPORT OF THE PRESIDENT'S COMMISSION ON NATIONAL GOALS

The Commission on National Goals was appointed by President Eisenhower, who requested that its work be administered by The American Assembly, a nonpartisan educational institution associated with Columbia University. The work of the Commission was financed by private foundations. It was submitted to The President November 16, 1960, signed by the members of the Commission as follows: Edwin D. Canham, James B. Conant, Colgate W. Darden, Jr., Crawford M. Greenwalt, Alfred M. Gruenther, Clark Kerr, James R. Killian, Jr., George Meany, Frank Pace, Jr., Vice Chairman, *Henry M. Wriston,* Chairman.

The Commission was assisted by an able staff and a qualified individual was assigned to write a special essay on each of the goals. The following is from the Report of the President's Commission on National Goals, Goals for Americans, *© 1960 by The American Assembly, Columbia University, New York. Reprinted by permission of Prentice-Hall, Inc., Englewood Cliffs, N. J. The Report was also published in instalments in* Senior Citizen *beginning in January 1963.*

The Report of the Commission and the essays associated with it will afford valuable guidance to citizens and leaders in public life for many years to come. The Commission Report follows:

Introduction—The paramount goal of the United States was set long ago. It is to guard the rights of the individual, to ensure his development, and to enlarge his opportunity. It is set forth in the Declaration of Independence drafted by Thomas Jefferson and adopted by the Continental Congress on July 4, 1776. The goals we here identify are within the framework of the original plan and are calculated to bring to fruition the dreams of the men who laid the foundation of this country. They stated their convictions quite simply:

"We hold these truths to be self-evident, that all men are created equal, that they are endowed by their Creator with certain unalienable Rights, that among these are Life, Liberty, and the pursuit of Happiness. That to secure these rights, Governments are instituted among Men, deriving their just powers from the consent of the governed."

It was a mighty vision. In the echo of those fateful words can be heard the onrolling thunder of a new age. It was an even broader and bolder declaration than those who made it knew. Its soaring vision enabled our society to meet the trials of emerging nationhood. It placed the young republic securely behind the principle that every human being is of infinite worth. In time it led the nation out of the morass of human slavery. It inspires us still in the struggle against injustice.

To make this vision a reality, a framework of selfgovernment was established nationally and in each state. It rested upon two fundamental principles—the election of representatives from among competing candidates, and the constitutional limitation of power of those elected.

The way to preserve freedom is to live it. Our enduring aim is to build a nation and help build a world in which every human being shall be free to develop his capacities to the fullest. We must rededicate ourselves to this principle and thereby strengthen its appeal to a world in political, social, economic, and technological revolution.

In the 1960s every American is summoned to extraordinary personal responsibility, sustained effort, and sacrifice. For the nation is in grave danger, threatened by the rulers of one-third of mankind, for whom the state is everything, the individual significant only as he serves the state. These rulers seek the "peace" of a Communist-oriented world, in which freedom is suppressed and the individual permanently subordinated. Supporting their aim are the Soviet Union's great and swiftly growing strength, the industrial and military progress and potential of Red China, a great capacity for political organization and propaganda, and the specious appeal of Communist doctrine to peoples eager for rapid escape from poverty.

Meanwhile, weapons of cataclysmic power have come into existence. A major nuclear conflict would be a world catastrophe; violence even in or between small nations could involve the great powers and spark the holocaust.

The Sino-Soviet threat and modern weapons present great dangers; we have equally great opportunities. With the increase of knowledge and material resources, we have achieved a standard of individual realization new to history. We can continue to improve our own way of life, and at the same time help in the progress of vast numbers in the world whose lives are blighted by chronic sickness, hunger, and illiteracy.

Since 1946, foreign rule has ended for more than one billion people in Asia and Africa. Much of their yearning for independence, for respect, and for abundance has been inspired by Western and especially American example. Nevertheless, historic resentments, inadequate economies, inexperience in selfgovernment, and excessive expectations offer fertile ground for Communist persuasion and conquest. This restless tide of events defines the magnitude of our problems and the scope of our opportunity.

To preserve and enlarge our own liberties, to meet a deadly menace, and to extend the area of freedom throughout the world: these are high and difficult goals. Yet our past performance justifies confidence that they can be achieved if every American will accept personal responsibility for them.

This Report identifies goals and sets forth programs. It is directed to the citizens of this country, each of whom sets his own goals and seeks to realize them in his life, through private groups, and through various levels of government. Choices are hard, and costs heavy. They demand subordination of lesser goals to the greater. But the rewards are beyond calculation, for the future of our nation depends on the result.

At the same time, the United States cannot attain its goals alone, nor by offering the free world grudging alms or condescending leadership. We must lead, but in a spirit of genuine partnership. Together, the free peoples of the world can develop unmatched strength and vindicate the mighty vision of the Declaration.

PART I. *Goals at Home*

***Goal 1. The Individual*—The status of the individual must remain our primary concern. All our institutions—political, social, and economic—must further enhance the dignity of the citizen, promote the maximum development of his capabilities, stimulate their responsible exercise, and widen the range and effectiveness of opportunities for individual choice.**

From this concern springs our purpose to achieve equal treatment of men and women, to enlarge their incentives and to expand their opportunities for selfdevelopment and selfexpression. From it comes our insistence on widely distributed political and economic power, on the greatest range of free choice in our economy, and on the fair and democratic exercise of public and private power. It underlies the value we put on education. It guides the pursuit of science. It is the source of our interest in the health and welfare of every citizen.

The great ideas that have moved the world have sprung from unfettered human minds. The spirit of liberty, in which they thrive, makes one man hesitate to impose his will on another. It relies on the conviction that the truth will emerge from free inquiry and exchange of views.

The notion that ideas and individuals must be rejected merely because they are controversial denies the essence of our tradition. Schools and institutions of higher education, and the trustees, board members and legislators responsible for them, have a particular responsibility to ensure freedom of expression by students, faculty and administrators alike. We must bring up young men and women to believe in the individual and to act upon that belief. There are subtle and powerful pressures toward conformity in the economic, social, and political world. They must be resisted so that differences of taste and opinion will remain a constructive force in improving our society.

Unity of purpose must never be confused with unanimity of opinion. Vigorous controversy and the acceptance of dissent as a positive value will renew our strength and demonstrate to the world our calm confidence that truth and reason prevail in a free society.

***Goal 2. Equality*—Vestiges of religious prejudice, handicaps to women, and, most important, discrimination on the basis of race must be recognized as morally wrong, economically wasteful, and in many respects dangerous. In this decade we must sharply lower these last stubborn barriers.**

Progress toward realizing these ideals in practice has been extraordinary. We have ever more closely approached a classless society; there has been a revolution in the status of women; education is more nearly available to all; most citizens have opportunities which a century ago were dreamed of by only a handful.

Respect for the individual means respect for every individual. Every man and woman must have equal rights before the law, and an equal opportunity to vote and hold office, to be educated, to get a job and to be promoted when qualified, to buy a home, to participate fully in community affairs. These goals, which are at the core of our system, must be achieved by action at all levels.

Primary responsibility rests with individuals. Habits of prejudice and fear of social and economic pressure restrict employment opportunities and housing choices, cause exclusion from eating places, hotels, and recreation facilities, and inhibit the free action of public officers. No American should remain within the grip of these habits and fears.

The right to vote is basic. Private pressures and discriminatory administration of registration laws must not continue to obstruct it. Predominant state control of voting qualifications is traditional; but if necessary, the basic democratic right to vote must take precedence.

One role of government is to stimulate changes of attitude. Additional municipal, state, and federal legislation is essential. The federal government should enforce the principle that federal funds shall not be disbursed to employers who discriminate on the basis of race. Similar policies should progressively be applied to federal grants for universities, hospitals, and airports, and to federal housing programs.

By 1970 discrimination in higher education should be entirely overcome. Every state must make progress in good faith toward desegregation of publicly supported schools.

***Goal 3. The Democratic Process*—The degree of effective liberty available to its people should be the ultimate test for any nation. Democracy is the only means so far devised by which a nation can meet this test. To preserve and perfect the democratic process in the United States is therefore a primary goal in this as in every decade.**

The democratic process functions only when the individual accepts his full responsibility as a citizen by forming considered opinions on public policy and by active participation in the choice of public representatives.

Democracy gives reality to our striving for equality. It is the expression of individual selfrespect; it clears the way for individual initiative, exercise of responsibility, and use of varied talents. It is basic to the peaceful adjustment of differences of opinion. It must not be curtailed out of impatience to find quick solutions.

The institutions of the federal government require improvement but not drastic change. As Mr. Rossiter's chapter points out, the conduct of the office of the President and the presence of high-quality people in key executive departments remain principal sources of effective policymaking and administrative performance.

Changing times require that the Congress reassess its procedures. Multiple hearings upon the same issue by several committees put an undue burden upon administrative officers and legislators. Congress could be more effective by focusing its attention on the determination of broad policies. Legislation has become unduly detailed. Congressional committees and their staffs too often encroach upon the administrative function. In the interests of efficiency and economy, Congress might well experiment with an occasional bill authorizing the President to eliminate or reduce specific items, subject to reversal by concurrent resolution.

Improvement of the democratic process requires a constantly better-informed public. Mass circulation periodicals have opportunities beyond their current performance. Television, altho it has improved, can do better still in communicating serious ideas. In far too many communities, newspapers are inadequate in their coverage of significant public affairs. The problem of interesting and informing mass audiences, which most media must serve, is a constant challenge. The American people remain among the best informed in the world, but their sources of information must steadily be enriched to cope with ever more complex problems.

Private interest groups exemplify the rights of assembly and petition. Thus, the functioning of pressure groups of many kinds has become a part of our democratic process. Special interest groups must operate legitimately. The program of any particular group can be opposed most effectively by the formation of a counter group. There is need for more which represent broader interests such as consumers and taxpayers.

The vastly increased demands upon the federal government require at the higher levels more public servants equal in competence and imagination to those in private business and the professions. This involves a drastic increase in their compensation. The President should be given unequivocal authority and responsibility to develop a true senior civil service, along the lines suggested in Mr. Sayre's chapter. The executive branch must also place greater emphasis on the recruiting, training, and stimulation of career employees.

Employee organizations, dealing with the executive branch on wages and conditions of work, can play a constructive part.

National, state, and local governments collaborate and share power in many domestic concerns. To ensure dispersion of power within the system without obstructing solution of pressing national problems, we must pursue the following primary objectives: enlarge local discretion, as for example in the handling of matching federal grants; increase the financial re-

sources of state and local governments; represent urban populations more equitably in those state legislatures where they are now under-represented; further develop limited metropolitan authorities or governments.

Shared power (in Mr. Grodzins' phrase) is the key to the miracle of effective democratic government of a vast and diverse country. Our major cities and suburban areas need to find means to coordinate numerous local governments for the solution of common problems. State and local governments are increasing their activities more rapidly than the domestic sector of the federal government. Their load will continue to grow, and their capacity to meet it must be strengthened.

***Goal 4. Education*—The development of the individual and the nation demand that education at every level and in every discipline be strengthened and its effectiveness enhanced. New teaching techniques must continue to be developed. The increase in population and the growing complexity of the world add urgency.**

Greater resources—private, corporate, municipal, state, and federal—must be mobilized. A higher proportion of the gross national product must be devoted to educational purposes. This is at once an investment in the individual, in the democratic process, in the growth of the economy, and in the stature of the United States.

Education is primarily a responsibility of the states. They have delegated responsibility for public elementary and secondary education to local authorities, and have chartered colleges and universities. This is the firmly established pattern; it can be made to function satisfactorily to meet the needs of our vast and diverse nation.

In a few states four-fifths of the youth complete four years of high school and one-half enrol in an institution of higher education. This is a majestic accomplishment. However, in many states less than half complete four years of high school and less than 20% enter college. Clearly the goal is to bring every state nearer the present standard of the best. Within the next decade at least two-thirds of the youth in every state should complete twelve years of schooling and at least one-third enter college.

There must be more and better teachers, enlarged facilities, and changes in curricula and methods. The enrolment in professional schools should be increased. Above all, schooling should fit the varying capacities of individuals; every student should be stimulated to work to his utmost; authentic concern for excellence is imperative.

Among the important things that should be done, along lines urged in Dr. Gardner's chapter, are the following:

[1] Small and inefficient school districts should be consolidated, reducing the total number from 40,000 to about 10,000. The local school district remains the key to good public education. Local boards should be greatly strengthened.

[2] Every state should have a high-level board of education.

[3] Teachers' salaries at all levels must be improved.

[4] Two-year colleges should be within commuting distance of most high school graduates.

[5] Graduate school capacity must be approximately doubled.

[6] Adult education should play a vital role, stressing a new emphasis on education thruout life.

Financial Support. Annual public and private expenditure for education by 1970 must be approximately $40 billion—double the 1960 figure. It will then be 5% or more of the gross national product, as against less than 4% today.

Most of these funds must continue to come from state and local governments, tuition payments and gifts. State and local appropriations have more than doubled since 1950. The federal role must now be expanded. Total government expenses at all levels must amount to $33 billion for education by 1970.

Federal aid to higher education must include increased scholarship and loan funds, support of research as an essential part of the educational process, and direct assistance for buildings and equipment.

The federal government should supplement state funds where per capita income is too low to maintain an adequate school program. It should also offer matching grants, for educational purposes to be determined by the states. Since the Northwest Ordinance of 1787, the federal government has participated in the support of education without destroying local initiative and responsibility. In the future those values should still be safeguarded.

Goal 5. The Arts and Sciences—Knowledge and innovation must be advanced on every front. In science we should allot a greater proportion of our total effort to basic research, first, to realize fully the rapidly unfolding opportunities to extend still further our understanding of the world, and second, to enrich applied science and technology so essential to the improvement of health, to economic growth, and to military power.

Today we must give high priority to those aspects of science and technology which will increase our military strength, but for the longer term we should recognize that our creative activities in science and all other fields will be more productive and meaningful if undertaken, not merely to be ahead of some other nation, but to be worthy of ourselves.

These objectives should govern our civilian space programs and policies. We should be highly selective in our space objectives and unexcelled in their pursuit. Prestige arises from sound accomplishment, not from the merely spectacular, and we must not be driven by nationalistic competition into programs so extravagant as to divert funds and talents from programs of equal or greater importance.

We should ensure that every young person with the desire and capacity to become a scientist has access to the best science education our leading scholars can devise. Given the availability of such education, science will find its fair share of the pool of talent. But this pool of talent must itself be enlarged to the maximum, by seeing to it that those who have the capacity for the rigorous academic discipline required for all the professions start their course of study early, are offered opportunities to develop their talents, and are urged to continue to do so.

We must use available manpower more efficiently. The practice of wasting highly trained people in jobs below their capacity, particularly in some defense-related industries, must be eliminated. On the other hand, we must recognize that many workers have potential for higher positions. We must intensify the practice of upgrading men and women who may not have had advanced training but who have demonstrated capacity.

As Dr. Weaver's chapter suggests, we should allot a larger proportion of federal research and development funds to basic research. The total program of basic research in industry and other institutions should be increased.

The federal government supports more than half of the research and development in the United States. It is of urgent importance that the administration of its scientific and technical programs be strengthened, but without resort to bureaucratic overcentralization and planning.

The humanities, the social sciences, and the natural sciences all are essential for a rounded cultural life. Literature and history are vital to understanding, to capacity to feel and communicate, to a sense of values. Economics, psychology, all forms of study of human relationships, have become more urgent as the conditions of living have become more complex; our progress in dealing with national economic policy is an indication of what may be achieved by continuing to give these studies full weight. Our worldwide responsibilities require fresh emphasis on foreign languages and continued improvement in teaching them.

The arts are a vital part of human experience. In the eyes of posterity, the success of the United States as a civilized society will be largely judged by the creative activities of its citizens in art, architecture, literature, music, and the sciences. While an encouraging creative surge in the arts is already manifest, our society must, as Mr. Heckscher's chapter urges, stimulate and support richer cultural fulfillment. Our theater must be revitalized; it must have the kind of support in universities, colleges, and communities that will give it greater strength at the roots. Professional artists require rigorous discipline; provision should be made for the long years of training which are required. We should raise our critical standards and widen the area and depth of public appreciation. Thus far, television has failed to use its facilities adequately for educational and cultural purposes, and reform in its performance is urgent.

Goal 6. The Democratic Economy—The economic system must be compatible with the political system.

The centers of economic power should be as diffused and as balanced as possible. Too great concentrations of economic power in corporations, unions, or other organizations can lead to abuses and loss of the productive results of fair competition. Individuals should have maximum freedom in their choice of jobs, goods, and services.

Government participation in the economy should be limited to those instances where it is essential to the national interest and where private individuals or organizations cannot adequately meet the need. Government, of course, must maintain its regulatory control in areas such as antitrust laws, collusion, and protection of investors and consumers. We must take special precautions to prevent government officials from being influenced unduly by the sectors of the economy they regulate.

Collective bargaining between representatives of workers and employers should continue as the nation's chief method for determining wages and working conditions.

Conferences among management, union leaders, and representatives of the public can contribute to mutual understanding of problems that affect the welfare of the economy as a whole.

Corporations and labor unions must limit the influence they exert on the private lives of their members. Unions must continue to develop adequate grievance procedures and greater opportunities for legitimate opposition. Professional organizations and trade associations should conduct their affairs on a democratic basis.

Pension rights should vest more rapidly and fully, to improve the mobility of employees.

Barriers to the employment of women and older workers must be removed. While women will maintain and enrich the home and the family, those whose children have left home for school, and those who are not married, are increasingly able to contribute their talents to jobs and voluntary organizations. They may well be the country's largest pool of inadequately used ability. Their enlarging opportunity will help significantly to meet the nation's needs.

***Goal 7. Economic Growth*—The economy should grow at the maximum rate consistent with primary dependence upon free enterprise and the avoidance of**

marked inflation. Increased investment in the public sector is compatible with this goal.

Such growth is essential to move toward our goal of full employment, to provide jobs for the approximately 13,500,000 net new additions to the work force during the next ten years; to improve the standard of living; and to assure the United States' competitive strength.

Public policies, particularly an overhaul of the tax system, including depreciation allowances, should seek to improve the climate for new investment and the balancing of investment with consumption. We should give attention to policies favoring completely new ventures which involve a high degree of risk and growth potential.

In practice, we must seek to keep unemployment consistently below 4% of the labor force. Reduction in unemployment and operation of the economy closer to its capacity require steadily growing consumer demand, and proper management of interest rates, money supply, and government budget surpluses and deficits. If Congress were to raise or lower tax rates more readily, stabilization of the economy would be facilitated.

Increased reliance on research and improved technology will provide opportunity for American industry to expand its markets by producing new and authentically improved products rather than by too great a dependence on superficial changes in style. To these ends, universities, research institutes, governments, and industries should greatly increase basic research, the ultimate source of new ideas and new products.

Education at all levels should aim at a more capable and more flexible work force.

There is no consensus among the economists as to the growth rate those measures will produce. The chapter by Messrs. Stein and Denison presents carefully documented evidence indicating an annual increase in the gross national product of 3.4% without extraordinary stimulating measures. Other estimates made with equal care indicate higher growth rates up to 5% annually. The higher the growth rate, the fewer additional extraordinary measures will be necessary. If the growth rate is lower, it will impel consideration of higher taxes, increased quantity of labor, and the greater individual effort and sacrifice exemplified by forced savings and reduced consumption.

There is no merit in a statistical race with the Communist nations. The real test is capacity to achieve our own over-all goals. Our economic decisions must be governed by ability to meet our needs for defense, for education, for a healthy private economy with rising standards of living, and for foreign aid.

Goal 8. Technological Change—Technological change should be promoted and encouraged as a powerful force for advancing our economy. It should be planned for and introduced with sensitive regard for any adverse impact upon individuals.

Education on a large scale is provided by many industrial firms for their personnel. Such activities combined with advance planning can minimize unemployment due to rapid technological change. Where reemployment within the industry is not possible, retraining must be carried out thru vocational programs managed locally and financed through state and federal funds.

Private initiative can accelerate technological change in our non-military economy.

In our military economy, the federal government must strengthen the management of its programs in technology by improving its supervisory and contracting procedures. It must avoid undertaking impracticable and unnecessary projects and thereby wasting scientific and engineering manpower. Both government and industry need to encourage that combination of engineering and management talent which can master our increasingly complex technology.

We must continue to adapt the management and organization of the Department of Defense to changing military needs. We must encourage fundamental advances in military technology and their rapid introduction. Thru bold and tough-minded management we should reduce lead-time in bringing new weapons to operational use. Civilian and military leaders, with the help and understanding of Congress, must make and make stick the difficult interservice decisions required for the selection of major weapons systems from among available alternatives. The increasing complexity of these systems, the time required for their development, and their fabulous cost give these decisions overriding importance. Conservation of time is critical; it may be more important than the conservation of funds. Saving time is likely to save money.

Thruout the economy, collective bargaining between management and labor will have a marked influence on the process of technological change. It should anticipate needed adjustments, thru retraining and transfer policies, and, if layoffs become necessary, by such means as severance pay. Problems of technological change will require far-sighted planning by industry, labor, and government on a cooperative basis.

Public and private leadership are required where whole areas are economically distressed. As Mr. Watson's chapter suggests, measures to encourage industries to move to such communities and relocation programs for individuals are justified. Consideration should be given, where necessary, to state and federal government participation in loans and grants to aid community efforts and to underwrite support for programs of retraining.

***Goal 9. Agriculture*—The relative financial return to agriculture in the economy has deteriorated. The ultimate goal must be a supply-demand equilibrium to permit the market, with a fair return to farmers, to determine the manpower and capital committed to this sector of the economy. To avoid shock to the economy, this goal should be approached by gradual stages.**

A separate problem concerns the 50% of farmers who operate at subsistence levels and produce only 10% of farm output. For them new opportunities must be found thru training and thru location of new industries in farm areas. During this decade nonfarm jobs must be found—where possible locally—for about 1.5 million farm operators who now earn less than $1,500 a year.

Mr. Soth's chapter makes clear that farm industry is a notable example of rapid technological change and difficult adjustment. Productivity in agriculture rose in the last decade about three times as fast as in the economy as a whole. Therefore, more resources—more people, and more investment—are employed than are required to meet our domestic and foreign needs.

Farmers are leaving the industry. There are a million fewer families operating farms than there were in 1950, a decline in the decade of about 20%. This shift of occupation contributes to our economic growth, and ultimately to a healthy farm industry.

Major measures to reduce oversupply must include much increased retirement of farm land, with emphasis on whole farms. To increase demand we need energetic development of overseas markets. Agriculture could be competitive in world markets if there were reciprocal lowering of quotas and other trade barriers. In selected areas, our surpluses can meet human want without disrupting the markets of other nations. Improvement of nutritional levels for many Americans would not only increase the work efficiency of our population but also reduce farm surpluses.

Government programs of help for farmers, including price supports and other means to prevent collapse of incomes, will continue to be necessary for some time; they must be so managed that they cushion the shock of the transition, without unduly slowing the pace of necessary fundamental adjustments.

***Goal 10. Living Conditions*—We must remedy slum conditions, reverse the process of decay in the larger cities, and relieve the necessity for low-income and minority groups to concentrate there.**

We should also seek solutions for haphazard suburban growth, and provide an equitable sharing of the cost of public services between central cities and suburbs. In many parts of the country, the goal should be a regional pattern which provides for a number of urban centers, each with its own industries, its own educational, cultural and recreational institutions, and a balanced population of various income levels and back-

grounds. The needs of a growing population for parks and recreation must be met.

To these ends, we need dedicated private leadership, together with public and private action to provide improved services and facilities for residents of slum areas, stepped-up urban renewal programs, and an increased rate of construction of lower-priced homes and apartment units. Effective regional planning is essential, and there should be fresh emphasis on considerations of beauty. We should seek elimination of racial discrimination in housing.

Experience in the past decade has taught us some of the steps which must be taken. Further urban renewal programs, costing as much as $4 billion per year, are needed to purchase city land, clear it of dilapidated buildings, and make it available for residential and business use. Roads and rapid transit facilities should be planned and financed as a unit, and effective regional planning should deal with all transportation, industrial location, and government-assisted housing plans. Services to residents of slum areas, including particularly education, need the same emphasis as slum clearance.

Because experimentation is needed and solutions to these problems may well vary from place to place, federal housing policies should permit local authorities much more discretion. Where local laws prohibit discrimination, federal officials should withhold assistance from housing projects that violate the local fair housing policies. Consideration should be given to federal support, for a limited period, of an intensive moderate-cost housing program, as Mrs. Wurster's chapter recommends, under which state and local governments could experiment with mortgage insurance, low-interest loans, nonprofit corporations and other forms of industry-municipal cooperation.

Private and civic initiative are vital to such programs. The attainment of these goals will involve massive investment. In the long run this will pay handsome social and economic dividends.

***Goal 11. Health and Welfare*—The demand for medical care has enormously increased. To meet it we must have more doctors, nurses, and other medical personnel. There should be more hospitals, clinics and nursing homes. Greater effectiveness in the use of such institutions will reduce over-all requirements. There is a heavy**

responsibility on the medical and public health professions to contribute better solutions.

Federal grants for the construction of hospitals should be continued and extended to other medical facilities. Increased private, state and federal support is necessary for training doctors.

Further efforts are needed to reduce the burden of the cost of medical care. Extension of medical insurance is necessary, thru both public and private agencies.

As our need for doctors rises, the number of applications to medical school is declining. To meet our medical needs, analyzed in Dr. Dixon's chapter, we must not only increase the number of places in medical school by about one-half in this decade; we must also make it much more practicable for young men and women of talent and modest means to enter the profession. Scholarships during medical school and internship training are necessary.

The study of environmental health measures should be increased. We need to mobilize our resources better to understand such problems as air and water pollution, radiation hazards, and food additives. This is necessary in order that the government may formulate wiser policies of regulation.

Some 17 million persons suffer from mental illness in this country; it costs state governments over $1 billion per year. A maximum research effort, a substantial increase in the number of mental health clinics, and further progress in improving state mental hospitals are all part of the necessary effort to cope with it.

An important welfare objective is to learn more about the causes and methods of prevention of juvenile delinquency and family breakdown. There is great need for sustained study in order better to understand this complex community problem. It requires cooperative attention and action by many professions, community services and organizations. It also requires special measures to find jobs for youth, while maintaining labor standards. Additional trained social workers are urgently needed. Church and neighborhood action must continue to play a major part.

Continued attention should be paid to the social insurance system. The federal government, having relinquished to the states 90% of the unemployment compensation tax, should encourage the states to meet a minimum standard of adequacy of benefit levels, duration, and fiscal solvency. In addition, there should be established a federal re-insurance program for states with temporary acute employment problems. Public and private arrangements for maintaining income during sickness should be improved.

PART II. *Goals Abroad*

***Introduction*—The basic foreign policy of the United States should be the preservation of its own independence and free institutions. Our position before the world should be neither defensive nor belligerent. We should cooperate with nations whose ideals and interests are in harmony with ours. We should seek to mitigate tensions, and search for acceptable areas of accommodation with opponents. The safeguarded reduction of armaments is an essential goal.**

The United States, tho omnipresent, is not omnipotent. We and the nations which share our basic aims cannot hope always to prevent violence, the corruption of nationalist movements to Communist ends, or other adverse developments.

Whether nations will prefer freedom to totalitarianism is a vital issue. The free nations must exert themselves to the utmost to influence that choice, by assistance freely given to help develop political stability based on progress and justice, and to ease economic pressures. They must seek to prevent the denial of choice by Communist expansion.

Our goals abroad are inseparable from our goals at home. We must strive toward an open and peaceful world by making democracy ever more effective and individual life freer and more rewarding.

Information programs should be made more effective in counteracting distortion and presenting a balanced picture of American life and policy to people in foreign lands.

***Goal 12. Helping To Build an Open and Peaceful World—Foreign Trade Policy*—The healthiest world economy is attained when trade is at its freest. This should be our goal. The United States should join with**

other free world industrial nations in seeking a gradual reduction of tariffs and quota restrictions. We should seek this goal while safeguarding the national economy against market disruption, against destructive competition as a result of grossly lower unit labor costs, and to preserve national defense. We must effectively counter totalitarian trade practices. While many underdeveloped nations will insist, as the United States did for many years, upon tariffs and other forms of protection, we should continue to seek lowering of trade restrictions elsewhere in the world, especially barriers by larger regional trading groups. Our export trade must be conducted with ingenuity and vigor.

If the United States is to participate effectively in this process, some revision in our trade legislation will be required. Mr. McCloy's chapter makes clear that the socalled "peril point" and "escape clause" provisions may need some modification, since they put a floor on the reduction of tariffs, which has now been reached in many areas.

Elimination or modification of these restrictions might lead to imports taking larger shares of particular domestic markets. Normally the reductions should be undertaken step by step. Where the impact of a tariff reduction is such that an industry or community cannot absorb it unaided, temporary government assistance toward retraining, relocation, and reinvestment is warranted.

Tho the trend should be downward, there may be rare cases where increases will be necessary in the national interest.

Altho exports have slightly exceeded imports in recent years, expenditures abroad for economic aid, military bases, private investment, and foreign travel have led to a deficit in international payments of about $3.5 billion in 1958 and 1959, and perhaps higher in 1960.

This unfavorable balance of payments is caused by many factors, some of which do not relate to foreign trade policy. At least three steps are essential to rectification: a much higher export surplus; larger participation of other developed nations in assistance to the underdeveloped; and more equitable sharing of defense costs among the Allies.

The principal Western European nations are capable of larger capital export and aid to underdeveloped nations; this is notably true of the German Federal Republic. Similarly, it may be necessary for the United States to seek greater sharing of the cost of new weapons systems by the nations of Western Europe.

***Aid to Less Developed Nations*—Our principles and ideals impel us to aid the new nations. The preservation and strengthening of the free institutions of underdeveloped countries, and the defense of the free world, require a substantial increase in the amount of foreign aid, to be equitably shared by the major free nations.**

International economic organizations, such as the World Bank, deserve our support. We must devise new forms of cooperation, in which developing countries have opportunities for participation.

The success of the underdeveloped nations must depend primarily on their own efforts. We should assist by providing education, training, economic and technical assistance, and by increasing the flow of public and private capital.

Thru investment of about $20 billion a year, three-fourths of it from their own savings, the underdeveloped countries are increasing their production at an average rate of about 2%. However, this economic growth is nearly balanced by population growth, so that the rise in living standards is barely perceptible.

Doubling their economic growth rate within five years is a reasonable objective. This could be accomplished if the developing nations increased their own yearly investment by about half, and if foreign investment rose from the present approximate $5 billion a year to about $9 billion in 1965—roughly 1% of the Western industrial nations' combined gross national product. The United States share of such an effort would require by 1965 an outflow of $5 to $5.5 billion per year of public and private capital, as compared with $3.4 billion per year in the 1956-59 period.

Government funds for roads, port facilities, utilities, educational facilities and other institutions should account for a high proportion of these totals. The balance can and should be supplied by private investors. Broader guarantees and incentives will be needed to induce the required volume of private investment.

Better coordination of the assistance programs of the industrial nations will be necessary. The newly proposed Organization for Economic Cooperation and Development is a promising instrument for stimulating cooperation among the North Atlantic industrial nations, and with the nations to be assisted. The World Bank and International Development Association, with wide membership from both groups and high technical competence and experience, can and must continue to expand. Our special relationship to Latin America will call for an increasingly close cooperation on the basis of partnership.

We must encourage far larger numbers of qualified Americans to live and work abroad.

Half a million American civilians live abroad, as a result of private and government employment. Their number and their ability to represent the United States creditably must rise rapidly in the next decade if we are to attain an adequate level of exports and foreign investment and carry out programs for training and technical assistance. Universities, businesses, and the federal government should each in appropriate fields greatly increase language and other specialized training for such work.

***Goal 13. The Defense of the Free World—The Soviet Threat*—Communist aggression and subversion, fully analyzed in Dr. Langer's chapter, threaten all that we seek to do both at home and abroad. Consequently, the maintenance of our independence and way of life, as well as our concern for the freedom of other nations, require the most effective counter-measures.**

The power and opportunities of the Sino-Soviet nations are such that it will be a major task to prevent their expansion in the coming decade. Nevertheless, we must never lose sight of our ultimate goal: to extend the opportunities for free choice and self-determination thruout the world.

We must stand firm wherever, as in Berlin, our commitments and interests are squarely opposed to those of the Soviets. At whatever cost, we must maintain strategic and tactical forces of sufficient strength to deter the Communist powers from surprise attack and to cope with military aggression even on a limited scale. A secure deterrent is essential. We must meet Communist military threats used for political purposes. We must be ready to make the sacrifices necessary to meet the rising costs of such military capabilities.

We must also meet subversion by cooperation with other nations, by direct help on request, and thru economic programs which, in addition to other purposes, reduce conditions favorable to subversion.

Nonetheless, we should try continually to find a basis for mutual tolerance and reduction of tensions. We should be prepared to negotiate on any reasonable basis. We should enlarge personal and cultural contacts.

Communist China—Communist China's blatant hostility to the United States makes it especially urgent to strengthen our Pacific defenses and our ties with our Pacific allies.

Over the next decade, Communist China may be more aggressive than the U.S.S.R. Within a few years, Peiping may have the capacity to produce atomic weapons. Its strong conventional forces and rapid industrial progress already exert great impact in Asia.

Our policies in the Far East must include maximum cooperation with Japan in solving its difficult economic problems, continued support for the Republic of Korea and the Government of the Republic of China, programs of military and economic assistance to the free nations of South-East Asia, major assistance toward the economic development of India, and the maintenance of our own military forces.

Military Alliances—For the common defense, we must maintain and strengthen our military alliances. Our commitment to NATO in particular must remain firm. We should encourage the trend to greater military integration among the European members and the assumption by them of greater responsibilities. Our other military alliances and relationships in the Middle East and Asia must likewise be reaffirmed and strengthened. The Organization of American States must continue to have our unstinting support.

In support of these alliances, and in a few nations not covered by them, the United States must continue to furnish military assistance. To the extent that other nations gain strength, and local dangers diminish, it may become possible to reduce such aid. But major reductions are not in prospect. In some instances, our military aid is essential to progress toward political stability on an increasingly democratic basis.

Communist-dominated Areas—In nations subject to Communist domination or influence, our hope must be that the right of self-determination will ultimately be achieved. Trade, cultural exchanges, and occasionally technical or financial aid may be useful policies toward Communist-dominated peoples who are not hostile to us.

Goal 14. Disarmament—Since a major nuclear war would be a world catastrophe, the limitation and control of nuclear armament is imperative. Disarmament should be our ultimate goal. It cannot be attained without eliminating the sources of distrust and fear among nations. Hence, our immediate task must be the step-by-step advance toward control of nuclear weapons and their means of delivery, with effective international inspection. A safeguarded agreement to suspend nuclear testing may well be the first step, and would tend to limit the number of nuclear powers.

In view of the complex interaction of arms control and national security, we must organize a major government effort for the study and analysis of political, military, and technical issues in order to provide a sounder basis for policy formulation and negotiation.

The essential condition of any stabilizing agreement must be that neither side be left in a position of significant advantage. Inspection measures providing adequate safeguards must be accepted by both sides, but we should recognize that any inspection system will have risks which must be balanced against the advantages of arms limitation agreement.

A real difficulty in progress toward arms limitation is to induce the Soviet Union to overcome its long habit of secrecy. The United States and its allies should emphasize their readiness to accept international inspection, altho it will mean a degree of foreign presence and activity that will be novel and distasteful even in our open societies.

***Goal 15. The United Nations*—A key goal in the pursuit of a vigorous and effective United States foreign policy is the preservation and strengthening of the United Nations. Over the next decade, it will be under tremendous strain. However, it remains the chief instrument available for building a genuine community of nations.**

This requires constant strengthening of world law, thru the discovery and adoption of legal principles common to all or at least to many cultures, thru improved methods for making existing international law accessible, and thru the further development of the International Court of Justice.

Thru various specialized agencies the United Nations does significant work in many fields. It shows increasing effectiveness in technical assistance to new nations, and often assumes a major role in the control of violence and the settlement of disputes.

In a world in social, economic, and political ferment, international violence is a constant threat. Since nations have become so closely interlocked, there is danger that local violence will induce widespread conflict. Without abandoning, in justified cases, our right to unilateral action, the United States should join with other nations in seeking resolution of as many issues as possible through the United Nations, the Organization of American States, and other international agencies.

It must be recognized that the United Nations provides a forum for Soviet propaganda and tactics of dissension, and an opportunity for Soviet vetoes to block or delay free world advances. On occasion, the growing bloc of votes from the new and uncommitted nations may turn a decision in the United Nations against our interests. Nevertheless, we should give the world community, as represented by the United Nations, our steadfast support.

PART III. *A Financial Accounting*

Resources are a crucial test of a nation's ability to attain its goals.

At the present time, federal, state, and local governments are spending about $135 billion each year, of which about $99 billion represents purchases of goods and services (as opposed to social security and similar transfer payments). These totals are 27% and 19% respectively of our total gross national product. We cannot now determine whether this proportion of our national product will be adequate for the role of governments in the Sixties.

The increase in defense expenditures is difficult to predict. National security expenditures, exclusive of veterans' benefits and interest costs due largely to prior wars, account for 36% of the total amount spent at all levels of government. Foreign aid should be raised over the next five years, and there is little prospect for reduction in other national security expenditures.

Domestic expenditures are also hard to estimate. For education, we shall need a large additional sum. Expenditures at all levels of government for health, urban renewal, housing, transportation systems, and reservation of open space will certainly rise materially, and federal government support for basic research must be increased.

Economies can and must be made. Some savings in the federal agricultural program may be possible, and greater efficiency thruout government would reduce costs. But these savings cannot be counted on to offset rising expenses.

We therefore face the prospect, tho by no means the certainty, that aggregate tax rates will continue at something like their present level thru the decade, and may even have to be increased. We must face squarely the issue: if attaining the goals outlined in this Report should require a somewhat higher level of taxation, can we bear this level without consequences which themselves make the goals more difficult to reach?

Provided that economic growth proceeds at an annual rate of 3.4% or higher, there is no doubt that we can do so. In aggregate terms, increasing public expenditures are very unlikely to reduce the level of average individual consumption in this country; the average citizen's standard of living would continue to rise, tho perhaps at rates below those of the recent past. A moderate increase in tax rates need not, if its necessity were understood, materially impair the incentive or the morale of the American people, nor alter the primary reliance of the economy on private choice.

Tax systems which must allocate for governments about one-fifth of the national product must be both fair and designed to reduce to a minimum the impact of taxes upon growth.

A substantial reform of the tax systems is essential, whether

public expenditures must be increased or can be reduced. It will facilitate the attainment of many national goals.

The federal tax system should be revised to eliminate unjustified exceptions to its general rules, to assure equitable treatment of all types of incomes, to encourage the accumulation of risk capital so vital to economic growth, and to remedy the many contradictions and flaws which have grown up within the system.

Many state governments must find new tax sources. Local governments must be freed of unnecessary restrictions on taxing and borrowing powers, and the pronounced inequalities in the property tax bases of local jurisdictions should be corrected.

If these reforms are made and the minimum growth rate we postulate is achieved, it is this Commission's conclusion that the levels of public spending we would need to realize the recommendations of this Report are attainable. There must be no ideological preference for public spending as such. Costs must always be carefully weighed. But the needs outlined in this Report are themselves vitally related to ultimate freedom and individual development. We should not fail to meet them.

A Concluding Word—The very deepest goals for Americans relate to the spiritual health of our people. The right of every individual to seek God and the wellsprings of truth, each in his own way, is infinitely precious. We must continue to guarantee it, and we must exercise it, for ours is a spiritually-based society. Our material achievements in fact represent a triumph of the spirit of man in the mastery of his material environment.

The family is at the heart of society. The educational process begins and is served most deeply in the home.

From the first days of our history, every American has been responsible for his own life and livelihood, and for his family's, and has shared responsibility for his neighbor's. In our early years, the perils which threatened were close at hand, and the responsibility was inescapable. Now dangers, and opportunities as well, come from greater distance, and more subtly. But they are just as real. And it is as true as in the days of the frontier that the goals for Americans cannot be won without the efforts of all.

The major domestic goals of equality and education depend overwhelmingly on individual attitudes and actions.

It is the responsibility of men and women in every walk of life to maintain the highest standards of integrity.

American citizens will in this decade have countless opportunities to take the national interest into account in deciding their course of action. Negotiators for labor and management affect the growth of the economy and its ability to compete with industry abroad when they reach a decision on compensation and working conditions, and thus influence the rate of technological change. Young men and women will help shape the course the United States will take by deciding in what occupation they will spend their lives. Americans who live or travel abroad can persuade countless people of the sincerity of American ideals and the values of democracy, or they can tarnish the nation's reputation. Voters will determine whether schools will be built, teachers' salaries raised, foreign assistance enlarged, defense needs fulfilled. Our goals will be attained and our way of life preserved if enough Americans take the national interest sufficiently into account in day-by-day decisions.

The American citizen in the years ahead ought to devote a larger portion of his time and energy directly to the solution of the nation's problems. There has been repeated occasion in this Report to emphasize the overriding importance of contributions by private groups and individuals. Many ways are open for citizens to participate in the attainment of national goals. To mention but a few: they may help to control delinquency by organizing a boys' club, serve on a school board, accept a tour of duty with government, participate actively in politics thru parties or interest groups.

Above all, Americans must demonstrate in every aspect of their lives the fallacy of a purely selfish attitude—the materialistic ethic. Indifference to poverty and disease is inexcusable in a society dedicated to the dignity of the individual; so also is indifference to values other than material comfort and national power. Our faith is that man lives, not by bread alone, but by selfrespect, by regard for other men, by convictions of right and wrong, by strong religious faith.

Man has never been an island unto himself. The shores of his concern have expanded from his neighborhood to his nation, and from his nation to his world. Free men have always known the necessity for responsibility. A basic goal for each American is to achieve a sense of responsibility as broad as his worldwide concerns and as compelling as the dangers and opportunities he confronts.

Goals of America—AND WHAT SCHOOLS CAN DO TO ACHIEVE THEM

This statement was condensed by Willard E. Givens, Executive Secretary of the NEA, from the report of the Committee on Social-Economic Goals of America of the National Education Association. The Committee was appointed in 1931 and made its report in 1937. The members were: Fred J. Kelly, Chairman; John Dewey; Dr. Givens; Leon C. Marshall; Robert C. Moore; and Edward A. Ross.

AS WE face the future, toward what kind of a civilization shall we bend our efforts? What shall the goals be? How shall we work out on this continent the historic purpose of "life, liberty, and the pursuit of happiness" as the right of every citizen? How shall we apply the aspirations of the Founding Fathers to the opportunities and resources of a new age? We tend to become what we will to become, what we sacrifice for, and what we work toward. The things which our parents emphasize and which our schools attach importance to become the values toward which we work. What shall those values be? What are the abiding values of civilization?

Several years ago the NEA Committee on Social-Economic Goals of America set forth the following ten goals, which, it is believed, thoughtful Americans desire for themselves and their posterity:

Goals in a Nutshell

[1] Hereditary strength—the right to be well-born.

[2] Physical security—the right to protection from accident and disease.

[3] Skills and knowledge—the right to mastery of skills and knowledge necessary for enjoyment of group culture.

[4] Values and outlooks—the right to possession of cultural values necessary for proper social adjustment.

[5] An active, flexible personality—the right to opportunity for growth.

[6] Suitable occupation—the right to appropriate training and guidance.

[7] Economic security—the right to a job and fair standard of living.

[8] Mental security—the right to affection and understanding of life needs.

[9] Freedom—the right to the widest possible freedom.

[10] Fair play and equality of opportunity—the right to expect fair play.

[1] *Hereditary Strength*

The future of our country is vitally involved in education for hereditary strength. As links in the chain connecting past and future, each of us is a trustee for our country's welfare. Everyone should be well-born under conditions which will conserve his innate strengths and capacities. The building of a sense of individual responsibility for the future of the race is education's obligation. We must create thru education a sense of responsibility for the future of the race [*hereditary-conscience*] which will move our strongest men and women to bear children. One child in every hundred in the United States is as far above average as the feeble-minded child is below average. The rearing of children by these highly gifted young people would greatly improve our national stock.

[2] *Physical Security*

"If the general public were to take advantage of all the attributes of scientific medicine and public health that are available at the present time," observes the California State Department of Health, "the immediate advancement of our civilization would be so astonishing as to be beyond the comprehension of the average individual."

The most effective way to apply this knowledge is in the field of preventive medicine, and next to the home the best place to begin is in the schools thru:

[1] *School sanitation and healthful school living,* [2] *Physical education,* [3] *Health instruction,* and [4] *Health services.* The school should provide for periodical health examinations and inspections, control of communicable disease, and classification of students. Health examinations should be made *each year* by qualified physicians.

[3] *Skills and Knowledges*

The school is the instrument thru which most people come into possession of the group culture. It must apply the best in the culture of the past to the solution of civic, social, and economic problems. The school will then become a means of evolving a finer culture.

The skills, technics, and knowledges which every individual should have in order that he may enjoy the culture of the group and cooperate in making a better culture and society are: language, reading, science, mathematics, art, music, social interdependence and the social studies, truth and civic education, and history. The school is only one agency for selecting, transmitting, and evolving culture. Other agencies include the motion picture, radio, press, home, and church; all should be strengthened and utilized.

[4] *Values and Outlooks*

Contemporary values and goals shift and change with changing conditions. But there is a set of standards nearly universal which include: justice and fair dealing, honesty, truthfulness, observance of covenants, recognition of regularly constituted authority, due regard for the rights and feelings of others, cooperation and mutual help, disposition to carry one's own load, tolerance, and respect for individuality.

Assuming that means are adopted to insure understanding of these standards, there remain certain technics which may supplement understanding by stimulating emotions and thus produce attitudes. Among these technics are: ritual, music, drama, literature, art and architecture, sportsmanship, hero worship. Of course such technics will come to be viewed as means and not ends. It is important that all social institutions come to be regarded in the same light.

[5] *Active, Flexible Personality*

Participation in our cultural resources should promote personalities who are active, not passive and inert; who are motivated by intelligently chosen purposes, not by misguided impulse from within or casual pressure from without; who are not set and rigid, but who readapt flexibly to social change and to the consequences of their own prior conduct; who express their individual differences, but who do it in ways that are cooperative and socially contributory, not in ways that are self-centered and egoistic.

The school itself must be made over into a way of life in which active, flexible personality, in the democratic sense, may be realized. In all its activities the school will provide situations in which thought and action are each developed in terms of the other. Young people will be encouraged to share with their elders in enterprises for the common good.

[6] *Suitable Occupation*

The guidance and counseling work of the schools should be integrated with the public employment service and the community occupational life to provide *vocational guidance, training, placement, and advancement.*

The special function of *guidance* is to help the individual marshal the facts about himself and about occupations, in terms of a plan of life to be lived by him. In formulating a program of *training* several factors must be considered: The length of the youth's dependency; his ability to profit by various types of instruction; his willingness to sacrifice to acquire training; the number of persons that can be absorbed in a given vocation. To make *placement* that will provide the individual with present satisfactions and opportunities for *advancement*, it is necessary to analyze his skills and qualities, and the requirements and possibilities of work opportunities.

[7] *Economic Security*

The individual is today a pawn of forces which he neither recognizes nor understands. Here lies the deepest cause of insecurity and here lies the task of the school in helping people understand the causes and possible remedies of economic insecurity.

Whether or not our economic system can be made to provide greater economic security has become an all-engrossing issue, upon which, apparently, the future of our civilization hangs.

The role of the government must be analyzed. The part of political agencies must be weighed, and the value of individual initiative appraised. The school is in no position to write any neatly detailed prescriptions, but it must seek to clarify central issues and to provide that background of critical experience without which there cannot be intelligent judgment and purposeful action.

[8] *Mental Security*

Students of human conduct tell us that delinquents, and others who violate the laws or customs, are really the victims of the fears and anxieties inflicted upon them in early childhood. From this viewpoint the need of prevention is clear, thru a saner, wiser, and more affectionate child care, and a revision of our concepts of human nature and conduct. The individual's conduct needs to be understood in the light of his personal history.

We suffer from the consequences of failure to provide tenderness and toleration to children, adolescents, and adults. To supply such affection the schools should play a major part. This step calls not so much for a change in subjectmatter as for a warm, human concern and respect by teachers for the personality of the child and a recognition of the life concerns of the student as his most urgent educational need.

[9] *Freedom*

Freedom is an eternal goal which must be forever won anew, and the ultimate stay and support of freedom is in the schools. For it is they more than any other single agency who are concerned with the development of free inquiry, discussion, and expression. The schools have the responsibility of seeing to it that those who graduate from them have ideas that are worth thinking and worth being expressed, as well as having the courage to express them against the opposition of reactionaries and standpatters.

Unless the spirit of free intelligence pervades the organization, studies, and methods of the schools themselves, it is idle to expect them to send out young men and women who will stand actively and aggressively for the cause of free intelligence in meeting social problems and attaining the goal of freedom.

[10] *Fair Play*

The principle of fair play may be stated as follows: "Men must play the game of life so that *each* will get as much as possible out of it." There must be fair play in all fields of human activity—domestic, social, religious, esthetic, educational, political, and economic—and everybody must be admitted to the game.

Two methods of securing fair play at present are: the compulsory method, fair play laws; and the voluntary method, selfdiscipline by organized groups. But fair play, particularly that represented by the concept of social justice, can be secured lastingly only by a shift from narrow individualistic and group loyalty to a loyalty to the common good.

The Four Freedoms

IN THE FUTURE DAYS, which we seek to make secure, we look forward to a world founded upon four essential human freedoms.

The first is freedom of speech and expression—everywhere in the world.

The second is freedom of every person to worship God—in his own way everywhere in the world.

The third is freedom from want—which, translated into world terms, means economic understandings which will secure to every nation a healthy peacetime life for its inhabitants everywhere in the world.

The fourth is freedom from fear—which, translated into world terms, means a world-wide eduction of armaments to such a point and in such a thoro fashion that no nation will be in a position to commit an act of physical aggression against any neighbor—anywhere in the world.

That is no vision of a distant millennium. It is a definite basis for a kind of world attainable in our own time and generation.—*Franklin Delano Roosevelt, January 6, 1941.*

Education for All American Youth

The following discussion is from the report of the Educational Policies Commission, Education for All American Youth, *which was published in 1944 by the National Education Association.*

IS THE task of providing education for all American youth a hopeless one? Can any program or series of programs be devised that will meet all, or even a majority, of these bewildering human needs, complicated as they are by vast differences of economic circumstances? . . .

The task can be met: first, by identifying the major types of educationally significant differences found among American youth; second, by noticing the equally significant characteristics that all or nearly all youth have in common; third, by devising and inaugurating educational programs and organizations that provide for the common needs of all youth and the special needs of each individual.

How Youth Differ

[1] Differences in *intelligence and aptitude* will exist, regardless of modifications in the environments of individuals. While certain portions of these differences are inherited, even these cannot be predicted from parentage. These differences require different educational procedures, content, and standards of speed and achievement.

[2] Differences in *occupational interests and outlooks* are both desirable and necessary. They require guidance

to match abilities against the requirements of the job, desires against opportunities. They require curriculum adjustments that provide the necessary preparation for thorough workmanship in all occupations. They require administrative arrangements that will remove or minimize undemocratic "social-status" distinctions among occupational fields and their corresponding educations.

[3] There are differences in *availability of educational facilities,* differences caused either by location of residence or family economic status. The elimination of these differences is an entirely practicable matter of administration and finance, involving the proper organization and location of schools, and the provision of transportation and student-maintenance facilities, of state and federal equalization funds, and of public or private scholarship funds.

[4] There are differences in the *types of communities* in which youth reside. Insofar as these differences are educationally significant, they can be met by a guidance program providing information and outlooks which transcend community barriers, and by curriculums which are adjusted to the needs and opportunities of diverse communities.

[5] There are differences of opportunity resulting from differences in *social and economic status,* often aggravated by differences in *race*. The removal of such inequalities is a difficult matter, often requiring basic social and economic changes in the community. Yet, even so, these differences can be measurably reduced by wise educational leadership and administration, and by the objective study of community problems in schools.

[6] There are differences in *parental attitudes and cul-*

tural backgrounds. In many cases, cultural differences can be utilized for valuable education purposes. In other cases, where differences give rise to conflict or jeopardize the proper development of children and youth, the undesirable effects may be minimized through a program of home visitation and parent education.

[7] There are differences in *personal and avocational interests.* Within reasonable bounds, these differences may well be encouraged by a broad curriculum with opportunities for some selection of studies.

[8] There are, finally, differences in *mental health, emotional stability, and physical well-being.* Extreme disabilities must be compensated for in special schools and classes. Other temporary or less serious deviations from normal health may be met by appropriate adjustments in curriculum and regimen and by remedial health instruction and school health services.

What Youth Have in Common

The common qualities of youth are fully as important to education as their differences. For example:

All American youth are citizens now; all (or nearly all) will be qualified voters in the future; all require education for civic responsibility and competence.

All American youth (or nearly all) are members of family groups now and will become members of other family groups in the future; all require an understanding of family relationships.

All American youth are now living in the American culture and all (or nearly all) will continue to do so in the future; all require an understanding of the main elements in that culture.

National Citizenship Day

Observed Annually on September 17

JOY ELMER MORGAN

THAT the Congress of the United States require, and make provision for, all youth as they approach voting age to receive specific preparation for active citizenship as voters is a goal for Americans that should be fulfilled without delay. Formal initiation ceremonies and a suitable certificate of recognition should be awarded the youth on completion of this preparation. As community problems become more complex and difficult with population increase and urbanization, it becomes urgent that every citizen shall accept his moral obligation to vote and to do so intelligently with some appreciation of the common good. This movement for universal preparation may well be related to the proposed Constitutional Amendment to set the voting age at 18. It may well reach its climax each year on September 17 which Congress has set aside as Citizenship day "in commemoration of the forming and signing, on September 17, 1787, of the Constitution of the United States and in recognition of all who, by coming of age or by naturalization have attained the status of citizenship. . . ."

The idea of initiating youth into the responsibilities of adult society is as old as civilization. In the United States, plans to initiate youth into citizenship have been suggested at various times. The resolutions of the National

Joe Di Dio, National Education Association

WILLARD E. GIVENS [LEFT] AND
JOY ELMER MORGAN, 1968

Education Association, for example, in 1932 read: "Provision should be made to receive all persons into citizenship with suitable ceremony."

Nothing was done about this resolution, however, until a unique experience impelled me to take up the cause thru the *NEA Journal* which I was then editing. In the fall of 1937, the Board of Education of Lorain, Ohio was sponsoring a public recognition service of young citizens who had spent a year in preparing themselves for citizenship. They asked me to deliver the address for the occasion. The experience in that ceremony made such an impression on me that I resolved to do whatever I could to promote the spread of the idea.

I began by publicizing the Lorain observance in the *NEA Journal* for November of that year.

As a followup I urged the appointment by the NEA of

a committee on new voter preparation and recognition. This committee, which became known as the Committee on Induction into Citizenship, was appointed and began its work in 1939 under the able chairmanship of Hugh S. Bonar, then superintendent of schools at Manitowoc, Wisconsin. I was able to support his work in three ways: thru *The NEA Journal;* the development of *The American Citizens Handbook;* and the publication of two leaflets in the *Personal Growth* series—number 70 entitled *Organizing New Voter Programs* and number 100 entitled *New Voter Preparation and Recognition*. These had wide circulation and helped to spread the idea. The movement made its best progress in Wisconsin, where the legislature passed a law aiding the cause, and the state university prepared special materials to acquaint citizens with their local and county governments.

One of the first acts of *The Committee on Induction into Citizenship* was to secure an act of Congress setting aside the third Sunday in May for the recognition of new citizens. This act, signed by President Franklin D. Roosevelt on May 3, 1940, was superseded on February 29, 1952, by a Joint Resolution signed by President Harry Truman changing the date to September 17.

The work of the NEA in this field eventually led to the formation of The National Conference on Citizenship, which was chartered by Congress in a bill signed by President Dwight D. Eisenhower on August 13, 1953. A moving spirit in the formation and work of the National Conference has been Judge Carl B. Hyatt, chairman of the Federal Bar Association Citizenship Committee, who in spite of limited funds has kept the conference alive with annual meetings attended by representatives of organizations interested in citizenship. The 23rd Conference was held in Washington September 15-18, 1968.

Altho here and there communities are doing a good job, especially with naturalization ceremonies, much remains to be done. The basic need is finance to recruit, train, and maintain a staff of leaders who can work with local and state leaders to develop plans and materials that will make induction into active citizenship a dignified, informing, and inspiring experience for the young people who will hold the reins of power in community, state, and nation and who will determine our role in world affairs. True, as in all great enterprises, there are many details to be worked out. There must be planning and replanning, trial and error, experiment after experiment.

In *Senior Citizen* for September 1962, Arthur P. Crabtree in an article on *The Americanization of the Native Born* writes: This title "is no attempt to coin a facetious phrase. Rather, it is perhaps, the most appropriate set of words with which to introduce the thesis of this article: namely that this nation conceived in a climate of human liberty betrayed the promise of its great potential, that the forces of American education aided and abetted the tragedy and, finally that the most imperative task facing education and, especially adult education in this hour is that of leading the American people back to the faith and dedication of the Founding Fathers."

In this spirit citizens should unite in an effort to have every community make the best use it can of National Citizenship Day and to urge Congress to add to the forward looking educational legislation of recent years provision for the development of a meaningful program of induction into citizenship.

ACKNOWLEDGMENTS

GRATEFUL acknowledgment is made to the following publishers and authors or their representatives for kind permission to use the copyrighted selections in this volume:

D. APPLETON-CENTURY CO.

"The Little Elf" by John Kendrick Banks; "To a Waterfowl," "Thanatopsis," and "Truth Crushed to Earth" by W. C. Bryant.

BOBBS-MERRILL CO.

"The Name of Old Glory" from *Home Folks* by James Whitcomb Riley; "When the Frost Is on the Punkin" by James Whitcomb Riley, from *Neighborly Poems,* copyright 1891, 1919.

DOUBLEDAY, DORAN & CO.

"Trees" by Joyce Kilmer; "If" by Rudyard Kipling, from *Reward and Fairies,* copyright, 1910, 1938, reprinted by permission of Mrs. Bambridge; and "Recessional" by Rudyard Kipling from *The Five Nations,* copyright 1893, 1933, reprinted by permission of Mrs. Bambridge; "L'Envoi" by Rudyard Kipling, from *The Seven Seas,* copyright 1893, 1933, reprinted by permission of Mrs. Bambridge.

E. P. DUTTON & CO.

"America the Beautiful" from *The Retinue and Other Poems* by Katharine Lee Bates.

HARPER AND BROTHERS

"How Big Are You?" by Edna St. Vincent Millay, from *Renascence,* copyright 1917.

HARVEY PARKER & CRAFTSMEN

"Today" by Angela Morgan, from *Gold on Your Pillow.*

HENRY HOLT

"Silver" by Walter de la Mare, from *Peacock Pie.*

ALFRED A. KNOPF, INC.

"The Spirit of the Worker" by Kahlil Gibran, from *The Prophet;* "Dreams" by Langston Hughes.

J. B. LIPPINCOTT CO.

"Tit for Tat" by Christopher Morley, from *Poems.*

LITTLE, BROWN, AND COMPANY

Emily Dickinson poems from *The Poems of Emily Dickinson,* edited by Martha Dickinson Bianchi and Alfred Leete Hampson; "October's Bright Blue Weather" by Helen Hunt Jackson.

MACMILLAN CO.

"Abraham Lincoln Walks at Midnight" by Vachel Lindsay, from *Collected Poems;* and "Barter" by Sara Teasdale, from *Collected Poems of Sara Teasdale.*

HOUGHTON MIFFLIN CO.

"Memory" by Thomas Bailey Aldrich; "Duty" by Ralph Waldo Emerson; "Friends" by Frank D. Sherman; "In School-Days" by John Greenleaf Whittier; "Inspiration for Living," "A Day in June," and "The First Snow-Fall," by James Russell Lowell; "Opportunity" by Edward Rowland Sill; "The Arrow and the Song," "The Ship of State," and "The Builders" by Henry Wadsworth Longfellow; "The Chambered Nautilus" by Oliver Wendell Holmes; "On the Firing Line," by Joaquin Miller.

F. A. OWEN PUBLISHING CO.

"This Land Is Ours" by Nona Keen Duffy, from the March 1941 issue of *The Instructor.*

CHARLES SCRIBNER'S SONS

"Requiem," "Rain," "My Shadow," and "The Swing" by Robert Louis Stevenson; "The Bill of Fare" by Eugene Field; "The Things I Prize," "Life," "Work," and "Keeping Christmas," by Henry van Dyke, from his book *The Spirit of Christmas,* copyright 1905; "God Give Us Men" by Josiah Gilbert Holland.

LOTHROP, LEE & SHEPARD

"The Better Way" by Susan Coolidge, from *Peace and Patriotism,* copyright 1919; "The Calf-Path" and "The House by the Side of the Road" by Sam Walter Foss, from *Whiffs from Wild Meadows.*

P. F. VOLLAND CO.

"A Song for Flag Day" by Wilbur D. Nesbit.

OTHERS

Irving Berlin for the song "God Bless America"; Elias Lieberman for "Credo"; Virgil Markham for "Lincoln, the Man of the People," "Outwitted," "Preparedness," "There is a Destiny" and "Leadership" by Edwin Markham; Mrs. Denis A. McCarthy for "This Is the Land Where Hate Should Die" by Denis A. McCarthy; Juanita Miller for "Columbus" by Joaquin Miller; John S. Montgomery for "What Does It Mean To Be American" by Roselle Mercier Montgomery; Aaron Metchik for "America, I Love You"; Berton Braley for "The Thinker"; Mrs. Hamlin Garland for "Do You Fear the Force of the Wind?" by Hamlin Garland; Ethel Blair Jordan "Disarm the Heart"; Mrs. A. L. Mosher for "A Little Song of Life" by Lizette Woodworth Reese; Margaret E. Sangster for "We Thank Thee"; Charles Merz for "This Land and Flag," an editorial in the New York Times, June 14, 1940; Edna St. Vincent Millay for "The Pear Tree," copyright 1919.

INDEX

THIS book was printed and bound by The Lakeside Press, R. R. Donnelley & Sons Company, 350 East Twenty-second Street, Chicago 16, Illinois, in their plant at Crawfordsville, Indiana. The text is in Garamond Linotype: 12 point on 14 point slug 23 picas [for example, page 3]; or 10 point on 11 point slug [for example, page 1]. Headings like "Part I" are in 14 point Garamond Linotype caps with the wording beneath in 24 point #252 Arrighi Italic Monotype.